In Defense of Honor

In Defense of Honor

Sexual Morality, Modernity, and Nation

in Early-Twentieth-Century Brazil

Sueann Caulfield

DUKE UNIVERSITY PRESS Durham & London 2000

2nd printing, 2002
© 2000 Duke University Press
All rights reserved
Printed in the United States of America on acid-free paper ∞
Typeset in Trump Mediaeval by Keystone Typesetting, Inc.
Library of Congress Cataloging-in-Publication Data appear
on the last printed page of this book.

For Matthew and Patricia Caulfield
For Elizabeth de Avelar Solano Martins
and for
Warren Dean, in memoriam

Contents

List of Tables

Acknowledgments

This book began as a doctoral dissertation at New York University. My greatest debt is to my adviser, Warren Dean, who left an example of scholarship and pedagogy that I struggle to emulate. I would also like to thank Professors Mary Nolan and Marilyn Young, who provided inspiration and assistance throughout my years as a graduate student, introducing me to gender history and helping shape the topic of my study. They and the other two members of my committee, Teresa Meade and Lila Abu-Lughod, were careful readers and supportive critics. Teresa also helped with ideas and access to resources for subsequent research.

Research for this book was completed with fellowships and grants from the Fulbright Foundation and the Rackham Graduate School, the Center for Research on Women and Gender, and the Program in Latin American and Caribbean Studies at the University of Michigan, Ann Arbor. I am also indebted to the archivists and staff of the National Archive and the National Library in Rio de Janeiro. Isaura Brasil, Alessandra Frota Martinez, and Lícia Mascarenhas provided competent and efficient research assistance during different phases of the project. Irfan Nooruddin ran the original statistical analysis presented in chapter 5; he, Tom Weiskopff, Maris Vinovskis, and David Lam helped interpret the results.

The project might never have been completed without the generous support and guidance I received from Brazilian colleagues and friends. Sidney Chalhoub guided me through the criminal record and government document collections on my very first day in the National Archive. Since then, he has become a dear friend as well as a source of intellectual inspiration and an instigating critic. I am especially grateful to Sidney for leading me to another intellectually and personally enriching friendship by introducing me to Martha de Abreu Esteves's work and arranging for me to meet her. I cannot begin to enumerate the many ways Martha helped me with this project, nor can I hope to thank her adequately here. The constant dialogue with her work that runs through this book attests to my intellectual debt; her personal support, warm generosity, and solid friendship were no less important.

Many other friends and colleagues in Rio de Janeiro have also provided indispensable intellectual support and exchange. Maria Fernanda Baptista Bicalho shared many hours of conversation about history and life; Rachel Soihet, Hebe Maria Mattos de Castro, and Magali Engel welcomed me into their lively seminars at the Federal Fluminense University. Miriam Chaves enriched my experience of Brazilian culture with an astonishing variety of extra academic activities and uniquely erudite conviviality. Keila Grinberg, along with academic collegiality and exchange, was responsible for my initiation into Sunday soccer with Rebola. I thank the Rebola players for their good-humored welcome; special thanks to Karola for her hospitality during subsequent research trips. Fellow *brasilianistas* Peter Beattie, Roger Kittleson, Maureen O'Dougherty, and Brodwyn Fischer must be included alongside this group of Carioca friends and colleagues. Roger has been a constant confidant and source of wisdom on scholarly and other matters over the past seven years. Maureen has accompanied the writing of this book at different stages, and it has benefitted from her critiques and her company. Brodie has added fresh insights and renewed enthusiasm. I also extend gratitude to Clara Rivera, Ken Silverstein, Saulo de Oliveira Guimarães, and Dona Geni for their support during the initial research in Rio de Janeiro. Silvia Hunold Lara and Maria Clementina Pereira Cunha opened their social history seminar at UNICAMP to discussion of portions of the text and gave insightful critiques. João José Reis provided another avenue of stimulating debate by inviting me to present portions of the book-in-progress in Bahia, and his careful reading helped sharpen the argument, particularly in chapter 5.

Colleagues and students at the University of Michigan, Ann Arbor, helped improve the book in a variety of ways. Since I first arrived in Ann Arbor, graduate students Lara Putnam and Aims McGuinness have challenged me to keep up with their enthusiastic intellectual curiosity and fresh interpretations; more recently, José Amador has joined them. The junior faculty reading group provided a lively forum for discussion of some of the book's central ideas. Frederick Cooper, Geoffrey Eley, Diane Hughes, Sonya Rose, Caroll Smith-Rosemberg, Hitomi Tonomura, and Maris Vinovskis improved the book inestimably through their comments on earlier versions of different chapters. Leslie Pincus contributed keen insights on culture and authoritarian politics as well as welcome alternatives to the academic milieu. Sue Juster and Val Kivelson shared critiques of the text and personal perspectives on gender politics and family values. Many conversations with Jane Burbank, who read key chapters and cotaught a course in comparative legal history with me, enriched the text immensely. Tomas A. Green also offered especially generous comments and helped me think and rethink about the analysis and presentation of issues in legal history. Peter Carl Caldwell read portions of the text early on, providing astute comments on the global context of Brazilian legal debates. I thank Maria Helena Machado and John Monteiro for their late-night house call with crucial last minute comments on the text as well as for their presence during other special moments while they were visiting in Ann Arbor. Laura Lee Downs, in addition to reading and rereading various chapters, has given constant inspiration and encouragement that influenced the book's development over the past five years; more important, she helped identify all that is funny and worthwhile about academia and life in general. Special gratitude is due Rebecca J. Scott. In addition to plowing through more than one unfinished version of the manuscript with her eagle eye and extraordinary intellect, she helped me weed through the morass of common academic preoccupations and keep sight of the goals and values that are fundamental to this endeavor. Along the way, her friendship has added invaluable warmth and camaraderie.

I am fortunate to belong to an especially active and supportive cohort of Latin Americanist, especially Brazilianist, historians in the United States. Susan K. Besse, Elizabeth Kuznesof, and Donna Guy included me in their projects and gave crucial advice and encouragement early on. Jeremy Adelman, Bert Barickman, Muriel Nazzari, and Stuart Schwartz generously read and critiqued part or all of the manuscript in earlier versions. Sandra Lauderdale Graham and Jeffrey Needell read each chapter with meticulous care, providing detailed and insightful comments as the book was nearing the end. The manuscript's final form owes much to the careful readings and valuable suggestions by Jeffrey Lesser and Barbara Weinstein, the two readers for Duke University Press. Finally, the book benefited greatly from the dedication and support of its editor, Valerie Millholland, and managing editor, Paula Dragosh, at Duke University Press. Cristiana Schettini Pereira did heroic work preparing the index, adding healthy doses of humor and inspiration during the final preparation of the manuscript.

The Avelar household—Dona Zizita, Mabel, Noga, Nolasco, Lele, e Zé, Rande, Dilson, Duda, Soraya, Juliana, Tato, Cleó, and Rita—engaged me in various levels of debate on Brazilian life and culture and made my daily life fun and comfortable as I completed the final stage of revision in Bahia. Last but certainly not least, I thank my own family members—Matt, Pat, Tricia, Dan, Matt, Jennifer, Danny, Nick, Ty, Zoe, and Matthew—for their good-humored endurance throughout this endeavor.

The book is dedicated to my parents, Matthew and Patricia Caulfield, for whom my love and admiration continues to grow with each unexpected turn of events; to Bebete, for sharing so much of this project and everything else; and to the memory of Warren Dean, whose tremendous impact on Brazilian history is equaled by the impact he made on individual lives such as mine.

Portions of chapter 5 appeared as "Raça, sexo e casamento: Crimes sexuais no Rio de Janeiro, 1918–1940," *Afro-Ásia* 18 (1996): 125–64; portions of chapter 3 appeared as " 'Que virgindade é esta?' A mulher moderna e a reforma do Código Penal no Rio de Janeiro, 1918 a 1940," *Acervo: Revista do Arquivo Nacional* 9, nos. 1–2 (1996): 165–202. Some of the material in chapters 1 and 2 appeared in "The Birth of Mangue: Race, Nation, and the Politics of Prostitution in Rio de Janeiro, 1850–1942," in *Sex and Sexuality in Latin America*, ed. Donna Guy and Daniel Balderston (New York: New York University Press, 1997), 86–100. Some of the material in chapters 3 and 4 appeared in "Fifty Years of Virginity in Rio de Janeiro: Sexual Politics and Gender Roles in Juridical and Popular Discourse, 1890–1940," *Luso-Brazilian Review* 30, no. 1 (1993): 47–74, coauthored with Martha de Abreu Esteves. All are cited here with permission.

In Defense of Honor

Rio de Janeiro 23-2-933.

Amigo Pires

Desejo que esta te vá encontrar perfeitamente bem, assim como a toda a tua familia etc.

Por minha parte vou-me encontrando bem de saude assim como todos os rapazes desta terra.

Participo-te que entreguei a carta ao Carvalho e que agradeceu. Estimei muito saber a tua vida actual que passas nessa terra. Pois a minha é bonita mas é em poucas atrapalhada.

Tu perguntarás pelo quê? Eu te explico como meu mais amigo, que até hoje o tive. Em Maio de 922. Amei uma pequena mas pouco tempo.

Depois deixei-a porque os pais queriam que eu casasse. Mas casar só pela pulícia! Em 4 de Setembro principiei a amar outra, até que breve

a vou deixar. Em 12 de Outubro de 922 principiei amar outra imagina faz hontem 130 dias quer dizer 4 meses e dez dias e pelo amor, rogo-te que nunca confesses nada a ninguem, mas tirei os tres ventos dela. Aqui aplica-se o nosso descanço. Hoje sinto o prazer ainda mas ando com um medo que até me dóe o coração.

Farei sempre tudo para me não casar, mas aqui é perigoso. O Salgueiro conhece-a muito bem, que ainda Domingo dia 18 andei com ela mais ela na Quinta da Boa Vista aqui no Rio. Não dês piada a ninguem quando escreveres para aqui porque até hoje ainda ninguem o sabe.

Eu fui sempre um pouco giro pela mulher apesar que não me dão prejuizo.

Amigo Pires

Peço-te como meu maior e meu amigo que nada digas porque se ai o souberem será um falatorio immenso.

Destes maiores segredos em breve sempre os haverei. Se enviar. Porque ai tambem saliamos da vida um do outro.

Lucrecio. Desejo que sejas sempre victorioso nestas coisas e que me participes todas as novidades que existam principalmente à finançada.

Peço-te para entregar tambem esta á minha familia que me desculpar em tudo.

Darás muitas lembranças dos meus aos teus Bartolomé

Darás à Ritinha etc.
Darás à tua Carina.
Desejo-te ser feliz com ela etc.
E tu recebe os meus perfeitos comprimentos bem como de todos os teus amigos etc.

Rio Caixa 1442

Desculpa peço e segredo de tudo que te enviar. Guarda as cartas e tudo até quando lá voltar.

Introduction

Rio de Janeiro
February 23, 1923
My Friend Pias,

I hope that this letter finds you and all of your family well.

As I write this letter I am in good health, as are all the young guys here.

I want to tell you that I delivered the letter to Carvalho, who was grateful. I was very happy to know about the life that you're living there. Mine is good, but a little muddled.

Why, you might ask? I'll explain to you as my best friend: that I've met up until now. In May of 1922, I loved a girl, but for a short time.

I left her because her parents wanted me to marry her.

But I'll marry only at the police station!

On September 7 I started to love another, but left her after a short time. On October 12, 1922, I began loving another imagine that as of yesterday that was 130 days that is four months and ten days well Lucrecio I ask you never to tell this to anyone, but I took her three pennies.

Here they call it the cherry.

Today I'm still feeling the pleasure but I am so scared that my heart hurts.

I will always do anything not to get married, but here it is dangerous.

Salgueiro knows her very well. On Sunday the eighteenth I went with her and him to the Quinta da Boa Vista here in Rio. Don't let out a word to anyone when you write, because up until today no one knows yet.

I have always been a little gluttonous for women, even though they only bring problems.

My friend Pias

I ask you as my best friend not to say anything because if they find out back there it will cause terrible gossip.

I will always have the pleasure of sending you my deepest secrets. Because back there we also knew about each other's lives.

Lucrecio, I hope that you are always victorious in these things . . .

I ask you to give this also to my family, that they forgive me for everything. (. . .)

And for you, my most respectful greetings, and greetings from all your friends, etc.

Manoel[1]

This letter, apprehended by police in Manoel Joaquim de Souza's boardinghouse room shortly after he wrote it, was about as incriminating a piece of evidence as one could get. What Manoel did not know was that as he was writing, his girlfriend, a nineteen-year-old Portuguese immigrant like himself who worked nearby as a maid, was tearfully relating the same deep secret to her employer, Senhora Maria Alícia Machado de Carvalho. Even worse, she added that Manoel had promised to marry her. Alarmed, Dona Alícia sent for the girl's father, a farmhand in the city's outskirts, who came immediately and filed a complaint with the local police. Manoel hauled into the third district police station on the charge of "deflowering a minor," confessed to the crime and married his victim, Maria Imaculada Martins Pereira, three weeks later.[2]

It was all in a day's work for the local police, although the letter must have made their work in this case easier than most. The scenario was common enough, although details were always unique. Some five hundred families a year, almost all of them working-class, appealed to the Rio de Janeiro police in the 1920s and 1930s because their daughters had been deflowered.[3] Contrary to Manoel Souza's perception, it was actually difficult for these families to prove that their daughters were "honest" and that the men accused were therefore guilty of offending their families' honor. Most men accused of deflowering and other sexual crimes were either acquitted or released without trial.[4] Nonetheless, Manoel Souza might have learned that it was dangerous to deflower an honest young girl in Rio de Janeiro from stories of other young men who had married "at the police station." Perhaps he had known such a young man; even if he did not, he certainly would have known of the stories relayed through the tabloid press or neighborhood gossip. There certainly would have been talk of young men in Manoel's situation whom police had beaten or threatened into marriage.[5] Still, Manoel might have been relieved that Maria's father went to the police rather than coming after him. Although bloody solutions to these kinds of conflicts were relatively uncommon, when they happened they received a great deal of space in the press. They were lumped together with accounts of men who got away with acts of domestic violence, most commonly wife-beating or murder, when they could prove that these acts were committed "in a justified state of uncontrollable passion," which everyone understood meant that the man had acted "in defense of honor."

Given the extraordinary level of public debate over sexual honor, not just in neighborhood gossip mills but in the mainstream press as well as in political tracts and specialized professional journals, it is not surprising that Manoel became nervous after he deflowered his girlfriend. It would have been difficult to live in Rio de Janeiro in the 1920s and 1930s without noticing that this topic preoccupied a great variety of people. They ranged from magistrates who wrote Brazil's legal codes and adjudicated court battles over lost virginity to local police officers who bullied recalcitrant young men into marrying their deflowered girlfriends; from working-class families who brought these cases to the police to middle-class reporters who blazoned their stories across the pages of the tabloid press; from intellectuals who campaigned to end press sensationalism and violent "crimes of passion" to housewives who rallied behind female "passionate offenders"; from fathers who struggled to support their families to sons who struggled to remain independent; from single mothers who taught their daughters the value of virginity to single daughters who gave up their virginity in bursts of adolescent rebellion. But although it seems clear that sexual honor was meaningful to most Cariocas (Rio de Janeiro natives) through the first half of the twentieth century, there was great disagreement about just what that meaning was. And although the valorization of sexual honor was a legacy from the colonial period (1500–1822), its significance in a city and nation that was precipitously "modernizing" was a problem of immediate concern and heated debate. Prominent turn-of-the-century intellectuals, professionals, and political authorities had considered the defense of sexual honor a central component of their mission to "civilize" the recently proclaimed Republic (1889–1930). Yet defining honor and civilization provoked intense controversy from the inception of republican institutions in the late nineteenth century to their transformation in the 1920s and 1930s. Along the way, the discourses of state and professional authorities both affected and responded to the attitudes and conflicts that poor residents such as Maria Pereira and Manoel Souza brought to their attention.

This book is about gender, honor, and nation-building in Rio de Janeiro, Brazil, from roughly the end of World War I to the early years of the Estado Novo (New State) dictatorship of President Getúlio Vargas (1937–1945).[6] My major concern is to understand the relationship between the

4

role of sexual honor in everyday personal choices and conflicts of people such as Manoel Souza and Maria Pereira and its role in public debates over the modernization of the Brazilian nation. For a great many contemporary religious authorities as well as political and professional elites, the relationship was simple: sexual honor was the basis of the family, and the family the basis of the nation. Without the moralizing force of women's sexual honesty, modernization—a catch-all term that meant many things to many people—would bring the dissolution of the family, rampant criminality, and general social chaos. What these elites did not recognize, or at least did not acknowledge, was that sexual honor stood for a set of gender norms that, with their apparent basis in nature, provided the logic for unequal power relations in private and public life.[7] Whether in relation to individual couples or the national social body, sexual honor was frequently used to reinforce hierarchical relations based not only on gender, but on race and class as well. In reality, of course, there was nothing natural about any of these three bases of inequality. On the contrary, all were constructed through dynamic and ongoing historical processes, which made each of the elements of honor potentially unstable. In the decades of political, economic, and cultural transformation that followed World War I, the concept of sexual honor became especially slippery, in both the private and the public realms. Contending parties in all sorts of conflicts could interpret honor in different, even contradictory ways, and changes in one realm were bound to affect the other.

Jurists play a central role in the pages that follow because they adjudicated private sexual conflicts (and thus documented them) and because they worked the hardest to articulate a clear definition of the state's role in defending family honor. In the first half of the century, and particularly in the 1920s, juridical thinking on issues such as virginity, consensual unions, and crimes of passion went in radical and conflicting directions. Faced with what seemed a chaotic liberation of social mores and a dangerous "emancipation" of "modern women," many threw up their hands and argued that protecting women's honesty was no longer possible. Others, applauding the modernization of social norms, believed that traditional notions of family honor were outdated. Still others insisted that new threats to older moral values made the defense of women's honor all the more urgent.

Despite formidable challenges, family honor not only survived in twentieth-century law, but gained new prominence as Getúlio Vargas consolidated power after 1930, when a civilian-military coalition brought down the First Republic and placed him at the head of a provisional government. After 1937, when Vargas proclaimed himself dictator and closed down political debate altogether, the state went to unprecedented lengths to enforce public morality and private family values, linking them explicitly to national honor. But Vargas's Estado Novo dictatorship did not invent sexual or family honor and impose it on an unsuspecting population. Nor did it simply revert to "traditional values" of previous generations. On the contrary, the effervescence of the previous decades had broadened both popular and juridical concepts of gender and family in ways that could not be reversed. These changes took a concrete form in the redefinition of family, honor, and sexual crimes in Brazilian law at the outset of the authoritarian period.

The period between World War I and the Estado Novo certainly did not mark the beginning of cases such as that of Manoel Souza and Maria Pereira. The scenario had been played out in ancient Rome courts and in medieval kingdoms ruled by canon law since well before the Portuguese first brought those legal traditions to Brazil in the sixteenth century. There are no statistics on the ebb and flow of complaints of stolen virginity and broken marriage promises to state or religious authorities over the centuries, but they seem to have been common from the colonial period up through the 1970s in diverse regions of Brazil.[8] The details of such conflicts, however, varied according to historical circumstance.

A number of recent studies of colonial Spanish and Portuguese America, for instance, have demonstrated that European notions of family honor and sexual morality were adapted in specific ways to the American colonies. Commoners in early modern Spain who testified before the Inquisition resisted the idea that it was sinful to have consensual sexual relations with prostitutes or nonvirgin single women. This attitude was probably common in Portugal as well.[9] Resistance to the church's moral prescriptions grew considerably in the Americas, where European men frequently considered it their right to take Indian or African women, and equated their status with that of single women, regardless of their virginity, previous marriage, or the terms of their consent.[10] Moreover, although the church struggled to teach colonists that sex outside marriage was sinful, particularly after the directives of the Council of Trent (1545–1563) were brought to the New World in the late seventeenth century, church officials were forced to acknowledge that there were not enough clergy to spread the doctrine, much less marry most of their brethren. This was especially true in Brazil. With its vast uncharted frontier, unsubdued indigenous population, and exotic African workforce, Brazil gained a reputation in Europe as a land of demons and temptation that heightened sensuality and bred immorality. Churchmen assumed that moral regulations would be bent in Brazil, and turned a blind eye to many sins of the flesh among commoners, and even among their own clergy. The church routinely forgave "simple concubinage," or consensual unions of marriageable couples, as well as various other sexual offenses widely practiced among the bulk of the population.[11] Most people seem to have placed a high value on legitimate marriage, for it helped to stabilize family units that were essential for social advancement, economic security, and even survival for all social classes, but the institution was frequently inaccessible for slaves and the free poor.[12]

In contrast, for elite families in Brazil and throughout Spanish and Portuguese America marriage alliances were crucial political and economic strategies up to the nineteenth century and even later in some areas. Parents chose children's, especially daughters', marriage partners with care. Legitimate birth and "purity of blood"—which came to mean the absence of African and Indian heritage—were essential elements of status, and hence family honor, although "stains" could often be washed away with money. Tremendous value was placed on the sexual chastity of privileged colonial women, who were generally considered white. Elite women's seclusion not only marked them as morally superior to common women in the eyes of their peers but, as Verena Martínez-Alier argues for nineteenth-century Cuba, ensured the endogamy of their class and race.[13] Elite men might take a number of lower-status women as concubines, and unless these men were nobles, they could "recognize" illegitimate children for purposes of protection and inheritance. Yet it was necessary for men's own honor that they fulfill promises of betrothal to elite women.[14] It was also often necessary for the preservation of their economic status that they marry a dowried woman of their own class.[15]

The elite, patriarchal family, held together by the gender norms that scholars of the Mediterranean and Latin America have termed the "honor/ shame complex," has long been recognized as the central economic, political, and social institution in colonial and nineteenth-century Latin America, and Brazil is no exception.[16] In Brazil, since the early 1930s, Gilberto Freyre's work on the role of the colonial plantation household in the development of Brazil's national character has been a constant reference for historians. Beginning in the 1950s, social historians have looked beyond elite families to find a variety of family organization, including, in many regions, high proportions of female-headed households. These scholars have shown that family organization was more diverse and society more dynamic than Freyre's model admits. Even members of elite families led lives that deviated from the moral requirements of this model.[17]

Scholars disagree about how to interpret this social reality, for both the colonial period and later. Some point to the high numbers of consensual unions, illegitimate children, and female-headed households to argue that the popular classes developed a set of alternative moral values in which patriarchal notions of family, women's subordination, and the moral ideals of marriage and women's chastity were relatively unimportant.[18] Others, most notably Ronaldo Vainfas for Brazil, argue that the church was successful in spreading the values of the patriarchal family, especially over the eighteenth century, although social inferiority and marginalization continued to make it impossible for many people to live by these values.[19] Still another position, defended by Sheila de Castro Faria, is that although patriarchy and marriage were crucial institutions for all colonial social classes, the value of these institutions was not merely moral, but economic.[20] What seems clear from this scholarship is that in Brazil, as in colonial Latin America in general, there existed what Asunción Lavrin calls a "dialogue" between values and behavior disseminated by church and state institutions and common practices and attitudes that transgressed ecclesiastical moral codes.[21] Both sets of social norms could influence the decisions and experiences of a range of individuals.

It is also clear that honor, with its overlapping components of gender, class, and race, was a central organizing principle of colonial society. Colonial codes of honor, written into complex laws regulating privileges and responsibilities of different groups, were a primary means of distinguishing among types of royal subjects and maintaining the cohesion of distinct social classes. Yet this cohesion was continually challenged by the development of colonial societies in which social boundaries were blurred. Racial and class identities fixed in law were more or less fluid in practice, depending on assorted historical circumstances. The same was true of the moral requirements of honorable men and honest women.

Royal concern with honor was apparently heightened in both Spanish and Portuguese America at the end of the colonial period, when social mobility increased and intermarriage among individuals of different social stations threatened to undermine the corporatist logic that sustained the monarchy. Both Crowns reacted to this upset to "the proper ordering of society" by prohibiting marriages among social "unequals" and strengthening parents' rights to impede their children's marriage in cases of "inequality."[22] The litigation between parents and children over marriage choices demonstrates quite explicitly that an individual's "quality," or social status, was measured by gendered notions of honor. The relative weight of different components of honor—race, class, wealth, legitimacy, behavior, reputation—varied over time and, as Susan Socolow shows in her comparison of disputed marriage choices in Córdoba and Buenos

Aires, even from city to city.[23] In any case, royal attempts to preserve the patriarchal, corporate social order by bolstering parental control of children were futile; the individualistic values of love and free will in marriage choice triumphed in the Americas, as was the case in modern Europe.[24] According to Muriel Nazzari, at least for São Paulo, this change in values was preceded by changes in the economic strategies of propertied families, which was reflected in the disappearance of the dowry in the nineteenth century.[25] Yet the movement away from clan-based social organization was far from complete. Entrenched political and social institutions ensured the survival of the extended family and personalized patron-client relationships as bulwarks of a tightly hierarchical social order through the twentieth century.

The relationship between sexual honor and state intervention in the social construction of gender, race, and class difference in Latin America also outlasted the institutions of colonial administration, although the place of honor in nationalist ideologies changed. Rather than serving as explicit means of maintaining social differences, concepts of sexual honor found a place in new ideologies of cultural unity and national identity. This is evident in the literature that Doris Sommer describes as the "foundational fictions" of Latin American nationhood, as well as in an array of political and urban professional campaigns to "moralize" and "modernize" Latin American cities by regulating and "sanitizing" public and private space. Denying the existence of racial and class cleavages while celebrating racial "improvement" through "whitening," many of Latin America's most prominent liberal nation-builders linked the notion of women's sexual purity, defended through patriarchal authority, to the advancement of civilization, social order, and state power.[26] Their notions of civilization and order, however, were imbued with class and racial prejudices, and the public policy these notions inspired seldom sought to eliminate social hierarchies.

Brazil was no exception, although the survival of slavery and the monarchy until 1888 and 1889, respectively, created unique challenges for liberal nation-builders. These institutions, together with the survival of a firmly family-based social hierarchy, helped sustain a social and political order based on dense networks of patronage and personalized and unequal social relations. Anthropologist Roberto da Matta, elaborating on Gilberto Freyre's analysis and the work by Mary Douglas on cultural notions of pollution, describes what he believes are the contemporary cultural manifestations of Brazil's social order through the metaphors of "house" and "street." The house is the private space of order and "natural" social hierarchy based on sex and age; the street, the public and unprotected space of disorder, anonymity, and physical and moral danger. A crucial function of male family members is to guard the house from penetration—symbolized especially by sexual intrusion on family women—by the elements of the street.[27] Da Matta's provocative and impressionistic work has inspired a number of historians to investigate the processes that have shaped this opposition in both public and private life. Peter Beattie has demonstrated that late-nineteenth-century military officials worked to change their corporation's abominable public image through a discourse of military masculinity and honor that associated the military with an honorable home and distanced it from the disorder and criminality of the street.[28] Works by Sidney Chalhoub, Martha de Abreu Esteves, Rachel Soihet, and Sandra Lauderdale Graham, in contrast, suggest that da Matta's broad interpretation does not describe the range of working-class attitudes toward the street in the nineteenth century, which in many ways contradicted elite assumptions.[29] I argue that competing attitudes about the street among people of different classes, generations, genders, and ideological positions generated a variety of conflicts in personal relationships as well as in municipal administration, law enforcement, and national image-making. Examination of these conflicts shows that the house/street binary is not a homogeneous or static cultural system. The values, practices, and relationships associated with each side of the binary change over time and vary among different social groups and individuals. The binary nonetheless remained meaningful in a society long dominated by the personalized power structures of family-based corporate institutions.

As historian Richard Graham has argued, it would have taken a revolution to change the paternalistic and hierarchical social order of the nineteenth century, and Brazil did not have a revolution.[30] Both slavery and the monarchy were overturned without major upset to the nation's social order over the long term. Likewise, the honor codes that had sustained the colonial social order were rewritten by imperial and republican jurists, but they did not disappear.

Chapter 1 of this book analyzes the ways Brazilian jurists "modernized" the legal defense of honor, especially sexual honor, under the Empire (1822–1889) and the Republic (1889–1930). Imperial and republican jurists believed that the history of civilization was marked by ever greater respect for the equality of individual citizens and state protection of women's sexual honor. These two principles proved juridically incompatible, since the defense of women's honor rested on the existence of the corporate institution of the family and gender inequality in constitutional, civil, and penal law. Moreover, even without knowing it, jurists who interpreted

Brazil's legal codes continued to imbue honor with its older racial and class components. Honor thus frequently obscured contradictions between official principles of universal citizenship, equal rights, and democracy, and the realities of gender, class, and racially based discrimination.

The defense of sexual honor was also a means by which jurists enhanced their collective role as a public power, a role challenged by the Catholic Church and other contenders to moral authority. As Martha de Abreu Esteves has shown in her study of turn-of-the-century juridical texts and deflowering cases, early republican jurists and legal-medical experts paid increasing attention to "scientific" measures of honesty, such as the physiological marks of virginity. In the process, they created more rigid categories of normal and deviant female sexuality. Adapting Michel Foucault's hypothesis for Western Europe, Esteves argues that this indicates that the republican desire to consolidate the bourgeois capitalist order in the aftermath of slavery required new forms of social discipline. Jurists, like other professional groups, used sexual categories and norms as both the base of a broader system of power relations and a means of disciplining individual families.[31]

I build on Esteves's research by tracing the progression of legal debates over honor in different branches of law before and after the crucial early republican period. By focusing on the fissures and major lines of theoretical and political differences among jurists, I explain changes in law not as a coherent response to the disciplinary needs of a new capitalist order, but as a complex process of negotiation and discord among professional experts. Thus, although criminal and civil law were meant to fix a coherent set of rules by which to judge family honor and punish its offense, jurists never reached complete consensus on how to interpret these rules. Constant debate on topics such as the boundaries of juridical authority in issues of morality or the meaning of legal terms such as "deflower," "seduction," and "honest woman" reflected political divisions among jurists. These debates also highlighted many of the social tensions that made it difficult for them to assert the primacy and objectivity of law. When social conflicts heightened in the 1920s and 1930s, debates over the definition of sexual honor and jurists' role in defending it intensified as well.

The transformation of legal notions of family honor, interesting in itself, also serves to frame the relationship between discourses of gender and nationhood and processes of broad social, cultural, and political change. In the heady nationalism that followed World War I, anxiety as well as excitement about imminent transformations in the nation's economic base, political system, and social hierarchies reverberated in debates over personal honor and women's sexuality. Western Europe and, increasingly, the United States clearly set the standards against which Brazilian professional elites measured their own country. Yet the liberal individualism and the class and racial conflicts of the industrialized West became as much a warning as a beacon for Brazilian observers.[32] While European capitals seemed to be falling into economic disarray and social debauchery, many Brazilian intellectuals and politicians boasted of their nation's moral and even material superiority, attributing both to the fortitude of the "traditional Brazilian family." Only by conserving the stabilizing force of "natural" social hierarchies epitomized by patriarchal honor, these men (and some women) argued, could Brazil's leaders promote progress and civilization. Yet those who wanted to transform the established political and social order often attacked older notions of gender and family honor as remnants of an outdated social system that kept Brazil from catching up with the "civilized" world. Political militants and progressive professional elites who opposed the nation's oligarchical political structures attacked what they came to consider archaic patriarchal traditions, including the veneration of virginity and the inflation of sexual honor. This position, supported by many feminists, held that "backward" notions of honor frustrated progressive efforts to modernize the family in ways compatible with social and economic advancement and contemporary global tendencies.

Chapters 2 and 3 explore these conflicting discourses from two different angles. Chapter 2 considers the ways that divergent ideas about what constituted an honorable people surfaced in controversies over how best to represent the capital city to visiting European royalty—King Albert and Queen Elisabeth of Belgium—in 1920. Official preparations for this event recalled Rio's traumatic recent history of urban renewal (1902–1910), when republican leaders had worked to transform the capital into a showcase of their "civilized" modern nation. After the rubble was cleared away, police and other public officials worked to enforce boundaries that segregated honest families and honorable public functions from the "dangerous classes" and dishonest public women. Ten years later, Rio received Belgian royalty with a magnificent display that seemed to validate these policies. Yet controversy over the visit foreshadowed the imminent eruption of long-simmering conflicts, conflicts that illustrate alternative visions of national identity, modernity, and the gendered boundaries of public space.

These conflicts were felt in renewed legal debates over sexual honor in the 1920s and 1930s. Chapter 3 describes these debates as they emerged from various social hygiene campaigns that mobilized a new generation of republican jurists. In their struggles to reform "popular mentality" or state actions in regard to issues such as prostitution, crimes of passion, and women's virginity, these urban professionals were no more unified than their turn-of-the-century predecessors. Yet in contrast to earlier legal debates over the meaning of sexual honor, which highlighted social tensions that arose from the process of legitimation of republican institutions, the debates of the interwar period reflected political battles that challenged the legitimacy of the Republic itself. Many young legal and medical authorities attacked the earlier belief that social preoccupation with virginity or sexual honor was a mark of advanced civilization and moral superiority, arguing to the contrary that it manifested the backwardness of Brazil's traditional political and social institutions. Like their more conservative colleagues, however, reformist jurists were concerned about the effects of "modern life" on women's moral and maternal functions, and thus on the nation's future generations.

Stories recounted in police and public health reports, newspapers, and deflowering complaints that flooded the Brazilian courts through the first half of the twentieth century suggest that unlike the professional elites, most of the city's residents did not ponder the exigencies of nation-building or moral uplift, whether in their everyday social interactions or at times of personal crisis that brought them to court as defendants, victims, or witnesses. Instead, they borrowed selectively from available notions of honor and modernity when positioning themselves in conflicts ranging from adolescent rebellion, domestic violence, and disputes over lost virginity to battles concerning regulation of work, housing, and leisure.

My analysis of the significance of honor in the everyday life of the city's working-class majority is based on a systematic analysis of 450 police investigations and trials of sexual crimes such as the deflowering of Maria Pereira described above. While chapters 1, 2, and 3 describe public debates about prostitution, personal honor, and crimes of passion, chapters 4 and 5 draw almost exclusively from criminal records of these sexual crimes to discuss the ways private citizens interpreted honor in their intimate relations and personal conflicts. These cases are particularly illuminating for two reasons. First, they represent one of the most common criminal complaints brought to police. Deflowering cases, as was mentioned above, numbered about five hundred a year between 1920 and 1940, compared to, for example, a yearly average of fewer than 150 homicide cases, a fraction of which might be considered crimes of passion. More important, as Manoel Souza's nervous letter suggests, deflowering cases generally involved conflicts common in most neighborhoods: sexual relations between young people followed by pressure on the reluctant man to marry the woman.[33]

Of course, precautions are in order when using criminal records of any kind as sources for understanding cultural values. First, there is the problem of official mediation. Unfortunately, letters like the one Manoel Souza wrote to his friend back home in Portugal are not available in most cases. Instead, we must rely on depositions and testimony recorded by police and court officials. The documents, written in the third person, exclude interrogators' questions and tend to use a formulaic technical language that probably obscures the nuances of the original speech. Moreover, people tell stories and perform roles in court that they hope will convince the police officer or the judge; they may or may not believe their own stories, and they might play different roles elsewhere. Finally, the courts tend to record exceptional situations. Judging from the ways witnesses describe the deflowering conflicts that did go to court, it is evident that most conflicts over virginity, particularly involving middle- or upper-class families, were resolved privately.

Criminal records provide, nonetheless, a uniquely rich source for social historians. It is possible to read between the lines of formulaic legal language to find evidence of how victims, defendants, and witnesses describe not only the events that brought them to court, but also diverse social relationships and actions that they consider right or wrong. Even when they lie or invent moral stances, they do so in ways that they assume will be credible, and that therefore help trace the boundaries of commonly accepted morality. A common criticism of criminal cases as sources for social history is that they record experiences of deviants rather than social norms. Yet by analyzing the social profiles of victims, defendants, and witnesses and by reading the records of sexual crime against other types of sources such as demographic data, newspapers, and other forms of social and political commentary, it becomes clear that these courtroom dramas seldom reflect merely the antisocial deviance of a marginalized sector of society. Instead, they generally emerge from unusual crises in relationships and conflicts that are otherwise common to the city's working-class population.

In recounting and analyzing these conflicts, I build upon a rich historiography on popular culture in Rio de Janeiro, mostly focused on the nineteenth and early twentieth centuries. A few works have used criminal records to analyze the cultural norms and values of the city's working class, including most notably Sidney Chalhoub's pathbreaking study of homicide records and Martha de Abreu Esteves's superb analysis of eighty-eight turn-of-the-century deflowering cases, as well as a joint study that compares Esteves's records to a subset of the records I consulted.[34] This book diverges, however, from these earlier works' emphasis on the cultural autonomy of "popular" and "elite," or "official," cultures. As Chalhoub recognized in later work, although this dual cultural process is a useful means of describing the distancing of social classes during the Old Republic and the role of poor residents in shaping their own lives, the concept of cohesive, autonomous cultures is of limited value in explaining processes of change.[35] It also does not help make sense of the stories that I found in court testimony.

In my reading of criminal records, I find that working-class victims, defendants, and witnesses, as well as lawyers, prosecutors, and judges, shared common vocabularies of honor and gender. They interpreted and deployed these concepts, however, in response to competing, sometimes contradictory demands and interests. Thus, and not surprisingly, I find little evidence that individuals who testified in court rejected the moral values or gender norms defended by the law. Yet their "strategic repetition" of these norms and values, to borrow Judith Butler's phrase, did not replicate the law exactly. Rather, individual interpretations of these norms and values varied, sometimes in patterns that contributed to the reshaping of the law.[36]

Like public officials, the private citizens who testified in deflowering cases frequently invoked values they considered "traditional," such as the confinement of women's sexuality within marriage. They also generally shared with jurists several basic assumptions about sexual honor. Deponents agreed, for example, that a young woman's honor was contingent on her submission to the vigilance of her protectors (usually family), whereas a man's honor was recognized as his freedom from such vigilance, and that a man who took an honest girl's virginity had a responsibility to "repair the damage" through marriage. Men and women (and their families) battled bitterly with one another, however, over the terms of the marriage contract. Moreover, these traditional values were countered by social institutions that have predominated throughout Brazil's history, such as premarital sexual relations and cohabitation, informal marriages, divorce, and female-headed extended families. Indeed, mothers of deflowering victims often challenged the notion that "family" was a patriarchal unit by asserting their role as authoritative heads of honorable families and defenders of their daughters' honor. At the same time, many young women insisted that their "liberated" behavior was "modern," not immoral; others used their virginity strategically in diverse power struggles, including rebellions against their mothers' authority. Taken together, their testimony suggests that some women's new attitudes and behavior were stretching the boundaries of acceptable gender norms, while other women maneuvered within these boundaries to increase their personal autonomy.

Similarly, deponents in deflowering trials constructed notions of honor that reproduced racial and class hierarchies. They did so, however, in response to interests and experiences that could simultaneously lead them to challenge these hierarchies. Stories of romance among individuals categorized in different "color" groups suggest that although racial endogamy seemed to be a social norm, notions of racial difference were complex. The general silence on race or color in the testimony as a whole was broken only by ambiguous references to racial stereotypes and scattered signs of moral indignation at the racist attitudes of opponents. Evidence from the criminal records as a whole suggests that although whiteness was valued, racism was recognized as morally reprehensible, and racial difference was an illegitimate basis of opposition to marriage partnerships.

By the late 1930s, the meaning of honor had stretched in so many ways that its effectiveness as a means of social differentiation had declined dramatically, so much so that jurists debated whether its legal defense served a legitimate "social purpose" and redefined it in the new penal code of 1940, which, among other changes, classified sexual crimes as offenses against "social customs," not "family honor."[37] This book concludes by considering this decline in light of the official ideology of state paternalism under dictator Getúlio Vargas after 1937, an ideology sustained by a fevered rhetoric of "organic" links between centralized state power, national honor, and the "traditional Brazilian family." In response to the anxieties unleashed by social struggles and populist experiments of the 1920s and 1930s, the Vargas regime reinvented honor as a mechanism for legitimizing authority. By exalting "traditional" family values, associating them with national honor, and identifying Vargas as the father of the nation's poor, the regime sought to naturalize centralized, hierarchical structures of authority and to ensure social order while promoting economic modernization. This represented a victory for conservative authoritarians, who were able to assert their vision of the "proper place" for different types of men and women through a rhetoric of national honor. The conservative triumph, however, was not unequivocal. Not only did struggles over the definition of gender and honor continue, but conservative ideology could not ignore the drastic changes in gender norms and in the meaning of female honor that had occurred in the preceding two decades—changes brought about in large measure through the everyday conflicts among people in Rio de Janeiro who held competing visions of their city and of the places of women and men in it.

1 Sexual Honor and Republican Law

✻

State power based in science → foc

At the end of the nineteenth century and through the first three decades of the twentieth, Brazilian legal-medical specialists produced a substantial literature on the study of the hymen, counting themselves increasingly among the world's foremost authorities on its morphology. Renowned practitioners such as Nina Rodrigues, Nascimento Silva, Agostinho J. de Souza Lima, Miguel Sales, Flamínio Favero, Oscar Freire, and later J. P. Porto-Carrero and Afrânio Peixoto published extensive studies aimed at correcting the "factual errors in the scientific notions" of not only Brazilian professionals, but also European masters.[1]

European science had not ignored the membrane. Brazilian legal-medical literature is replete with citations of nineteenth-century studies by French, Italian, and German pioneers who recorded and compared hymens observed in various categories of female bodies: prostitutes and virgins, married women and small children, fetuses and corpses, and an assortment of animal species.[2] Nonetheless, as late as 1934, when Peixoto published *Sexologia forense*, misconceptions about the relationship between virginity and hymen morphology persisted, resulting in tragic misdiagnoses.[3] Peixoto rested his authority on the matter on his experience as the founder and first director of the Medical-Legal Service (renamed Institute of Legal Medicine in 1922) in Rio de Janeiro, where, he explained, the demand for "deflowering examinations" was extremely high. His findings were far more conclusive than previous European studies because his sample was vastly greater in size. While he had personally observed 2,701 hymens from 1907 to 1915, European masters "could count fewer than 300, at the end of their lives, after thirty years as medical-investigators."[4]

At issue was the precision of medical proof of female virginity, or, more frequently, its absence, in legal disputes over lost honor. In Brazil and many European nations, this evidence was provided by state legal-

18

medical specialists in obligatory examinations of female victims of sexual crimes, even when the victim's prior virginity was supposedly not a legal issue, as was the case in most European nations.[5] In Brazil, prior virginity almost always was at issue, since deflowering cases such as the one involving Manoel Souza and Maria Pereira were overwhelmingly the most common "offense of honor" brought to trial. Providing deflowering examinations, as Miguel Sales pointed out in 1928, was one of the most important functions of legal-medical work in Rio de Janeiro.[6]

Peixoto believed that both demography and culture explained his advantage over the European experts. "In Brazil, principally in Rio de Janeiro," he posited, "the scarcity of women makes them so precious, that upon loss of virginity, they promptly demand due repair by marriage."[7] Furthermore, while Northern Europeans were indifferent toward the hymen, "Latins have a hymen fetishism: those of the Americas kill and die for it. For this reason, any loss of the jewel provokes a prompt complaint . . . up to 500 per year, in Rio alone."[8] Sales, reminding his readers that "we all know that the sexual preoccupation predominates in inferior types, in whom it constitutes a fixed idea," explained that the preoccupation with the hymen among the "Latin nations" was due to multiple factors "such as race, climate, upbringing, environment, ignorance and superstition of a great number of illiterates or individuals of a very rudimentary moral and mental culture."[9]

Neither Peixoto nor Sales offered convincing evidence for their explanations of why so many lower-class Brazilian women brought cases of lost virginity to the attention of the Institute of Legal Medicine. While the ratio of females to males increased to near equal proportions in Rio de Janeiro by 1940, there was no corresponding decline in reports of sexual crime. Furthermore, in her analysis of eighty-eight turn-of-the-century deflowering cases, Martha de Abreu Esteves found a variety of complex motivations and conflicts that cannot be attributed simply to "Latin" culture or ignorance.[10] In the chapters that follow, I argue this was true for the interwar decades as well. On one hand, the persistent valorization of female virginity and male sexual aggressiveness, coupled with a longstanding tradition of premarital sexual relations, gave men an enormous advantage over their female sexual partners before marriage. Some men, like Manoel Souza, preferred to maintain this advantage by putting off marriage indefinitely. Given the power inequality of such a hierarchical relationship, it is not surprising that women, or their families, frequently recruited allies from outside the relationship in cases of conflict.[11] Whereas middle or upper-class families might appeal to their male kin and private social networks in these kinds of conflicts, working-class daughters, particularly those whose fathers were absent, often turned to the local police. On the other hand, we shall see that the actual conflicts that led to legal action did not follow any set pattern. Young women mobilized resources, including their honor, their virginity, and the criminal justice system, in diverse ways to negotiate within a variety of hierarchical relationships. These included their relationships with parents and employers as well as with male sexual partners.

Although Sales's and Peixoto's observations do not explain why so many working-class women brought deflowering cases to the police, they do provide fascinating commentary on Brazilian law. Legal-medical specialists' studies of the hymen, which culminated in Peixoto's campaign against "hymenolatry," demonstrate a remarkable preoccupation among legal authorities with sexual honor and female virginity throughout the fifty-year reign of the 1890 penal code.[12] Although Sales's comments about "inferior types" were aimed at Rio's uneducated and racially mixed masses, it seems that "the sexual preoccupation" was particularly prominent among the self-defined elite group of jurists and legal-medical specialists who were his peers.

For Sales, Peixoto, and others writing in the 1920s and 1930s, excessive legal concern with physiological virginity (as opposed to "moral virginity") and defense of sexual honor was retrograde—evidence of Brazil's backwardness. The "anachronistic crime of deflowering," Peixoto argued, "is dying and will die here, as it has already in more civilized lands."[13] Peixoto's work to speed its demise was part of a broader movement to redefine sexual honor in the 1920s and 1930s.

The jurists who had shaped Brazilian law at the outset of the First Republic, however, had cited this same concern with sexual honor and virginity as evidence of Brazil's progress. Judge and law professor Francisco Viveiros de Castro expressed the sentiment of his turn-of-the-century peers when he proclaimed that "respect for the honor of women is not a sentiment innate in man, but rather a conquest of civilization, the victory of moral ideas over the brutality of the instincts."[14] According to Esteves, Viveiros de Castro's generation believed that although Brazilian legal codes had progressively "conquered civilization" since the colonial period by defending women's honor with increasing precision, the social and demographic transformations brought by the abolition of slavery made it necessary to reinvigorate the civilizing campaign.[15] Esteves concludes that jurists' attempts to impose "civilized" gender norms and contain popular sexuality within "hygienic" families were part of a wider project of social control under the First Republic. State and professional authorities, jurists among them, saw the family as the basis of their new nation, a social space that would produce an honest, disciplined, and self-sacrificing labor force.[16]

Despite a broad consensus on the importance of "civilized" family values, however, jurists and legislators of the early Republic disagreed about just what these values were and how the state should promote them. Their conflicting views on virginity and sexual honor reflected broader struggles over the power to shape the nation's political and cultural future. We shall see in chapter 3 that legal debates over how to define sexual honor and why it mattered demonstrate that both nationalist discourses and the power relations they supported were furiously contested in the decades between the two world wars. In the 1920s, a new generation of legal experts joined diverse groups of critics to challenge older definitions of sexual honor and family values as well as the moral authority of the Republic itself.

Before turning to post–World War I debates over honor and challenges to the political and juridical order of the First Republic, it will be useful to examine the struggle of turn-of-the-century jurists to consolidate that order. These men's attempts to define sexual honor and justify their role in defending it highlight many of the political and social tensions that accompanied the legitimization of state power after the fall of the Empire in 1889. Controversies over the rights and responsibilities of individual citizens and legal subjects, the state's power to regulate public and private life, and the role of jurists and other public officials in republican society were all played out in debates over sexual honor.

Jurists under the First Republic no longer dominated national politics to the same degree as their predecessors, who had run the imperial bureaucracy.[17] Their authority rested increasingly on their claim to professional expertise, and this claim did not go uncontested. Viveiros de Castro's cohort encountered resistance not only among their colleagues in the courts, law schools, and legislature, but also among the population they sought to perfect, which had developed diverse moral values and sexual norms that did not match the ideals of professional elites. Reform-minded jurists also had to justify their intervention into the realm of private morality against the claims of family and religious authorities. In the process, they found new ways to combine notions of family honor that formed the basis of Catholic, patriarchal social organization with concepts of personal honor that were more compatible with the values of a secular bourgeoisie. In this regard, they built on the work of generations of liberal jurists who preceded them and paved the way for more radical thinkers in the decades ahead.

The transformation of the legal concept of honor was not a linear movement from traditional to modern values, although many jurists saw it that way. Nor did Brazilians mimic foreign models, although they read the latest debates in European legal scholarship and adapted them to their own local concerns. Instead, jurists responded to difficult questions of culture and tradition that accompanied the construction of the new Brazilian Republic. Although nationalists of left and right agreed in theory that law should reflect the historical moral values of a republic's people, they disagreed about whether Brazil's racially mixed, illiterate population constituted a "people," and about which shared cultural traits or moral values deserved to be preserved in law. How could jurists attend to both "the customs, traditions, and juridical principles that are the legacy of our past" and the "demands of our progress and social evolution"?[18] Should jurists try to replace Brazilians' "propensity toward sensuality and love" with "modern" hygienic norms imported from Europe?[19] Should they appropriate the control mechanisms of the "traditional Brazilian family," or strengthen private control over these mechanisms?

Turn-of-the-century jurists defined their positions in these conflicts by evaluating and applying theoretical principles to their analyses of Brazilian society and to their judgments in individual criminal cases. In the process, they developed their own body of legal theory, which borrowed eclectically from diverse local and international sources. In the 1920s and 1930s, a subsequent generation would draw on their corpus to redefine the state's defense of honor and expand its intervention in the family while attacking what they saw as the oligarchical basis of state power and the patriarchal values associated with it. The earlier generation, in contrast, worked to reinforce key patriarchal traditions in ways that allowed them to sustain both liberal democratic ideals and the eugenic and disciplinary goals of the republican state.

Brazilian Legal Traditions: Liberalism, Classical Law, and the Imperial Penal Code of 1830

Like many of their European counterparts, reform-minded jurists of Brazil's early Republic worked to change a set of legal principles that had been passed down from the liberal heyday of the early nineteenth century. For the self-declared "new generation" of reform-minded jurists at the turn of the century, the influence of "classical law," as they termed Enlightenment legal principles such as individual equality before the law, free will, moral responsibility, and proportional punishment, had represented an early phase in their nation's moral progress from backward colony to modern nation.[20] This progress had begun with the liberal wave that swept through the Brazilian Empire a decade after its independence in 1822, leaving in its wake a new criminal justice system.[21]

Imperial criminal law was grounded in the criminal code of 1830.[22] The code, a bold expression of liberal legal philosophy that Europe's most progressive jurists were still struggling to implement in their nations, passed swiftly through the Brazilian legislature, replacing the criminal section (book 5) of the Portuguese Philippine Ordinances of 1603.[23] As contemporary jurists and politicians complained, corruption and problems of judicial procedure made it difficult to guarantee that criminal law would be applied effectively.[24] The new code was significant nonetheless, both for the principles it laid out and as a symbol of Brazil's new status as a modern nation. Later jurists, still eager to display Brazil's progress, frequently remarked that the 1830 code was one of the most advanced compendiums of its time and had earned Brazil the admiration of prominent European legal scholars.[25] As Latin America's first autonomous penal code, it also influenced penal law continent-wide, enhancing Brazil's leadership efforts in the region.[26]

The principles that grounded the 1830 criminal code revealed its authors' inspiration in the classical theory that was then taking hold in Europe. Equally important was the influence of the French Revolution and the desire of early imperial jurists to eliminate what they saw as remnants of the absolutist colonial regime: excessive power over the individual by the state, based in the king's claim to represent divine will; vindictive and arbitrary punishment, decided "at the king's mercy"; differentiation among classes of legal subjects that was the basis of aristocratic privilege; and the fusion of law and morality.[27] Although a series of royal decrees in the late eighteenth century had already ameliorated some of the penal excesses of church and state that liberals associated with Portugal's "dark ages," much of the legislation was unclear or even contradictory, and it lacked a coherent set of principles that justified and limited state authority.[28] Codification of penal law in 1830 aimed to resolve these problems. On the premise that the law should sacrifice individual freedom only to the degree necessary for greater social welfare, the new code specified the "common social good" served by repression of each "criminal act," defined minimal, fixed punishments for each crime, and established equal "criminal responsibility" regardless of the identity of the offender, with a few crucial exceptions.[29]

In practice, jurists could not establish objective distinctions between crime and immorality or uphold the equality of legal subjects in criminal law when social norms and civil legislation differentiated the rights of individuals by gender and status through the institutions of the family and slavery. Moreover, defining these legal categories and institutions was so difficult that legislators found it impossible to codify civil law, despite the efforts of successive juridical commissions.[30] In the absence of a civil code until 1916, books 1–4 of the Philippine Ordinances reigned by default, modified by scattered imperial decrees and by the *Lei da Boa Razão* of 1769, which allowed magistrates to use their "good sense" to adapt Roman and canon law to contemporary customs, especially in situations not specifically regulated by existing laws.[31]

It is not surprising, then, that the criminal code of 1830 did not completely erase the vestiges of medieval morality from criminal law. There were fundamental changes: the code eliminated punishment of sins such as sodomy and other "carnal conjunctions" between consenting unmarried adults, and it rescinded husbands' right to kill adulterous wives and their lovers, which the Philippine Ordinances had permitted unless the lover was "of higher quality" than the husband.[32] Yet although nineteenth-century liberals attacked the Philippine Ordinances for authorizing private vengeance and patriarchal privileges, they failed to purge the new code of the concepts of honor and morality that had provided the logical foundation for such privileges.

Like most other southern European legal systems, the Philippine Ordinances had recognized a variety of offenses to honor alongside different kinds of physical injury or material loss; laws punishing these offenses were thus interspersed throughout the civil and criminal sections. Some of these offenses were related explicitly to political authority and public order: slandering the king or his likeness was a capital offense, for instance, and insulting public officials was equivalent to resisting arrest.[33] The Crown regulated the markers and rituals of honor (titles, clothing, dueling, and, as we have seen, wife-killing), and punished gossip and insults under various circumstances.[34] Offenses to women's sexual honor were more complex: they might offend the moral authority of church and state, the inviolability and public reputation of a household, private paternal authority, individual integrity, or family patrimony.[35]

Under the 1830 code, honor was to become an expression of personal virtue rather than social precedence or religious morality. Ignoring rituals of absolute power and ascribed status, lawmakers created a chapter on crimes against individual honor, including slander, libel, and sexual offenses. Yet contrary to two of the code's fundamental principles—individual equality and the separation of crimes against the individual from crimes against the state—the laws ranked the seriousness of slander in descending order according to whether the victim was a member of the emperor's family, a public official or institution, or a private individual. The laws thus continued to invest honor/authority first in the monarch, then his representatives; secondarily, they protected the authority that rested on an individual's public reputation.[36]

The survival of older concepts of honor and morality was most evident, however, in the new code's definition of female legal subjects. As the code reduced the variety of moral offenses and the severity of punishments, it maintained the previous law's underlying principle of gender difference. Thus, murderous husbands could still cite their wives' adultery as an attenuating circumstance that could free them from punishment, and cuckolded husbands who chose not to murder could have their wives imprisoned.[37] The Philippine Ordinances had condemned adulterous wives to death, banishing to Africa only husbands who "kept and supported" a concubine. The 1830 code made the same distinction, changing the punishment to one to three years' imprisonment for both adulteresses and husbands who kept concubines.[38]

Punishments for sexual crimes had already been reduced by royal decrees in 1775 and 1784; they were lowered further in 1830. Rapists received the death penalty under the Ordinances; three to twelve years' imprisonment under the new code (one month to two years if the victim were a prostitute). The Ordinances had ordered any man who "slept with a willing virgin or honest widow" to marry the victim or provide for her dowry; lacking the means to do either, he received banishment to Africa and, if he was a plebeian, public lashings. The 1830 code retained the dowry payment for these crimes (now "defloration" and "seduction of an honest woman" younger than seventeen[39]), along with a blander exile of one to three years outside the offended woman's town. Marriage to the victim freed men of punishment for all sexual offenses after 1830; the Ordinances had granted this pardon only in cases of consensual sex, not rape.[40]

Clearly, sexual crimes represented both a different kind of affront and a different kind of honor than insults. The criminal acts were not verbal, but physical; the harm done was often not just moral, but material. Victims were exclusively female, and their honor was associated with sexual virtue and loyalty to husbands, not individual autonomy and public authority. This complexity was reflected in the code's vague and inconsistent definitions of sexual crime victims. Promiscuous women might logically be excluded, yet there was a penalty for rape of prostitutes. Seduction and rape laws requiring that the victim be "honest" did not stipulate whether the criteria were the same in each case; the deflowering law mentioned only the woman's prior virginity. Thus, although the victim's status was crucial to the definition of the criminal act, the law did not provide guidelines for evaluating this status.

In practice, moral virtue and other markers of honor such as color and class combined in ways that made it impossible to establish consistent and objective criteria for defending female honor. Could a master be convicted of raping his slave?[41] Could a minor who was immodest or who worked and socialized in public complain of deflowering?[42] Sixty years later, jurists would complain that the conceptualization of family, honor, and sexuality was confusing, the respective crimes illogically organized, and punishment poorly justified in the 1830 code.[43] Attempts to correct these errors would provoke contentious legal debates that outlived both the Empire and the Republic.

The incompatibility of slavery and the universal right to freedom provoked even greater legal conflicts.[44] Faced with regional and popular insurrections during the liberal 1830s, most legislators came to the conclusion that classical legal principles such as equality were incompatible with the "cultural level" and "social evolution" of Brazil's population. Brazil's population, they argued (and many who considered themselves liberals agreed), not yet a "people," was unprepared for a social contract and would revert to barbarism if not tightly disciplined.[45] Already in 1830, Conservatives used arguments of this sort to guarantee slaveholders' rights to apply private justice through corporal punishment and to maintain the death penalty for what they considered the most heinous crimes, including slave insurrection. Over the decades that followed, complaining that the law's "excessive liberalism" led to regional revolts, slave insubordination, and general social unrest, state and imperial legislators passed a number of decrees that modified the original code, differentiating among types of criminals and victims, imposing harsher punishments, and strengthening centralized state authority.[46]

At the same time, the contradiction between the Empire's slave-based economy and the principle of individual liberty that underlay its liberal legal codes resulted in what Keila Grinberg describes as "the law of ambiguity" regarding slaves' civil status. Even as the law continued to uphold the property rights of slaveholders over slaves, lawyers and magistrates could successfully evoke the liberal concept of universal rights to freedom in favor of slaves.[47] This contradiction was apparent to late-nineteenth-century liberals and abolitionists, who called for the revision of imperial law to eliminate the distinctions between slave and free persons and to respond to the new needs of a society of "free men."

Defining the Brazilian Family in Republican Civil Law

With the abolition of slavery in 1888 and the overthrow of the Empire the following year, the need to define citizens, legal subjects, and the relationship between state and society gained new urgency. In a climate of vigorous political militancy centered in Rio de Janeiro, arguments for citizenship rights for women and men of all classes were widely disseminated and debated, appearing in the press, in political rallies, and in the favored forum for popular political debates, Carnival parades.[48] Several radical members of the Republican Party, most of whom were urban professionals, supported women's suffrage, and it was debated in the 1891 Constituent Convention.[49]

The Constitution of 1891 proclaimed a republic of free and equal citizens. As was the case in nineteenth-century legislation, however, the Constitution failed to define equality and citizenship clearly. The Constitution itself did not mention gender, but referred to the Brazilian people with masculine collective pronouns ("all" [todos] were equal under the law; "citizens" [cidadãos] could vote). Although, as in all Romance languages, the masculine plural in Portuguese can include women and men, republican officials interpreted this wording to exclude women. By limiting "active" citizenship, which included the rights to vote and hold public office, to literate males twenty-one or older, legislators guaranteed continued rule by a privileged minority.[50] Along with children, the insane, beggars, illiterates, and Indians protected by the state, women became "inactive" citizens, subject to republican laws but denied rights to civic participation.

Proponents of women's rights also lost important battles over republican civil law. The young jurist Clóvis Bevilaqua, commissioned in 1899 by then Justice Minister Epitácio Pessoa to write the republican civil code, produced a document that most observers considered a compromise between reformists such as himself and those who fought to preserve "Brazilian traditions."[51] The legislature nonetheless passed Bevilaqua's proposal into law only after removing what Bevilaqua considered its firmest "liberal dispositions"—those that enhanced the rights of women and illegitimate children in the family.[52] While this demonstrated divisions among public authorities over the type of family to be defended, it also reinforced the continuing political importance of the institution. No one, and certainly not Bevilaqua, doubted that the family would remain Brazil's most important civil institution under the new Republic, nor that its "harmony" required maintaining distinctions between the rights of women and men.[53]

Although Bevilaqua and other young reformists agreed with more conservative lawmakers that preserving the family justified the suppression of women's individual liberties, the two sides disagreed on the extent of this suppression. Bevilaqua was eager to adapt civil law to what he considered the modern family—a family held together by love and mutual respect rather than the "egotistical authority" of archaic patriarchs. He believed that nature determined that men and women should play fundamentally different but "equally noble" roles in the family and in society. Since men were the natural heads of families, it was necessary to grant them certain authority over their wives, but this should not override the principle of legal equality.[54]

Following this principle, Bevilaqua wrote in an early draft of the civil code that equal rights and responsibilities applied to "all human beings." A congressional review commission changed the phrase to "all men." Bevilaqua explained that this change was merely philological and reflected a Roman juridical tradition that inferred inclusion of women in universal references to "man."[55] Yet the review commission also rejected—without so much as a discussion—Bevilaqua's proposal to concede married women the right to represent themselves legally. Over his protests, the civil code reproduced the gender distinctions that had distinguished between "capable" and "incapable" legal subjects in the Philippine Ordinances. Husbands were legally capable, which meant they could represent themselves and their wives and children in court and before other public institutions. As "head of the couple" and holders of *patrio poder* (paternal authority), husbands also enjoyed the power to determine where their wives and children would live, whether and when they would work, and how their property would be administered. Married women's "inactive" status in constitutional law was paralleled by their "incapacity" in civil law—again, a status they shared with minors, the insane, and state-protected Indians.[56]

Bevilaqua continued to defend his opus despite these modifications, explaining that "the need to harmonize conjugal relations" justified the "sacrifice of justice" for women. He insisted, moreover, that women's subordination to men was "very slight, almost merely formal" in the new code, since husbands were required to allow their wives to administer the household expenses and women had the power to control their husbands' financial transactions.[57]

Although none of these justifications satisfied Brazilian feminists, who mobilized to improve women's legal status almost as soon as the code was passed,[58] it must be noted that married women's property and custodial rights in the Iberian legal traditions that Brazil inherited were far superior to those of most contemporary European nations. In Brazil, husbands and wives had always been equal partners in ownership of communal marital property and wives retained ownership of their dowries. Under the Philippine Ordinances, husbands had administered common property, but needed their wives' permission for important transactions. Upon the death of either spouse, the survivor maintained half of the common property; almost all of the other half was divided equally among children or other heirs. These provisions, which were maintained in the 1916 civil code, contrasted starkly with patrilineal traditions such as those of Anglo-American common law, which granted husbands full testamentary freedom and unbridled power over common property.[59]

As Muriel Nazzari demonstrates, however, with the gradual decline of the extended family over the eighteenth and nineteenth centuries, making way for nuclear families headed by independent men, elite women lost their position of economic equality vis-à-vis their husbands, and this was reflected in civil law. Unlike earlier legislation, under the 1916 code women automatically took their husbands' surname and husbands were required to support their wives and children.[60] Commenting on these laws, Bevilaqua suggested that they demonstrated Brazil's progress, since in "modern society," it was a man's duty and honor to support his wife.[61] In any case, since relatively few professional options were open to women, the social and economic advantages of marriage remained considerable, and may even have increased, for elite women.

The 1916 code did not modernize the legal distinction between "honest" and "dishonest" women, nor the laws that guaranteed the benefits of family membership only for the former. As was true under Philippine law, husbands could annul their marriages if they discovered their bride's defloration or other evidence of prior dishonesty, now considered an "essential error" about her identity.[62] Under another law derived from the Philippine Ordinances, dishonest, or sexually immodest, daughters were subject to disinheritance; this condition did not apply to sons. Women's dishonesty was a serious offense: the only other behavior that resulted in the loss of filial rights was a criminal assault on a parent's honor or patricide.[63]

Following canon law traditions, imperial and republican legislators maintained the principle of free will in marriage partnerships.[64] A few radical legislators and jurists, joined by a small number of pioneering female professionals such as newspaper publisher and author Josefina Alvares de Azevedo and lawyer Mirtes de Campos, favored extending free will beyond marriage vows by allowing no-fault divorce.[65] Yet while debates over divorce were among the major causes of the delay in the passage of the civil code, opposition to it was overwhelming, and it was not legalized until 1977. Civil law did allow legal separation, prohibiting remarriage. If the wife were poor and innocent of offenses to her husband's honor, she had the right to receive alimony and child support from her husband.[66] Records of marital separation litigation reveal that the separated woman's subsequent dishonest behavior, or sexual relations with other men, could strip her of these rights.[67]

The rights of children born out of wedlock provoked even greater controversy than divorce. Iberian legal traditions were remarkably forgiving of illegitimate birth. Under the Philippine Ordinances, "natural" children, or those born to marriageable parents, possessed the same inheritance rights as legitimate children, as long as their parents were plebeians. Plebeian fathers could voluntarily recognize their natural offspring; if they did not, these children could prove paternity using various kinds of evidence. The law denied inheritance rights to "spurious" children, or those born of incestuous or adulterous unions, but the Crown could grant exceptions to this law along with a "certificate of legitimization." Likewise, nobles, who were not permitted to recognize illegitimate children (whether natural or spurious), could sometimes get around these restrictions by "legitimizing" their children.[68]

In a gesture hailed by some as enlightened, the imperial legislature eliminated distinctions between natural and spurious children and between nobles and plebeians in an 1847 decree. The same decree limited fathers' rights to voluntarily recognize illegitimate children and rescinded illegitimate children's right to sue for paternity all together. Against protests that this law was backward and cruel, punishing innocent children for their parents' sins, prominent nineteenth-century jurists and legislators defended it as necessary protection of "family peace, property, order and public morality" from the scandal and extortion of paternity suits.[69]

Some of these same men helped design the laws regarding illegitimacy in the 1916 civil code. Bevilaqua's original draft reinstated the traditional rights of illegitimate children—now including both natural and spurious—to paternal support and inheritance. To his immense frustration, however, the "reactionary influence" of his opponents resulted in restrictions that made the code "less liberal than the Philippine legislation."[70] Legislators reinstituted the Philippine distinction between spurious and natural children, now prohibiting recognition of the former unless the parents married (possible only if former spouses died). Fathers could voluntarily recognize natural children, giving them the same rights as legitimate children. Natural children could also sue for paternal recognition, but they usually had to prove that they were conceived while the father was "living in concubinage" with the mother, a task that was particularly difficult, since this condition was left undefined.[71] Over the first half of the twentieth century, judges came to distinguish between "honest" and "dishonest" concubines, granting paternal recognition and other only to the offspring of the former.[72]

While jurists, legislators, and the public engaged in fevered debates over the morality of paternity suits, the law that prohibited illegitimate children from suing married women for recognition went almost unnoticed, probably because lawsuits for maternal recognition were extremely rare. Surprisingly, given Bevilaqua's diatribe against the restrictions on paternity suits, the law restricting maternity suits was his own innovation. The law was unprecedented in Brazilian and Portuguese legal traditions, in which maternity was assumed to be obvious, and maternal recognition thus unnecessary.[73] The measure recalls, however, the social practice of concealing illegitimate children in order to protect the honor of women and their families, a practice that was probably common throughout Brazil's history.[74] As Bevilaqua explained, the reason for the new law was to maintain "family peace" by defending the dignity and reputation of married women—an argument he rejected as "reactionary" and "hypocritical" when made in favor of married men. Implicitly, he assumed that it was more damaging to attribute sexual impropriety to wives than to husbands, so much so that justice to the illegitimate children in question should be sacrificed to protect the honor of legitimate families. At the same time, while he held men responsible for their sexual conquests, he argued that family women who had born illegitimate children before their marriage might have been victims of seduction, and thus deserved protection.[75] Judging from its author's observations, then, the law reflected both traditional cultural values that condemned women's illicit sexual behavior, but not men's, as well as the traditional paternalism that diluted liberal principles of equality and responsibility.

Like the laws that defined the rights of legitimate wives and daughters, illegitimacy laws thus reinforced the principle of gender differentiation that emerged from the contentious and lengthy process of codification of civil law. Women did not share all of the rights of men, nor were they equal among themselves. Rather, they were capable or incapable; honest or dishonest, depending on their position in or outside a family.

Defending the Honor of Families: Positivist Jurists and the Classical Penal Code of 1890

Legislative and public debates over the new penal code were much less intense than those over the civil code. While jurists were exasperated at the legislative delays in passing the civil code—sixty-five years passed from the time the imperial legislature rejected the first of a series of commissioned proposals until the adoption of Bevilaqua's proposal in 1916—they complained that the penal code had been adopted too hastily. As had been the case in 1830, the legislature commissioned and passed the penal code in 1890 after little discussion. The penal code became the first compendium of republican law, preceding the 1891 Constitution by nearly a year. Unlike the 1830 criminal code and the 1916 civil code, which were widely hailed in and outside Brazil as models of modern juridical achievement, the 1890 penal code was attacked as poorly written and out of date from its very inception.[76]

In contrast to the explicitly political and economic issues that dominated debates over civil law and spilled out into newspapers and other public media, penal law debates were usually framed around theoretical precepts and tended to remain more firmly in the domain of specialists. At the heart of these theoretical debates, however, were the same concerns to maintain, in "modernized" form, the patriarchal institution of the family and the gendered concept of honor that sustained it.

Debates that placed positivist legal theory in opposition to Brazil's classical law tradition provide the most easily identified dividing line between the new and old generations of penal law professionals at the turn of the century. Young jurists such as Viveiros de Castro, many of whom divided their time between their Federal District courtrooms and legal scholarship, formed an elite among a growing group of urban professionals who believed themselves qualified to diagnose and remedy the social ills that obstructed the nation's progress. Indirectly and to varying degrees, these civilian professionals were inspired by the Comtean philosophical/sociological positivism that dominated military thinking and technical training in late-nineteenth-century Brazil. Although few jurists were members of the Positivist Church or supported the orthodox positivism of some of the radical factions within early republican politics, many espoused variations of Comte's laws of human progress and his belief that society could be studied and perfected through the rational application of scientific principles.[77]

Brazilian jurists, joined by colleagues in the medical field, found endorsement for their intervention in society and politics in the postulates of various European "positivist" legal and medical specialists of the late nineteenth and early twentieth centuries such as the Italian criminal anthropologists Cesare Lombroso and Enrico Ferri, leaders of the French or criminal sociological school such as Gabriel Tarde and Alexandre Lacassagne, or the German jurist Franz von Liszt. Despite enormous differences among them, these criminologists, identified collectively in Brazil as the positive school, or the "new school of penal law," shared a commitment to scientific method and a belief in inherent differences among individuals. They produced a phenomenal array of psychological, sociological, and physiological criteria for classifying types of criminals and "individualizing" sentences accordingly, in the interest of social defense ("regeneration" for "accidental" or "occasional" criminals; permanent seclusion for "habitual," "incurable," or "born criminals").[78]

Up until the late nineteenth century, European positivist criminologists faced formidable resistance from jurists schooled in classical law, who held a very different conception of the individual; the same was true in Brazil. By opposing classical principles such as free will and equality with the thesis that physiological and sociological factors caused deviant behavior and thus attenuated criminal responsibility, positivist legal doctrine provoked the most significant juridical debate of the second half of the nineteenth century all over the Western world.[79] Related to this debate was the question of natural law that had troubled Enlightenment philosophers: were there universal moral and legal concepts common to all rational men and civilized societies, or did morality and law evolve differently according to each society's history, culture, and national conscience?[80] For Brazilian positivist jurists who aimed to shape what they considered a yet unformed national conscience and civilization, these debates seemed particularly urgent. This helps to explain the remarkable prestige that the positive school enjoyed in Brazil by the first decades of the twentieth century, despite jurists' recognition that enthusiasm for the radical claims of scientific criminology was waning in Europe.[81]

It was not the classificatory systems of any one of the positivist criminologists that attracted Brazilian jurists, but rather their common use of modern science and the empirical method to refute what they considered utopian classical principles. Brazilian jurists anxious to promote social and racial advancement saw in positive law a rationale and a method for intervening in the nation's physical and moral development. If positive law promised, as Viveiros de Castro proclaimed, "the moral improvement of the species" in Europe, surely it could help Brazilian jurists reverse the cultural and physical degeneracy that otherwise might doom Brazil to perpetual inferiority.[82]

A few of the most important figures of late-nineteenth-century political and legal thought—most notably Nina Rodrigues, the pioneer of Brazilian anthropology and legal-medical science—adapted the work of Lombroso and other European scientific racists to the Brazilian reality to argue that Indians and "the black race" did not possess reason or free will and could not be considered responsible for criminal behavior. Penal law, Rodrigues insisted, should establish specific kinds of penal institutions and criminal sentences for these "inferior races."[83]

Explicit discrimination or "individualization" on the basis of race, however, never found a place in republican law. Brazilian jurists and legal-medical specialists avoided simple racial determinism, favoring theories that considered environmental and social causes of deviance.[84] In part, the absence of studies of physiological degeneracy and other "anthropological" causes of criminal behavior in Brazil was explained by a lack of technical training and resources. Although a few pioneers beginning with Rodrigues, began to classify Brazilian "ethnographic types" at the end of the nineteenth century, more systematic criminological studies were initiated only in the 1930s by police and legal-medical officials.[85] More important, jurists' preference for environmental, social, and cultural analyses of criminality mirrored the social and racial theories that were being developed in other Brazilian professional and intellectual circles. The medical-psychiatric notion that degeneracy was caused by social and environmental factors, and that races could therefore "improve," would become predominant among nationalist intellectuals and social reformers—including many jurists—in the decades ahead. As studies of medical and psychiatric fields have demonstrated, proponents of environmental explanations did not necessarily reject racist evaluations or policies.[86]

Clearly, turn-of-the-century jurists did not simply mimic European legal scholarship to form a homogeneous positive school. Rather, they analyzed Europe's various legal systems and read European scholars widely, choosing among them to justify their positions on different issues.[87] They employed positive science alongside classical and other juridical tendencies—including traditions derived from canon law, the Philippine Ordinances, and popular custom—to evaluate Brazilian society or pass judgments. Their "radicalism," moreover, was rather muted. Although they argued that the defense of Brazilian society required social reform, most believed this possible through defense of "traditional morality" within the Republic's existing liberal order.[88] And although jurists adapted elements of European positivist theory to argue that the law should recognize social inequalities, the most radical political implications of reformist ideas, including demands for much greater state intervention in the social and economic sphere, would gain force in Brazil only after World War I.

Nonetheless, many legislators, who represented powerful state "oligarchies" as well as religious and other conservative lobbies, along with classically inspired liberals such as the ubiquitous Rui Barbosa, were already suspicious of legal positivism in 1890. To the frustration of the

Republic's most prominent young jurists, the classically oriented penal code of 1890 represented little improvement over the previous code from the perspective of positive science, and the legislature rejected a series of proposals to replace it with a more "modern" document until 1940.[89] Although positivist jurists immediately attacked the code for what they considered its imprecise and outdated conceptions of the sexuality, family, and honor, they took advantage of the space that was left open for interpretation through scholarship and jurisprudence, where they left an indelible mark.

Defining Virginity and Defending Honesty

As had been the case in 1830, traditional concepts of honor and morality retained a central place in the new penal laws, and the defense of family honor became even more prominent than before. In response to criticism that the 1830 code failed to define a specific, logical social purpose for punishing sexual crimes, the defense of honor was reorganized. Libel and slander remained "crimes against honor and reputation," because cultivation of individual honor fostered civic values.[90] Following the trend of earlier legislation, the republican law lowered the penalties still further (now ranging from a fine to two years' imprisonment), maintaining the principle that printed libel of public authorities was a graver offense than verbal insult of private individuals. Sexual offenses, in contrast, were no longer crimes against individuals, but rather against "the security of the honor and honesty of families."[91]

The 1890 code dramatically reduced the maximum prison term for rape (from three to twelve to one to six years), which now included consensual sex with a girl younger than sixteen, and it eliminated punishment for seduction of honest adults. It raised the maximum age for def. victims from seventeen to twenty and increased punishment from one to three years' banishment to one to four years' imprisonment. Finally, the law stipulated that deflowering was a crime only if the young woman's consent was obtained through seduction, deceit, or fraud.

Efforts to establish logical principles and clear guidelines for defending family honor were in vain. Disagreements and uncertainty among jurists regarding technicalities of these laws surfaced immediately, providing fuel for larger debates over legal procedures and moral principles. Debates regarding the principles of moral responsibility and free will, for example, underlay jurists' disagreements over the law's protection of female minors. Many argued that women should assume responsibility for their sexual virtue at a much younger age than twenty-one, citing both the lower age limits in "the principal civilized nations" and Brazil's racial and climatic conditions, which they believed made its population more sensual at an earlier age. For the same reasons, many questioned the code's stipulation that girls younger than sixteen were incapable of voluntary consent; whether the girls had to be honest in these cases remained unanswered.[92] Some argued that legal age limits were arbitrary and should be replaced with a medical and psychological evaluation of maturity.[93] Finally, faced with the difficulty of how to determine a woman's age in a nation where the births were frequently not officially recorded, jurists argued over whether other kinds of documents or a medical evaluation could substitute for the birth certificate.[94]

Practical problems created by the term "deflowering" stirred more profound debates over the importance of philology, popular traditions, and medical evidence in criminal law as well as over the relationship between the abstract principle of moral virtue and the historical valorization of physical virginity. The verb "to deflower" was an innovation of the 1830 penal code. Roman law had used *desvirginatio* and *devirginare* ("devirginification" and "to devirginify"); the Portuguese Philippine Ordinances were less precise, condemning men who "slept with" or "corrupted" a virgin or honest widow.[95] Although most modern nations punished the seduction of minors under specific conditions, these generally did not include the women's prior virginity. Modern Portugal and some Latin American nations did pass specific laws against the seduction or rape of a virgin, but only Brazil went to the "extreme" of emphasizing the material element of the crime by specifying that the woman be "deflowered."[96]

Federal District magistrate and legal scholar Galdino Siqueira explained in 1923 that it was not juridical science or legal history but rather Brazilian "popular intuition" that justified the choice of the term "deflowering." This intuition was shared by other cultures and represented by a variety of rituals such as the Italian *camicia del onore* or the Middle Eastern bloodstained sheet, all of which equated loss of virginity with the rupture of the hymen. Although elsewhere Siqueira attacked the penal code for failing to accommodate scientific legal theory, his judgments in deflowering cases were based on the classical doctrine of strict adherence to the letter of the law. In his courtroom, virginity meant hymenal "integrity," and medical evidence of a lacerated hymen was indispensable.[97]

Most of Siqueira's peers rejected his position on the grounds that it ignored modern legal-medical science and the teachings of the Republic's major juridical scholars. By the end of the nineteenth century, legal-medical specialists Nina Rodrigues and Agostinho de Souza Lima had demonstrated that medical evidence of deflowering was imperfect, given the proven existence of the "complacent hymen" and the possibility, however rare, of the membrane's rupture by other means. Many jurists supported Souza Lima's plea to replace "deflowering" with "seduction" in order to eliminate this "extremely embarrassing ambiguity."[98] In the meantime, the leading magistrates and legal scholars agreed that deflowering should be interpreted to mean penetration by the penis, with or without hymenal rupture.[99]

Understanding of the complacent hymen, however, was limited to specialists, and legal-medical training was rudimentary up to the turn of the century.[100] Before the 1920s, the obligatory "deflowering examination" routinely evaluated virginity by criteria that included not only the state of the hymen (often incorrectly observed, according to Souza Lima and others) but also other evidence that legal-medicine had rejected, such as flaccidity of breasts and labia. Over the objections of leading experts on the matter, defense lawyers made good use of this evidence, which seems to have been especially effective before juries (individual judges tried these cases after 1911).[101]

Notwithstanding this technical imprecision, there were those who defended the wording of the 1890 code. Senator Rui Barbosa attacked Clóvis Bevilaqua's use of the term "devirginification" (*desvirginamento*) as one of the grounds for marital annulment in the civil code, arguing that the term "deflowering" was a more traditional and elegant juridical term.[102] Viveiros de Castro also defended the term "deflowering," even though he agreed that some deflowered women possessed intact hymens. Disposing of positivist principles in favor of classical objectivity, Viveiros de Castro insisted that "the judge cannot enter into psychological probing to examine the state of a soul. . . . The word virgin has here a physical, anatomical significance."[103] It was unthinkable for the courts to protect a woman who had been deflowered prior to her seduction, Viveiros continued, "for in every large city, alongside public prostitution, manifest in the light of day, there is clandestine prostitution, reserved, discreet, mysterious."[104] This clarifies the presumption that was implicit in the 1890 code: an unmarried woman who was not a virgin was a suspected prostitute.

Virtue and the Marriage Promise

Whether they preferred "deflowering," "seduction," or "devirginification," jurists unanimously agreed that what the law protected in punishing deflowering was a moral principle, not simply a physiological mark.

Defining this moral principle, however, proved even more difficult than delineating the material element of virginity.

Since, as jurists frequently complained, the penal code did not provide guidelines for how to judge offenses of family honor, jurists tackled the problem themselves, insisting that victims of sexual crimes display honesty and *pudor*. The precise meaning of these terms, however, was far from self-evident. The English term "shame" does not quite capture either concept, but it is not simply a problem of translation. Brazilian jurists themselves spent considerable effort trying to find precise definitions for these terms without great success. We shall see in the chapters ahead that common Brazilians could take advantage of the complexity of these concepts in legal disputes involving sexual crimes.

Pudor, a term common to several Romance languages and European legal codes, connotes sexual virtue, sexual decency, modesty, or shame. *Pudor* could refer to either a collective or individual attribute, hence the crimes of "offense of public *pudor*" and "offense of the *pudor* of a minor" meant an indecent public act and corruption of a minor, respectively.[105] The meaning of honesty was similar, but it was an exclusively individual attribute, and it was a highly gendered term.

Esteves demonstrates that discussion of male honesty rarely appeared in juridical texts, but it did arise in arguments for the defense in turn-of-the-century criminal trials. An honest man was hardworking, well respected, and truthful; he would not dishonor a woman or go back on his word.[106] Female honesty, in contrast, referred to moral virtue in the sexual sense, and it was a major topic of both theoretical and jurisprudential concern. It did not necessarily mean truthfulness, except in the sense that the testimony of a rape or deflowering victim was to be believed if she was honest and described honorable behavior. "Family girls," Viveiros de Castro argued in a frequently cited 1899 verdict, "living in the seclusion of the domestic home, under maternal vigilance, know to conserve the virginity of their bodies and the dignity of their sentiments. The offended girl, therefore, should be believed when there is no evidence against her honest precedents."[107] There were exceptions to this rule: For example, after first pointing to her fiancé, an honest girl might later attribute her defloration to someone else. If her "precedents" proved her honest, she should not be believed in such a case, since it was inconceivable that an honest girl would have sex except as a prelude to marriage.

The naïve innocence (*ingenuidade*) and predictability of family women was held in opposition to the cynical deceitfulness (*cinismo*) of women not subject to family controls, who were considered enigmatic and easily corrupted. Viveiros de Castro thus insisted that "the precedents of the offended woman and her family should be carefully examined, since they indicate whether she is an honest girl from a respectable and serious family or an already corrupted woman, brought up among people without morality or scruples."[108]

Honesty, then, was a social marker and a moral attribute, "sealed" by a physiological state (an intact hymen). A woman's "dishonor" on any of these three planes placed the other two in danger, but the rupture of the physiological seal was by far the most pernicious, because it was irreversible. Turn-of-the-century jurists, whether inspired by classical or positivist principles, medical science or "popular intuition," agreed that deflowering should be punished, because once a woman lost her virginity, she was at high risk of taking a "precipitous fall" into prostitution. Several jurists noted that one of the reasons for this was economic, since a daughter's loss of virginity often led her father to throw her out of the house. As we have seen, daughters' sexual impropriety was just cause for disinheritance under civil law.

Defining the "criminal means" of deflowering—seduction, deceit, and fraud—was at least as complex as defining "honesty" and "deflowering." Viveiros de Castro, once again, followed classical legal precepts, but his interpretations were more compatible with popular Brazilian traditions than with European theorists. Citing one of the major nineteenth-century interpreters of Italian classical law, Francesco Carrara, Viveiros explained that criminal seduction (as opposed to "vulgar seduction," which for him was not a crime) and deceit should both be understood as an unfulfilled marriage promise. Fraud consisted of a man's convincing a woman he was her legitimate husband when he was not. Thus, a woman's knowing acquiescence to extramarital sex was defensible only if she had been under the illusion that she was "advancing [her seducer] the rights of the husband," in which case—for Viveiros, not for Carrara—"the woman had every reason to consent."[109]

Again following Carrara, who insisted that the marriage promise be proven by witnesses and gift exchanges, Viveiros de Castro explained that the marriage promise should be "formal and serious." The Brazilian jurist, however, after years of experience on the bench, was obliged to incorporate more flexible criteria: "the marriage promise should be made under circumstances . . . that would lead the woman to believe it."[110] This would include the informal and private relationships particularly common among working-class young women and men of turn-of-the-century Rio de Janeiro, where Viveiros de Castro and most other prominent jurists gained their practical experience.

Judging Dishonest Women

Before the 1930s, only a few jurists disputed Viveiros de Castro's insistence that a marriage promise was the sole criminal means of deflowering honest young women.[111] There was much less agreement on how the law should protect "dishonest women." Some, like Galdino Siqueira, insisted that there were many women who "fell in between" the chaste honest woman and the dishonest prostitute, whereas others, following Viveiros de Castro, considered any single woman who had sex without a marriage promise a "clandestine prostitute."[112]

A clandestine prostitute was a promiscuous woman who might or might not receive payment for sex, but who did not publicly solicit clients.[113] As for "public prostitutes," or those who plied their trade openly, jurists cited St. Augustine more frequently than either positive or classical doctrine to argue that prostitution was a "necessary evil" that provided an outlet for uncontainable male sexual impulses and thus protected honest women and family honor. This attitude, as Donna Guy has pointed out, was common to most Catholic nations, including almost all of the Latin American republics.[114] In some cities, most notably Buenos Aires, where the massive immigration of single men was accompanied by an enormous demand for prostitutes in the late nineteenth century, public authorities created state-regulated bordellos, inspired by those that had existed in Paris since 1804. In Brazil, lobbying efforts for state regulation by many physicians and police officials failed. In part, this failure reflected the reaction to the Buenos Aires experience. State-regulated bordellos there became notorious throughout Europe for housing European women coerced into prostitution through the infamous white slave trade. Moreover, Brazilian physicians kept abreast of the work of leading French professionals, who became increasingly disillusioned with regulation in Paris. By the late nineteenth century, the vast majority of Brazil's public health physicians opposed both criminalization and state regulation of prostitution, a position that coincided with that of progressive European health professionals. Legislators of the First Republic thus followed their imperial predecessors: they neither criminalized nor regulated prostitution, but left the messy work of prostitution control to the Federal District chief of police, who worked under (or around) a series of nebulous municipal ordinances.[115]

In defense of honest women, however, the penal code criminalized pimping.[116] Antipimping legislation was made more severe in 1915, after Brazil signed a 1904 international anti–white slave trade treaty. The new law mandated deportation of foreigners who "facilitated prostitution" and made it illegal to "operate houses of tolerance" or "rent rooms to facilitate prostitution." The eleven-year gap between treaty and law was but one indication of the long-standing conflicts among jurists, police, physicians, and legislators on prostitution policy. Once passed, the law engendered scores of copious judicial opinions on what constituted a house of tolerance (many jurists argued that they did not exist in Brazil), what types of rentals were illegal, and whether police could deport foreigners without a criminal trial.[117]

In the meantime, police efforts to put their "discretionary power" into practice by regulating prostitution were often blocked by lawyers and judges who considered them illegal, since the state explicitly rejected regulation. Moreover, as the brilliant young socialist attorney Evaristo de Morais argued in a series of successful habeas corpus petitions on behalf of prostitutes at the end of the nineteenth century, police "moralization" involved violence against prostitutes and abuses of their civil rights.[118] Morais, however, did not represent the majority among jurists. Among his opponents was Aurelino Leal, who attacked the penal code on "scientific" grounds in 1896, arguing that its excessive liberalism obstructed social defense. As Federal District police chief two decades later, Leal convinced a group of the nation's most powerful jurists to reinforce the police's traditional discretionary power regarding public morality and prostitution.[119]

Conflicts over the rights of dishonest women also emerged in debates over rape. Following the imperial criminal code, the 1890 document punished the rape of prostitutes with a lighter prison sentence (six months to two years) than the rape of honest women. Following Viveiros de Castro and Souza Lima, many jurists opposed the inclusion of prostitutes as potential rape victims on both logical and moral grounds. Souza Lima simply reminded readers that rape was a crime against family honor; the logical exclusion of prostitutes was thus self-evident. Viveiros de Castro, using familiar positive school rhetoric, argued that the rape of prostitutes lacked "juridical sense" because "the act does not reveal in the delinquent a frightening or dangerous character, it does not cause irreparable damage to the victim, it does not hurt the interests of social defense."[120] Other jurists disagreed. Siqueira, always eager to support legal traditions, pointed out that the Philippine Ordinances punished the rape of prostitutes with the same penalty as the rape of honest women.[121] He and other supporters of the law cited the classical doctrine of individual rights to sexual liberty, and pointed out that this provision concurred with the most modern European codes.[122] None of these men, however, objected to the reduced penalty for prostitute rape. Clearly, the defense of "sexual liberty" was less important than the defense of family honor.

Repairing the Damages

Jurists' opinions on punishment and retribution of sexual crimes also demonstrate their greater commitment to protecting family honor than individual liberties. None seemed to object to the fact that the 1890 code had diminished the difference between sexual crimes committed with or without the victim's consent. Some, in fact, argued that since deflowering caused irreparable moral damage, it should be punished more severely than rape.[123] Yet although many complained that punishments, particularly for deflowering, were too light, almost all of the major jurists supported the provision that set free men who married their victims. Even Souza Lima, who opposed pardoning men completely because he believed this encouraged youths to have sex in order to marry against their parents' wishes, believed that penal sanctions should encourage marriage.[124] No Brazilian specialist supported the argument that giving men a choice between marriage and prison contradicted the principle of free will in marriage, although some recognized that this argument had won sway in Europe.[125] Instead, Brazilian jurists maintained the position held by Carrara and other Italian classical thinkers: marriage eliminated the need for punishment because it repaired the damages done to the woman, her family, and society.[126]

Souza Lima was virtually alone in his opposition to another law handed down from the 1830 code: the requirement that sexual offenders pay their victims a dowry. Souza Lima considered monetary compensation immoral because it encouraged "capitalist speculation" in virginity and degraded honest women.[127] But although the dowry payment had all but disappeared from modern European penal codes, most Brazilian jurists insisted that it represented fair indemnification for damages to the victim's honor and social position, and that it was up to the courts to weed out the speculators.[128] For Viveiros de Castro, this principle also justified indemnification for broken engagements, another provision that was rapidly dying in Europe.[129]

Once a woman married, her sexual liberty was even more subordinate to family honor than before. Brazilian jurists, following canon law precepts, agreed that while a husband could be convicted of "indecent acts" against his wife, he could not be convicted of rape under any circumstances, since he was within his "conjugal rights" in demanding sex.[130] Moreover, the 1830 adultery laws that distinguished between husbands and wives remained in place. This discrimination was well supported in modern European law codes, justified by the argument that only women could bring illegitimate children into honest families without their spouses' knowledge. By the beginning of the new century, leading penal law specialists opposed the criminalization of adultery and supported a civil solution (divorce), but, as we have seen, opponents of divorce overwhelmed its supporters in debates over republican civil law.[131]

Wife-Killers and Uncontrollable Passion

There was no question that the 1890 penal code, like that of 1830, would deny men the traditional right to defend family honor by killing adulterous women. The new code went further, eliminating the earlier code's recognition of "response to insult or honor" as an attenuating circumstance for all crimes. After 1890, only women who aborted or murdered newborn children could obtain reduced sentences if they acted "in defense of honor." Brazil's major jurists of both classical and positivist persuasion supported the latter provision in principle, disagreeing on the relative gravity of homicide, infanticide, and abortion, and on whether defense of family honor could attenuate punishment for infanticide by someone other than the mother.[132] In contrast, classical and positivist doctrine alike condemned the traditional defense of male honor through wife-killing. Yet both provided loopholes that allowed it to persevere in courtrooms around the Western world, including Brazil.

In his mesmerizing appeals on behalf of infamous wife-killers at the turn of the century, Evaristo de Morais—the same young trial attorney who defended prostitutes against police harassment and eviction—popularized the ideas of the Italian socialist and positivist jurist Enrico Ferri on "passionate offenders."[133] Building on Lombroso's criminological classifications, Ferri argued that certain individuals possessed a "passionate temperament" that, when provoked by extreme emotion, robbed them of reason. Morais agreed with Ferri that defending men who had killed their wives did not contradict a commitment to social justice. To the contrary, he considered this defense humane, since the men's actions had been provoked by a psychological response beyond their rational control. Moreover, as Ferri argued, the passions that inspired them—love and honor—were socially useful. Noting the decline of crimes of passion in Western Europe, he argued that the spread of modern, civilized moral values would eventually eradicate these crimes. In the meantime, it was unlikely that passionate offenders would repeat their crime, and thus it was unnecessary to protect society from them. Their condition might warrant psychiatric attention, but not incarceration.[134]

According to Morais, the jury was the only tribunal that recognized positive school doctrine—which was ironic, given the opposition to the jury by the great majority of positive school jurists.[135] Yet although Morais's arguments in jury trials worked to implant positive school concepts such as criminal classification, attenuated responsibility, and individualized sentencing into Brazilian legal practice, he insisted that his defense of passionate criminals ultimately rested on "the strict application of the penal code's doctrine of free will, taken to its logical conclusion."[136] Classical masters such as Carrara, searching for a way to justify leniency for men who killed adulterous wives, suspended the attribution of free will, and hence criminal responsibility, to those suffering from a "blind passion" that rendered them incapable of reason.[137] Following this logic, Brazilian law forgave those who acted "in a state of complete deprivation of the senses."[138] After Morais became famous for his "passionate offender" defense, lawyers routinely argued that men who had "washed their honor in blood" did so because their "intense passion" had deprived them of their senses.

While classical and positivist jurists debated the relevance of psychological perturbations that led to socially useful or antisocial passions over the first three decades of the twentieth century, countless cases of domestic violence became front-page headlines in Rio's popular press. Popular opinion did not interpret stories of juries that freed wife-murderers as the triumph of modern criminology. Instead, most Cariocas saw these stories as evidence of the persistence of the notion that men's honor was determined by their women's sexual fidelity, and that Brazil's criminal justice system still permitted men to defend this honor violently. The persistence of popular notions of honor that condoned wife-killing, and of legal loopholes that permitted its impunity, was common to contemporary European nations as well.[139] Yet the highly publicized success of Morais and other defenders of passionate killers provoked alarm about the backwardness of Brazilian society and the corruption of Brazil's legal and political institutions. By the 1910s and 1920s, outrage over the survival of these notions would explode in impassioned protests against the impunity of wife-killers as well as to the institution of the popular jury.[140]

Conflicts over how the law should intervene in family relations and define honesty and virginity resulted from the coexistence, in law and jurisprudence, of two competing notions of honor: the patriarchal notion of honor as a family resource and the bourgeois notion of honor as an individual virtue. As anthropologist Julian Pitt-Rivers observes in his classic essay on honor, the latter notion corresponds to "communities of equals" and was thus compatible with the First Republic's democratic principles. Yet although republican jurists supported the liberal ideals that held honor to represent personal virtue, they were unable to expunge from their writings on sexual crimes an opposing conception of honor as precedence, ascribed in social status, which corresponded to the social reality of unequal, paternalistic power relations. The combination of these two notions worked to reinforce the family values that Pitt-Rivers describes as characteristic of "Latin countries": honor as precedence was the prerogative of men, honor as sexual purity was restricted to women, and the defense of female honor was a male responsibility.[141]

Competition between classical precepts and positivist innovations were thus not the only problems jurists faced as they attempted to establish a coherent rationale by which to identify and defend sexual honor. They also faced their own reluctance to let go of notions of morality and authority that contradicted precepts of modern juridical science. At the same time, they engaged in power struggles between and among private, religious, and public authorities. To resolve these problems, jurists resorted not only to diverse legal theories, but also to both Christian and scientific social analyses. In the process, they created a body of legal thought that fit within the parameters of what later jurist Roberto Lira called the "Brazilian school of social humanism.[142] Because they believed that adverse social conditions, such as what they perceived as Brazil's widespread cultural backwardness and ignorance, produced criminal behavior and the spread of moral degeneracy, they acknowledged the inequality of legal subjects and the need for individualized punishment as well as a more vigorous state role in social defense.

Public Action versus Private Authority and the Brazilian School of Penal Law

Like the 1830 code, the 1890 code defined crimes against personal and family honor as "private" offenses. The public prosecutor could not intervene unless the victim's life or health were "severely threatened" by the offense, the offender was the victim's legal guardian, or the victim's family were "impoverished," that is, if the expenses of a lawsuit would strain family resources.[143] Under any other circumstance, the victim's legal guardian could choose whether to file suit. Although "private criminal law" was intended to leave the power to guard family honor in the hands of family heads (fathers), in practice, the public prosecutor intervened in almost all cases of sexual crimes, since the overwhelming majority of families who brought complaints to the court's attention were impoverished.[144]

There was great uncertainty over the victim's rights in these cases. In private suits, the complainant had the right to drop charges at will or to pardon the offender; in state-prosecuted cases, she did not. Should the prosecutor act as simply a state-financed advocate for impoverished victims of sexual crimes, who should retain the prerogatives allowed them in private suits? Or was the victim stripped of the rights of a private complainant once public intervention was established? As Esteves has demonstrated, most turn-of-the-century jurists not only supported the latter supposition, but sought to eliminate private law from the penal code altogether, arguing that the social interest in bringing sexual offenders to justice was too great to justify leaving the prosecution in private hands.[145] Moreover, legal initiatives by private citizens were motivated by subjective personal interests rather than objective "social interests." Only trained specialists could define the latter, since law had become "a science of profound complexity."[146]

This task was crucial, moreover, because it represented jurists' contribution to the advancement of Brazil's civilization. Observing his countrymen's "propensity to sensuality and love," and the rise of immorality in Rio de Janeiro in 1898, Viveiros de Castro outlined a key question for further research: was this "merely an exuberance of the sexual instinct" provoked by the sensual tropical climate, poor education, and the cultural legacy of slavery, or was the Brazilian population degenerating because of biological miscegenation? The answer, he implied, should guide legal science and practice.[147]

Viveiros de Castro regretted that existing data were inconclusive, but he and his colleagues over the next few decades worked on the theory that Brazil's "race" was "improving," and that further social evolution would depend on the dissemination of civilized moral habits. Several jurists, again following Viveiros de Castro, prefaced studies of sexual crimes with an overview of the evolution of sexual morals in human societies, concluding that respect for female honor through the valorization of virginity was a mark of civilization unknown to "primitive peoples."[148]

Although these analyses of social evolution were secular and scientific, they were in no way anticlerical. To the contrary, the Catholic Church loomed large in jurists' explanations of the evolution of *pudor* and the origins of respect for women's honor. Perhaps conscious of the church's resentment of republican encroachment in its traditional domain, they emphasized the complementary role of religious and state efforts.[149] Viveiros de Castro, for example, downplayed the German sex-

ologist Krafft-Ebing's criticism of the church's misogyny, insisting that
Catholic moral teachings and the sacrament of marriage had "elevated
women [and] protected feminine honor." Criminal law would follow, defining and punishing acts that threatened these Christian values.[150] Oscar de Macedo Soares agreed that Christianity—specifically the Catholic
Church—was the major force behind the evolution of *pudor* and the valorization of female chastity "from primitive peoples of antiquity [and] from
the savages of the inferior races that exist today, to the most civilized." He
explained that "this evolution began in Muslim, then Roman law . . .
then in canon law . . . and finally in all the modern codes."[151] Writing in
1920, Crisólito de Gusmão summarized the position of the Republic's
major jurists on the congruence of science, law, and Christianity in promoting the evolution of *pudor*, the "substratum" of virginity and fidelity.[152] Gusmão cited Lombroso, Spencer, Krafft-Ebing, and other European
scientific authorities to explain that *pudor* had evolved to much greater
intensity in women than men as protection against primitive man's violent sexual instinct. Yet it was the Catholic Church, particularly through
St. Augustine's position on virtue and the sanctity of virginity, that spread
the principles of *pudor* throughout the civilized world. *Pudor* formed the
basis of individual morality, which in turn formed public morality, "the
guarantee of all civilization." It was therefore in the interest of the state to
promote Christian morals, for they protected civilization against "retrogression to the savage state."[153]

Not surprisingly, jurists' attempts to civilize the federal capital's population by identifying and protecting honest women revealed racial and
class biases. Viveiros de Castro explained that the defendant in an infanticide case could not have acted to hide her dishonor, because "she was
not a family girl nor a respectable wife, obliged to guard her honor before
society. From her humble position, a cook, . . . with no family, making
her own living, the accused did not have social conventions to respect."[154]
Esteves finds that juridical definitions of honest female behavior in cases
of deflowering from 1900 to 1911 also included restrictions that were
impractical or impossible for most poor young women: honest women
were kept under stringent maternal vigilance, did not go out of the home
unchaperoned, did not pursue courtship, and did not attend popular festivals. Most important, honest women did not live in immoral homes
such as the squalid and overcrowded communal *cortiços* and squatter
settlements that filled the downtown, and they did not have immoral
families, which might include parents or siblings living in consensual
unions. Nonetheless, Esteves shows that prosecutors and judges often
energetically defended poor young women complaining of deflowering

who did not quite meet their standards of honesty, particularly if the young women were white.[155] —→ low class could be white?

By establishing "civilized" codes of honor and enforcing them through the courts, this first generation of jurists to interpret the Republic's legal codes thus took on pedagogical and eugenic responsibilities in keeping with the motto emblazoned on the new nation's flag, "Order and Progress." These pedagogical and eugenic functions and their positivist precepts, however, collided with the egalitarian ideals that inspired republican civil and penal codes, which held law to be a social contract written to reflect and uphold universal rights and the ethical and moral standards of the nation's citizens.

Turn-of-the-century jurists did not come to a complete agreement on how to distinguish among Brazil's unique cultural traditions, the natural evolution of modern moral norms, and social and biological degeneration, but they were certain that the law's defense of sexual honor represented the continuation of the march toward higher levels of civilization, a march begun centuries earlier by the Catholic Church. Yet jurists were unsuccessful in their attempts to modernize honor and establish objective, coherent standards for defending it. Instead, diverse social and political conflicts were played out in debates over gender and honor from the very inception of republican law. When social and political conflicts heightened in the 1920s and 1930s, these debates intensified. By then, a new generation of jurists would take the social consciousness that their turn-of-the-century predecessors developed in analyses of Brazilian penal law to more radical extremes, with both authoritarian and radical progressive implications.

she was
low-class,
citizenship?

2 National Honor, the Family, and the Construction of the Marvelous City

Turn-of-the-century jurists were not alone in their belief that protecting family honor was crucial to the defense of civilization and the construction of a modern nation. Already in the nineteenth century, urban planners, municipal and federal politicians, public health physicians, and the police agreed with jurists that it was their collective duty to preserve female honesty by segregating "the families"—by which they meant "honorable," privileged families—from the "dangerous classes" in Rio de Janeiro. The advent of the Republic in 1889 gave a boost to their efforts. Federal and municipal funds poured into a project to renovate, "sanitize," and "moralize" the city's physical space, as persistent problems of overcrowding, poor hygiene, epidemic diseases, and an insufficient commercial infrastructure were blamed on Brazil's backward colonial and imperial heritage. In practice, defending the family and "civilized morality" through urban policies, like defending family honor in the law, provoked a great deal of conflict. And although the early decades of the century saw dramatic transformations in the city's social geography, not everyone agreed on what kind of modern civilization had emerged, or should have emerged. In the period that followed World War I, shifting international trends and a new nationalist spirit led many Cariocas to debate what kind of national image their city should represent.

The visit of King Albert and Queen Elisabeth of Belgium to Rio de Janeiro in September 1920 throws these debates into relief. The event provided an arena in which to display the virtues of Brazilian culture and civilization. It was a public relations triumph, mobilizing massive, enthusiastic participation on the part of Rio's population and earning broad coverage by Brazilian and Belgian communications media. Yet the government's investments in preparing the city "for the King to see" also provoked tremendous controversy. It was not only the expense, censorship,

and general police repression surrounding the visit that angered cr
Conflicts also erupted over the ways the city and the nation were ʋ ʋ
represented. Should Brazil shake off its lingering, humiliating status as a
former colony by entertaining royalty with the European-style splendor
and refinement that its capital could display? Or was it, as many intellectuals and popular artists argued, precisely the ludicrous attempts by elites
to "Europeanize" Rio de Janeiro and hide the city's poverty and its authentically Brazilian culture that made Brazil vulnerable to ridicule and con-
tempt? Why, after all, should the Brazilian Republic bow to European
royalty? And what was it about Albert, Elisabeth, and the civilization
they represented that was worthy of veneration? The impassioned responses these questions generated leave no doubt that defining national
identity preoccupied a diverse array of Rio's citizens.

The theme of honor was prominent in the political maneuvering and
cultural debates that Albert and Elisabeth inadvertently incited. In an era
of liberalization of social norms in Western societies (which, Brazil's political leaders insisted, included Brazil), the preoccupation with honor
might seem anachronistic, reactionary, or, as some Brazilian critics complained at the time, an indication of the nation's cultural backwardness.
The publicity the visit generated, however, illustrates a new urgency in
debates over honor in Rio at the end of World War I, precisely when the
need to modernize the nation became a nearly universal dogma in Brazil.
While preparing the city to receive the royal guests, public officials and
their supporters in the press evoked honor in ways that they hoped would
both support new configurations of national and international power and
reinforce traditional hierarchies of class, race, and gender. Other pros-
pective hosts, including the opposition press, popular artists and enter-
tainers, and residents of lesser renown, also evoked honor in their proposals to provide an "authentically Brazilian" reception, one that was
emphatically egalitarian.

Many of the Cariocas who vied to represent the nation before the
European king and queen concealed their class and racial ideologies behind a rhetoric of honor, while celebrating the gender ideologies that this
rhetoric highlighted. Gender, in fact, was a privileged category of social
differentiation in the Brazilian nationalist version of the discourse of liberal democracy that emerged victorious from World War I—a discourse
that characterized "modern civilization" and, at least theoretically, guaranteed the sovereignty of honorable nations.

The salutary effect of the republican concern with modernity and
civilization will become clear as we follow the king and queen on their
official tour of Brazil's scenic capital. At the same time, the mirth that

surrounded the visit points to the less laudable outcome of policies designed to "moralize" and "civilize" the city. We shall see that the defense of "family values" and sexual honor played a role in shaping both the "marvelous city" that Albert and Elisabeth were shown in 1920 and the shameful aspects of the city's social geography that were hidden from royal view.

"For King Albert to See": An Official Version of the Marvelous City, 1920

King Albert and Queen Elisabeth's visit was by far the city's most celebrated public event of the year. The excitement began months in advance. By May, one newspaper reported, "official concern with doing everything possible to surround the visit of the royal guests with the utmost splendor and comfort is so great that it is no exaggeration to say that every government ministry and all public services have been mobilized for this purpose."[1] In April, after agreeing that the dreadnought São Paulo would carry the royal entourage to Rio, military officials sent the vessel to England, where it was transformed into a "floating palace."[2] It was even rumored that the navy, whose recruits were considered predominantly black, selected lighter-skinned sailors to crew the ship. A few months later, similar rumors circulated with regard to the selection of soldiers for guard duty during the reception.[3] Military and government officials indignantly denied the allegations.

Meanwhile, the federal and municipal governments financed improvements in the capital that would "render the city worthy of the monarch's visit," according to a newspaper report published in June. The port and other federal properties were renovated, the Congress building recarpeted, and several railroad cars custom-built or refurbished for transporting the monarchs to the neighboring states of Minas Gerais and São Paulo when they departed Rio. City workers built a special box in the Municipal Theater, cleaned and painted public fountains and statues, landscaped plazas and planted gardens, and replaced gas lighting fixtures with electric street lamps along Rio Branco Avenue.[4]

Since the Belgian royalty would promenade down Rio Branco Avenue upon departing the port, it was fitting that it received special attention. Moreover, investments in the appearance of "the Avenue" had tremendous potential to impress the Europeans with Rio's—and Brazil's—sophistication. In 1920, it housed the headquarters of Rio's most formidable commercial and industrial firms, military and high-society social clubs, and the city's most elegant public buildings, including a quasi-circular concentration of palatial structures in French Beaux-Arts style: the School of Fine Arts, the Municipal Theater, the National Library, the Municipal Council building and, at its southern extreme, Monroe Palace,[5] home of the Federal Senate. Several movie houses, which in the weeks leading up to the royal visit billed Belgian historical dramas and documentary clips alongside the usual Hollywood features, clustered amid these stately public edifices on a plaza filled with sidewalk cafés, reinforcing the avenue's deliberately cosmopolitan ambience.

Just beyond this strip of movie houses, Rio Branco Avenue intersected with Beira Mar Avenue, which followed the contours of the bay shore to the affluent neighborhoods of Rio's South Zone. South Zone neighborhoods were favored, not for the first nor the last time, with a large share of available public funds. In Laranjeiras, one of the more traditional domains of Rio's upper-class families, First Lady Mary Pessoa personally directed the renovation of the nineteenth-century palace that would house the Belgian king and queen. Gas lamps were replaced along Pinheiro Machado Street, which Albert would travel each morning from the palace to the road leading to Copacabana, the seacoast south of the bay, for his daily swim. Farther down the coast, all along the sparsely settled beachfront areas of Copacabana, Ipanema, and Leblon, workers paved roads, laid the city's trademark black-and-white stone sidewalks, and resumed construction of the spectacular Niemeyer Avenue, a project that had been halted years earlier for lack of funds. The new road, completed in time for Albert to tour in the automobile provided for his inner-city travel, was chiseled around the seaboard face of Dois Irmãos, the twin stone mountains that separate Leblon from the sandbanks of lower Tijuca at the city's southern extreme.[6]

The "marvelous city," as Rio had been dubbed after completion of the urban renewal project a decade earlier, was resplendent when the *São Paulo* reached Guanabara Bay on September 19, 1920, a radian Sunday morning. Yet panoramic coastal highways, landscaped plazas, and breathtaking natural beauty were not the most crucial components of the capital that officials wanted the European royalty to see. It was more important that the city's population represent the nation's social harmony and cultural advancement.

A few days before the royal couple's arrival, President Epitácio Pessoa and Mayor Carlos Sampaio summoned "the Brazilian people of all classes" to join in "the elation the government feels at the eminent distinction that their majesties the King and Queen of Belgium have conferred upon us by visiting our country" and urging the population to gather to greet the sovereigns along their route from the port to Guanabara

Palace.[7] Newspapers echoed the summons, proclaiming that the reception was "not merely official, but should involve all our people," and that all should cooperate in giving the monarchs "a perfect vision of our culture, our disposition, and our hospitality."[8]

The appeals were wildly successful. It seemed that the city's entire population mobilized to welcome the king and queen, making their arrival "a virtual apotheosis."[9] The "popular masses . . . bursting with joy and enthusiasm" turned out early in the morning, "conglomerating" behind rows of soldiers and police along the route the king and queen would travel.[10] Families crowded at the windows of their homes in the buildings above and in clusters of chairs along fashionable Beira Mar Avenue. Dove keepers and children armed with roses and jasmine lined the road that led from Beira Mar to the palace. Five hundred schoolgirls from the National Institute of Music, primed to intone the Belgian national anthem, gathered in the palace yard, where guards struggled to exclude gatecrashers.

As the *São Paulo* neared the harbor, dozens of ships offered salutes and airplanes circled and dipped overhead, "cutting through space in all directions, sometimes coming so close to the *São Paulo* that it seemed they would crash into her."[11] No such calamity occurred (although one plane did crash on takeoff), and the king and queen emerged unscathed before the cheering throngs. Escorted by the president's family, the mayor, and the chief of police, the royal entourage then paraded by horse-drawn carriage down Rio Branco Avenue and along Beira Mar Avenue, where buildings and the new arched lampposts were adorned with banners, flowers, and Belgian and Brazilian flags.

More impressive than fine buildings and festive decorations, according to the press, were the people lining the streets. "The behavior of the popular mass deserves praise," one report crowed. "The people lived up to our customs, thus honoring, with dignity, the Belgian sovereigns who distinguish Brazil with their visit."[12] Popular enthusiasm remained high for the duration of the visit. Everywhere the king or queen went, jubilant crowds instantly appeared, prompting a reporter to comment that "with good reason our people are called essentially carnivalesque. It was a kind of carnival."[13]

Family Values and National Honor

The population may well have been attracted to the streets by the promise of a spectacle—a taste of Carnival five months early, with a real-life king and queen.[14] Massive publicity, including film clips of each royal event projected in theaters almost immediately afterward, certainly contributed

to the aura of excitement. But the press and the government official
put such energy into preparations, as well as the numerous private organizations that published greetings of welcome, considered the reception of
the Belgian sovereigns a significant civic duty, not simply popular enter- *masses*
tainment. Indeed, as many of their manifestations pronounced explicitly,
nothing less than Brazil's honor—and hence the nation's strength and
independence—was at stake. The visit would give Brazil the opportunity
to demonstrate its status as a budding great power that deserved the recognition and even the admiration of European kings and queens.

And Albert and Elisabeth were not just any king and queen. Public
statements by state officials and reports in the city's major journals portrayed the royals as symbols of the values Brazil held most dear: honor,
morality, and modern civilization. Newspaper accounts glorified Albert
as "the most honored sovereign in the world," and defender of "the peoples who are the principal representatives of our civilization." As trium-
phant king of a small nation victimized by barbarous imperialism, Albert
represented the victory of moral fortitude over military force.[15] Nowhere
was there any mention of Belgium's notorious reputation for especially
barbarous forms of imperial domination in the Congo prior to World
War I, although several features mentioned the couple's visit there and
Albert's "modern" administration of his African subjects. Instead, officials and the press presented the Belgian monarchy as the kind of civilizing force Brazil's leaders sought to emulate.

To live up to this example, Brazil would need to shake its reputation
as a tropical wonderland populated by primitive natives, lest it be associated with Belgium's colonial possessions rather than her metropolis. "It is
essential," began a front-page report instructing the Carioca population
how to behave on the day their majesties arrived, "that our guests learn
quickly that aside from the prodigies of this marvelous natural setting . . .
there is the spirit of a race worthy of the civilization [the king and queen]
symbolize."[16]

The civilization Albert and Elisabeth symbolized, at least for their *Belgians*
Brazilian hosts, combined cosmopolitan modernity with a firmly patri- *were*
archal conception of honor and nationhood. "The King is the head, but the
Queen is the soul," one journal explained in a historical feature. "Their
royal motto is liberty and family.'"[17] A popular weekly magazine called
the Belgian sovereigns "the figures who symbolize masculine honor and
feminine virtue all over today's world."[18] Both President Pessoa and his
political rival Rui Barbosa called Albert "the incarnation of honor," echoing journalistic reports of Albert's "virile" defense of Belgian autonomy
during the German invasion.[19] Reports on German-descended Elisabeth's

male honor, female virtue
inclusion/exclusion?

loyalty to Belgium during the war associated her patriotism with her marital fidelity and maternal qualities. "He, the hero that in defense of law and justice, threw his throne to the fate of war, . . . preferring to be king in a small village, with honor, than a dishonored monarch in his palace. She, the heroine, who knew how to show to all wives the sublime example of fidelity and demonstrated the same love for the nation she reigns as for the princes she mothers."[20]

Brazilian newspapers also cited gender norms to describe—with evident relief—the civilized deference displayed by Rio's "popular mass." The *Correio da manhã*, for example, gave the following account of the public reception:

> Defying the unpleasantness that usually marks popular festivals—the pushing and shoving, the shouts, etc.—it was beautiful to see among the multitude, innumerable *senhoras* and *senhoritas*. And even more beautiful to admire the composure of the people, who behaved like gentlemen, in a clear demonstration of their consciousness of what they were at that moment: a family honored with a visit worthy of the greatest appreciation. We thus have the pleasure to record the fact that the multitude defended yesterday, gallantly, our traditions of respect and order.[21]

The image of the respectful and orderly popular mass on the streets representing the national family, and of its novel "gentlemanly" composure, did not signify a democratic leveling of social classes. To the contrary, the descriptions of Rio de Janeiro at its best illustrate the ways that the concept of the family served to symbolically and spatially segregate women from men and the city's working classes (referred to as "the popular mass," or "the people"),[22] from more privileged social sectors, including the traditional upper class and the expanding middle class—who in contemporary estimations represented less than 20 percent of the city's population.[23]

"The families" was a term that referred to this privileged sector, which identified itself as "respectable society"—more civilized, more culturally European, and racially whiter than the popular masses. Although privileged men might occupy diverse urban spaces, their *senhoras* and *senhoritas* generally did not "conglomerate in the streets," but occupied protected private space, gathering at the windows or in chairs at the front of their homes.

For the *Correio da manhã* reporter cited above, however, the possibility that honest women could occupy formerly male social space suggests that the gender norms of the family could be conceived as an instrument of social discipline for the lower classes. The reporter made this explicit by counterposing the image of the happy Brazilian family described above to Europe's "social convulsion": "Someone arriving from the volcanic countries of Europe, where the agitation of anarchist ideas of social convulsion multiplies and accelerates, can appreciate the atmosphere of calm joy, the equilibrium of the atmosphere, the happiness . . . that exist here."[24] By upholding the behavioral norms of the Brazilian family, the popular masses provided evidence that Brazil had achieved a social order superior even to that of Europe.

"Civilizing" the Marvelous City: Gender and Public Space during Rio de Janeiro's "Belle Époque"

This portrait of Rio as a shining showcase of the Republic and of its people as representatives of a civilized "Brazilian race" contrasts sharply with earlier official characterizations of the city and its people, particularly in the downtown the king found so inviting. While jurists were busy elaborating and interpreting republican law in the late nineteenth and early twentieth centuries, municipal administrators enacted a series of authoritarian measures aimed at creating the "Europeanized" modern city King Albert and Queen Elisabeth saw. Acting in the interests of the minority that conceived itself as elite white families, urban authorities worked to clear prime downtown real estate not only of unsightly and unsanitary streets and buildings, but also of the population they saw as an unruly black and mixed-race mass.

According to historian Sidney Chalhoub, nineteenth-century urban authorities saw Rio's downtown as a "theater of vice."[25] Chalhoub argues that under the Empire, slaves and freedpersons, who at times composed more than half the population, created their own "black, separate, and alternative city" in the center of Rio de Janeiro, one with identifiable social and cultural practices that seemed uncivilized and dangerous to those charged with enforcing order.[26] Many conceived the city as polarized into two opposing social spaces that Chalhoub describes as "the city constructed by blacks and the codified city desired by whites."[27] Yet it was impossible to demarcate racial categories and cultural differences with precision.[28] Over the course of the nineteenth century, as the influx of poor European immigrants swelled downtown tenements and squatter communities and as slaves were more and more successful in achieving material conditions and lifestyles that approximated those of the free poor, public officials concerned about degeneracy and the dangerous masses were more apt to decry the city's "promiscuous mixture"—of slaves and the free poor, of different racial and ethnic groups; of male and female family members; of honest and prostituted women—than to bemoan the proliferation of a homogeneous "black" population.[29]

Over the second half of the nineteenth century, as a series of epidemics ravaged the population, increasingly aggressive groups of urban professionals—physicians, police, jurists, urban planners—extended their authority to broader areas of urban policy. Following their counterparts in many European capitals, these professionals integrated notions of moral and physical health in projects to "sanitize" the downtown. Policies enforced in the name of "social hygiene" as well as public health, such as campaigns against wet-nursing, imposition of sanitary codes in housing and laundry services, regulation of Carnival and other public leisure activities, prosecution of sexual crimes, and control of prostitution, sought to put an end to "promiscuous mixing" by segregating public and private space and establishing control over both by white professional men.[30]

As was true in most of the Western world in the nineteenth century, gender oppositions were central to Brazilian conceptions of public and private space. Brazilian medical and psychiatric authorities, following their European counterparts in their attempts to sanitize and modernize bourgeois households in Rio de Janeiro, reached conclusions very similar to those of the jurists who defined the family in imperial and republican law. The maternal instinct and an innate sexual inhibition made "normal," healthy women submissive and sexually chaste, while their physical weakness and impressionability rendered them susceptible to physical and moral contamination. Women were naturally suited to the home, where they became a moralizing force. Public space was the domain of naturally dominant and aggressive men. Men's more developed sexual instinct and less developed morality (pudor) justified their sexual liberty; indeed sexual abstinence was considered unhealthy for men.[31]

The overlap of gendered notions of private and public space and pure and impure women was evident not only in elite women's activities, but also in the way elite households administered their female domestic servants. According to Sandra Lauderdale Graham's study of domestic service in Rio from 1860 to 1910, families classified servants as either "indoor" or "outdoor." Indoor servants, generally young and inexperienced, were much more severely restricted and usually confined to their employer's house, whereas outdoor servants, implicitly not virgins, worked and socialized in the street.[32] The criminal justice system also associated sexual impurity with unprotected exposure to public space. Examining court cases of sexual crime from 1900 to 1911, Martha de Abreu Esteves found that the question of whether a woman "went out alone" was considered a key indicator of her sexual "honesty."[33]

Both Graham and Esteves find that working-class women did not understand the opposition of private and public space in the same way as doctors, jurists, and other defenders of the "hygienic" family. Graham argues that while "conventional design of safe and dangerous, clean and dirty, valued or demeaning" coded the house as safe and the street as dangerous, for domestic servants these meanings were inverted. Domestic servants were often subject to unsafe conditions and physical and sexual abuse in the houses where they worked, while the street provided the security of relative autonomy from employers and contact with their own communities.[34] Similarly, Esteves finds that working-class women openly socialized and courted in public, and were often unaware that admitting to going out alone could compromise their reputation in a court of law.[35]

Despite efforts to codify and sanitize Rio de Janeiro, then, alternative uses and conceptions of public space by those who did not live by the norms of the hygienic family continued to develop through the late imperial and early republican periods, as the population soared.[36] Most of the population that flocked to the city to escape slavery or in search of opportunity after abolition in 1888 crowded into squalid downtown tenements or hillside squatter communities with little or no privacy or access to public services. European immigrants, most of whom were young Portuguese men, found themselves living in better, but still dismal conditions.[37]

One of the housing priorities for poor residents was a location near sources of work. For men, jobs were more plentiful at the docks, the rail yards, or in downtown workshops and commercial establishments. Most women performed domestic services, either cleaning and cooking in the homes of wealthier residents or washing laundry in tenement courtyards or in public plazas. Some women worked as petty vendors, hatmakers, or seamstresses. At the end of the century, many found work in the expanding textile and consumer goods industry. By the early twentieth century, large numbers of relatively privileged working-class young women of "good appearance" (usually a euphemism for "white") were employed as salesclerks in the fashionable shops and new department stores catering to mostly wealthier female consumers.[38] Because these professions placed young women in public space, they subjected them to suspicion of "clandestine prostitution" by police and other public officials.

Public prostitution was another source of female employment, one that was highly stratified and particularly unsettling to the forces of moral order.[39] Prostitutes had figured prominently in both negative and positive images of Rio's tropical sensuality throughout the nineteenth century. Slave women who were forced into prostitution by their owners provided

58

fuel for abolitionists who depicted Rio as corrupted by Brazil's slave system.[40] Yet many upper-class men received lessons in cosmopolitan fashion and social mores from high-class European, especially French, coquettes.[41] High-class coquettes, paid concubines, and elegant bordellos, often run by European madams and modeled after Parisian establishments, were a prominent feature of upper-class men's social and political life in the late nineteenth century.[42]

The great majority of prostitutes in the late Empire and early Republic, however, were neither slaves nor sophisticated *francesas*. Instead, lower-class Brazilians were joined by large numbers of poor foreign women, predominantly from Eastern Europe. It is not possible to determine how many European prostitutes came to Rio, whether independently or through the so-called white slave trade, as international prostitution rings were known. Although *francesas*, along with the most privileged or lucky Brazilian *mulatas*, were tolerated or even admired and protected by some of the city's most influential men, the presence of *polacas* (a derogatory term meaning Polish), or lower-class Europeans who worked alongside poor black Brazilian prostitutes, provoked tremendous consternation. By the early twentieth century, they had become a source of national embarrassment.[43]

Given the widespread belief in men's irrepressible sexual instinct, most physicians and police officials, like legislators and jurists, considered prostitution a necessary evil. But the absence of clear legal mandates for regulating prostitution did not mean that Brazilian authorities believed in a completely hands-off approach. As in many other nineteenth-century cities, the concern to sanitize the family was accompanied by an increasing preoccupation with prostitution as a source of moral and physical contagion. Most public authorities recommended some sort of control, most commonly the confinement of prostitutes to specific city zones in order to avoid contact between public and family women.[44] Yet even before the Buenos Aires and Parisian experiments in state-regulated brothels had failed, imperial and republican legislators consistently rejected proposals by physicians, police officials, and private citizens for prostitution-control policies. In the words of an 1879 Municipal Council report, "the government should not officially recognize nor legalize under any condition a vice that corrodes the moral bases of society, replacing the family . . . with sterile and brutal sensuality."[45] Legislators defined "the problem of prostitution" a matter for the local police, to whom they occasionally conceded reasonable discretionary power for dealing with prostitutes.[46] In its justification for granting this power, the 1879 report made explicit the ideological relationship between physical and moral contagion: "Just as certain infractions of individual liberties are rightly pe[r]-mitted, exceptional measures when it is urgent to attend to the manifest and imperious necessities of health in cases of epidemics and contagion, it is also legal to employ extraordinary repressive measures against the corruption of customs and affronts to public decorum."[47] In contradiction to the antiregulation position of Brazilian law, police began to delineate areas where prostitution would be tolerated and to regulate the trade in those areas, but their efforts were frequently frustrated by changes in police personnel or setbacks in court. The boundaries as well as the regulations (including, for example, rules about hours for opening and closing window shutters) fluctuated erratically and arrests and relocations were arbitrary and inconsistent, as individual police officers, police chiefs, magistrates, and municipal legislators failed to establish which practices constituted "reasonable discretionary powers."[48]

Although poverty, disease, prostitution, and other social ills were not new, with abolition of slavery and the population boom of the late nineteenth century these problems seemed increasingly threatening. As overcrowding and poor sanitation services exacerbated the effects of periodic epidemics of plague, yellow fever, smallpox, and tuberculosis, police, professional organizations, and the press registered increasing alarm over rampant prostitution and the proliferation of vagrants, criminals, and beggars.[49] Poor living standards, epidemics, political militancy, and diverse forms of popular resistance to moral hygiene campaigns combined in the minds of many residents, foreign visitors, and administrators, creating the perception that the streets of Rio were dangerous territory.

With the advent of the Republic in 1889, changing this perception became not only a public health imperative, but a matter of national honor. The city's racial composition, the visibility of prostitution, abject poverty, and disease, and widespread norms of public decorum and private morality that differed from Europeanized moral standards defended (if not always upheld) by middle- and upper-class families led to pessimistic appraisals of Brazil's progress by republican intellectuals and politicians. As jurist and national intellectual Alberto Torres pointed out in 1914, in a period of aggressive imperialism, when political and economic domination was justified by notions of racial and cultural superiority, Brazil's reputation as an uncivilized and backward former colony was a threat to national sovereignty.[50]

Although political and economic power after the turn of the century was concentrated in the agricultural-exporting states, particularly São Paulo, the federal government poured monies for renovation into Rio de Janeiro. In addition to its symbolic importance as the nation's capital and the cosmopolitan reputation it had earned since its days as the seat of the entire Portuguese empire (1808–1822), Rio de Janeiro was an important financial, commercial, and administrative center and a major port, which attracted influential foreign visitors. Since the agricultural export sector depended on foreign, mostly European, credit and investments in infrastructure, its capital city, government leaders believed, should inspire European confidence and admiration.

Converting Rio into a showcase that would help secure Brazil's position among the independent, honorable, and civilized nations of the West required the "Europeanization" and "modernization" of its physical space and its population. Public authorities frequently obscured the causes of poverty, inadequate housing, and epidemic disease by associating them with moral depravity, licentiousness, and racial inferiority. At the same time, the power and size of the Federal District civil police, responsible for enforcing public morality, increased steadily under republican administrations.[51]

A project of massive urban renewal from 1902 to 1910, modeled after the Haussmann project for Paris, was the most spectacular episode of what historian Nicolau Sevcenko terms "aggressive cosmopolitanization" during Rio's belle époque.[52] Working-class living quarters and the shops and kiosks that catered to common Cariocas were demolished. As the mostly poor, ethnically diverse occupants relocated to hillside favelas and to the more remote suburbs of the North Zone, the beautiful areas of the downtown were occupied by elite commercial, cultural, and social establishments. After the project was completed, police worked to keep "moralized" areas clear of prostitutes, vagrants, dandies, and others whose presence was an affront to the honor of bourgeois family women, who made appearances in increasingly broad areas of public space.[53]

Much of the population, however, remained unconvinced that moralizing efforts worked to their benefit. Although moralizers had lobbied their causes for decades, only the silencing of political opposition and the imposition of virtual martial law in the Federal District after 1902 made it possible to implement the more draconian "civilizing" measures, and even then there were limits to what Rio's people would put up with. In the most dramatic expression of popular resistance to authoritarian implementation of public policy, a four-day revolt sparked by opposition to an obligatory smallpox vaccination campaign (known as the "vaccine revolt") nearly toppled the government in 1904.[54] Citizens of various classes also objected to failures of public services, massive evictions, demolitions, or arbitrary police repression that accompanied the capital's transformation by signing petitions, writing letters to newspapers, organizing neighborhood protests, and refusing to cooperate.⁵⁵ These citizens frequently gained the support of elite professionals and politicians. Military officers and Positivist Party legislators joined the vaccine revolt, for example. Even prostitutes had influential allies, whether among their clients or among progressive legal professionals such as Evaristo de Morais, who at the turn of the century successfully defended prostitutes against police harassment and eviction from their downtown residences.⁵⁶

Nonetheless, there was a great deal of agreement among middle- and upper-class residents, expressed through the mainstream press, that the "civilizing" reforms, and even their authoritarian implementation, were necessary to make the city physically and morally safe. By justifying "moralization campaigns" of police, public health officials, and urban planners as the defense of the family and of Brazilian civilization, republican authorities could disregard their own racial and class biases. Here they encountered firm ground, since in law, medical literature, and urban planning, protecting the family was presented as the defense of a natural social and sexual order, an interest common to all of society.

The urban renewal project of 1902–1910 demonstrates explicitly that for turn-of-the-century republican policy makers, "to civilize" meant to emulate the social order of modern industrialized Europe through the construction of a modern capital city.⁵⁷ This explains the special significance of the visit, two decades later, of a royal couple that officials and the media glorified as symbols of the family values that sustained civilization. The euphoria surrounding the visit of King Albert and Queen Elisabeth was much less an homage to Belgian glory than a celebration of Brazil's national honor.

Self-congratulatory descriptions of the popular mass behaving like a civilized family, and the juxtaposition of images of "calm joy" of Brazilian families with the "volcanic countries of Europe" illustrate the dawn of a new spirit of nationalistic optimism in post–World War I Brazil. Over the course of the 1920s, widely divergent nationalist movements mobilized against the social and economic orientation as well as the political leadership of republican civilizers. But in 1920, those with a stake in the status quo saw the Belgian visit as a confirmation of their nation's progress. Brazil was a country of the future, a nation whose youth and vigor could sustain the progress of its transplanted European civilization, even as Europe itself entered into decline.

King Albert and Queen Elisabeth proved most obliging guests. Themselves models of sporty and elegant modern youth, they sped about the city, each in their own automobiles, demonstrating their appreciation of the salubrious environment. Despite uncooperative weather (periodic rain after the first day), the king and queen conspicuously enjoyed their tours, viewing all that was prepared for them to see and making flattering remarks along the way. They charmed their hosts with their "simplicity" and informality—characteristics Cariocas commonly attributed to themselves—as well as their regard for all that was distinctive of the tropical city. Indeed, they clearly preferred the regional cuisine and natural environment to the European fare and the ceremonies prepared for them, delighting locals and prompting criticism of official pretensions.[58] Moreover, their patronizing attitude toward the Brazilian popular classes was compatible with that of Brazil's upper classes. They were especially pleased by what they saw as the innocence and humility of the masses. President Pessoa's daughter remembered twenty years later that the maternal Elisabeth was particularly enchanted by black Brazilian children, constantly exclaiming, "Look how funny they are!" Playing with a black toddler at one of their train stops, she remarked that she would take one home "if only they didn't grow up."[59]

Rio had dazzled the Europeans, not just with its natural splendor, but, more important, with its civilization and potential as a great power, equal in status to "noble, industrial Belgium," as Albert's kingdom was described in one of the mayor's speeches. King Albert not only behaved "with the modesty and discretion of a simple Brazilian citizen,"[60] but, in a speech at Monroe Palace, recognized and lauded Brazil's historical "civilizing mission," quelling any misgivings about the path to progress republican leaders were following by emulating Europe and by sustaining Brazil's agricultural exporting model of development.[61]

You cleared the virgin forest, you scaled the mountains, you explored the riches of your soil and subsoil, handing over to the service of humanity inestimable forces and reserves. . . . You transformed sickly agglomerations into cities known for their healthiness. Here is a great example that can inspire the nations of the old world. . . .

You eliminated civil wars, nearly abolished party divisions, and achieved harmony and prosperity . . . you have followed progressively and surely your natural destiny, which is to implant civilization in the heart of the American continent.[62]

Albert did not stop at praising Brazil's historical progress. Quite explicitly, he legitimized the burgeoning nationalist view of Brazil as a country of the future, a nation whose youth and vigor would solve the problems faced by civilization and overcome the decadence and decay of Europe:

Gentlemen! . . . The old world has been severely punished by the war. . . . The new world finds itself in all the vigor of its robust youth. We depend upon you, we count on you to help us in the terrible crisis we are going through. And the close collaboration between America and Europe can save civilization.[63]

Albert received several ovations from his audience of public figures, including the president and the mayor, senators and congressmen, supreme court justices, and their wives. The speech was reprinted in several Brazilian and Belgian newspapers, along with reports of the unanimous approval by the Brazilian audience. "Brazil's senators and deputies all agree that the king's speech was a masterpiece of historical analysis," a Belgian reporter exulted, "and that never before have Brazil's achievements and the profound meaning of her institutions been better understood or so precisely and eloquently elucidated."[64]

"For King Albert Not to See": The "Authentic" Rio of the Popular Masses

With the hindsight of Brazil's political and economic history, the euphoric response to King Albert's speech seems ironic. Despite Brazil's participation in the Allied cause, it was not favored by the reordering of the world capitalist economy after World War I, and its export sector was hit particularly hard by the depression. In all of Brazil's major urban centers, both the economic orientation and the model of civilization pursued by republican governments came under attack in the press and on the streets, in fine arts and in popular festivals, and through political militancy and military revolts. Diverse groups opposed not only political rule by regional oligarchies and economic structures favoring export agriculture, but also the conceptual and moral basis on which the nation had rested. Far from political harmony and prosperity, a state of siege was declared from 1922 to 1927 on account of military and regional unrest. In 1924, junior officers and the crew mutinied on the very ship that had brought Albert and Elisabeth to Rio, the São Paulo, and sailed into exile in Uruguay. The First Republic was overthrown in 1930 by another revolt that ushered in a broad coalition held together by Getúlio Vargas. Fervid debate over the definition and resolution of "the social question" and the "moralization of Brazil" marked the interwar period, and reverberated in various issues of urban administration.[65]

But King Albert cannot be held entirely responsible for his overly optimistic reading of Brazil's social reality. After all, authorities had carefully constructed an image of the capital "for the king to see," as innumerable headlines pointed out. Even the Belgian press picked up on the phrase. It played upon a popular aphorism, "for the English to see." The aphorism originated with an 1831 law that banned slave traffic, passed for the sole purpose of appeasing the British. Imperial officials continued to tolerate the notorious African slave trade centered under their noses in Rio de Janeiro, and it actually increased between 1830 and 1850. The law displayed to the English was therefore an artifice that concealed Rio de Janeiro's social reality. Likewise in 1920, as critics insinuated, primping Rio's glamorous exterior diverted European eyes from the less "noble" or "civilized" aspects of the city, not to mention government abuses of civil rights guaranteed by Brazilian law.

In an article published two months after the king and queen's departure, Evaristo de Morais was more pointedly ironic in his attack of the role of the police in preparing the city for the royal visit.[66] Police, he explained, concerned that "the scandal of poor prostitutes would demoralize us before King Albert," had carried out one of their periodic moralization campaigns, making arrests and forcing prostitutes from their homes on selected downtown streets in the commercial area just west of Rio Branco Avenue.[67] Morais's invective linked the illegal coercion and violence used against prostitutes to the hypocrisy of the Republic's veneration of European royalty. "Of course," he reasoned sarcastically, "the motive for this situation was a greater international cause, a cause that is unarguably supreme, absolute, the same cause that lowered Congress to the feet of the president, sanctioned all kinds of exploitation and subterfuge, and provoked general disorientation: the arrival of King Albert."[68]

Morais's mention of exploitation and subterfuge refers to complaints that police took advantage of the extraordinary security measures in place for the royal visit to arbitrarily arrest political militants. This, he complained, like the arbitrary power police claimed over prostitutes, was illegal and coercive, a reflection of the hypocrisy of Brazil's ostensible democracy, under which individuals were protected by laws the state did not respect. Brazilian legislators explicitly and emphatically rejected state regulation of prostitution, yet police enforced their own regulations, delineating zones, registering prostitutes, and abusing civil rights.[69]

Police cleanups of the downtown were not only coercive, violent, arbitrary, and illegal, Morais argued, but they were ineffectual, even counterproductive, as a measure of "moral hygiene."[70] The vast majority of prostitutes were never affected by police regulation. Prostitution was not officially tolerated in the commercial center of the city, but despite sporadic cleanup campaigns, it continued to coexist with businesses, residences, and leisure establishments. The "moralized homage to the hero-king" that police prepared was thus nothing more than a temporary facade. "If it weren't forbidden," Morais remarked, referring to press censorship, "we would say it was all for the king not to see."[71]

Behind this facade lay a city that had not been constructed by urban planners or "disciplined" by police. Dividing their time between official events, nature hikes, and the South Zone beaches, Albert and Elisabeth did not have the opportunity to wander just north of the port, into the neighborhood of Gambôa, or further inland, through the neighborhoods known as the Cidade Nova (New City). Neither did they climb any of the city's characteristic hills such as Favela (officially Providência), just behind the train station, which gave its name to Rio's infamous hillside slums; Mangueira, not far north of the Quinta da Boa Vista; Santo Antônio and Castelo, flanking either side of Rio Branco Avenue; and many others scattered throughout the city, even in the South Zone. According to several opposition papers, if the royal couple had visited these poor neighborhoods, they would have seen Rio de Janeiro's—and Brazil's—disgraceful social reality. "The royal visitors would be horrified," one report clamored, if they saw "the indecorous contrast of rising misery, in the very heart of the city, with the majestic opulence of marble palaces on the avenues."[72]

One thing Albert and Elisabeth might have noticed was that most of the city was not organized into discrete zones conforming to city planners' blueprints. In fact, much of the population, particularly in favelas and in the more inaccessible suburban areas, squatted or rented illegal properties in unnumbered houses on streets that did not appear on official maps. Even in the renovated area, which had previously been known as the Cidade Velha (Old City), the airy modern avenues and plazas were flanked by centuries-old narrow winding streets and shadowy blind alleys. The favela atop Castelo Hill, the most egregious mark of contrast between the persistence of widespread poverty and the desired image of modernity, survived the era of demolitions until 1922, when the entire hill was finally flattened and converted into a pavilion for an international exposition marking the centennial of Brazilian independence.[73]

Visible signs of poverty such as malnutrition, vagrancy, lower-class prostitution, and the same overcrowded "beehive" tenements and rooming houses that had been condemned as unfit for human occupation twenty years earlier could still be found bordering and spilling over into the sections of the city that had been cleaned up for occupation by "families." Although public health campaigns had made important gains in con-

66

trolling smallpox, cholera, yellow fever, and bubonic plague, the world-
wide outbreak of Spanish influenza in 1918 devastated Rio, and other
diseases such as tuberculosis continued unabated, taking their heaviest
toll on the lower classes. Immigration from Europe had slowed after the
start of World War I, but migrants from the interior continued to flock to
the city until jobs dried up in the late 1920s. The wealthier families of
the middle and upper classes avoided the downtown and North Zone suburbs, preferring the tranquillity and comfort of the South Zone, which
was flooded with public and private investments. Middle- and upper-class
residential developments served by new tunnels, highways, and utilities
multiplied in Copacabana and Ipanema in the immediate post–World
War I period. At the same time, the supply of low-income housing shrank,
and that which existed lacked basic services such as running water, sew-
ers, electricity, garbage collection, paved roads, and adequate access to
transportation.[74]

Many among the popular masses who gathered to greet the Belgian
royalty in 1920 had come from the North Zone and the suburbs farther
out, generating substantial profits for the Central rail station.[75] Families
of the expanding lower-middle class and relatively well-off working class
had moved from the center to modest houses in less crowded northern
outskirts in the first decades of the century, where they were joined by
poor migrants from the interior. By 1920, the North Zone suburbs were
the fastest-growing areas of the city. With the housing shortage of the
following two decades, the suburban population closest to railway lines
would expand enormously, straining meager transportation and public
services, while other suburban areas remained primarily rural. Workers
who were unwilling to commute to the suburbs or unable to afford transportation crowded into tenements, rooming houses, or decrepit old man-
sions downtown or joined the growing squatter communities in hillside
favelas.[76] Labor mobilization and protests against inadequate social services and living conditions were brutally repressed in the immediate postwar period, as republican governments continued to consider "the social
question" a police issue.

In 1920, the new police chief, jurist Geminiano da Franca, outlined
his goals to combat what he considered a "degrading spectacle" in Rio's
downtown: new gains of anarchist propaganda; abandoned children, especially girls, who were easy prey to the growing numbers of foreign and national pimps; malnourished and diseased vagrants begging in the streets;
the spread of prostitution; and the proliferation of communal residences,
"lacking the most rudimentary hygiene, [which] constitute, because of
the promiscuity of their tenants, true dens of vice in their most abject

modality." Franca launched a renewed police moralization campaign with the arrests and forced relocation of downtown streetwalkers and anarchist militants in time for the Belgian sovereigns' visit. Once again, the goal of moralization was to ensure that the living conditions of the city's poor women, men, and children did not threaten the tranquillity or the image of the city's honorable families.[77]

Evaristo de Morais's attack on the government's hypocrisy during the visit of the Belgian sovereigns, however, was but one piece among a multitude of evidence that few Cariocas supported, or took very seriously, the moralizing pretensions of police and government officials or their supporters in the press. In fact, it is likely that many apparently progovernment journalists did not take these pretensions seriously either, since reporters often wrote for more than one journal, worked around unofficial censorship, and saw their trade as a combination of artistic creation and detached objectivity—characteristics that would soon come under attack by a public campaign against press sensationalism. A good portion of the reports on the visit seemed to be at least slightly tongue-in-cheek, whether applauding or attacking the preparations.

The ridicule of official pretensions reflects a broader critique of what was perceived in the 1920s as Brazil's political and cultural elite. Increasingly, intellectuals and others involved in diverse artistic and political movements insisted that the authentic Brazil had been devalued, its cultural expression repressed, by this elite's feeling of inferiority vis-à-vis Europe. Over the next two decades, it was the celebration of the African impact on Brazilian civilization, and not the nation's emulation of Europe, that would earn Brazil the international (that is, European) acclaim that turn-of-the-century republican leaders had so avidly sought.[78] As was the case with the white reception of jazz and soul music in the United States, an avant-garde among privileged Brazilians considered Afro-Brazilian artistic expression truly authentic, raw and primitive, closer to "true" human emotion.

Unlike jazz in the United States, however, samba, the musical style associated with poor Afro-Brazilian neighborhoods and bohemian spaces in Rio de Janeiro, became a quintessential symbol of Brazil's miscegenized national culture in the interwar period.[79] Anthropologist Hermano Vianna argues that nationalist intellectuals and artists searching for authentic Brazilian culture "discovered" it in samba.[80] After much concerted effort on the part of many working-class Afro-Brazilian *sambistas*, samba schools that "descended from the hills" such as Mangueira, Salgueiro, and São Carlos, along with those formed in the Cidade Nova or in working-class suburbs such as Portela, became an important presence in Carnival, the city's largest public festival, by the 1930s. Samba schools integrated into and eventually replaced the upper-middle-class *grandes sociedades* ("grand societies," the social clubs that organized Carnival balls and paraded elaborate floats down Rio Branco Avenue on the last day of Carnival) and the more modest lower-middle- and working-class *ranchos* (small groups of organized musicians, dancers, and revelers). After the populist-reformist government led by Mayor Pedro Ernesto took over the city's administration in 1930, the samba schools—and their poor black participants—received official sponsorship, and they have been promoted as a local tradition, emblem of collective identity, and tourist attraction ever since.[81]

At least three popular tunes, two sambas titled "For King Albert to See" and a *cateretê* (a popular music and dance style with rural origins) called "For King Albert to Hear," made fun of the glamorous facade created for the royal reception in 1920 when most residents endured dismal living standards. The third made its own call to mobilize the population that would represent Brazilian civilization: "Let's loaf and get drunk for King Albert to see; Who knows, once here, so maybe will he."[82] But this mockery by no means meant that popular artists rejected the opportunity to form part of the "official" image of Brazil. The Oito Batutas, a soon-to-be-world-famous popular band that already played samba and *choro* for fashionable audiences in the movie theaters on Rio Branco Avenue, took good advantage of an opportunity to play for King Albert, calling itself in later publicity "the acclaimed troupe that played for King Albert!"[83] The following year, the band was billed as "the patriotic group that will go to the United States on the patriotic mission to publicize our [popular music]! A brilliant group of genuinely Brazilian artists!"[84]

Catulo da Paixão Cearense, a well-known interpreter of the popular Northeastern folk music called *sertaneja*, disagreed. Catulo considered it "a lack of patriotism" for the Batutas to play two of his songs at a luncheon, while he was invited to give a more precarious performance atop a boat in the less elegant "Venetian festival." The Batutas, he claimed, would degrade his folkloric poetry—"a poetry known all over Brazil and appreciated by both the intelligentsia and by the popular soul" by mixing it with their lowbrow tunes.[85]

Catulo's repudiation of the popular, carnivalesque aura around the Venetian festival, in turn, must have provoked the ire of Angelo Lazzary, artistic director for one of Rio's prominent *grandes sociedades* and one of the festival's three designers. Lazzary defended the event against accusations that its evocation of Carnival would reveal the coarseness of Rio's lowbrow popular culture, insisting repeatedly that "it is not exactly a carnival . . . but something more elevated, of great artistic expression." He described the festival with the superlatives typical of the city's general mood: "it is the greatest apotheosis ever achieved, on the world's most beautiful bay, for the greatest soldier of the European conflagration."[86]

The Homosocial Space of Bohemian Rio

Lazzary removed from his Venetian festival the scantily clad women of dubious reputation who usually adorned Rio's Carnival floats. While these women probably participated in the festivities from the sidelines, the poorer prostitutes that Police Chief Franca's forces picked up were relocated to Mangue, an area of the Cidade Nova decidedly excluded from royal tours.

The king and queen did see Lapa, the city's other "zone," during their first auto tour of Rio by night. Located just west of Rio Branco Avenue, a few blocks above Beira Mar, Lapa had been included in urban renewals of earlier decades, when it was designated for family residence and decorous commerce. Although the most unsightly tenements were demolished, however, Lapa was not surrendered to the forces of moral hygiene. Remembered as "our little improvised Montemartre in the tropics," the neighborhood included an assortment of "German bars," or beer houses, pool halls, cabarets, and café-concerts evoking Old World charm with names like "Blue Danube," "Viena-Budapest."[87] Lapa's fame, however, derived from its white-suited *malandros* (rogues or con-men), *mulatas,* and samba music—all of which later became icons of Brazilian popular culture. In Lapa, symbols of European erotica blended into a distinctively Carioca space of moral transgression, a place where middle- and upper-middle-class men, including some of the city's most influential intellectuals, artists, journalists, and politicians, escaped the confinement of bourgeois family life. The neighborhood characterized Rio de Janeiro's sensual identity for the men who gathered to drink, eat, listen to samba, rub elbows with *malandros*, enjoy the paid company of waitresses and prostitutes, or purchase sex.

Younger and poorer men frequented the less distinguished and more remote streets of Mangue, where police vigilance was more intense, and the establishments less varied. The neighborhood, which covered about the same geographical area as Lapa (six or seven city blocks long and two blocks wide), held a higher number of prostitutes: in 1923, police registered 436 in Lapa and 674 in Mangue. While Lapa was perceived as the territory of sophisticated *francesas* and exotic *mulatas,* Mangue was the reputed home to *polacas* and *pretas* who served lower-class men.[88] Like

Lapa, Mangue had its share of samba musicians and *malandros.* In fact, the zone was adjacent to "little Africa," the lower-class, largely Afro-Brazilian neighborhood where samba was born. Nonetheless, many of Mangue's houses were frequented by sons of the middle classes, and several modernist artists depicted the zone in paintings over the next few decades. Nelson Werneck Sodré, a young military officer who frequented the zone in the 1920s, remembered this period in Mangue as "a splendid phase, with such outstanding and picturesque aspects that Mangue was even a tourist attraction."[89] Among the picturesque aspects he mentioned were frequent street fights between clients, particularly soldiers and sailors.

Partly because of its rowdiness and the class and racial makeup of its prostitutes, and partly because it was considered a remote area where "scandalous" activities would not offend families, Mangue became the center of increasingly systematic police regulation, beginning with Albert and Elisabeth's visit.[90] As Evaristo de Morais argued, the vast majority of prostitutes in Rio were not confined by police zoning policies or regulation. Many worked in unregulated brothels in the center of town, subject to sporadic police cleanup campaigns. Most, however, worked independently of brothels, through "clandestine" rendezvous and other arrangements.[91] Notwithstanding this reality, police zoning policies confined certain kinds of "public women" to spaces reserved for male leisure, on the grounds that their presence there satisfied male instincts without posing an affront (or a temptation) to honest women or the family.

The necessary corollary of prostitution zoning was therefore the exclusion of family women from these spaces of male leisure. This was not only a police policy, but the practice of many of the men who sought bohemian life in Lapa. Luís Martins, for example, a nostalgic self-identified bohemian who frequented Lapa in the 1920s and 1930s, recounted his discomfort when, in 1937, he was asked to accompany a group of modern artists, including the painter Tarsila do Amaral and two other women, on a tour of Lapa nightlife. "I always disapproved of mixing people and places," he explained. "I thought that a place for carousal was no place for the family, and it made me uncomfortable to direct ladies to bars where I would prefer to be alone or with the company of my own sex."[92] Men like Martins, who considered themselves socially transgressive bohemians, generally upheld normative standards of sexual honor for the women in their families.

In Martins's account, prostitution facilitated male bonding, although he insists that it was merely "an accessory." He and his buddies frequented "the other Lapa" (the brothels, as opposed to the bars) individually and in voyeuristic groups. In the latter case, they acted "as if it were austere observers of vice," or so he claims, and prostitutes did not interfere in "that group spirit, of sociability, of collective bohemia that defined our conviviality in bars."[93] By creating strictly homosocial erotic leisure spaces, men could satisfy their desires for male bonding and transgressive sexuality outside the family without challenging the control of female sexuality within it.

"Where Men Enter, Women Can Enter Too": The Feminine Invasion of Masculine Space

The Lapa King Albert and Queen Elisabeth saw would soon become part of a folkloric past, as did the idea that "ladies," by definition, stayed at home while men went out to work or carouse. In the interwar decades, highly visible middle- and upper-class women stretched the conceptual boundaries that excluded them from wide areas of public space. Their rebellion took various and sometimes conflicting forms. Most women who called themselves feminists, along with many who did not, publicly demanded women's rights to political equality with men, but studiously disavowed "the right to licentious liberation of customs" or "to imitate men in their errors," in the words of L. V., writing in the conservative *Revista feminina* in 1923.[94] Working through several women's journals or small but well-connected feminist organizations, the most successful of which was the Brazilian Federation for Feminine Progress (*Federação Brasileira para o Progresso Feminino;* FBPF), middle-class feminists lobbied congressmen and other politicians for equal property rights, education, access to professions, and suffrage (the latter was won in 1932). Other women intellectuals such as political activists and writers Patrícia Galvão (known as Pagu) and Maria Lacerda de Moura, and painter Tarsila de Amaral shunned the organized feminist movement, condemning it as bourgeois.[95] They called for more radical political and cultural transformations, among which the destruction of the patriarchal family and women's sexual liberation. Some of these women lived and worked outside Rio de Janeiro, but the influence of their ideas and lifestyles was felt in the capital. Not only were their work and details of their personal lives publicized, but artists, intellectuals, and political activists from all over Brazil made at least occasional appearances in Rio, which, despite strong competition from São Paulo, was still considered the nation's cultural center in the 1920s.

Notwithstanding the considerable impact of new intellectual currents on social norms, many middle- and upper-class women were less

less interested in feminist organizations or radical politics than in earning a living or following the fashions and behavior of the "new women" they saw in European and United States cinema and advertising. Whatever their ideological or practical motivation, many middle- and upper-class women physically occupied wider areas of public space, joining men of their class in work and leisure. Gilka Machado, a writer known for her sensual poetry, made explicit her desire to tear down the gendered spatial boundaries that restricted women's access to power. "I am for women in Parliament," she explained in a 1920 newspaper interview, "because I understand that where men enter, women can enter too."[96]

According to Luís Martins, the entry of "ladies" (*senhoras*) in nocturnal leisure space led to the death of "the old Lapa" and transformed Rio's bohemian experience for the younger generation. Mourning the death of Lapa, Martins attributed it to the "mass exodus" of the intellectual bohemia to Copacabana, an atmosphere "very different from our Lapa, because ladies participated in it."[97] Copacabana, Martins claimed, was "killing Rio little by little," replacing the "picturesque," run-down brothels and other places unfit for honest women with new, bright, and healthy spots, including the beach and commercial establishments, where honest women mingled with men.

King Albert's morning workouts and Queen Elisabeth's afternoon dips in the waves at Copacabana in 1920 lent prestigious approval to what was fast becoming a fashionable leisure space for men and women of diverse social classes. Beach activities and "maillot," or one-piece French-style bathing suits, which had seemed scandalous just a few years earlier, became commonplace for women of the 1920s and 1930s. The beach provided visible evidence that modern notions of salubrious public leisure were replacing the traditional seclusion of honest women, just as critiques of the dubious morality of the traditional patriarchal family became popularized. According to intellectuals such as Gilberto Freyre, who wrote in the early 1930s, the seclusion and repression of elite women in Brazil's colonial households had reinforced the unrestrained tyranny of polygamous patriarchs, produced lazy, portly, frigid, and vindictive matrons, and victimized *mulata* slaves who were the objects of the patriarchs' sexual desire and the mistresses' wrath.[98] Rio's new image as a modern, cosmopolitan metropolis demanded the presence of respectable and healthy family women. To Luís Martins's dismay, the boom in cosmopolitan heterosocial leisure, not just for "literary bohemians" in Copacabana but for diverse social groups all over the city, would transform the urban landscape in the 1920s and 1930s.[99]

Gilka Machado attributed women's traditional exclusion from male

space to the backwardness of the Brazilian people and the "inferior eroticism" of their blood. "For the organized races that have progress as a
permanent concern," she explained, "sexual prejudice is not an obstacle to
working together toward a progressive goal. This is how the Americans
think."[100] This association of the United States with modern gender roles
was not limited to middle-class feminists demanding the right to work
alongside men. With its aggressive marketing of cultural exports, especially movies, the image of the assertive new woman represented in
Hollywood productions became an important symbol of modern leisure
for the post–World War I generation in Rio.[101] While more traditional,
male-centered establishments frequently sought to reproduce a sultry
Old World atmosphere, new types of establishments that appealed to
both women and men often invoked the image of the fast-paced, widely
accessible leisure spaces that for Brazilians typified the United States.
Many such spaces were collectively called, in English, "dancings" or
"jazz-clubs."

The association of the modern youth culture with the United States
did not put an end to the prestige of Europe. Several new social spaces that
appealed to the 1920s spirit of moral transgression were exclusively accessible to the upper classes and reflected their European taste. The best
example is probably the Hotel Copacabana Palace, designed by a French
architect in Louis XVI style, opened in 1923. The hotel's casinos, operat-
ing under a special government license, were the object of tremendous
moral debate until they were finally outlawed in 1946. There, as well as in
older upper-class clubs, "new women" scandalized conservatives with
racy clothing and dances and by taking on masculine habits such as drink-
ing, smoking, and stalking the opposite sex.

A major attraction of these places of leisure was their cultivation of
an aura of sensual excitement and transgression of moral codes. The pursuit of illicit sensuality had long been part of male leisure in the city. The
novelty in the 1920s was the deliberate moral transgression of adven-
turous middle- and upper-class young women who frequented areas of the
city newly open to them. For some, like Gilka Machado, changing gender
roles and increasing sexual liberties for women were a sign of progress,
demonstrating the advancement of civilized societies such as the United
States, which was not overwhelmed by the "inferior eroticism" of Brazilian culture. For others, women's sexual liberties signaled the victory
of the disorder and vice of the black lower class over the civilized refinement of elites. Many conservatives, citing the sexual impropriety of high-
society women as evidence of the immorality and decadence of the nation's ruling classes, would call for greater assertion of moral authority by

74

police and military forces, whose leaders were drawn largely from the middle class. Commenting on the scandalous attire and behavior of high-society ladies in the Jockey Club in 1926, for example, a conservative police journal argued that these women, "forgetting their dignity and the respect they owe to others," were "lowering themselves" to the level of their social inferiors. "The 'clubs' of the kinky-haired people should be proud," the journal sneered, "for they have imitators . . . in Rio de Janeiro's most elegant society."[102] The journal, like several mainstream papers, lobbied for better moralization efforts by police, including censorship of the media, control of prostitutes, and patrolling of leisure establishments.

Against the protests of conservative mouthpieces such as this journal, however, cultural forms emanating from lower-class neighborhoods were increasingly embraced by the upper classes and by populist politicians who came to power in the 1930s, as symbols of a shared Carioca culture. Samba was the most salient symbol of Carioca, and even Brazilian, culture to arise in the 1920s and 1930s. To guarantee broad acceptance in citywide Carnival celebrations, samba leaders went to great lengths to shed their association with disreputable *blocos sujos*, the older, more ragtag groups of mostly young male revelers. A major achievement was to convince parents in the poor, largely Afro-Brazilian neighborhoods where samba developed that their activities were not dishonorable entertainment for daughters.[103] When samba schools paraded down the Avenue, they were accompanied not by the high-class prostitutes that had adorned the grand societies' floats, but by young women and men from "honest" working-class homes.

Besides the samba schools, diverse establishments catering to working-class or mixed crowds, specializing in "popular" music and dances including samba, tango, and jazz, also proliferated in the 1920s and 1930s. In dance schools (*escolas de dança*), middle- and working-class patrons danced to jazz, tango, samba, and maxixe. *Gafieiras*, establishments inspired by suburban neighborhood dances that featured regional Brazilian music, were favorite spots for lower-class families.

The proliferation of both popular and elite leisure establishments, together with middle-class women's growing presence in the workplace, led to the perception among commentators that modern women were abandoning the home and invading masculine public space. Lower-class women, however, had long occupied the streets of Rio. Despite official intentions to segregate public areas for leisure, commerce, industry, and family residence, these spaces continued to overlap in most working-class neighborhoods. Moreover, as in the nineteenth century, women and girls commonly worked and traveled unaccompanied through various zones of the city, where they were often diverted by new beaux or old acquaintances.

Stories of social and sexual encounters related in criminal trials of deflowering (taking the virginity of a minor woman) suggest that even though parents or employers often did not allow virgin daughters to go out with boys or men, they were frequently unable to prevent these meetings, especially in cases in which the young women worked far from home.[104] Maria Pereira, for example, went out to deposit her paycheck in the bank when she met her boyfriend Manoel Souza, who convinced her to step up to his boardinghouse room, where "he said he had something to show her."[105] Fifteen-year-old Edith Martins, for example, was selling theater tickets by herself in 1927 in the Quinta da Boa Vista—a few train stops away from her home in the North Zone suburb of Meyer—when she met nineteen-year-old Salústio de Castro. Castro, the son of a Portuguese store clerk, offered to buy all of her tickets if she would spend the afternoon with him (he failed to keep the promise).[106] A few months later, Izaltina Moreira, a seventeen-year-old who delivered laundry for her mother, a washerwoman, took advantage of her trip from her home, also in Meyer, to the homes of downtown clients to flirt with a taxicab driver who took her for a ride around the city.[107] Edneia Nazareth de Marcondes, twenty, met Paulo Silveira de Mello on the commuter train she took from the North Zone to work in a downtown laboratory in 1936 and, like countless others, took advantage of the voyages to and from work to flirt and develop a romantic relationship.[108]

Courtship, as in earlier decades, often took place in public. In records of sexual crimes the witnesses' testimony demonstrates that it was commonly accepted for young women to receive their beaux at the gate of their own or their employers' homes. Character witnesses for Arminda da Silva, for example, testified in 1933 that her father "did not even allow her to talk to boys at the gate" as evidence of her unusually strict upbringing.[109] Increasingly over the course of the 1920s and 1930s, young women were allowed to go out socially with their suitors, and many young women frequented a variety of dance halls or nightclubs. Since money was scarce, however, and not all parents allowed daughters to frequent dances, clubs, or movies, most dates consisted of walks through the woman's neighborhood or in public parks, or outings by streetcar to public festivals.

These public settings did not prohibit private romantic and even sexual encounters. Judging by the complaints brought to the courts, young women commonly "gave themselves" to their boyfriends in public places such as empty lots or public parks, on the beach, against the wall of a church, behind the bleachers at a soccer stadium, under the tarp covering a construction site, in a train cabin, "in the bushes," or in "a secluded spot" in one of the alleyways leading off the windy, narrow streets that public authorities considered dangerously obscure.[110]

Conclusion

One thing is clear from all the arguments over what King Albert should and should not see in Rio de Janeiro: Rio de Janeiro's unique identity and "authentic" Brazilian culture was under debate, among both elite and popular interpreters. For many of them, the royal visit threw into relief a dichotomous social geography, which, in turn, revealed an enormous economic and cultural distance between a Europeanized elite and a popular mass. A parallel dichotomy separated private homes and "moralized" areas of the city that were safe for white, privileged honest women from professions and leisure spaces reserved for men, public women, and the black and mixed-race lower class. Divergent notions of how the government would or should represent Brazil and its people, however, make it difficult to delineate the two sides of these dichotomies with any precision. Debates over the king and queen's reception suggest, in fact, that the blurring of spatial and cultural categories was generating a great deal of anxiety, and that there was little agreement over how the boundaries should be redrawn. As was the case in turn-of-the-century urban reforms, a preoccupation with gender categories and sexual honor was a privileged means of expressing this anxiety, particularly since class and racial hierarchies were attacked as illegitimate, undemocratic, and "un-Brazilian" bases of power.

The contrast between images of Rio de Janeiro deemed "fit for a king" and those concealed "for the king not to see" in 1920—and the conflicts that arose over the construction of these images—foreshadowed conflicts that would characterize subsequent decades. First, political battles over the form of Brazil's governance and legal system—dictatorial or constitutional and representational—were played out over the issue of who should be first in line to represent the nation and the city. The choice of the first family and the chief of police over congressional and judicial representatives symbolized, according to critics, the government's option for patriarchal authority imposed by force. Evaristo de Morais insinuated as much when he linked extralegal police action against prostitutes to the hypocrisy of the Republic's veneration of European royalty. Yet the Catholic, patriarchal civilization that Albert and Elisabeth represented was precisely the model that had inspired turn-of-the-century republican officials as they set out to moralize the nation's capital.

Second, the mirth of samba composers and the general carnivalization of the royal visit, together with the delight that many took in the royal couple's interest in authentic Brazilian culture was emblematic of growing criticism of Brazil's political and cultural elite for its Europeanizing pretensions. For the post–World War I intellectual vanguard as well as for the Oito Batutas, and, presumably, the multitude who sang and danced to their music, the lifestyle and values of the mixed-race popular masses represented the nation's "true" identity.

Third, the accusation that the navy was "selecting for color" in assigning the crew of the *São Paulo*, and the defensiveness of the navy's response, was a sign of increasing public intolerance for overt racism, attacked as hypocritical and anti-Brazilian. Already in 1920, progovernment sources insisted that Brazil's honor rested on its repudiation of racism. In the 1930s, the thesis that Brazil was a "racial democracy," a nation free of racial prejudice, would become an official credo, even as racial discrimination persisted.

Finally, conflicting visions of moral ideals and national honor were symptomatic of the growing political discord between reformist professionals such as Evaristo de Morais and the public officials he considered elitist and authoritarian. The 1920s and 1930s would see unprecedented attempts by opposition politicians of diverse platforms to garner the support of the popular masses. Many on the right promoted "the popular family" and linked patriarchal authority in the home to the authority of the nation's rulers. Resistance to authoritarian and patriarchal institutions marked the period just as decisively, however. This resistance ranged from feminist demands for legal and political rights for women and women's challenge to older moral norms in dress, work, and leisure, to partisan struggles to eradicate the power of what came to be identified as the "traditional oligarchy."

The chapter that follows argues that the shifting political and cultural conflicts that shook Brazil in the period between the two world wars were played out in battles over the enforcement of sexual norms and family values in the capital city. Nowhere was this more evident than in debates over the meaning of honor, status, and citizenship in national law. Groups of jurists and other professionals would attack what they considered retrogressive and perverse traditions of sexual honor that were sustained in penal law, as well as the roots of these traditions in the patriarchal and authoritarian rural oligarchies that, they insisted, continued to rule the nation. Socially conservative groups, particularly those linked to the Catholic Church or the military, also called for the nation's "modernization," but insisted that it be accompanied by moral and political authority that could maintain tighter social order. They commonly defended authoritarian politics and corporatist social institutions with warnings that without them, women's sexual honor and the traditional Brazilian family faced imminent degradation. Both positions, and many others in between, emerged within the loose alliance that came to power after the overthrow of the First Republic in 1930. Social reformers and conservatives alike took part in campaigns to support state interventionist family policies, to redefine legal definitions of honor, and to empower judges to use their own discretion, particularly in judgments of the honor of "modern women" in their claims against allegedly abusive or criminally deceitful men.

3   *"What Virginity Is This?":*
Judging the Honor of the Modern Woman

I n 1898, Viveiros de Castro attributed what he perceived to be an increase in crimes against the honor of women to the changes brought
by turn-of-the-century urban life. Factory work and "modern upbringing" were leading women from "the silent intimacy of the home" and exposing them to "all kinds of seduction." The rise of new attitudes among
women was the most damaging effect of these changes. The "modern
woman," he warned, "dominated by the erroneous, subversive idea of her
emancipation . . . does all she can to lose the respect, the esteem and the
consideration of men."[1]

To some nostalgic jurists of the 1920s and 1930s, however, Viveiros
de Castro's era seemed one of innocence, a time when women were "zeal-
ously preserved in ignorance of the evils of the world."[2] Judges needed to
adapt the 1890 penal code to the realities of their day through "creative
interpretations," according to post–World War I legal authorities such as
judge Nelson Hungria, because "the modern social environment, with its
complacency and licentiousness, presents us with a very different type of
young woman than that of a half-century ago."[3]

Yet Hungria's description of new "modern women" would sound familiar to Viveiros de Castro. "Modern girls," Hungria explained in a 1937
compendium, "have participated actively at the vortex of daily life, spreading out into offices, public buildings, and commercial establishments, and
they have thus lost . . . that feminine reserve that was their greatest en-
chantment, and constituted, at the same time, the inhibiting force of
shame. They removed themselves from the vigilance and discipline of the
family and became precocious in the science of sexual mysteries."[4]

Apart from the occupational classification of "modern women"—
factory hands in Viveiros de Castro's day, white-collar workers forty years
later—the rhetoric of these prominent representatives of two generations

of jurists on the lost innocence of independent working women is strikingly similar. It may be that for Brazilians, as anthropologist Michael Herzfeld argues for rural Greece in the late twentieth century, "women were 'always' more chaste in the preceding generation." Herzfeld believes that the "lament for lost virtue" is a rhetorical device, a means of justifying a frequently transgressed moral system, which "would otherwise seem an unreasonable and unrealistic morality" by alluding to past traditions.[5] Both jurists, however, were writing about the urgent need to establish new guidelines for distinguishing between honest and dishonest women in trials of sexual crime. Viveiros de Castro argued for the need to defend what he considered the civilized moral standards upheld in the 1890 penal code against the threat posed by women's factory work. Hungria, however nostalgically, expressed the consensus among jurists of the 1930s that the 1890 code must be repealed because of its antiquated moral concepts. In 1939, Hungria would join fellow appeals court judges Vieira Braga and Narcélio de Queiroz and public prosecutor Roberto Lira on the commission that worked under Justice Minister Francisco Campos to produce the final draft of Brazil's new penal code of 1940.

The ways that witnesses, victims, and defendants describe honest, dishonest, and commonplace behavior in these trials suggest that in many ways, working-class young women of the post–World War I period were not, in fact, radically different from women of preceding generations. To a great extent, their behavior and attitudes were compatible with long-standing popular social institutions such as premarital sexual relations, consensual unions, and female-headed households. But although the lifestyles and morals of working women of the postwar era were not so very different from those of their mothers or grandmothers, the context in which their behavior was interpreted *had* changed radically, and in ways that made jurists such as Hungria even more uncertain than his predecessors about how the courts should defend sexual honor.

The Rio de Janeiro that King Albert and Queen Elisabeth saw in 1920 had been transformed since the nineteenth century, not just by massive turn-of-the-century urban renewal projects but also by demographic, political, social, and cultural forces. In particular, immigration, rural to urban migration, the resulting population boom, and economic fluctuations of the belle époque and World War I contributed to greater individual autonomy and mobility in the city, and to a general sense of instability. Contemporaries frequently blamed this instability on the dissolution of the family and traditional morals. Meanwhile, in a trend that began at least a century earlier, horizontal ties of solidarity gained importance relative to vertical ties of patronage, as the extended productive household gave way to the nuclear family, and the paternalistic social relations characteristic of rural society were slowly replaced by more impersonal capitalistic relations. Women from increasingly varied socioeconomic strata joined the wage labor force, filling not only the factory floors of Viveiros de Castro's era but also the shops and offices that Hungria mentions.[6]

Both turn-of-the-century factory workers and "office girls" of Hungria's times were a small, privileged minority of the female labor force, but they occupied a large space in the public imagination. Most working women continued to perform low-paid domestic labor throughout the twentieth century, and it was these women who were most likely to go to the police with deflowering complaints. Nonetheless, the chapters ahead demonstrate that women and men who appeared in Hungria's courtrooms took advantage of the new meanings that could be attached to women's employment, leisure activities, and independence in order to position themselves advantageously in conflicts of various kinds. In this sense, both jurists were correct when they complained that the women they observed were behaving in ways that transformed popular and even legal notions of virginity and honor.

The broad social and economic changes that preoccupied Viveiros de Castro and Hungria were uneven and took place over several decades, which might explain why the two men held similar impressions of modern women. After World War I, however, fashion, leisure, the labor market, and the communications media were swiftly and dramatically transformed, leading Hungria and his contemporaries all over the Western world to perceive their era as one of unprecedented changes in gender norms.[7] The term "modern woman" in the 1920s connoted not just a factory worker but a flapper—racy, flirtatious, assertive, androgynous. Much of the Brazilian discourse about her echoed that of contemporary Europe and the United States: she symbolized the transformations of the new century, much accelerated after World War I, and she defied the male dominance and patriarchal family values that had seemed to cement an earlier social order.[8] Brazilian versions of this discourse, however, reflected broader conflicts over the nation's cultural identity and political and economic future that surfaced at the time of King Albert and Queen Elisabeth's visit in 1920 and intensified over the following two decades. Was this new woman a welcome symbol of Brazil's youthful and cosmopolitan modernity? Or did she represent Brazil's lamentable mimicry of European decadence? Did she incarnate a uniquely Brazilian blending of the cultures of different social and racial groups, or the degeneracy of Brazil's traditional family values, contaminated by the nation's lowest elements?

Although Hungria's lament for lost virtue may seem timeless, his preoccupation with the need to redefine sexual honor in Brazilian law was firmly positioned within these post–World War I cultural and political conflicts. In contrast to turn-of-the-century legal debates over the meaning of honor, which had highlighted social tensions that arose as jurists struggled to legitimize republican power, the debates of the 1920s and 1930s reflected political battles that would topple the liberal political order of the First Republic. In widely publicized campaigns against prostitution, crimes of passion, press sensationalism of sex scandals, and hymenolatry, prominent male professionals such as Hungria, public prosecutors Carlos Sussekind de Mendonça and Roberto Lira, and legal-medical specialist Afrânio Peixoto attacked the belief that a society's concern with virginity and sexual honor was a mark of advanced civilization and moral superiority. Rather, they argued that this widespread preoccupation was a manifestation of the backwardness of Brazil's traditional political and social institutions.

Grappling with women's assertion of new public identities in the 1920s, jurists reinterpreted concepts of honesty and virginity in ways that could either encompass or exclude "modern women." Many, lamenting the decline of the family and "traditional" values, categorically declared modern women devoid of virtue. Others—including both conservatives who deplored the effect of modernity on gender roles and more progressive professionals who welcomed it—argued that because modern women were no longer secluded in the home, they were knowledgeable enough to guard their own virginity.

Still another group of jurists sought to preserve the normative function of law by reconceptualizing sexual crimes in ways compatible with interventionist state paternalism—and with the demands of the mothers and fathers of hundreds of young girls who were deflowered in the nation's capital each year. These jurists, voicing the position that would prevail after 1940, argued that the criminal justice system should continue to protect virginity, even that of modern women. They often cited Freud to defend the theory that even honest women possessed sexual instincts, however latent, and that seduction could therefore be interpreted as physical arousal and not solely a marriage promise.[9]

Jurists and other reformers of all three positions agreed with Hungria that a postwar "crisis of morality" (crise de pudor) threatened women's honesty and, hence, the family.[10] The danger, they insisted, did not arise from modernity itself, but rather from the Brazilian masses' unpreparedness for the new liberties of modern society. It was necessary to educate women to resist the temptations to which they were newly exposed, and to subdue men's hyperstimulated sexual instinct, which incited them to barbarous passionate crimes and predatory sexual attitudes that ruined innocent girls.

Unlike some prominent female professionals and radical men,[11] these men did not champion women's autonomy. On the contrary, by taking charge of campaigns to combat what they considered anachronistic notions of sexual honor and by modernizing legal and medical concepts of the female body, reformist lawyers, judges, and legal-medical specialists sought to reinforce gender hierarchies and their own moral authority while challenging the power of the nation's traditional economic and political elite. In doing so, professionals of diverse political positions helped institutionalize new, state-interventionist social and legal policies. These policies, products of social-reformist urban movements that flourished after the overthrow of the Republic in 1930, would be appropriated by the authoritarian Estado Novo, which sought to put an end to what conservatives and positivists alike long considered the "excessive liberalism" of Brazil's political and legal institutions.

Interwar Politics of Social Reform

Debates over sexual honor reflected reformist professionals' positions in the political upheavals of the interwar period. In Rio de Janeiro, as in many other Western capitals, movements for social reform expanded after World War I and formed a vital part of the opposition to the political order of the *belle époque.* In Brazil, a number of reformist urban professionals participated in diffuse, often opposing, movements to depose the political block dominated by the state of São Paulo that had monopolized state power during the First Republic. Although power in São Paulo had begun to shift from the traditional coffee-exporting sector to newer commercial, professional, and industrial elites by the late 1920s, opponents of the regime continued to characterize the Republic's rulers as representatives of backward rural "oligarchies."[12]

Many reformist professionals joined political movements such as the Liberal Alliance and participated in the civilian-military revolt that brought Getúlio Vargas to power in 1930. As a result, Rio was administered in the early 1930s by a team of populist social planners, led by Pedro Ernesto, a physician and public health activist.[13] The response of these reformist professionals to "the social question" and "the woman question" revealed their desire to modernize Brazil in more than mere outward appearance. They sought to replace the traditions of patriarchal authoritarianism they associated with oligarchical agrarian society with a system of expanded democracy, physically and morally "hygienic" nuclear families, and social welfare. Rather than resolving social problems with police violence, the favored response of the governments of the First Republic, reformers generally hoped to head off labor militancy with benevolent reforms. Their reform organizations also sought to keep the social effects of new economic and cultural stimuli under the control of professional authorities. They called for the intervention of middle-class professionals in working-class families through social service, especially public health, housing, and education.[14] Pedro Ernesto's government also intervened in working-class cultural production and celebrated Afro-Brazilian contributions to Carioca identity by sponsoring samba schools and guaranteeing them expanded space on Rio Branco Avenue during Carnival. Attacking republican authorities for their elitist and Eurocentric notions of civilization, populist reformers such as Ernesto looked to the mobilized popular masses for an authentic cultural identity as well as a source of political support.[15]

Social reformers who sought to modernize Brazil by challenging patriarchal and authoritarian social traditions were not the most powerful of the groups who mobilized in the new political climate. Vargas's major base of support outside the capital came from the traditional rural oligarchies in Vargas's home state of Rio Grande do Sul and in Minas Gerais—two of the three states that had dominated republican politics—along with powerful Northeastern politicians, reformist young army officers, and conservative groups linked to the Catholic Church and the military hierarchy. Many of his supporters admired elements of European fascism and mobilized around the motto "God, Family, and Fatherland." They were not eager to liberalize either politics or gender relations.[16]

In Rio, right-wing factions were represented by imposing figures such as the revered Cardinal Leme, who erected the city's landmark statue of Christ on Corcovado Hill in 1931 and mobilized lay activists to lobby against Communism, progressive public school reform, and the "immorality" of Carnival, movies, and other popular cultural activities.[17] Another representative was Rio's notorious police chief, Filinto Müller (1933–1942). Müller's brutal campaign against what he considered political and moral subversion placed him in fierce opposition to Mayor Ernesto, whom Müller helped force out of office in 1935.[18]

Like middle-class professionals calling for social reform, these conservative groups sought to assert their own authority by reinterpreting the concept of honor and controlling "popular" passions. Rather than reject the authoritarian past, however, right-wing factions of the Vargas coalition drew on the patriarchal structure of an idealized "traditional Brazilian family" for a model of social organization that would maintain stable social hierarchies while Brazil modernized economically. Many among these factions would triumph after 1937, when Vargas declared himself dictator.

Juridical discourse on sexual honor was influenced by both liberal-reformist and authoritarian ideological trends that arose amid the heightened nationalism of the 1920s and would vie for precedence, within and outside the Vargas coalition, after 1930. Some influential jurists such as the socialist public prosecutor Roberto Lira positioned themselves decidedly in the reformist camp; many others followed leaders such as Nelson Hungria, who reconciled strongly traditional views with a progressive self-image. Despite philosophical differences, however, they were united in their belief that the production of juridical knowledge lay outside the realm of politics. Moreover, jurists of various political tendencies shared class- and gender-based anxieties about what they saw as the destabilizing force of passions unleashed by populism and modernization. Common fears that the "popular masses" and modern women threatened social order often outweighed the differences among jurists and allowed them to work together on various campaigns to "regenerate" Brazil.

Social Hygiene: Campaigns against Prostitution, Crimes of Passion, and Press Sensationalism

There was a general consensus among jurists of the 1920s and 1930s that modern society, with its "sensual stimuli," such as new heterosocial leisure and the mass media, brought new threats to the nation's social order and progress. Not all of Hungria's generation, however, shared his nostalgia for the traditional Brazilian family. Roberto Lira, for instance, blamed the repressive traditions of patriarchal society for what was widely perceived as a popular obsession with sexual honor and an explosion of domestic violence and sensationalist sex scandals in the period following World War I.[19]

There were other differences between jurists nostalgic for a golden age of female virtue such as Nelson Hungria and more forward-looking professionals such as Roberto Lira. Lira, a young socialist reformer, viewed the judiciary as a progressive institution opposed to the autocratic police regime that governed the city's streets. Hungria, in contrast, began his career as a police official. As chief inspector (*delegado*) in Lapa in the early 1920s, Hungria was in charge of regulating prostitution in that neighborhood, a policy he continued to support as a judge. Along with an increasing number of judges in the 1930s, he endorsed the de facto police regulation and

zoning of prostitution in Rio on the grounds that prostitution was necessary for the defense of honest women's virtue, and that its confinement to
particular zones protected public morality in the city.[20] This position was
vehemently attacked by Lira and several colleagues who joined him in
forming the Brazilian Council for Social Hygiene (Conselho Brasileiro de
Higiene Social; CBHS) in 1925.[21]

The CBHS was a cosmopolitan group of elite professionals whose position on prostitution matched that of many progressive reformers throughout Western cities in the early twentieth century. Most notably, Jewish,
socialist, and feminist, and other activists in neighboring Buenos Aires
had mobilized since the turn of the century to combat state-regulated
prostitution and the white slave traffic, which had stained Argentina's
modern reputation abroad and exacerbated local moral and public health
problems.[22] Since state regulation was never enacted in Brazil and feminist
and socialist groups were less prominent than in Buenos Aires, mobilization on the prostitution issue was not nearly as vigorous in Rio de Janeiro.
Yet while Brazil's representatives boasted of their nation's progressive
"abolitionist" legislation on prostitution at international public health
and anti–white slave trade conferences in the early decades of the century,
Foreign Ministry officials and young professionals such as Lira complained that little was done to help prostitutes or curb police abuses in the
capital city.[23]

Complaints multiplied at the end of World War I, when the League of
Nations sponsored a commission to investigate the international trade
and as the traffic between Argentina and Brazil appeared to increase.
The London-based Association for the Protection of Girls and Women,
alarmed at what it considered the failure of local authorities to address the
problem, focused its efforts on Brazil in 1925.[24] At the same time, Brazilian Jews organized committees to keep pimps and prostitutes out of
their community and to intercept single Jewish immigrant women who
arrived at the docks.[25]

Many years later, Jewish community leaders claimed victory in its
campaign to protect immigrant girls from the agents of vice in post–World
War I Rio de Janeiro.[26] The professionals who set out to moralize poor
Brazilian prostitutes were less satisfied with the results of their efforts.
Writing in the 1970s, Roberto Lira acknowledged that the CBHS attempt
to "radically combat prostitution" made little impact.[27] Initiated by the
eminent public health physician and radical political activist Belisário
Pena, the campaign mobilized a handful of recent law school graduates
who set out to study the causes of prostitution by interviewing bemused
prostitutes who, as it turned out, lacked serious interest in their project.

Campaigners proved unable to produce even a rough outline of the "social reality" of Carioca prostitution—how many prostitutes, how many pimps, their national origins, the relationships among them—much less make honest women of them or protect them from unsanitary or exploitative working conditions.[28]

Physicians who worked in a progressive public health project to combat venereal disease, initiated in 1923 through the private Gaffrée-Guinle Foundation, made more energetic efforts to sanitize prostitution. To the tremendous frustration of the public health workers, however, police vigilance over prostitutes in specified "toleration zones"—Mangue, Lapa, and, periodically, a few of the streets surrounding Tiradentes plaza, known for its popular *gafieira* dance halls, movie theaters, and other nightspots—made headway over the course of the 1920s. Arbitrary harassment and periodic round-ups and relocation of prostitutes wrecked havoc on physicians' attempts to map syphilis outbreaks in prostitute zones and to convince prostitutes to participate in long-term treatment programs. As legal-medical specialist Leonídio Ribeiro Filho explained in a 1931 public debate on police reform, public health physicians, working toward "the patriotic goal of defending the destinies of our people and the health of our race," rejected police regulation of prostitution as arbitrary, ineffective, and retrograde.[29]

Although intervention by these public health and legal professionals tempered police actions through the 1920s and early 1930s, prostitutes and bohemian nightlife were among the victims of the heightened police repression after Police Chief Müller took control in 1933. By the late 1930s, of course, with the advent of the Estado Novo, open dialogue on the topic of police reform and police powers had shut down along with many unregulated bars, bistros, cabarets, and brothels.[30] Under the command of auxiliary police delegate Anésio Frota Aguiar, police embarked on a new moralization campaign that sought to simultaneously free prostitutes from pimps and clean up the downtown by more frequent expulsion of foreign pimps, arrests and detention of prostitutes, mandatory registration, and restriction of the trade to specific zones, most notoriously Mangue.[31]

The struggle over prostitution policy did not simply pit conservative police against liberal professionals. Many jurists, especially judges such as Hungria and Eurico Cruz, another former police inspector, established jurisprudence over the 1920s and 1930s that supported police policies.[32] In part, they rested their arguments on the historical precedents of legislative and juridical support for police enforcement of public morality. A few judges had attended the Juridical-Police Conference in 1917, where, in the face of widespread labor agitation, then Police Chief Aurelino Leal convinced a group of the nation's most prominent legal authorities that broad "police discretionary powers," including the power to control prostitutes, were crucial to public order in modern cities.[33] Even CBHS founding member Carlos Sussekind de Mendonça, frustrated with the inefficacy of the judicial process and reform efforts, cited these legal precedents in support of Aguiar's campaign in the late 1930s. Sussekind defended Aguiar against the criticism of other CBHS members such as Lira, who remained fiercely opposed to police prostitution control measures.[34]

Given the profound disagreements among jurists over how to combat prostitution and the "social reality" associated with it—which in the minds of many authorities included general criminality, poverty, and by extension, labor activism—the failure of the CBHS attempt to reform "public women" is not surprising. Jurists as a whole were more receptive to the CBHS campaigns to sanitize private life by modernizing the Brazilian family and channeling unruly passions into rational and hygienic sexual relations. While for Nelson Hungria this meant enforcing sexual fidelity and indissoluble marriage and for Roberto Lira it meant decriminalizing adultery and permitting no-fault divorce, both men agreed on the need for state intervention to control erotic desire.[35]

According to Lira, the CBHS's most successful undertaking was the battle against the perceived epidemic of crimes of passion, or violent crimes motivated by romantic or sexual conflicts.[36] As we have seen, although Brazil's penal codes of 1830 and 1890 had unequivocally rejected colonial legislation that permitted husbands to murder adulterous wives and their lovers, defense lawyers were frequently able to exonerate "passionate murderers," or at least dramatically reduce their sentences, by arguing that they possessed a "passionate temperament" that in the face of a "grave affront" to their honor had temporarily deprived them of their senses.[37] Since Evaristo de Morais—whose reputation as both a great trial lawyer and socialist defender of the rights of the socially excluded was well established by the 1920s—had provided the formula for the classic crime-of-passion defense by adapting the arguments of European positivist criminologists, it carried the weight of both social justice and theoretical sophistication and was not easy to combat.[38]

The CBHS's celebrated campaign against crimes of passion indicated a shift in the focus of juridical concerns about sexual honor. If turn-of-the-century jurists had set out to educate the population in what they considered civilized moral values, including the valorization of female sexual honor, as a means of establishing order and progress, their efforts had apparently backfired. Intense preoccupation with sexual honor among the masses, according to leading legal specialists, was verging on the pathological. Although complaints of deflowering, or seduction, as it was termed in most European penal codes, were on the decline in "the civilized nations," young working-class women in Rio continued to inundate police stations with these appeals for the defense of their honor.[39] Moreover, many observers came to associate Brazilians' hymenolatry, or veneration of women's sexual chastity, with an escalation of murders related to sexual honor. Writing in 1926, prosecutor Carlos Sussekind de Mendonça described the mounting "love murders" as "a horrendous calamity that has assailed our social organism."[40] A little over a decade later, Lira, who was then working on the commission that produced a new penal code in 1940, blamed the calamity on existing laws. The 1890 penal code's definition of sexual crimes and the family perpetuated the "medieval notion" that "women's honor is a membrane" as well as the "primitive concept" that linked women's sexuality to men's honor.[41] Lira and his CBHS colleagues emphatically rejected turn-of-the-century analyses that concluded that the valorization of sexual honor was a mark of progress and civilization. They saw it instead as an outdated notion that encouraged popular hypersexual tendencies, led to lawlessness and violence, tore apart the family, and exhibited Brazil's backwardness.

Historian Susan Besse argues that the CBHS campaign against crimes of passion, led entirely by men, enveloped efforts begun a decade earlier by writers, many of whom were celebrated female intellectuals, who published in women's journals and the popular press.[42] These writers, skilled in the sensationalist journalistic style favored by their contemporaries, had sparked public outrage over what they described as an "extraordinary proliferation" of violence against women and the impunity of "wife-killers."[43] In the absence of reliable criminal statistics for the period, it is difficult to determine whether these types of crimes or their perpetrators' impunity actually increased in the early decades of the century. They were certainly made more visible by the 1920s, when many writers saw them as paradigmatic of wider political or cultural aberrations.

Lira's attack on the 1890 penal code—one of the last vestiges of republican order—was characteristic of contemporary analyses of the issue. Before 1930, activists of left and right took the opportunity to criticize the Republic and promote their political views while mobilizing against crimes of passion. The Catholic *Revista feminina* (1914–1927), the nation's most widely circulating women's journal, provides a good example. As Besse has shown, under editor Virgínia de Souza Sales, the journal promoted modern education and professional opportunities for women, insisting that they were compatible with traditional gender roles in the home.[44] Salles's son, the playwright Claudio de Souza, writing under the pseudonym Ana Rita

Malheiros, likewise suggested that women's political mobilization need not disrupt their natural domestic and moral functions—a strategy that was common to contemporary Catholic organizations.[45]

Leading the journal's campaign against "women-murderers," Souza implored his readers to use their "hidden force" to combat immoral republican institutions.[45] Among the worst of these institutions, for Souza and other *Revista feminina* writers, was the judicial system, particularly the popular jury. In a 1920 report of a wife-murder case in which the defendant cheered the Republic when the jury acquitted him, for example, the author attacked the jury as "the most immoral and shameful institution of our unscrupulous republican politics." The "ignoble Republic," by destroying "morality, the family, energy, civic virtue, and all the attributes that make up strong races," had allowed the murder of women to become a "national institution."[46] The article, signed by Carolina Pereira, mirrored Claudio de Souza's ongoing series on the issue. A few months later, in a typical piece, Souza argued that juries always acquitted woman-murderers because men controlled public opinion and wrote the law. Moreover, the Republic's characteristic corruption allowed competent professionals to escape jury service, leaving it in the hands of "the riffraff." The solution was in the hands of women, who should use their natural moral superiority not only to combat the victimization of their sex but to preserve Brazilian civilization against barbarous and violent men.[47]

Since women were excluded from juries until 1932 and were in the minority on juries in subsequent decades, male gender identification may well have been one factor in jurors' sympathy toward passionate criminals (jury decisions were based on majority, not unanimous, vote). Women, however, could also benefit from juries' benevolence in cases involving sexual conflicts. According to CBHS campaigners, the 1920s saw an alarming rise of cases in which passionate women killed men. In one incident that occupied headlines for years, a group of women organized in support of Sylvia Seraphim, a writer from a "respectable" family who in 1929 killed the scion of one of the most important journalist clans in the city, Roberto Rodrigues, for printing a scandalous account of her marital separation (she was acquitted).[48]

It is not clear whether the group that supported Seraphim or other female passionate criminals included the same women who called for an end to male violence against women in the press campaign that Besse has studied. It is certain, however, that as gender identification coalesced around the issue of crimes of passion, some women writers became increasingly aggressive in rhetorical tactics. Publicizing cases of women's retaliatory violence against men, writers such as Chrysantheme threatened that unless crimes against women were halted, intense female resentment and hatred of men that was already brewing below the surface of seemingly serene domestic relations would explode in even greater violence.[49]

Writing in the 1930s, Roberto Lira suggested that this situation had indeed come to pass. Passionate female "man-killers" had joined the male "woman-killers" in the crowded crime sections of the city's dailies.[50] Among those who responded to the new publicity were groups of women who mobilized in support of passionate female defendants. Understandably, prosecutors voiced especially harsh criticism of these women, since their objective was to undermine the prosecution.[51] Prosecutors were undoubtedly also troubled by these women's assertion of an independent, gender-based political identity. Mendonça, for example, believed that domestic violence was rising because of a general crisis in traditional family values, created by women's new public roles.[52] Even Lira, who considered himself a proponent of women's rights, repeatedly berated feminists who demanded equality with men. He suggested that women should aspire to "relative emancipation," that is, they should study and work in ways that would fulfill their natural role as man's companion and inspiration, and "never for liberation."[53] In an appeal for women's education, he warned that uneducated working women, devoid of "family ideals" and self-control, "have only one road to take in response to the quivering of their provoked sensibility: perdition."[54] Lira explained that although women's sexual instinct was naturally dormant, their limited reasoning capacity made them particularly vulnerable to corruption by exposure to inappropriate stimuli. This was especially true in Brazil, given the nation's "mimetic tendency" in relation to imported culture. In an article calling for censorship of movies, Lira argued that "Brazilian girls arbitrarily . . . accept and copy everything foisted upon them with the irresistible label of novelty."[55]

Besse argues that attitudes such as these distinguished the mostly male campaigners for social hygiene from earlier female writers, some of whom linked domestic violence to women's subordination and demanded political and economic equality. Liberal professionals such as Lira and Mendonça also avoided the rabble-rousing discourse of Cláudio de Souza and other more conservative Catholic militants. Instead, they argued that violence against women demonstrated the need to substitute the power of the elite and its patriarchal traditions for a more rational control of the volatile popular masses.[56] Although a series of celebrated cases of middle- or upper-class wife-killers—precisely those most likely to win an acquittal— had sparked the outcry against this kind of crime in the early decades of the century, most passionate criminals who appeared in the press and behind prison bars were lower-class men, often men of color. These men were the major focus for professionals who lobbied for social reform. Writing for a broad audience through the press, or, more frequently, for each other in specialized journals, jurists, physicians, and legal-medical experts cast themselves as intellectual leaders whose duty it was to suppress the overindulged sexual instinct of the masses in the interest of survival of the greater social body.

Although many professional elites agreed with Cláudio de Souza and other Catholic thinkers that the clemency granted wife-killers by the popular jury reflected the ignorance of jury members as well as the general corruption of the Republic, they disagreed about how to resolve the problem. The controversy did not end with the overthrow of the Republic in 1930. On the contrary, the jury remained a major point of contention among the politicians and jurists who worked to build the new regime. Their debates demonstrate that the tension between liberal democratic ideals and hierarchal, authoritarian social structures that had erupted in conflicts over the jury since its creation in 1822 remained unresolved more than a century later.[57]

Progressive jurists rushed to the jury's defense in the early 1930s, as both the scientific determinism and the anti-jury position of earlier positivist criminologists become associated with European fascists and the extreme Catholic right. Supporters of the jury followed the lead of activists such as Roberto Lira and Evaristo de Morais as well as Jury Tribunal Judge Magarinos Torres and Supreme Court Justice Firmino Whitaker, all of whom insisted that the institution was among the most important of the nation's liberal democratic traditions.[58] Earlier efforts to "moralize" the institution by making it more efficient and by enlisting men from more elevated social positions quelled the misgivings of some of their more conservative peers, while the inclusion of women on juries and the dissemination of jury tribunal statistics that showed high conviction rates helped to quiet attacks on the institution by those who had mobilized against wife-killers.[59] Yet although the Constitution of 1934 mandated maintenance of the jury, the issue continued to divide jurists and other professional elites. When renowned legal-medical expert, scholar, novelist, and essayist Afrânio Peixoto, for example, refused to heed the summons to jury duty in 1935 because his "scientific convictions" opposed the institution, Judge Torres levied a hefty fine against him and published an indignant reprimand.[60] While Nelson Hungria continued to insist that only those of elevated culture, preferably trained specialists, should be allowed to pass judgment, Roberto Lira argued that the jury should be composed of the defendant's true social peers.[61] In 1938, the new Estado Novo regime sought to resolve the controversy by decreeing that appeals court justices would make final judgments if they determined that jury decisions "diverged from the evidence presented in the proceedings." Although the decree followed appeals court jurisprudence that had responded, in part, to criticism of the jury's leniency with wife-killers in the 1920s, progressive jurists of the late 1930s attacked it as another instance of authoritarian intrusion on civil rights.[62]

While jurists and other professionals continued to debate the wisdom of the popular jury, there was a clear consensus that much of the blame for the frenzy over crimes of passion and other sex scandals fell on irresponsible journalism. The sensationalist press, they argued, catered to the instinctual vulgarity and excitability of Brazil's uneducated masses. Carlos Sussekind de Mendonça, for example, suggested in a 1927 article that although the generalized "neurosis" that caused the proliferation of passionate crimes might be linked to "organic defects of the [Brazilian] race," the press exacerbated these defects by "openly preaching subversive ideas, . . . that easily infiltrate unenlightened heads" and by printing detailed dramatizations of gory passionate crimes.[63]

In 1933, Mendonça organized a conference on sensationalism that brought together a group of prominent jurists, journalists, politicians, and other intellectuals. Throughout the published collection of papers, speeches, radio broadcasts, and journal articles that resulted from this conference, the masses emerged as a volatile and pliant "other" in need of mastery and guidance. Interestingly, most of the authors did not discuss the issues of gender conflict or violence against women, although the discussion revolved around crimes in which these issues were usually defining features. Several writers, however, imbued the masses with feminine characteristics—they were governed by emotion, easily influenced, and dangerously susceptible to seduction and subsequent degeneracy—while depicting themselves as rational men responsible for social control.

Mendonça's discussion of the power of the press, for example, used implicitly sexual language. "The newspaper," he argued, "lowers itself to the level of the public, courting its passions. . . . But by giving in to the public . . . unfeelingly, it defaces it, subjugates it, dominates it."[64] Célio Loureiro, speaking in a radio broadcast, expounded upon Mendonça's observations, exploring the sexual imagery more explicitly. "The collective soul that dominates the masses," he announced, "is of a truly feminine primitivism, and, thus, just as we men enslave women by satisfying their whims, the newspaper dominates the people by satiating their passions."[65] Like women, according to these intellectuals, the masses did not reason but mimicked the behavior to which they were exposed. Without enlightened moral guidance, they threatened order and civilization. "There is nothing more dangerous, nothing more frightening," proclaimed one orator, "than the false judgments and absurd and ignorant mental intoxication of the masses, or better yet, of the people, who believe they are sovereign and independent! They are . . . the true Apocalyptic Beast of these modern times, the threat to social stability, the bottomless pit of the universal cauldron in which the future of the worlds boils!"[66] The solution to the crisis, according to these public figures, was censorship of the media, especially the tabloid press and movies, singled out as particularly pernicious because of their mass appeal. "The notion of freedom," Loureiro concluded, in reference to the freedoms of speech and the press, "must be subordinated to the social good if we are to progress."[67]

Lira agreed that the masses lacked a "cultural level" that would allow them to filter information rationally. He therefore recommended "hushing up acquittals, cases thrown out of court, and cases delayed past statute of limitations" (in other words, evidence of the public prosecutors' failures), and "publication of arraignments, indictments, and convictions, so that punishment exercises in all its plenitude its role of example and intimidation."[68]

Although there was a consensus among this self-identified intellectual elite that they had a responsibility to "free" the masses from moral degradation by censoring mass media, there was less agreement about how the population should be reeducated. Some, like Mendonça, believed that "the education molded in the austere customs of our forbears" would provide "the only components capable of making a society strong, healthy and balanced."[69] Others, however, pointed to the "austere customs" of Brazil's traditional patriarchal family as precisely the cause of present hyperstimulated passions and resulting degeneracy. Lira's contribution to the volume was an analysis of mass psychology that linked sexual repression to traditional structures of political domination. In a variation on the generally more celebratory "melting pot" theories that were popularized in the 1930s, he argued that the Brazilian "subrace" was "born of the mixture of three ethnic elements that were suppressed through centuries of relentless oppression: black slaves, Portuguese exiles [*degredados*, or criminals banished to the colonies], and dispossessed Indians." Worse, the declaration of the Republic in 1889 did not represent freedom and democracy but rather "dictatorship, *caudilhismo* [rule by local strongman] and the rod." Lira believed that the most pernicious legacy of Brazil's past was its oligarchical tradition, in which marriages were key political and economic strategies. This "tyranny of marriages arranged by fathers," sustained by religion and law, produced the "psychic disequilibrium" of a suppressed "national Super-Ego." Lira concluded that rampant neuroses, not to mention widespread attraction to sensationalism, resulted from "the imprudence with which the aggressive and sexual instincts were governed" through centuries of political repression. Collective rebellion agains this repressive patriarchal tradition led to the sensual excesses and vices that plagued post–World War I Rio de Janeiro.[70]

The solution, however, was not simply to eliminate patriarchal repression and to allow individual will to replace the interests of the extended family in determining marriage partners. "Individual will," Lira declared in a 1939 publication, "is unimportant before the general good." Instead, the rational education and guidance that legal authorities could provide should replace patriarchal repression. He noted, approvingly, that the state regulated and taxed marriage, "breaking up romances in the name of health, discipline, morality," and for economic reasons.[71] On this principle, in Lira's view, the state should promote "healthy and balanced marriages, in which reason is associated with sentiment, in the interest of the children," and it should deny marriage licenses to couples who want to marry because of their passionate feelings for each other. The state should not yield to "amorous intrigue," but defend "the conservation of life, the perfection of the species, social organization, civilization" by promoting "hygienic" marriages and permitting their dissolution.[72]

Lira and his colleagues in the CBHS, like the pioneering generation of republican jurists who preceded them, saw themselves as modern nation-builders working to control Brazil's uneducated and volatile masses, partly by disseminating civilized standards of sexual behavior. In their analyses of Brazilian society, the family continued to represent the basis of order and discipline, and women's independent activity outside the family was a constant threat to its integrity. Both the definition of civilized morality and the means of achieving social order, however, were contested by campaigners for social hygiene in the 1920s.

In Viveiros de Castro's day, debates among jurists over sexual honor were contained within a discourse of linear human progress in which Western Christianity was the harbinger of civilized morality and social order, a progress marked by ever increasing respect for female sexual honor. In the post–World War I period, many Brazilian nationalists, including Lira and Afrânio Peixoto, Lira's collaborator in the fight for social hygiene, explicitly challenged this version of social progress through a new discourse of sexual honor.

Afrânio Peixoto and the Campaign against Hymenolatry

Afrânio Peixoto's fight to eradicate hymenolatry was both an attempt to provide rational education and moral guidance to the population as well as an attack on the conceptions of honor, civilization, and the female body that informed republican law. On the basis of his observation of 2,701 hymens in eight years as a legal-medical examiner, Peixoto argued that physiological evidence was a poor measure of virginity. He was particularly bent on proving that the complacent hymen was much more common than previously believed. It was, therefore, senseless to define loss of virginity by the absence or rupture of the "flower."

By 1934, when Peixoto published his assault on hymenolatry, *Sexologia forense*, many Brazilian legal-medical specialists had already criticized both the wording of the penal code and poorly trained legal-medical practitioners for spreading erroneous notions about the hymen's characteristics.[73] Even those who supported the use of the term "to deflower," such as Viveiros de Castro, acknowledged that the crime could occur without hymenal rupture. Galdino Siqueira's literal interpretation of deflowering was a minority position, and one that had been largely discredited before Peixoto's antihymenolatry crusade of the 1920s. In contrast to cases of sexual crimes during the first decade of the century, by the 1920s and 1930s, legal-medical reports of complacent hymens were common. "Flaccidity" of breasts and labia, commonly reported in deflowering examinations through the 1910s, was eliminated from the legal-medical vocabulary, at least in Rio de Janeiro, by the 1920s.[74] Peixoto himself concluded that recent (1931–1932) jurisprudence had marked "the twilight of hymenolatry."[75]

If the issue was moot by the time Peixoto wrote *Sexologia forense,* why did he persist in his antihymenolatry campaign? Peixoto did lament the tragedies caused by ignorance of the general public about the hymen, such as brides returned to their families or even murdered because their new husbands mistook a complacent hymen (which permitted intercourse without bloodshed) for an absence of virginity.[76] Peixoto's diatribe against hymenolatry was not, however, motivated solely by the concern Souza Lima had expressed in 1905 for scientific accuracy in examination techniques. More than educating his peers on hymen morphology, Peixoto wanted to demonstrate that the very concept of physiological verification of honesty was absurd. Although *Sexologia forense,* like Peixoto's earlier *Medicina legal,* was a professional guide, cited by jurists as the authoritative work on the subject for decades, it can also be read as political satire. Peixoto ridiculed not only widespread ignorance of hymen morphology but also the national fixation on the hymen and the idea that respect for virginity was a mark of progress and social order. In the process, he attacked the Catholic Church and the moral basis of the Republic's oligarchical political traditions.

Like his predecessors, Peixoto provided a historical analysis of the evolution of sexual mores, but his conclusions inverted earlier tenets. Listing the taboos of diverse ancient and contemporary societies, he concluded that "the promiscuity supposed by sociologists and dogmas does not exist among any barbaric peoples; it is, rather, modern and civilized."[77] If promiscuity was modern, veneration of the hymen was a relic of the ancient and primitive past. Peixoto agreed with earlier Catholic scholars such as Macedo Soares and Viveiros de Castro that virginity was fundamental to the values of Christian civilization, but disagreed that this demonstrated progress. Rather, he explained Brazil's "cult of the hymen" as a result of the tenacity of ignorant ideas about female anatomy and the persistence of brutal rituals practiced by the ancient Romans, Jews, "and other primitive peoples," who placed in the hymen "all that is most sacred in woman, or humanity."[78]

This sanctification of the hymen was based on the erroneous idea that the hymen was "a seal (*natura scelleta*, for Cicero), which closes (*natura perclusa*, for Pliny) the feminine 'tabernacle.'" Although the idea that the hymen formed an unbroken seal ("like a kind of drum") was still current in popular belief, and one European specialist claimed to have observed a hymen of this type, Peixoto insisted on the basis of overwhelming empirical evidence that it did not exist. The Catholic Church, in making marriage "a sacrament that rests on the integrity of the hymen," thus perpetuated a cult based on ignorance. This religious cult was also founded on "cruel pleasure and erotic and perverse sadism." "Brutal, primitive pride" obliged husbands to be "the bloody initiators" and to desire "the animal 'glory' of rupturing a membrane, causing pain, spilling blood."[79]

After describing the barbaric history of hymen veneration, Peixoto refuted earlier theories that indifference to the hymen was a mark of "primitive peoples." Dividing the peoples of the world in two groups, hymenolaters and mishymenists (*misimenists*), or peoples who disdained the hymen, he placed "civilized" and "primitive" peoples in both groups. Contemporary hymenolaters included the cultural descendants of the Romans, the "Novi-latins of Europe and America," whose hymen veneration derived from ancient religious exaltation and state sanctification of virginity. *Misimenistas*, in contrast, including Asians, Hindus, Nordics, and Anglo-Saxons, represented "primitive peoples from the four corners of the earth in fraternity, in this disregard for the hymen, with the most civilized peoples of today's world."[80] Peixoto predicted that this fraternity would not last long, for modern civilization was clearly moving away from hymenolatry and toward hymen disdain. "Honor will change its residence," he predicted, "from below the abdomen to the soul."[81]

Echoing Lira, Peixoto refuted the idea that the natural brutality of Brazil's masses was gradually being tamed by the historical civilizing efforts of Eurocentric ruling elites. He held the highest church and state authorities responsible for perpetuating and disseminating hymenolatry through catechism and law. Furthermore, although women who filed deflowering suits were overwhelmingly working class, Peixoto's examples of the slander of innocent women because of the erroneous evaluations of virginity by new husbands involved upper-class couples. In one case that suggests that less public means of dealing with conflicts over virginity were available to the upper classes, Peixoto was consulted by the lawyer of a well-to-do man who was uncertain of his bride's virginity. Finally, Peixoto concluded that Brazilian research had corrected "grave errors" of European legal medicine.[82]

Notwithstanding his defense of women victims of hymenolatry and his attack on patriarchal traditions, Peixoto did not advocate women's sexual liberation. Instead, he believed that the law should both discipline women and protect men from the rising numbers of "semi virgins" (a term Peixoto and other jurists borrowed from the French novel by Marcel Prévost, Demi-vierges [Paris: A. Lemerre, 1894]), or women whose "loose habits" rendered them dishonest even though they had preserved the integrity of their hymens.[83] His call for the elimination of legal emphasis on what he called material virginity in favor of moral virginity reflected a shift in legal practice. The jurisprudence that would orient the 1940 penal code established that what the law sought to preserve in protecting virginity was not simply sexual abstinence among unmarried young women but their moral rectitude; the law should protect "the membrane with virtue." This orientation allowed judges to adapt the law to "scientific acquisitions" (e.g., knowledge of hymen morphology) and to the "social development" of modern times.[84]

In the context of political and sociological analyses by intellectuals and professionals such as Peixoto and Lira, new legal interpretations of honor also suggest that since the turn of the century, liberal bourgeois notions of honor as individual virtue had gained ground against patriarchal notions of honor as a birthright and family resource. Yet new considerations—such as the growing intervention in social and family relations by a paternalistic state and jurists' reaction to new challenges to gender and class hierarchies—made legal interpretations of honor even more complex as jurists struggled, once again, to rewrite the nation's penal law.

Modern Times and Impure Virgins

By the mid-1920s, Brazil's most powerful judges agreed that the nearly half-century-old penal code should be adapted to conform to modern times. Modernity, however, was an extremely ambiguous goal for reformers, for although they sought to replace ascriptive bases of power with bourgeois notions of individual merit, they were preoccupied by postwar challenges to the social hierarchies that supported their own privileged position.

This ambiguity was expressed through gender. In some instances, modernity connoted social and economic progress and healthy and rational sexual and family relations, but it could also signify moral degeneracy, the degradation of traditional family values, and the dissolution of "customs." When applied to men, modernity was generally understood in its positive sense of progressive rationality. When applied to women, however, modernity usually implied loose morals and a dissolute lifestyle.

We have seen how this gendered conception of modernity worked symbolically to justify the tutelage of the feminized popular masses by male intellectuals. It also worked to justify women's subordination to men. According to the right-leaning weekly *Revista criminal*, a journal that covered police activities and the criminal justice system, for example, "modern judges," such as José Duarte Gonçalves da Rocha, Eurico Cruz, and Barros Barreto, were those who took into account "present sociomoral conditions" in their verdicts in cases of sexual crime, drew from psychology and sociology rather than jurisprudential precedents, and ruled that modern women were morally suspect and did not merit legal protection, regardless of prior "material virginity."[85]

This gendered conception of modernity allied jurists such as Lira and Peixoto, who considered themselves avid antitraditionalists, with some of Rio's most conservative judges, men even more nostalgic for traditional family values than Nelson Hungria. More strikingly, reformists and traditionalists expressed a common hostility toward independent women.

Peixoto concluded *Sexologia forense* by applauding judgments passed by Cruz, Duarte, Barreto, Ary Franco, and Firmino Whitaker, who granted impunity to men for deflowering women who "were accustomed to being loose [*acostumadas à soltura*]."[86] In precedent-setting legal opinions, these judges argued that the innocence presumed for turn-of-the-century maidens was incompatible with modern society. As Duarte argued, "modern girls familiar with modern society's extravagance, scandalous newspaper reports, uncensored magazines, immoral films, lewd dances, . . . lust and the temptation of harlots, adultery, illegitimate children," knew all too well "the value of virginity, the purpose of copulation and the consequences of a sexual union not preceded by marriage."[87] Their sexual acquiescence demonstrated not men's abuse of their innocence, but their own depravity or their cynical machinations to force unwary men into marriage.

Judges had long accused some women of using deflowering cases to force men to marry them. Viveiros de Castro, for example, identified two types of women in deflowering cases: "those who suffer, and those who speculate."[88] The semivirgins of the 1920s and 1930s—modern, independent women who might as easily gamble their virginity as lose it capriciously—were more careless. As Peixoto described them, their loose behavior halved the value of their virginity, and the other half came cheap: "on a day with more excitement, dancing, or alcohol, or, with forethought, with a police and judiciary complaint in mind, which is often worth a marriage, . . . she comes forth with the other 50 percent."[89] Similarly, the jurist C. A. Lúcio Bittencourt, criticizing a 1936 Federal District Court of Appeals decision for its "retrograde and archaic hymenolatry," claimed that in modern times, women were careless with their virginity because "all women think . . . that the 'Police,' or the law 'forces' the seducer to marry and that, by giving themselves sexually, they will be more secure. . . . It is an indirect method of 'tying down' an undecided boyfriend."[90]

Modern girls were guilty not only of cunning and other indecorous knowledge afforded by their environment, but of activities that freed them from the discipline of the family. One judge, citing Cruz and Duarte, explained in a 1929 sentence that "a woman older than sixteen, who frequents poorly lit cinemas, public dances, taking part in modern dances, who goes on excursions in automobiles, unchaperoned . . . lives the liberated life of the modern woman."[91] Parents who permitted daughters "a disorganized life . . . outside the sanctuary of the home" did not deserve legal protection in cases of sexual crime. Liberty, the judge concluded, borrowing a contemporary antifeminist slogan, led to licentiousness and made the modern woman "responsible and not a victim of the crimes that occur during the new phase of her activity."[92] In this sentence, as in countless others, modernity for women became synonymous with independence and liberty, which led women, as Roberto Lira noted in another context, "down the road of perdition."

The association of women's freedom with sexual dishonor was not entirely novel. The phrase "free woman" (*mulher livre*), used interchangeably with "public woman," had signified prostitute in popular and juridical usage in the late nineteenth century (which was paradoxical, since many masters forced slaves into prostitution before abolition in 1888, and the importation of foreign prostitutes was known as the white slave trade). What had been a euphemistic association became explicit and formulaic in 1920s juridical literature, when it was no longer limited to prostitution. "Emancipation," "liberation," and "independence"—precisely the language used by contemporary feminists to challenge women's subordination—came to be used interchangeably to mean the corruption and promiscuity of women who exposed themselves to immoral movies, literature, or dance halls. The independent woman disregarded the spatial and moral boundaries of the family, giving up her innocence and naïveté in exchange for the knowledge and experience available in public spaces of leisure. To counter the "dissolution of the family," judges established through jurisprudence the concept that "emancipated" women, although not prostitutes, were neither pure nor innocent and should not be considered virgins.[93]

The word "emancipation" had another, seemingly less value-laden meaning in law: the age of legal majority or adulthood. Women and men were fully "emancipated" from paternal tutelage at twenty-one, although women gave up their legal emancipation upon marriage. Jurists of the 1920s and 1930s continued earlier debates over whether a woman who was not yet legally emancipated for other kinds of responsibilities should be responsible for preserving her sexual honor. Still struggling to determine the age at which girls were capable of consensual sexual relations, a few judges continued to argue for a lower age because ethnicity and the tropical climate made Brazilian girls mature quickly. The most pressing argument for lowering legal ages of consent, however, was that modern times made girls mature psychologically at an earlier age than girls of previous generations. The age limits for both seduction and presumed violence should be lowered, in this view, because modern girls, "precocious in the science of sexual mysteries," lost their ingenuousness and were capable of taking responsibility for their own virginity well before they reached the age of legal majority.[94] An important contingent of jurists, led by Hungria, opposed lowering the age for deflowering victims on the grounds that pubescent girls were vulnerable precisely because of their heightened sensuality.[95] After the Constitution of 1934 lowered the age for civil and criminal responsibility to eighteen, however, it seemed even more illogical, as Justice Minister Campos pointed out in 1940, to assume women's "psychological immaturity" until the age of twenty-one.[96]

The concept of emancipation as maturity was clearly intertwined with the notion that a woman who was either free or knowledgeable was morally suspect. If this was only insinuated by the argument that the immorality of modern times made girls grow up faster than the supposedly innocent generation that preceded them, it was explicit in debates over whether sex with an "already corrupted" minor should be punishable by law. Contradicting the principle that the law should protect girls who were too immature, physically and emotionally, for consensual sexual relations, jurisprudence of the 1920s and 1930s established that fictive violence did not apply to prostitutes, who were in this sense considered emancipated regardless of their age.[97] The language jurists used to describe virgins and nonvirgins also carried the implication that maturity and independence were incompatible with sexual virtue. Except in the wording of the actual law, the term "virgin woman" rarely appeared in juridical literature. Instead, when describing a virgin, jurists usually called her a girl (moça, moça virgem, or donzella). Conversely, the term "deflowered girl" did not even seem to exist; once deflowered, the girl became a woman (mulher deflorada or mulher desvirginada).

Jurists' disapproval of women's emancipation or liberation revealed their anxiety about women's rejection of the patriarchal tutelage and dependence that these sexual ideologies perpetuated. For many, Viveiros de Castro's fears that modern ideas of emancipation could render women unworthy of men's esteem and respect had indeed come to pass. Modern women were not only working outside the home, but they were blurring the boundaries of social identities and perverting femininity by mixing with prostitutes in public places of leisure and by demanding equality with men. As in Europe and the United States, there was great concern in Brazilian cities that postwar fashion and habits created an androgynous being, or "woman-man," who would challenge the most fundamental and seemingly natural basis of social differentiation.[98]

This concern was illustrated by Judge Cruz in what was unquestionably the most celebrated deflowering verdict of his time. Arguing for the acquittal of the defendant in a 1926 case, Cruz maintained that modern women stripped themselves of their own moral virginity by becoming men's equals and inverting natural sexual roles. "In carnal conjunctions between individuals of different sexes," Cruz explained, "the woman, normally, is the one . . . to whom nature itself has given the trait of total passivity. It is possible that individuals of the female sex, after various sexual congresses, instigated by lasciviousness, could assume in the sexual act gestures and attitudes that are peculiar only to the unashamed and innate boldness of the male, but only exceptionally; however, what is inadmissible . . . is that the woman, during the first coitus, deny the normal passivity of her own sex—the fragile sex— . . . especially since, in the first sexual union, it is suffering, more than pleasure, that she is due."[99]

The belief that women deserved to suffer during their first sexual encounter and that they were naturally passive was, of course, not new. Jurists such as Cruz were not the only ones who felt compelled to defend this belief in the 1920s, however. Dissemination of Freud's work led to a wide acceptance of the idea that normal women possessed a libido, but many legal and medical scholars continued to publish scientific evidence that supported their belief that sexually assertive women were aberrant. The noted physician and legal-medical expert Oscar Freire, for example, published a study of the "insensibility of female genital organs" in the same year as Cruz's famous verdict that concurred with Cruz's conclusion of women's natural sexual passivity.[100] Psychologist J. P. Porto-Carrero, arguing in 1930 that women's desire for emancipation was "nothing more than penis envy," expounded a similar theory: "If we observe the psychological attributes of the sexes, we see that it is no different from the physical in the amorous act. The woman is the being who waits, who initially resists . . . who finally gives in, opens, accepts the aggression; the man is the being who pursues, excites, penetrates, attacks. . . . She gives herself, is 'possessed'; he pursues and 'possesses.' "[101]

The women Cruz encountered in his courtroom, however, defied this medical fact, in ways that stimulated his imagination. The complainant in the 1926 case, for example, testified that she was deflowered while standing in front of her seated boyfriend.[102] In a dramatic re-creation, Cruz described her "dominating the scene, in the act in which she should be overcome by shame and physical and moral pain; assuming the active role, the thrusting, and the male, in a passive role . . . no modesty, no holding back, no refusal, but unnaturally, fearlessly, furiously dominant," and he asked himself, "what virginity is this that devirginifies itself?"[103]

Cruz responded to his own question with a rambling diatribe against independent women, social mixing, and retrogression to primitive savagery. Although there was no indication that the couple in question frequented public dances or cabarets, and their sexual relation took place in the woman's living room, Cruz blamed the immorality and lasciviousness of modern dancing and heterosocial leisure for creating "the atmosphere that generated the present case," in which "the sexes face one another as equals." He used the case as evidence that the penal code was out of date in its protection of virginity. "It was a different virginity," he concluded, "over which, forty years ago, the penal code extended its cloak of protection. Mothers' vigilance was different and girls did not dare do so much."[104] If for earlier jurists, "the innocence and purity of the virgin are legal dogmas,"[105] modern women blurred female types, producing the previously inconceivable "impure virgin" (a catchphrase used by defense lawyers), just as they blurred gender and sexual roles.

Cruz, Duarte, and other conservative judges joined Peixoto's crusade to do away with the crime of deflowering, not because they agreed with Peixoto that veneration of virginity was barbaric, but because they believed that modern women did not deserve legal protection of their honor. The law should protect only those young women whose innocence and naïveté led them to believe promises of marriage and to commit acts they did not fully understand. Men, in contrast, should be freed of any responsibility for their relations with knowledgeable liberated women, who, fully aware of the consequences of their acts, calculated their deflowering in order to force a man to marry them or, worse, gave in "to their own repressed desires, which are exacerbated more and more each day."[106] In the modern environment, Cruz ruled, "there is no longer anyone to seduce, nor any need to seduce."[107]

Hundreds of working-class Carioca parents who filed complaints against the seducers of their daughters each year apparently disagreed.

4 Single Mothers, Modern Daughters, and the Changing Politics of Freedom and Virginity

For all their talk of how traditional notions of virginity were being subverted by women's "excessive liberty" in the nation's capital, jurists and legal-medical experts could not deny that popular recourse to the law in cases of lost virginity remained extremely important throughout the interwar period. Far from a remnant of the past, deflowering complaints poured into local police stations at a higher rate than complaints of any other sexual crime up until the 1970s. They were, in fact, among the most frequent criminal complaints of any type through the 1940s, outnumbered only by physical assault and robbery.[1]

Young women of the 1920s and 1930s interpreted their relationships with boyfriends and with their own families in ways that reflected a variety of new images of appropriate female comportment. Nonetheless, the general characteristics of deflowering records remained the same throughout the period the 1890 penal code was in force (1890–1940).[2] Working-class young women, or, more frequently, their parents or guardians, appealed to the police and the courts for arbitration in disputes involving the women's virginity, usually with the hope that the authorities would pressure or force their deflowerers to marry them. The relationship between the offended women and the men they accused in cases of sexual crime ranged from casual acquaintance to formal engagement. Their personal conflicts ended up at the police stations for various reasons: the man abandoned the young woman after deflowering her, or he found another girlfriend; the couple argued; gossip about the deflowering began to circulate in the neighborhood; the young woman's parent or employer found out about the deed; the couple ran away together; the young woman ran away alone; the young woman became pregnant. The proposed resolution of most of these predicaments was marriage. Almost all of the deflowered women, whether spontaneously or after prompting by the police, claimed that their deflowerers had promised this to them.

In all but four of the 450 cases consulted, the young women were declared "impoverished" by police officials, which meant that the police determined that the cost of a lawsuit would present a hardship to their families. Their cases were therefore converted from private lawsuits to public criminal investigations headed by the attorney general's office.

It is difficult to generalize about the level of impoverishment these young women suffered. Their parents' professions were not consistently recorded, and when they were, they were often vague. Most mothers were called "domestics," without explanation, and some of the fathers were simply "employees" or "functionaries" of different private or public organizations. Subsequent testimony does not always clarify their positions. Statistical comparison of victims' parents' professions is therefore not illuminating. Many of the young womens' families lived in the hillside slums or downtown collective-residence tenements that were the exclusive domain of the city's lower class, but others lived in neighborhoods, particularly those in the northern suburbs, that were home to a differentiated lower-middle- and working-class population. Although 53 percent of the young women were themselves employed in working-class occupations such as domestic service, factory work, or dressmaking, 39 percent were classified as "domestic," which usually seemed to mean that they did not work outside their own homes.[3] In one of the latter cases, the accused man tried unsuccessfully to argue that his accuser, whose father was a tailor and owned some property, was not impoverished.[4]

With notable exceptions, including seventeen cases of domestic servants who pointed the finger at their employers, the young women usually accused men whose class and racial categorization seemed similar to or slightly higher than their own. Slightly more than half of the accused men were either military recruits or worked in trades or manual labor, some apparently in skilled positions. Twenty-eight percent stated that their profession was either white-collar, technical, or "commercial employment," which usually meant store clerks, waiters, or various other relatively high-status working-class occupations, and 6 percent were men of the middle or upper-middle class.[5]

The literacy rates and "color" categorization of offended women and accused men also suggest that the young women were of slightly lower status, as a group, than the accused men. The offended women's literacy is slightly lower and the color classifications attributed to them by legal-medical examiners were slightly darker than those shown in the 1940 censuses for the city's general female population, while the accused men's literacy and color classifications (usually provided by police) were closer to the census data for the city's male population in 1940.[6] The problem of analyzing social status in relation to the color categories and racial attitudes that appear in these cases is complex, warranting a separate discussion in chapter 5. Nonetheless, beneath the formulaic patterns of testimony, it is possible to ascertain that individuals classified in different color categories and who held an array of lower- and lower-middle-class occupations shared a set of expectations regarding virginity, honor, and marriage—and disagreed among one another about how to meet these expectations.

The very prevalence of these court battles suggests that a great many working-class people, like juridical authorities, valued female virginity and believed that under certain circumstances, seducers should be held responsible for the honor of women they deflowered. A close look at individual cases, however, reveals that in at least one respect, Judges Viveiros de Castro and Hungria were both correct in their assessment of "modern women," whether those who might have been factory or domestic workers when Viveiros wrote in 1898 or their daughters and granddaughters of the 1920s and 1930s. Women of both generations did, in fact, challenge the notions of virginity and family honor that jurists considered "traditional." At the same time, however, women preserved or recast traditions that made these notions meaningful in their own lives. Working-class mothers and daughters who appeared in legal disputes over lost virginity invoked traditional or modern values in a variety of strategic ways to narrate stories of their encounters and conflicts with men and with each other. Jurists responded to the women they encountered in their courtrooms, as well as those they saw on the streets, at the movies, and presumably in their own homes, as they debated how to redefine the legal defense of female honor.

Before turning to these women's stories and actions, I outline the ways that their actions were interpreted by their mostly male opponents in deflowering trials: the young men they accused, defense witnesses, and lawyers. These men's statements, like those of women deponents, produced multiple, often contradictory images of appropriate gender roles and conflicting attitudes about honor. Despite considerable disagreement about the boundaries of honorable behavior, however, deponents who wished to denigrate young deflowering victims consistently recognized and used the notion, well-supported in Federal District jurisprudence, that modern women who demanded freedom were not honest and did not deserve men's respect nor the protection of the court.

108

Defense Strategies

Defendants in deflowering cases made ample use of a discourse that associated women's liberation or freedom and the absence of virginity or honor. Many admitted having had sex with their accusers, and all seemed to agree that a man who took an honest girl's virginity had a responsibility to repair the damage through marriage. They refused to do so, however, on the grounds that the young women had either lost their virginity previously or misbehaved in ways that relieved the men from the responsibility for having taken it.

Defense lawyers' statements differed slightly from those of their clients. Unlike their turn-of-the-century predecessors, lawyers of the 1920s and 1930s did not mention a woman's bodily flaccidity or failure to bleed upon the first sexual contact as evidence of her prior state of dishonesty. Instead, they generally portrayed the young woman as morally "corrupted" and focused on the "irregular" situation of her family. They frequently argued that the "pseudovictim" or "impure virgin" was permitted "excessive liberty" by her family[7] or was "not educated in an atmosphere conducive to modesty" or that she "did not have the necessary maternal assistance."[8] This might mean that she lived in a tenement occupied by black washerwomen and single soldiers or "on a street that is known to be a prostitute area";[9] or that her sister had died during an abortion, had married already pregnant, had been involved in a deflowering case, "went for automobile rides with young men," or was "living in concubinage";[10] that a brother was a drunk, "sexually inverted," or "brought his mistress to the home";[11] or that a mother was separated from her husband, engaged in "illicit liaisons," or was even "a low-class prostitute."[12]

Defendants' testimonies were usually less condemning than lawyers, and rarely described the woman as essentially corrupt because of inadequate living quarters, which in many cases must have resembled their own. Like lawyers, however, defendants frequently cited the young woman's "excessive liberty," or her "free upbringing" as the reason they believed she was not a virgin and did not want to marry her. In 1923, for example, thirty-two-year-old textile worker Sebastião Almeida claiming his relationship with the eighteen-year-old *parda* ("brown," a color category between black and white used in official data; see chap. 5) seamstress Deolinda da Glória Nunes was purely sexual and involved no commitments of any kind, much less a promise of marriage, justified his behavior by explaining that "he was sure that he was dealing with an entirely liberated woman [*tinha certeza de tratar de uma mulher inteiramente liberada*]."[13]

Castro's elaboration on why he believed Deolinda da Glória Nunes was liberated provides a key to understanding the opposition of liberty to female honesty. He explained that he knew Nunes was not a virgin because although she was frequently out with him until late at night, "he never heard of any complaints from her family, whose duty it would be to forbid these outings if she were, in fact, a minor and a virgin." A witness in the same case described the young woman as "a person without commitments," whose "unconcealed liberty" demonstrated she was not an honest virgin.[14] For these young men, an honest woman was clearly not independent.

Severino de Souza Ferreira, a twenty-one-year-old white army soldier made a similar argument, arguing that he had assumed that his girlfriend was not honest because "he always had total liberty with Maria, whether to go to the movies . . . or during Carnival festivities."[15] His statement is revealing of the different meaning of "liberty" in regard to men. Not surprisingly, many activities considered disreputable for women were not so for men. One man claimed, for example, that he believed that the young woman was loose because he met her in a dance hall "that was frequented by men and easy women"; another stated that he had believed the woman was not a virgin because she drank beer at a Carnival club and let him walk her home although they were not well acquainted.[16] In a third case, a witness stated, as evidence of the victim's dishonesty, that "he knew that the offended minor came home late, even as late as 3:00 A.M., because as a single man he also came home late sometimes and saw her."[17] In sum, a single man was expected to be free to enjoy the nocturnal leisure that marked a woman as dishonest.

More significantly, when witnesses said that a young man "enjoyed a great deal of liberty in the young woman's home," or that a girl's parents gave a young man "liberty to go out with her," it meant that the man was considered honorable and deserving of the parents' trust.[18] Statements of this kind were often made by witnesses for the prosecution, who condemned the man for betraying this trust. Male honor and female honesty were thus both tied to social connectedness—but whereas a young woman's honesty was contingent on her submission to the vigilance of her protectors (usually family), a man's honor was recognized when he was no longer subject to such vigilance, but imposed it himself.[19]

Most of the alleged deflowerers acknowledged that they had taken liberties with their accusers, having dated them for at least a month. Many claimed that they had initially courted the young women with honorable intentions, but abandoned marriage plans when their girlfriends frequented dance halls and clubs in their absence or attended parties or

Carnival festivities with other men.[20] Although these men acknowledged their initial obligation to "repair" the honor of the women they deflowered, they claimed that the women's independence, misconduct, or contact with other men canceled this obligation. José de Oliveira, a twenty-five-year-old painter (probably of buildings), was clear about the terms of the marriage promise he made in 1938. By his own account, after he had sex with his girlfriend, fifteen-year-old white Lea Camilo Henrique, he announced to her and her mother that although he had "verified that she was not a maiden," he proceeded to "live maritally" with her in her mother's home, paying the rent and promising "to marry her provided she remained well-behaved." He later reneged on his promise to Lea because he "discovered what had happened between Lea and the shopkeeper" who he claimed had deflowered her.[21] In a 1927 case, Topásio Pimenta, a twenty-eight-year-old white mechanic, admitted deflowering his fiancée, but declared that his responsibility to her was revoked when, during Carnival, "she went out with whomever she wanted," against his wishes.[22] Odiomar Santos Teixeira, a twenty-five-year-old white driver (probably of a taxi) likewise admitted "that in fact . . . he had intended to marry Maria de Lourdes Cardoso; that in fact he deflowered Maria de Lourdes . . . that the declarant later found out that Maria de Lourdes was misbehaving and was frequenting dances, from which she went on automobile rides with young men . . . that in these circumstances the declarant, who even heard from Maria de Lourdes that she had been with a young man who played in a band, resolved not to marry Maria de Lourdes, which he decided . . . after an argument with Maria de Lourdes."[23] In the first of these three cases, José de Oliveira was acquitted, and Lea Camilo Henrique and her mother were left to raise his son without his assistance. In the other two, the young men apparently gave in to pressures—which included twenty-eight days in jail in Pimenta's case—to marry their former fiancées.

Unlike lawyers, who set out to convince the court that the offended woman was an essentially corrupt being and thus place the offended women in the legal category of "dishonest woman," defendants often described specific conflicts over gender roles and responsibilities. These conflicts might be resolved with the couple's (apparent) reconciliation through family mediation or police intervention. They could also end more tragically. In 1933, for example, João Dionízio Fernandes, a black mason's assistant, admitted deflowering his companion of two years and fathering her child, but stated that "as time went on . . . Menemozine began to disobey him and to behave dishonestly" and that "tired of being humiliated in this way in front of his friends and acquaintances, he decided to separate from her definitively." Menemozine, along with her father and friends who testified on her behalf, considered his abandonment "unjustified," and complained that she was left without means to support their child. Condemned to two years and six months of prison, Fernandes requested permission to marry Menemozine Peçanha da Silva after serving fifteen days, but for unspecified reasons he was unable to do so. Instead, he died in prison of tuberculosis three months later.[24]

Although some men defined their responsibility to their partners as contingent on the women's obedience or deferential public conduct, deflowering cases demonstrate that men were also preoccupied with the material virginity that Afrânio Peixoto and other jurists had so disparaged, at least in their public writings.[25] It seems that most men both insisted on marrying a virgin and recognized a moral code in which they were responsible for repairing the honor of women they deflowered, although they did not always live by either of these provisos. Deflowered young women frequently claimed that they consented to sex because their fiancés had demanded "proof of virginity" as a condition for marriage, and sometimes the men confirmed these claims. In a typical scenario, Theonília Maria Vieira's fiancé took her to a dark alleyway in 1919 and "proposed that she let him deflower her, with the allegation that only thus would he marry her, because he wanted to be certain that she was a virgin." Apparently unsure of his commitment, Theonília filed a deflowering complaint at the local police station the next morning. Her boyfriend, arrested and interrogated that very afternoon, confirmed her account and then proceeded to marry her, thus putting an end to the case.[26] Likewise, twenty years later, the soldier Severino Souza Costa explained that "he in fact was the deflowerer of the minor Dyonísia Souza de Andrade, but he did this deliberately, with the intention of joining with her through the bonds of marriage, so much so that he was already making preparations for the occasion, getting together the respective papers."[27] He, too, made good on his promise. In another case, the defendant denied having previously promised marriage, but said that "since the act was done, he intended to marry her."[28] Another man assured his girlfriend that "she should not worry" about losing her virginity, "for he was not some kid" and would live up to his responsibility to her, which in fact he did, after some prodding from her mother and the police.[29]

Of course, harmonious accounts and happy endings are not common characteristics of conflicts narrated in criminal records. More frequently, the woman claimed she gave her fiancé the proof he demanded, but the man countered that he "verified that she was not a virgin" by having sex with her. Antônio Sampaio, for example, explained that after asking his fiancée if she was a maiden (se era donzella), to which she responded yes, he convinced her to let him "certify the truth of what she said." Since he found it easy to "introduce his virile member," he broke his engagement, "declaring to her and her parents that he would no longer marry her, and still intends not to, since he was not the cause of her dishonor."[30] Floriano Peixoto Soares also admitted that he convinced his girlfriend to "accede to his desires" on the first night of Carnival in 1927 by promising that he would marry her "as long as she was a virgin." Although the couple maintained an active sexual relationship for several months after the initial contact (which led to her pregnancy and her mother's police complaint), Soares refused to marry her, "because he noticed that she was not a virgin when he copulated with her the first time."[31] Most men appeared quite confident of their verification techniques. The defendant in a 1921 case, for example, defiantly declared that he would marry the offended woman if the medical examination confirmed recent defloration, "but he knew it would not because he found her quite wide [*bastante larga*]."[32] Twenty-year-old Severino de Oliveira, however, seemed less certain. There was "something strange" about his sexual encounter with his eighteen-year-old girlfriend that made him think she was no longer a virgin.[33] Her mother's police complaint apparently helped him overcome his doubt, for the couple married before the case went to court.

Other men claimed that they had sex with their fiancées only after the women "confessed" that they had already been deflowered, a confession that the men assumed annulled their marriage promise. Manoel Virgílio, a twenty-two-year-old taxicab driver, claimed that he had sex with his fiancée, a seventeen-year-old domestic servant, only after finding out "through her own confession" that she had been deflowered by a previous boyfriend. As further evidence, he added that "he did not notice his fiancée lost any blood as a result of the carnal copulation." Insisting that he was innocent, he argued that the marriage "did not take place only because of the fact he discovered."[34]

This defense strategy was based on a moral standard that allowed men to engage in sexual relations with impunity, as long as their partners were not virgins or someone else's wife. This impunity freed men from the responsibility for more than damaged honor: 26 percent of the offended women were pregnant when they sought the police. Unless she were living "in concubinage" with the father or could prove that he had sequestered her when the child was conceived, a woman and her children born out of wedlock had no way of obtaining material assistance from a father who refused to legally recognize his paternity in writing (usually on the child's birth certificate).[35]

For many men, it was only natural that a man would have sex when the opportunity arose. Salústio de Castro's lawyer expressed this concept clearly in 1927, when he argued that since fifteen-year-old Edith Martins's willingness to have sex with nineteen-year-old Salústio after an acquaintance of one afternoon proved she was immoral and dishonorable, Salústio, in doing the same, "did what any man of his age and marital status would do without reluctance."[36] In defense of Salústio's friend, Luiz de Oliveira Marcondes, who was indicted as an accomplice because his boardinghouse room was the scene of the crime, a witness stated that "when Luiz said that he had permitted [Salústio] to spend the night with that woman in his room, he assumed she was . . . a woman knowledgeable about life, and if he had thought she was a virgin girl [uma donzella], he wouldn't have permitted it."[37]

Of course, one might suppose that young men who stood accused of deflowering, or their witnesses, would express moral standards that they hoped would convince legal authorities to free them from prison or marriage. Some of these men may have professed values and cast judgments that they would not have upheld outside the police station or courtroom. In other cases, police may have coerced men to confess their crime and promise repair, as a few of the men claimed in later testimony.[38] But although many accused men's moral righteousness may well have been opportunistic, the values they evoked were not alien to them, for they expressed these values in diverse circumstances, and in ways that were consistent with one another and with the values described by other deponents, including their accusers.

Jurists versus Declarants: Competing Conceptions of Sexual Honesty

Whatever the reason, most alleged deflowerers testifying before police and judicial authorities performed the role of machista moralist, upholding a double standard of sexual discipline, the concept of sexual "possession" of women, and differentiated and unequal gender norms. Most important, men defended themselves by insisting that women's honor depended on their submission to patriarchal vigilance, whereas freedom from this vigilance was an important component of male honor. In many ways, their attitudes were compatible with the norms prescribed in law and juridical discourse.

If the definition of moral norms and social values protected by law was a source of constant struggle among jurists, however, the battlefield was widened considerably by the attitudes and norms found in court testimony. At times, the people who testified espoused a sexual ideology that fit within the parameters of juridical debates, but at other times—or simultaneously—they expressed attitudes that contradicted this ideology.

For example, as Esteves finds in turn-of-the-century cases, the concept that a virgin girl should feel shame at exposing her body and submitting to her man's passions appears frequently in judges' statements, but is absent from defendants' testimonies. Also absent is the prostitute/mother dichotomy in which an unmarried woman who was not a virgin was "already corrupted," or on the way to becoming a prostitute. Defendants did classify women as either virgin girls or liberated women, but both categories were broad, and sometimes they overlapped. Only three of the men characterized their accusers as prostitutes. More typical was the testimony of Marcos Leopoldo, who as a witness asked to comment on Edith Martins's moral standing, responded that "his impression was that she wasn't a prostitute but she wasn't a virgin either."[39]

In several other cases, witnesses for the prosecution asked to comment on the young woman's honor did not limit their observations to the characteristics described in juridical tracts, such as her sexual virtue, her sense of shame, or her ignorance of the world outside her door. Rather, some witnesses reported that the young woman was "an honest girl who never went out alone and was a very hard worker";[40] "an honest girl, a very hard worker, always willing to perform any kind of task";[41] "a well-behaved girl, living with her mother and working to help support the household";[42] "an honest girl, a very hard worker."[43] Witnesses for the prosecution might make similar remarks regarding the victim's mother, particularly if the defense focused on the absence of "maternal vigilance" in her upbringing. In a 1937 case, for example, a witness testified that "Imperalina's mother is employed in a clothing factory, living from the product of her work, and in the neighborhood is taken to be an upright woman of good habits [bons costumes].[44] The statement demonstrates that a woman did not necessarily have to emulate the idealized mother of juridical texts to earn a good reputation in her neighborhood. Imperalina's mother had borne at least two children out of wedlock, beginning at the age of sixteen. Despite the absence of marriage and husband, neighbors referred to her household as an "honest family."

Although some men seemed to value submissiveness and physiological "purity" in their female partners, then, there is no evidence that they believed that a woman's independence or assertiveness necessarily led her down the road to perdition. Nor did they seem to believe that deflowered unmarried women were antithetical to mothers. Two cases illustrate. The first is that of twenty-eight-year-old Euzébio da Cunha. In 1922, he "made a home" (*montou uma casa*) with his fiancée, fifteen-year-old Marietta da Conceição Salles, a *parda* domestic servant, with whom he had two children. Two years later, when Marietta's father instigated a deflowering case against him, because "he had not fulfilled his promise to marry Marietta," Euzébio defended himself with the following story:

> The first time he had sex with her he noted she was not a virgin, and upon his severe interrogation, Marietta informed him that she had taken her own virginity by inserting a candle into her vagina; . . . he therefore resolved not to marry her but instead to live with her.[45]

In the second case, Almir Serra Cardoso gave the following testimony in 1928:

> In October of last year, the declarant began courting the minor Glória, whom he intended to marry; . . . in February of this year, having sexual relations with Glória, he verified that she was not a virgin; . . . interrogating Glória, she, after some reluctance, ended up confessing that she had been deflowered by her brother-in-law Raymundo, when she was twelve years old; . . . for this reason the declarant resolved not to marry her, but to live maritally with Glória, in the house he gave as his residence.[46]

Almir's involvement with the police was limited to his testimony as a witness in the deflowering case against Glória's brother-in-law.

These cases contain values that were contradictory in the logic of judicial authorities. The "hymenophilia" that, according to judicial experts, characterized the "average morality" of Brazilian society was accompanied by the defendants' willingness to accept exclusive unions and form households and families with nonvirgin women, which was immoral in the eyes of the courts. The sexual "education" the courts sought to disseminate was aimed precisely at curbing informal conjugal relationships by either forcing men to formalize them or marginalizing from "honorable" society women who accepted them.

Defendants were not the only ones whose positions undermined attempts to convince the population that living together was immoral. Many of the parents and witnesses who testified that the offended girl was honest and therefore deserving of marriage were themselves living in consensual unions.[47] There were several cases in which couples "lived maritally" in the woman's family's home after her defloration, usually with the understanding that marriage would follow.

Men frequently explained that they could not afford to marry, and proposed to their girlfriends that they live maritally until they could. The marriage ceremony itself was free, but it could be difficult and expensive to obtain, notarize, and file the necessary documents, such as birth certificates or proof of age, certification of residence, and written proof of the absence of impediments to marriage if one of the parties resided outside the state for most of the preceding year.[48] Nearly all of the defendants who confessed to their crime and expressed a willingness to marry stated that they had arranged for someone to get the papers together (*tratar dos papéis*), and a few mentioned that they had borrowed money to do so. Jerônimo Antônio de Souza, a twenty-three-year-old mason, and his fifteen-year-old fiancée, Albina Melo de Batista, who lived maritally with their son and Albina's mother, explained to the police that they had been planning to marry for more than a year, but could not because Albina was having trouble "getting her documents together." Albina's mother went to the police when the couple moved from her home to Jerônimo's mother's home.[49]

As is often the case in present-day Brazil, some Cariocas apparently found it necessary to hire a professional expediter (*despachante*) to help them through the complexities, or corruption, of civil and criminal bureaucracy. In a 1938 deflowering case, a man who made his living by providing these kinds of services was on hand at the police station to serve as a witness to Waldemar Genaro Martins's confession. Questioned in court by Martins's lawyer, who claimed that the confession had been extracted through coercion, the man, Fernando de Souza, explained that his profession was "dealing with papers" in police stations and the courts.[50] According to the lawyer, Souza hung around police stations "waiting for marriages he could expedite." When the defendant refused his services as marriage broker, the lawyer claimed, Souza "even offered his services to have the case assigned to a judge who was a 'comrade.' "[51]

According to the Federal District attorney general in 1935, thousands of people resorted to fraud in order to obtain the documents necessary for marriage.[52] Paying civil registry officials, judges, and expediters such as Souza was not likely to be inexpensive. Putting off the expense of marriage did not always mean waiting for the man to save or move up to a higher salary, which was particularly unlikely in the depression years of the late 1920s and early 1930s, and even more so for Afro-Brazilian men. Rather, couples often economized together in preparation for their marriage. When Pedro Martins de Araújo was confronted by the mother of his twenty-year-old girlfriend about her deflowering, for example, he told her "that he could not get married at the moment, but he was prepared to move in with her and finalize this fact [*finalizar esse facto*], both of them saving to get married."[53]

A more critical obstacle to marriage than the expense or bureaucratic complexity of obtaining a civil marriage was the previous marriage of one of the spouses. Several of the defendants in deflowering cases were already married, but separated from their wives. These men often proposed informal unions to their girlfriends, which was a common solution to the absence of legal divorce in Brazil (until 1977). In a few cases, the victim claimed that the man lied to her about his marital status, and deflowered her "under a promise of marriage," only later suggesting a consensual union.[54] Others told the truth from the start, and ended up at the police station either because the woman complained that they failed to fulfill a promise to live together because parents or guardians were unhappy with the arrangement.[55]

Parents, of course, preferred legal marriage to informal unions for their virgin daughters, as is evidenced by the very existence of most of the deflowering cases. But although they protested when their daughters consented to informal arrangements or when the man dallied in getting together the paperwork to formalize them, many parents seemed to accept the situation once it was in place. As Menemozine Peçanha da Silva's father stated, explaining why it took him two years to file the complaint against her companion, "since the two lived in good harmony," he had accepted their union.[56] Generally, the cases of consensual unions reached the police not because of problems inherent in this arrangement, but because of a crisis in the relationship: the man abandoned the woman, became engaged to another, or argued with his "mother-in-law." In Menemozine Peçanha da Silva's case, her father filed the complaint because João Dionízio Fernandes abandoned his daughter "without a justifiable motive." The same was true of Marietta da Conceição Salles's father, who explained that although he had been after Euzébio to "fulfill his promise" to marry his daughter for two years, his complaint was motivated by Euzébio's abandonment of her and their two children.[57]

As would be expected in records of this type, most of the young women involved expressed not only a desire for formal marriage, but the feeling that they were entitled to it in exchange for their virginity. Some, however, resigned themselves to consensual unions instead. In a letter to Rodrigo Noronha Filho, a *pardo* municipal guard, Jacy de Abreu Olinda—a nineteen-year-old *parda* domestic servant who claimed she was pregnant by Rodrigo—begged him not to abandon her because of the deflowering case her mother opened against him. "Don't blame me . . . the police delegate made me sign the accusation. I don't want to marry you by force, and I know you didn't promise to marry me," she wrote. "I went to your room because I wanted to. Because I want to live with you . . . I love you and I want to live with you." Jacy told the judge the same story, and Rodrigo was acquitted. The couple did not move in together, at least not by the time of the trial in 1936, one year after Jacy wrote the letter. This is not surprising, since Rodrigo insisted that although he had been having sex with Jacy every Sunday for several months, he "always assumed she was a woman without commitments, because she frequented night clubs by herself."[58]

Eighteen-year-old Isabel de Oliveira, also a *parda* domestic servant, seems to have had a happier experience. She explained to police that she had allowed her boyfriend, a black railroad conductor, to deflower her because he promised to marry her, but that after she moved in with him, "the hardships of life" kept him from keeping the promise. After five months, her mother grew impatient and filed a deflowering complaint, but Isabel told the judge that "she resigned herself to this explanation and continues living with the defendant, and even prefers this situation to marriage."[59] There were also cases in which the young women moved in with the defendant sometime after filing the initial police complaint, and were no longer interested in prosecuting when the case came to trial, sometimes many months or even years later. In a case initiated in 1919 and brought to trial in 1924, for example, judicial officials searched unsuccessfully for the victim and defendant, finding only a few witnesses who testified that the couple had moved in together and left the neighborhood.[60] Another couple did the same in 1930, but officials were able to locate them a year later, when they finally married.[61] The latter couple was probably prompted by the court action to formalize their union.

Judging from a 1984 survey of girls and women aged fifteen to fifty-four, it was common, at least in later decades, for couples to live maritally for a period of time and to formalize the union later—precisely the arrangement proposed by many defendants in deflowering cases in the 1920s and 1930s.[62]

Since young women commonly accepted consensual unions in lieu of marriage, or while waiting for marriage, it is not surprising that several deflowering complainants stated that they had "given in" sexually because the defendant had promised to live maritally with them, apparently considering this contract binding.[63] Judges and prosecutors, however, were generally not sympathetic to these grievances. Prosecutor Sussekind de Mendonça, for example, arguing in 1925 for the dismissal of a case in which the woman stated that she had sex because her boyfriend promised to live maritally with her until they could afford to be married, equated the acceptance of this promise with prostitution: "The offended woman . . . sold her birthright for a plate of lentils, a paid room and a remote marriage."[64] Judge Emmanuel de Almeida Sodré likewise ruled against a woman whose boyfriend had promised to live maritally with her in 1939, arguing that "the profound difference between a marriage promise with the vision of a life-long, stable union and the launching of concubinage, always precarious, with no guarantee whatsoever of permanence, capable of ending at any moment, escapes no one."[65] Sodré considered the woman's pregnancy her sole responsibility, despite her boyfriend's statement that he was "absolutely certain" that the unborn child was his.

As is evident from the marital status of some of the young women's mothers, although informal unions might indeed be transient, they often constituted stable marriages in the conception of those involved.[66] Although only twenty-nine mothers reported that they lived in a consensual union with the victim's fathers, it is likely that many of the mothers who declared that they were married to the fathers did not distinguish between formal and informal unions. In one case, the victim's mother's companion (who was not the victim's father) filed the police complaint, unaware that he was not the girl's legal guardian—and did not have the power to defend the family's honor—until the complaint was deemed invalid. There were other instances of informally married people who did not distinguish their relationship from a formal one. In one case, for example, the victim's sister's companion, who represented the victim because she was orphaned, called himself her brother-in-law and acknowledged that he was not legally married to her sister only after the defendant's lawyer challenged him.[68]

If consensual unions could be either transient or stable, the same was true of formal marriage. Despite state attempts to mandate the indissolubility of marriage—including a constitutional provision upholding indissoluble marriage after 1934—people commonly separated, formally or informally, and lived with subsequent partners. Moreover, according to the attorney general of the state of Rio de Janeiro in 1942, marriage annulments were commonly (and fraudulently) granted in the 1930s, and presumably earlier, on the grounds that the woman's consent had been obtained through coercion, resulting in "a truly unique situation: the common practice of *divorce by mutual consent*—something that does not exist in any civilized nation."[69] Although divorce was legalized only in 1977, most working-class Cariocas were aware well before then that it was impossible for the state to force people to remain in marriages against their will when there were various other options available to them.

In accepting both consensual unions and the idea that sexual relations and cohabitation were justified by a promise of formal or informal marriage, the people who testified in deflowering cases were following patterns common to most Latin American nations and that date to the early colonial period. Informal unions were compatible with medieval Portuguese law, which considered couples that lived together as husband and wife to be legally married. Even after the Council of Trent mandates were brought to Brazil, neither church nor state persecuted "simple concubinage" vigorously or systematically.[70] Along with the marriage promise and informal unions, however, the desire for legitimate marriage also seem to have precedents in colonial Brazil. The static image of generalized bastardy of the Brazilian colonial population, which has been widely disseminated since the publication of Gilberto Freyre's work in the 1930s, has been challenged by new local studies that demonstrate tremendous variation in illegitimacy levels by region and social group and over time. Yet formal marriage rates seem to have plummeted in the nineteenth century, especially among the slave and free-poor population in the dynamic and unstable center-south.[71]

Although marriage rates increased in the first half of the twentieth century, particularly in urban areas, demographers agreed that consensual unions remained a norm for a significant portion of the population.[72] According to census data in 1940, 13 percent of all families in Brazil were joined by "free unions"; another 22 percent by religious marriages. Fewer than 65 percent of Brazilian families were headed by legally married couples.[73] Census bureau officials noted that since many women who lived in consensual unions declared themselves married, the actual proportion of "free unions" to legal marriages was certainly higher.[74] Based on studies of unpublished data from the 1940 census together with estimates from earlier censuses, officials concluded that the prevalence of free unions was "a constant characteristic of Brazilian demography over the previous fifty or sixty years."[75]

Early-twentieth-century women who consented to sexual relations upon the man's promise of a life together, whether state-sanctioned or not, and took their deflowerers to court when the promise was broken, thus followed both common contemporary practices and long-standing customs. Yet while premarital sexual relations and consensual unions were not ignominious, neither were they ideal. Adolescent girls, and especially their mothers, were aware that marriage brought advantages and that virginity was an important resource. The ways some of them used this resource, however, stretched the parameters of juridical concepts of female honor, virginity, and freedom.

The Importance of Virginity for Deflowered Women

Loss of virginity was a critical event in a single woman's life, provoking gossip in her neighborhood (or sometimes even newspaper reports) and warranting action as severe as a lawsuit against the deflowerer. Euphemisms used for "deflowering" suggest that it both victimized and stigmatized a young woman in the eyes of the friends, relatives, and neighbors who testified on her behalf. Witnesses described the young woman as "disgraced," "dishonored," or "abused." There were also cases of young women like fifteen-year-old Olívia Pereira, a white, illiterate domestic servant, who sought to escape this sort of stigma by going to the police and the Institute of Legal Medicine to prove she *was* a virgin, "despite what people said about her" in her neighborhood.[76] Medical proof of virginity was also important for middle-class families, many of whom paid for private examinations at the institute.[77] In rare cases, middle-class fathers such as military officer Adalberto Carvalho sought this proof through a police complaint. His nineteen-year-old daughter Arlene swore before the police that she was a virgin, "as the examination . . . will prove." She was vindicated at the Institute of Legal Medicine. Her examination discredited her father's "vehement suspicion" that she had allowed her ex-boyfriend to deflower her.[78]

Despite Afrânio Peixoto's exhortations about the limitations of the medical examination for proving lost virginity, it remained through the 1920s and 1930s a powerful means not only of validating deflowering complaints, but also of disciplining young women. Parents such as Arlene Drumond's father sometimes submitted their daughters to an examination or threatened to do so in order to extract a "confession," usually in arguments provoked by a daughter's prolonged absence from home. In one 1927 case, seventeen-year-old Luiza Moreira's mother, a washerwoman, went to the police because her daughter refused to submit to an examination in her neighborhood clinic.[79] Apparently, legal-medical officers were more practiced at performing examinations on reluctant subjects, although in Moreira's case the exam was inconclusive because her hymen was elastic (*complacente*). Several young women simply did not appear for their examinations at the Institute of Legal Medicine. Apparently, their complaints at the police station were sufficient to push wedding plans ahead, and they married their offenders before the investigations proceeded further.[80]

There were five cases in which the young women appeared at the Institute of Legal Medicine as instructed by police, but once there refused to be examined.[81] This annoyed examiners and especially prosecutors. Until the 1930s, the majority opinion among jurists was that once a woman complainant was declared impoverished, and her case taken over by the public prosecutor, she lost the right to desist in her complaint or to pardon the accused. Impoverished young women were obliged to provide the testimony and documents necessary for the prosecution, including most crucially the deflowering examination.[82] This explains prosecutor Maximiano José Gomes de Paiva's attitude when he chided medical examiners for failing to examine seventeen-year-old Maria Gonçalves, who refused to submit to the examination in 1927. Paiva demanded that they try again, insisting that "the examination is the essential basis of the prosecution and the illustrious examiners have the means to perform it, even against the will of the offended minor." If these means existed, they were not employed. Maria Gonçalves followed police instructions to return to the institute, but once again refused to be examined, and her case was closed.[83]

Impoverished women could also intervene in the prosecution of their deflowerers in other ways. Some simply failed to appear at the trial (sometimes they moved away with the defendant or for some other reason could not be found by officials delivering summons) or gave testimony in court that differed wildly from their statements to police. Before the judges, a few women blamed someone other than the defendant for the deflowering, and a few others tried alternative strategies such as portraying themselves as dishonest or even as a prostitute. An example is the case of twenty-year-old Perfeita Nunes, a white factory worker. Perfeita's sister and brother-in-law filed a deflowering complaint at the local police station when Perfeita ran away to live with her boyfriend José Santos, a twenty-nine-year-old married army sergeant who had separated from his wife. Perfeita escaped her sister's and the court's protection and freed her boyfriend from prosecution by portraying herself as a woman who "had always had a free life [vida livre], and thus began frequenting nightclubs such as Pingão Fidalgo, Cananga do Japão, Bohêmios, Recreio das Flores, and Zuavos."[84] By providing the names of the clubs and insisting that she had been deflowered by someone she had been with only one evening, Perfeita was able to convince the public prosecutor to drop the case without any investigation, even though her sister and brother-in-law insisted she was lying to protect José. Although juridical theory held that "honest" women should not be believed in such cases, performances like that of Perfeita Nunes usually made conviction impossible.[85]

By the late 1930s, jurists began to reverse earlier precedents and recognized the right of poor women's legal representatives to intervene to stop the prosecution of their offenders, or even to pardon them. The new tendency was sustained in a 1937 appeals decision, in which Federal District justices allowed a young husband to pardon his wife's deflowerer, releasing the convict from a two-year jail sentence. To do otherwise, the justices argued, would signify a legal bias against poor families.[86]

Unlike this and other reluctant or repentant complainants, most of the deflowered women did not express a desire to pardon their deflowerers. They willingly submitted to the medical examination, hoping it would substantiate their complaints. In these complaints, the young women expressed an acceptance of the concept that virginity was a prerequisite for marriage, and that honest women "gave themselves" only to please their future husbands. Of course, it is logical that women who were aware of the legal meaning of "deflowering" and who hoped to earn the protection of the court would cooperate with judicial officials and would create an identity compatible with the court's definition of an honest woman, as they understood it. Undoubtedly prompted by police officials who, versed in the legal definition of the crime, recorded their initial testimony, deflowered women almost always asserted that they had consented to having sex only "on the basis of a marriage promise" (*sob promessa de casamento*). Typically, they described their first sexual encounter as painful and bloody and their role in the act as passively submissive.

The bloodshed and pain reported by deflowering victims diminished over time, corresponding to the dissemination of medical research on the subject. At the turn of the century, according to Esteves's study, women commonly described blood that spilled over all of their clothing and pain that lasted longer than a day.[87] In the 1920s and 1930s, most women (78 percent of the cases observed) reported pain and bloodshed, but described more moderate reactions, a few as mild as "some pain, but not much" and "a small blood stain," or "a little blood, like when you cut a finger," and one even reported "no pain whatsoever nor any bloodshed."[88] Jurists did not give up their attempts to grasp objective "material evidence." In a 1931 case, the defense lawyer argued that a young woman who "boldly and brazenly" claimed that her deflowering caused a great deal of pain and stained her clothing with blood was clearly dishonest, since her hymen was "extraordinarily complacent."[89] The judge ignored this argument, but a few years later it became commonplace to discredit deflowering victims' testimony on these grounds. By 1934, a judge could rule decisively against a woman in a similar situation by stating that it was "well-known that complacent hymens permit painless and bloodless copulation."[90] This knowledge was not based on empirical studies. In fact, the cases consulted suggest that women's association of pain and bloodshed with the loss of virginity apparently had only slight relationship to the configuration of their hymens. The proportion of women reporting these reactions was only 6 percent greater among the 269 women with ruptured hymens than among the 109 with complacent hymens (83 and 77 percent, respectively).[91] In any case, as was true of other juridical means of determining honesty, judges applied this precedent selectively in their verdicts.

Like their turn-of-the-century predecessors, deflowered women of the 1920s and 1930s generally described their deflowering as something done *to* them, if not exactly against their will, at least without their participation. Surprisingly few of the cases, even among those tried as rape rather than deflowering, involved force or violence, and only a handful involved rape by a stranger. If it is true that rapes were rarely reported because rape victims and their families felt that the publicity of a trial would only increase their dishonor and humiliation, as jurists reasoned when they determined that prosecution of sexual crimes must be initiated by the victim's complaint, then deflowering must not have carried the same sense of shame. It is probable, however, that many victims and their families went to the police because they hoped legal action might lead to the repair of the deflowering through marriage, whereas they would be less likely to desire a young woman's marriage to a rapist. But in some deflowering cases, there was little or no likelihood of this kind of resolution, such as in the twenty-six cases in which the men were already married, or in the two in which they had sailed off to Portugal,[92] or when the woman did not wish to marry her deflowerer. The young women, or their parents, nonetheless seemed to feel that it was possible to "guard" the women's honor (*resguardar a honra*) through a public affirmation that they had given their virginity in good faith, or at least that it had not been taken from them in a dishonorable way. Thus, although forty-two of the young women complaining of deflowering mentioned the use of physical force by the defendant, most of them (thirty-one) emphasized that this force was accompanied by romance, seduction, and a promise of marriage.

Most young women did not report the use of force by their deflowerers, but instead described themselves as passively acquiescent. Three even claimed that the defendant "took advantage of her deep sleep" to satisfy his lascivious desires.[93] A typical scene was that described in the testimony of an eighteen-year-old domestic servant in 1926: "promising marriage . . . he laid her down on the floor and pushing up her clothing introduced his virile member in the vagina of the declarant, deflowering her, causing her pain and soiling her clothes with blood."[94] As Esteves argued for her turn-of-the century data, the formulaic nature of many of the descriptions of initial sexual contacts, along with the use of technical language ("introduced his virile member," "vagina," "deflowering") suggests that police recorders "helped" the young women recount their experience. The case of Jacy de Abreu Olinda, who told a judge that the police delegate had "mixed up her words" and made her sign testimony that incriminated her boyfriend in her deflowering, provides particularly strong evidence of police interference. Of course, we do not know whether the story was true. The judge was so outraged by the allegation that he ordered an investigation; unsurprisingly, the delegate and his clerk swore that Jacy was lying.[95]

Jacy's case is unique. More commonly, police probably wrote down testimony in language that the young girls would not have used. Not only some of the terms ("virile member," "vagina," "hemorrhage") but some of the phrases used by different victims in initial testimony were suspiciously similar from one generation to the next. In a 1908 case quoted by Esteves, the testimony of a fifteen-year-old black washerwoman's daughter explained that her boyfriend "grabbed her, laid her down on the bed and held his hand over her mouth so that she wouldn't scream, pushed up her clothing and introduced in her vagina his virile member causing her pain and hemorrhage."[96] Thirty-one years later, another fifteen-year-old domestic servant testified that "Argemiro, lying the declarant down on her bed, pushed up her clothing and, under promise of marriage, introduced his virile member in the vagina of the declarant who felt slight pain and hemorrhage."[97]

Yet even taking into account possible police intervention in favor of the prosecution, it is clear that most of the young women were aware of ideals that held honest women to be sexually passive. Most victims recounted the stories of their initial police testimony in less technical language in statements before judges, which were frequently made months or even years later. Furthermore, variations in the deflowering scenarios, male and female roles that contradicted juridical ideals, and occasional slips that suggested that some young women might not have been as passive as they claimed, are evidence that they re-created, or at least helped re-create, the images and sexual roles that appear in their testimonies.

More striking than the offended women's descriptions of their sexual passivity was their acknowledgment of the importance of virginity in determining their marriageability. This was expressed clearly in the case against Antônio Ramos, a thirty-year-old textile worker accused of deflowering his cousin, twenty-one-year-old Olívia Ramos in 1927. Olívia's mother, Elvira Rosa Ramos, explained the situation:

Her daughter had been courted for the past year by Luiz Sinhorelli, who recently wanted to marry Olívia; . . . only then was Olívia obliged to confess to the declarant that she couldn't marry Sinhorelli because her cousin and the declarant's nephew Antônio Ramos, one year ago, had deflowered Olívia.[98]

Similarly, when public functionary Hernani Ribeiro proposed marriage to seventeen-year-old black Jurema Barros, Jurema also confessed to her mother "that she had been deflowered two years earlier during Carnival by Jorge Portella . . . and thus could not accept Hernani's proposal." Jurema herself explained that when Hernani proposed, she "confessed her secret to him and to her mother . . . because she did not want to deceive him." Seventeen-year-old white Jandyra Marinho also found a suitor— Manoel de Oliveira Carvalho, a twenty-two-year-old Portuguese commercial employee—after she had been deflowered, but according to her friend and confidant, "she did not take him seriously, for she knew she could not marry him since she had already been deflowered" by a previous boyfriend, José Gracioso.[99] In all three cases, the suitors rescinded their marriage proposals when they heard their fiancées' confessions, and appeared in court as witnesses against the accused deflowerers. In the first case, the judge acquitted Antônio Ramos because he had not promised to marry Olívia (he was already married). In the second case, Jorge Portella agreed to marry Jurema, but she refused, and he was given a one-year prison sentence. In the third case, José Gracioso married Jandyra Marinho, even though he insisted that her boyfriend Manoel Carvalho was responsible for her defloration.

Clearly, it was commonly assumed that a man would not marry an already deflowered woman, although there is some evidence that this was not true of all men. Twenty-three-year-old Marcos Gonçalves, for example, stated that he had had sexual relations with his fifteen-year-old girlfriend and planned to marry her, "although he did not notice whether she was a virgin."[100] In a few other cases, the young woman married a third party while the case against her deflowerer was underway.[101] This situation was not unprecedented. In fact, the question of whether a deflowering case should proceed after the offended woman married a third party arose frequently in Brazilian jurisprudence between 1890 and 1938.[102] Nevertheless, the belief that a woman was eligible for marriage only to the man who first "possessed" her was present in the minds of many working-class women. This belief might place women in a "desperate situation," as one lawyer described a woman's defloration, and could even lead the woman to attempt suicide, as occurred in one case and was com-

monly reported in scandalous newspaper accounts. Its corollary, however, was that the deflowerer had the responsibility to repair the young
woman's honor, which was the premise behind almost all of the deflowering suits. As we shall see, women could use this sexual ideology to
strengthen their position in various sorts of domestic disputes.

Arguments for the Prosecution

Like the defendants and their lawyers, the offended women and their
families also linked women's liberty with sexual experience, frequently
insisting that the young women were strictly supervised and "not permitted any liberty" as evidence of their virginity. In parents' absence, employers were often expected to guard a girl's virginity. Upon employing
their daughters in the service of "honest families," some parents specified
that they should be "rigorously supervised," or that "maximum precau-
tion" should be taken with them.[103] Several of the domestic servants also
stated that their employers "did not allow [them] any liberty" as evidence
of their virginity, explaining that they were not allowed to talk to boys at
the gate of the house, or that they were only allowed to go out alone on
their day off (once a fortnight) and then only to visit their parents.[104]

What liberty meant was not always clear. For example, when a lawyer
tried to establish the victim's lack of moral guidance in a 1940 case by
asking whether she was given "liberty" to go out alone, her grandmother
answered in puzzlement, "that of course Maria had permission to go out
alone because she had to work."[105] This lawyer's strategy was unsuccessful. In a city in which women were increasingly absorbed into the urban
labor force, few, even among lawyers and jurists, still held the nineteenth-
century notion that a virgin girl would never venture out onto the street
unaccompanied.

Women's participation in public leisure was more problematic. Some
young women were apparently not aware that unchaperoned excursions
to dance halls, movie houses, Carnival festivities, or rides on streetcars or
even automobiles with girlfriends or boyfriends were signs of excessive
liberties that put their family's morality and their own virginity into question, for their testimony is full of such excursions. Frequently, the excursions were made possible by attracting a young man who could pay the
way. The young women, and their witnesses, countered accusations of
excessive liberty with alternative interpretations of the women's actions,
and often of common working- and middle-class leisure. "Esther's Carnival costume did not demonstrate a lack of honesty," one witness protested, "but merely a lack of good judgment, childishness," and the Car-

nival "block" she danced with "did not practice excesses that would blemish the honor of the young ladies."[106] A distraught father justified his daughter's unchaperoned outings with her deflowerer by explaining that "he was intimate with [the boy's] family."[107] A mother explained that her daughter "amused herself by going to the movies, like the other girls from the neighborhood."[108]

Although deflowering victims did not hide the ways that their daily lives provided a wide margin for independence and even assertiveness, they were especially careful to downplay their own sexual freedom, describing their role as passively submissive and often explaining that they had "given in" to their deflowerers only under coercion—he would marry her only on this condition; if she refused it was because she did not truly love or trust him; or, most commonly, he would marry her only after "verifying that she was a virgin" by having sex with her. Some of the women even explained that their deflowerer had used force to overcome their resistance; indeed, from the way sex is consistently described by young women in these cases, male aggressiveness, and even violence, must have been widely considered to be a common, or at least potential, feature of heterosexual relations. But if one reads beyond the young women's reiterated descriptions of themselves as passive victims of male passion and their own incredulity, it is possible to detect varied and complex motives for the women's actions. The loss of virginity was an important event for these women, but often for different reasons than those foreseen by their parents, their deflowerers, or the courts.

"Desires Similar to Those of the Man": Sexual Excitement in the Testimony of Deflowered Girls

Evidence that young women's own libido influenced them to have sex contradicted many of their assertions of passivity and single-minded pursuit of marriage. Although it seems likely that sexual excitement and pleasure influenced many adolescent girls' decisions to have sex with their boyfriends before the 1920s, Esteves found only sparse and indirect evidence of these sensations in her analysis of turn-of-the-century deflowering cases.[109] She did not find cases in which women openly acknowledged their own sexual arousal or described themselves as the "active" partner. Her study corroborates the observations of judges such as Eurico Cruz, who, scandalized by the audacity of modern girls of the 1920s, declared that these girls' acknowledgment of their physical excitement and assertiveness was unprecedented. There is little evidence to support Cruz's claim that modern girls were unabashed in their quest to satisfy their licentious desires and then turn to the courts for protection from their own promiscuousness. Nonetheless, it is clear that increasingly over the course of the 1920s and 1930s, offended women's testimony contained a new language of sexual arousal in addition to the older references to female passivity and male agressiveness. In 1940, for example, eighteen-year-old white commercial employee Judith Valézia Raposo described her defloration as follows: "after renewing the promises [of marriage] that he was always making and caressing her, exciting her a great deal, he deflowered her." Arlette Moreira, a seventeen-year-old black domestic worker made a similar statement in 1932: "the act was preceded by formal promises of marriage and caresses which induced the declarant to permit the act to take place."[110]

In these testimonies the male was depicted as sexual protagonist. At the same time, sexual foreplay (or "preparatory acts," as it was termed in the testimony of one woman) was described in ways that contradicted images of the honest woman as passionless and motivated solely by an irresistible promise of marriage. This, together with descriptions of unconventional positions (eight of the women gave descriptions similar to the one that horrified Eurico Cruz in 1926, in which the woman stood or sat in front of or on top of her partner) contradicted the images of passivity that were constructed in the same testimony.[111]

Young women's increasing acknowledgment of the role of physical arousal and pleasure in their decision to "give in" provoked both their condemnation by jurists such as Eurico Cruz and the opposing juridical tendency to interpret seduction in its "vulgar sense," or as physical stimulation.[112] Yet while some young women acknowledged that they felt the pressure of their own libido, sexual desire rarely seemed to be the sole factor that influenced their decision to give up their virginity.

Women's Struggles for Authority

In 5 percent of the cases consulted, the women had sex with their boyfriends in order to force their parents to accept a forbidden relationship. Although by law, parental consent was required for marriage of those younger than twenty-one regardless of virginal status, conventional wisdom held that parents lost authority over their daughters upon the girls' defloration. The testimony of sixteen-year-old Olga Xavier de Costa, who ran away from home because her mother objected to her relationship with Manoel Ribeira, illustrates this wisdom. Olga explained that Manoel's seventy-eight-year-old brother-in-law Almir da Costa Ferreira "advised her to give herself to her boyfriend because that would be the way they could get married independently of her mother's consent."[113] This case, along with all of the other cases in which the couple had sex in order to overcome parental opposition to their marriage, was resolved by the marriage. It seems likely that this strategy, registered in colonial litigation in various regions of Latin America and involving people of diverse classes, remained common in twentieth-century Rio de Janeiro, although only a tiny fraction of the cases ever reached the courts.[114]

The symbolic sexual possession by a man of a woman took a concrete form in these cases, as men who "possessed" a virgin woman sexually came to take authority over her away from her parents. "To possess" in the sexual sense was an explicitly gendered verb: men possessed women, never vice versa. Brazilian law legitimized this "possession." Legally, women were under the tutelage of their fathers, the holders of *pátrio poder* in the family, until the age of twenty-one; if a woman married, this authority passed to her husband. In these relationships, the protagonists, that is, those taking authority, were theoretically always male.

In contrast to these male-centered symbolic power relationships, the deflowering cases consulted suggest that in practice, conflicts of authority involving a girl's loss of virginity usually involved female protagonists on both sides. The mother was the major authority figure for most of the young women involved; fathers appeared in only 27 percent of the cases consulted. This figure in part reflects the historically high occurrence of consensual unions and female-headed households among working-class families in Brazil. In many of the cases, fathers or stepfathers may have been present in the home, but do not appear in these documents.

In any case, single mothers were a favorite target for lawyers seeking to denigrate deflowering victims by arguing that they lived free of the constraints that honest families placed on their women. José Joaquim Marquês Filho's attack on Magdalena Teixeira Alves is a good example. Alves brought the soldier Urbano Rodrigues to court over the deflowering of her seventeen-year-old daughter Arlette in 1936. Representing Rodrigues, Marquês Filho did not deny that his client had been engaged to Arlette and had had sex with her. He argued, however, that Arlette's downfall was entirely her mother's fault. By separating from her husband and relocating her family from a small town to Rio de Janeiro, Magdalena Alves had both broken the law and thrown her daughter into "a life of dangerous liberty."[115]

The lawyer described the tenement where the Alves family lived as "that pigsty on Estâcio Street," and insinuated that their neighbors, with whom the family shared sanitary facilities and cooking space, were disreputable laundresses and "single soldiers of the military police," a category of men known for their disorderliness and immorality.[116] Magdalena Alves's refusal to submit to the authority of her husband, the lawyer alleged, had brought her family to live in these despairing conditions. This morally questionable environment was not, the lawyer argued, the family's legitimate home, for it was "not chosen by the person with the legal right to choose—the girl's father." Magdalena Alves could not possibly head a respectable household, according to Marquês Filho, for "the conjugal home determined, as it is, by the husband, is always subordinated to the spirit of domestic-economic expediency and propriety, and central to this spirit is the supreme control of the family's destiny . . . by the father, who, invested with the powers conferred by law, is the head of the family."[117] Because the mother had "fled [evadida] the conjugal home," it was preposterous for her to defend her daughter's honor "as if the greater honor, that of the family, were not already destroyed to its foundations by the irregular situation [of the mother]." To proceed with the case, the lawyer argued, would set "a dangerous precedent, disrespecting the explicit imperatives of the law, and would also take from the man, head of the family, the traditional prerogatives that are attributed him in Society, from remote times."[118] It was not only the liberty of the minor girl, but also that of her mother that was dangerous to tradition, family honor, and social order.

The judge in this case acknowledged that the lawyer was correct when he called Magdalena Alves "an amorphous entity," a nonperson who was legally incapable of defending herself or her family. Magdalena Alves's complaint was declared invalid because she had had no right to move her family from the home her husband had established or to go to court over her daughter's deflowering.

Although the lawyer and the judge acted on solid legal grounds in the Alves case, the invalidation of cases of sexual crime on the grounds that the mother was not the legitimate legal representative of her daughter was rare. Mothers, regardless of their marital status, commonly acted as heads of their families and guardians of their daughter's honor, both in and out of court. At least in the cases recorded in criminal records, mothers rarely depended on male protectors, but took action themselves—interrogating their daughters' deflowerers, demanding some sort of settlement (usually a marriage promise), and going to the police to seal the agreement or when the promise was not kept.

Most of these mothers headed their households. Fathers appeared to file charges, often accompanied by mothers, in only 27 percent of the cases; mothers appeared alone in 45 percent.[119] If we exclude the remaining 28 percent, in which the deflowered girls were orphans or lived far from their parents, the numbers shift: 63 percent of the girls were represented by their mothers; 37 percent by fathers.

The families of deflowering victims were not highly unusual among the general population. In the 1940 census, a third of the city's mothers declared themselves single (10 percent) or widowed (23 percent), proportions only slightly lower than those found among the mothers in the criminal records (12 percent single and 29 percent widowed).[120] The proportion of married mothers in the criminal records was probably inflated by women who declared themselves married but actually lived in "free unions," as officials believed was true of census data.[121]

We might suspect nonetheless that the prevalence of female-headed families in these cases reflect men's preference to defend their family's honor personally rather than by relying on public authorities.[122] In contrast to wife-killings, however, which filled the pages of the tabloid press and preoccupied a variety of observers, evidence of this kind of violence is sparse. Stories of this type appear in the press, but only occasionally; the scenario is seldom pondered by the jurists who debated passionate crimes. In a cursory search through fifty randomly selected boxes of jury trial records from 1918 to 1940, no murders or attempted murders of deflowerers by fathers of dishonored girls were uncovered among the 366 records, in contrast to forty-one murders of wives or lovers.[123] One of the latter cases, however, suggests that fathers might have exerted other kinds of pressure. A jockey who killed his wife in a jealous fit in 1931 claimed that he had always suspected she was dishonest and had married her eleven years earlier only because her father intimidated him with threats of violence as well as by filing a deflowering complaint with the police. In another case, reported in the tabloid *A notícia* in 1921, Anna Ramirez's father filed a complaint against her deflowerer, but the police informed him that Anna was too old (she was twenty-two) to qualify as a deflowering victim. According to the reporter, Anna's father then went after the young man, a fruit vender, with a shotgun; in the ensuing struggle, the young man, his mother, and two passersby were wounded.[124]

Fathers might also defend their daughters' honor without resorting to violence, as seems to have been the case in most middle-class families. Some evidence of this emerged in a 1923 marital separation case involving what seems to have been a lower-middle-class family. One of Iracema Valdés Mendes's complaints against her husband was that he had refused to press charges against their daughter's deflowerer, delaying her marriage. The husband's lawyer retorted that the husband had defended his daughter's honor as well as his own by settling matters quietly with the girl's fiancé and his father.[125]

Both the prominence of matrifocal families among Rio de Janeiro's working-class population and men's recourse to extralegal strategies for defending honor probably help to explain why mothers or other women (aunts, sisters, or employers of domestic servants) play leading roles in these honor dramas. Yet the deflowering records suggest that mothers, too, employed diverse strategies, and they were protagonists even when men were present. Unlike Iracema Valdés Mendes's husband, male protectors who were involved in the cases often reported that they acted on the instructions of the girl's mother. Magdalena Alves's son, for example, reported that his mother sent him out to look for his sister's deflowerer and question him on his intentions. Even the fathers who filed police complaints often testified that their wives or partners had learned of the deflowering and advised them on how to proceed.

In one case, police officials sent a mother home to get her spouse so as to avoid an outcome like that of Magdalena Alves's, but in sixteen others, women who were married to and living with their daughters' fathers successfully filed complaints.[126] The same was true of twelve of the eighteen mothers who declared that they were married to but separated from their daughters' fathers.[127] These women were evidently not aware that their marriages made them "amorphous entities," incapable of representing their families in court. It might be assumed that in the cases of the separated mothers, the fathers' whereabouts were unknown, in which case the law granted the mother the right to represent her family.[128] What is interesting, in any case, is that mothers acted as legal representatives for their daughters much more frequently than fathers, and did not feel the need to explain or justify their role as family heads. In short, contrary to the gender basis of legal subjectivity, mothers existed as individual subjects who asserted authority, alone or with their partners, in both public and private. At least in the cases recorded in criminal records, it was usually women, not men, who were responsible for guarding their family's honor.

Adolescent daughters sometimes used the ideology that demanded their submission to family vigilance in rebellions against authority—often that of their mothers. Since much of the discipline imposed on young women was justified as the defense of their sexual honor, which required the preservation of virginity, many came to view the rupture of their hymens as liberating. Having sex was, for many young women, an act of defiance.

The complaint filed in 1929 by Honorina da Silva Gonçalves, mother of Esmarina Maria Gonçalves, an eighteen-year-old black factory worker, is revealing:

> On the morning of March 5, the declarant was at home, as was her daughter Esmarina, [who] for a trifling reason responded rudely to a comment made by the declarant; . . . the declarant therefore said to her daughter that she was obliged to obey her until she got married; . . . Esmarina responded that all she had to do was leave with Urbano, because "she was already his"; . . . the declarant, suspicious of these phrases from Esmarina submitted her to a rigorous interrogation, obtaining the confession from her that she had been deflowered by Urbano.[129]

In this and many other cases, the major conflict was not between "victim" and "accused." Parents or guardians and daughters were often the combatants. After "rigorous interrogation," sometimes accompanied by beatings, many parents went to the police and filed complaints that seem to have been retaliation as much against their daughter as against her deflowerer. In several cases, angry parents accused their daughters of sexual misconduct when family conflicts flared, often over daughters' courtship choices. Arlene de Carvalho Drumond, for example, whose virginity was verified by the Institute of Legal Medicine in 1938, had run away from home because "she was very badly treated at home because of her courtship."[130] Izaltina de Souza Leite's stepfather and mother, during the course of the defloration case they opened in 1927 against Izaltina's boyfriend Leandro Braga, a thirty-one-year-old sailor, attempted to have Izaltina confined to a juvenile detention center. Izaltina, a fifteen-year-old domestic servant who had run away from home on her own accord and without Leandro's assistance (according to both Leandro's and her own testimony), escaped her mother's and the court's governorship by having sex with and then marrying Leandro.[131] Fifteen-year-old white Maria Cândida Dias attempted a similar strategy nine years later. Maria's father, a middle-class businessman who was separated from her mother (with whom Maria lived), tried unsuccessfully to force her to undergo a deflowering examination by a private doctor and then to intern her in a religious boarding school when he discovered the "liberties" her mother allowed Maria and her boyfriend, a white Naval Academy cadet. When Maria refused to undergo the examination and escaped from the school, her father cut off the child support he provided her mother. At this point, Maria decided to begin a sexual relationship with her boyfriend and accepted the monthly allowance he offered to help pay her family's expenses. Her boyfriend proved unwilling to marry her, but apparently helped her move out of her mother's apartment to a boardinghouse.[132]

Clearly, deflowering victims did not necessarily feel subjugated or enslaved after being possessed by a man. Rather, this possession some-times symbolized liberation and a breaking of bonds of dependence. This is not to idealize sexual freedom, or to claim that independence, partic-ularly economic independence, always resulted from liberated sexual behavior. Maria Cândida Dias, for example, who was unemployed, would probably have found it difficult to support herself without her boyfriend's help. Judging from the unflattering statements he made about her in his testimony, it seemed unlikely that his help would continue for long. Furthermore, contraceptive use was limited (though mentioned in three cases), and it was extremely difficult for a young woman to support a family alone. Many women lost their jobs when they became pregnant and continued living with their parents, with or without the fathers of their children.

The difficulties of single parenthood were all too familiar for many of the girls' mothers, which explains in large part the urgency of mothers' attempts to force the deflowerers to marry their daughters. But in a so-ciety in which survival strategies for the majority of the population in-volved intricate networks of interdependence and solidarity, economic independence was rare for anyone. By giving up her virginity, a young woman did increase her power to choose her survival strategy. In some cases, this strategy might even have included marriage against her par-ents' or her partner's will.

In any case, the point remains that when the need to protect virginity was eliminated, much of the constriction imposed on young women was no longer justified. White nineteen-year-old Georgina Medeiros was clear on this. On September 19, 1935, Georgina ran away from home, only to be found later in the afternoon by her father, who convinced her to return home. According to her father's testimony, Georgina told him "that she had left home because she considered herself to be entirely free, be-cause she had been deflowered by an individual by the name of Amaro Cavalcanti."[133]

Georgina Medeiros, like Esmarina Maria Gonçalves, thus strategi-cally deployed the gender ideology that associated women's loss of virgin-ity with freedom. Also like Esmarina, Georgina's rebellion was directed against her mother's vigilance. In her testimony, Georgina explained that "desiring to get away [se afastar] from her mother . . . she informed her mother of her state as a deflowered woman [seu estado de mulher de-

florada], because her mother refused to allow a single girl to live far from her."[134] In the ensuing trial, Cavalcanti was acquitted at the lower court on the grounds that Georgina's "desire to be free" disqualified her as an "honest woman." Prosecutor Roberto Lira successfully appealed the case with the argument that it was Cavalcanti who had provoked this "desire for freedom" in Georgina, and had thus committed a crime:

> The attempt to leave home after being deflowered, because she considered herself entirely free as a consequence of this deflowering having become irremediable by the attitude of the defendant, does not mean that, before the fact, this liberty existed. Much to the contrary, it was the defendant who created this situation, dishonoring his girlfriend and dragging her into a desperate social position.[135]

Medeiros, Gonçalves, and many other young deflowering victims encountered in court records of the 1920s and 1930s were probably not interested in jurists' debates about the relationship between modern life and women's excessive liberty. Their actions and choices were clearly inspired by personal concerns. In making and explaining these choices, however, the girls responded to both historical precedents and new ideas about the freedom of modern women in ways that placed them at the center of public debates. Most significantly, they cast themselves as independent and sexually active women without accepting the dishonor that was supposed to accompany women's liberation. Explicit references to sexual arousal or the desire for liberty identified some of them unmistakably as the modern woman—a figure that occupied an enormous space in the public imagination and on the city's streets, movie screens, beaches, and dance halls during these tumultuous decades. And, as we have seen, jurists engaged in the raging debate over state protection of female honor worked on the premise that modernity posed a threat to women's honor.

The young women, however, did not seem to perceive modernity as incompatible with or even particularly threatening to their honor. More common than the explicit demands for liberty made by some was the less explicit insistence by most of the offended women that their daily activities were not dishonorable. They felt entitled to the respect of the men who accompanied them on the streets, in streetcars, and in the workplace; or who invited them to movies, dance halls, or for rides in taxicabs; or who convinced them to enter into sexual relationships and even consensual unions. In their behavior and in their sense of honor, these young women at once replicated the lives of their mothers and grandmothers and responded to new ways of occupying a rapidly changing city.

That is, they sought out new spaces of public leisure, appropriated some of the images about the modern woman they found there, and introduced a new language of liberty and desire into their affective and sexual relationships. At the same time, they continued traditional patterns of premarital sexual relations, consensual unions, and matrifocal family formation, as well as survival strategies and community networks centered on poor women's occupation of public space.

These young women did not, then, step outside socially and historically constituted gender roles. Rather, they told stories, argued with their mothers or their boyfriends, and otherwise lived their lives in ways that, without contradicting the logic of gender identities found in legal and popular discourse, nonetheless continually reshaped these identities.

Given the generational conflict that is a central drama in many of the deflowering stories, it is ironic that the girls modeled themselves after their mothers and grandmothers in another way. In the language of both juridical literature and testimony, the terms *moça* and *donzella*, literally "girl" or "young woman," both signified virgin in popular usage and implied puerility, dependence, and tutelage. In contrast, *mulher desvirginada* signified an independent adult, with responsibilities and liberties not permitted a young virgin. This status, of course, brought stigma and certain disadvantages for single young girls—otherwise, these criminal records would not exist. It was not, however, necessarily equated with the status of prostitutes. In fact, it could be equated with their antithesis: mothers. Many young women, even if unconsciously, followed in their mothers' footsteps and chose the relative independence this status brought over the protection they could earn by preserving the integrity of their hymens (to use a contemporary medical phrase).

Like many of the mothers who defended their daughters' honor in court, these young women deviated from prescribed gender norms and attitudes, performing roles and expressing values that helped stretch the boundaries of what it meant to be a mother, an honest girl, and a free woman. By the late 1930s, jurists found themselves increasingly obliged to respond to these new boundaries in individual cases, as well as in their proposals for revising the legal provisions for the defense of family honor.

The Marriage Promise or the Art of Don Juan?
Adapting Legal Theory to Modern Women

In 1936, ten years after Eurico Cruz's celebrated deflowering sentence, in which the judge ruled against a young woman because she had not been sufficiently overcome by shame and suffering on the "first coitus," another Federal District judge passed a similar verdict against a daring modern girl. Antonietta Gomes had accused her boyfriend Fligialdo Gerson Lyrio of seducing her by promising marriage. The judge (unnamed in the published appeals sentence), finding the promise insufficiently "solemn," acquitted the defendant on the following grounds:

> Excepting . . . the case of a serious promise, of unquestionable commitment, the presumption that should be made from the fact [of the deflowering] is that, as long as normal people are involved, the woman gave into the impulses of her instinct, to her sensuality, accepting all risks inherent in the sacrifice of her virginity.[136]

Though unsympathetic to Gomes's complaint, the judge expressed a new, significantly more benevolent attitude toward women's sexuality than had existed in earlier jurisprudence. Whereas turn-of-the-century jurists had denied that women possessed sexual desires and judges such as Cruz in the 1920s had labeled female sexuality aberrant, this 1936 verdict described woman's sensuality as an instinctual impulse of "normal people." The judge nonetheless upheld the precedent that women who gave in to that instinct should not be protected by law. He based his verdict on the understanding of criminal seduction as defined by the nineteenth-century Italian legal scholar Francesco Carrara: it was a crime to seduce a minor by promising marriage and then to break this promise after deflowering her. Girls who gave in to other, "vulgar" forms of seduction had none but themselves to blame.

This verdict, then, was not entirely novel. Although it was not written into the 1890 penal code, turn-of-the-century legal scholarship and jurisprudence was virtually unanimous in defining the first two of the three criminal means of deflowering (seduction and deceit) as a marriage promise (the third, fraud, was to pose as a legitimate husband). Turn-of-the-century Brazilian judges, however, discarded the Italian master's criteria for an acceptable marriage promise. They followed, instead, Viveiros de Castro's opinion that publicity and witnesses were not necessary.[137] Elaborating on this point in his classic work on crimes against female honor, Viveiros de Castro described a hypothetical case of "true criminal seduction": a young man, after courting a young woman for some time, finds her at home alone. After an ardent declaration of long-standing love, "he solemnly, energetically, swears he wants to marry her . . . and he thus is able to delude the girl."[138] This was precisely the story of Antonietta Gomes's deflowering in 1936, recounted by the judge as evidence that she had *not* been criminally seduced.

The notion that seduction was a crime only when it involved a publicly acknowledged marriage promise was not a remnant of the past. To the contrary, it was a novelty of the 1930s, when some of the nation's most progressive jurists, including those who were commissioned by the government to draft two successive proposals for a new penal code after the overthrow of the First Republic.[139] Both proposals equated deflowering with breach of contract and stipulated that a public marriage promise should be the sole, indispensable element defining criminal seduction.[140] The definition of seduction, however, provoked heated debates in legal journals and at the Brazilian Conference on Criminology; a substantial majority of jurists favored a broader interpretation of criminal seduction of minor women. The jurists who produced the new penal code of 1940 followed the majority opinion and made no mention of the marriage promise.[141] A broader, more highly subjective interpretation of seduction prevailed: criminal seduction was defined as "taking advantage of the inexperience or justifiable trust" of a minor in order to strip her of her virginity.[142]

The new law responded to developments in jurisprudence and legal scholarship of the preceding twenty years. Several jurists had attacked the notion that a marriage promise, in itself, justified a woman's sexual acquiescence because, as Judge Perdigão Nogueira argued, "to accept seduction on the sole basis of an engagement is to accept the RIGHT of engaged couples to the precipitation of carnal congress," when the law should discourage such "indecorous precipitation."[143] In fact, Brazilian jurisprudence had, though unintentionally, legitimized the widespread practice of premarital sexual relations and cohabitation that the Catholic Church had attempted to curb (though the Church's attempts were halfhearted) for centuries. This was not considered a problem, or at least it was not denounced, until the late 1930s.

A more frequently cited argument against limiting the potential victims of deflowering to the formally betrothed was that the need to counter the contemporary "dissolution of customs" required that the law expand and not reduce its protection of female virtue. As Judge José Mesquita declared, in opposition to the 1933 Sá Pereira proposal, "the social conditions of today, the growing moral liberty [*liberdade crescente de costumes*] . . . require even greater amplitude for the concept of seduction, not restrictions."[144] The law, argued Mesquita and many others, should not lower its principles to match a debauched society, but rather should broaden its conception of sexual crimes to protect women from the dangers this debauchery posed to their honor.

The argument for a broadened understanding of seduction, firmly established in Federal District jurisprudence by the late 1930s, corresponded to the increasing acceptance of Galdino Siqueira's formerly little-heeded technical criticism of the standard interpretation of seduction as a marriage promise. In 1923, Siqueira pointed out that seduction could not have deceit "as its indispensable substratum" (a tenet in Carrara's thought), for this would signify an illogical redundancy in Brazilian law, unacceptable to jurists concerned with "good hermeneutics."[145] If deceit was understood as an unkept marriage promise, seduction must mean something else.

Siqueira, rejecting the reigning jurisprudential distinction between the "vulgar" and juridical meaning of seduction, insisted that both good hermeneutics and Brazilian legal tradition demanded that seduction be understood in its "vulgar usage." Seduction was "the employment of methods with a tendency to influence the minor's will, disposing her to give in solely to serve and be pleasing to her seducer." It could include "insistent pleas," "blandishment," or "the disorienting influx of the more exigent sensuality."[146] Although sexual desire was latent in honest women, men could employ their superior intelligence to influence the naturally more sentimental and impressionable woman, inducing in her "desires similar to those of the man."[147]

Siqueira's definition was introduced into jurisprudence in an appeals court decision of 1925, and appeared with increasing frequency over the following decade.[148] This jurisprudential tendency was cited by the appeals court justices who overturned Fligialdo Gerson Lyrio's acquittal for the deflowering of Antonietta Gomes in 1936. Criticizing the original verdict for "failing to attend to jurisprudential guidelines regarding the conceptualization of seduction," the justices described these guidelines:

> What is definitely established in the most recent decisions of the Court of Criminal Appeals is that the seduction that is required to influence the spirit of the minor, convincing her to give in, is not . . . a marriage promise . . . but rather vulgar and generic seduction, it is any seduction capable of deceiving a virgin woman and making her accept the carnal contact.

This new understanding of seduction was clearly influenced by more than Siqueira's concern for good hermeneutics. By the late 1930s, jurisprudence favored the view that the law had to adapt to modern times not by denying modern girls the right to defend their honor, but by expanding its definition of seduction. Judges were urged to draw from "sociological and psychological intuition" in order to integrate modern understandings of female sexuality and to counter the kinds of dangers faced by modern girls. Nelson Hungria's opposition to the call for lowered age limit for victims of deflowering illustrates this tendency. He claimed that the law protected women between sixteen and twenty-one "not because of their psychic immaturity, but because, above all, in this phase of vivacity of the senses, of inquietude of the sexual instinct, she can be an easy prey of seducers. It is a question of special psychological conditions, independent of greater or lesser mental development."[149] Since, as Judge Waldemar Couto argued in 1934, modern society "saturates men and women with sexualism [sic]" and "contemporary man, especially, sees everything through a veil of flesh, and discovers in a woman's every act, every word, every glance, an invitation to the sexual act," it was necessary to define seduction in a way that would protect fragile women from this sexual saturation.[150] Elaborating on Siqueira's interpretation in 1935, Hungria described the definition of seduction current among his contemporaries:

> It is the enticement of the fragile will of the woman exclusively through suggestion. It is the persistent pleading, the enveloping blandishment, the reiterated protest of love, the madrigalist phrase, the hot language of unsatisfied desire, the persuasive caress, the exciting prelude of kisses, of increasingly indiscreet touching. In a word: it is the refined art of Don Juan.[151]

Hungria accepted the notion that even honest women possessed a sexual instinct that, awakened by a skilled seducer, could induce them to serve him sexually. Like less sympathetic judges who considered women who demonstrated an awakened sexuality undeserving of legal protection, Hungria feared that women's sexual arousal outside marriage resulted in their degradation and represented a threat to public morality. Rather than ostracize these women, however, he argued for increased judicial intervention. To fail to punish seducers who "knew how to arouse the sexual instinct," Hungria argued, "is to encourage crimes against the honesty of families, indirectly favor prostitution, augment this wind of lasciviousness that seems to be presently subverting women's most precious and cherished virtues."[152]

Virginity Revisited: A Dam of Moral Containment

Although jurists had difficulty defining virginity and honest female behavior and continually debated whether the law should defend the "minimal ethical standard" of civilized society or the "average morality" of Brazil's population, none ever doubted that lost virginity greatly reduced a single woman's chances of marriage and decent family life and that unmarried sexually active women threatened social order. The justification of juridical intervention to protect virginity was based on these assumptions. The law was more concerned with women's reproductive and moralizing mission than with their individual rights.[153] As a 1921 appeals decision stated, the law punished deflowering because it "obstructs or impedes [women's] social function" in "the legally and morally constituted family" and led to her prostitution.[154] Innumerable legal and medical studies of prostitution likewise argued for increased prosecution of deflowerers as "social prophylactic" for the prevention of prostitution.

Jurists thus justified their intervention in the realm of morality by condemning sexual crimes as offenses against larger social institutions, not as physical assaults against individual citizens. As we have seen, the 1890 penal code defended family honor by prosecuting sexual offenses. In the 1930s, when jurists targeted family honor as a symbol of antiliberal oligarchical power, they recommended replacing it with the notion of "social customs" or "morality" (costumes). "Criminal law does not protect individual rights per se," explained Hungria, explaining the new code, "but rather because and when they coincide with social and public interest."[155]

It was also in the public interest, according to the viewpoint that prevailed in the 1940 penal code, to protect female virginity.[156] Many jurists found a new language to justify continued juridical intervention in the realm of morality. For example, the notion that virginity lost outside marriage led to prostitution was often explained as a natural psychological process: once women's naturally latent sexuality was awakened, if not sublimated through wifely and maternal duties, women would follow their base sexual drive to indulge in increasingly depraved activities. In cases of vulgar seduction, which did not involve a marriage promise, a seducer destroyed the feminine pudor, or natural repulsion of immorality, that shielded honest women and "civilized love."[157] Once this shield was lowered, women became more and more promiscuous. Nelson Hungria described what he believed was a typical scenario: "abandoned by the man who initiated her in lasciviousness, she begins giving herself to others. It is the gradual road toward the bordello, where, finally, the poor creature will be transformed into a sewer up for rent."[158]

Thus, although an intact hymen was not a foolproof sign of purity, one ruptured outside marriage provided an entryway for moral corruption. Explaining how new theories could simultaneously reject the veneration of material virginity and yet provide for its legal protection in the 1940 penal code, legal-medical expert Hélio Gomez argued that although it was possible that a single young woman with a ruptured hymen could be honorable (digna), this was an exception. "As a rule," Gomez continued, "the preservation of hymenal integrity is an extremely powerful dam of moral containment. When the membrane breaks outside marriage, experience has shown that the physical rupture is perhaps the first symptom of a moral rupture, which from then on widens to social deviation."[159]

Traditional cultural values, according to many legal and medical authorities, reinforced this natural process. Even jurists who, citing Peixoto, criticized traditional values as excessively repressive, agreed that prevailing social attitudes required that the law continue to protect female virginity.[160] According to many officials, families (especially fathers) often threw deflowered daughters onto the street. Since no man would marry a woman who was "already ruined" (já estragada) by a seducer, she had no recourse but the brothel.[161] Thus, whether for natural or cultural reasons, lost virginity converted women from "angels of the home" to independent, liberated, and corrupted beings who caused social depravity and, by spreading venereal disease, even physical degeneration of Brazil's future generations.

Modern Judges, Legal Positivism, and the "Tutelary Function" of Law

It is clear that turn-of-the-century positivist jurists had left their mark on subsequent generations. The positive law doctrine that legislators had ignored when they passed the classically inspired 1890 penal code was solidly integrated into Brazilian jurisprudence by the late 1930s. Moreover, as jurists trained in modern criminology integrated positivist notions into penal law, they unabashedly enhanced their own authority. Even conservative jurists such as Nelson Hungria, who considered himself an opponent of positive law doctrine, proclaimed that judges had a moral and professional obligation to mold the law to specific situations through "adaptive interpretations."[162] Judges should take into account not only changing moral norms and scientific advances but the characteristics of the individuals involved in each case. Criminal law, Hungria insisted, was not simply punitive, but normative; it was up to judges to apply the law in ways that fulfilled its "tutelary function of social discipline."[163] As Judge Aderson Perdigão Nogueira explained in an influential 1937 deflowering sentence: "If the law is inhuman, the judge should interpret it by diminishing the rigid rigor of formulas and understanding it according to social development. The modern judge is no longer . . . a simple machine that registers sentences and follows legal texts blindly."[164]

Some judges' "adaptive interpretations" in cases of sexual crimes countered the letter and the spirit of the classically inspired 1890 penal code. Yet judges and other judicial authorities applied new jurisprudential precedents selectively; depending on the situation, they might also resort to older classical tenets. Thus, although flexible legal principles and modern women led jurists to broaden the legal conception of female honesty, they could choose among a wide range of criteria to defend or condemn specific individuals. In practice, jurists often used their new interpretive powers in ways that reflected traditional social prejudices, such as the prejudice against women of color.

5 Honorable Partnerships:
The Importance of Color in Sex and Marriage

Despite the relevance of racial ideologies in determining status in a society that had abolished slavery only one year before the declaration of the Republic, and despite police and legal medical experts' increasing emphasis on the scientific determination of race as a tool for identifying and classifying individual subjects, the jurists who interpreted and revised republican penal law were remarkably silent on the relevance of race to their determination of criminal responsibility. At the same time, the questions Viveiros de Castro had posed in 1898 about whether slavery, race, and miscegenation had harmed Brazil's collective morality became a central preoccupation for the Republic's major intellectuals—many of whom were law school graduates, if not jurists. Their responses created a climate of increasingly vigorous nationalist and even official celebration of Brazil's supposed "racial democracy."[1]

By the time King Albert and Queen Elisabeth prepared for their visit to Rio de Janeiro in 1920, Brazilian nationalists were already boasting that the absence of "hateful inequality on the basis of race or color" was evidence of their people's moral superiority.[2] The progovernment press denounced rumors that the army and navy were "selecting for color" as "anti-Brazilian" and calumnious, since "the honor of [Brazilian] culture" rested on its unparalleled resolution of racial tensions.[3] Not only were Brazilians "a people who could never harbor savage [racial] prejudices," but there had never been "any sign of discrimination against men of color" by any of the nation's leaders since abolition.[4]

It is reasonable to interpret these proclamations regarding the absence of racism in Brazil as yet another effort by republican officials to hide the heritage of Brazil's slave past behind the modern facade created "for the king to see." Yet, Brazilians' distinctive attitudes about race and specifically about interracial sexual relations have fascinated and confounded observers in and outside Brazil since the early colonial period. Racial ideology in Brazil was perceived as unique by the colonial church as it struggled to convince white men that sexual relations with black and indigenous "single women" were sinful; by nineteenth-century travelers describing a racially based slave society in which a good portion of the population was neither "white" nor "slave"; and by UNESCO officials searching for a model of racial democracy in the hopeful post–World War II era. In the early 1960s, the persistent emphasis on sexual mixing as the key to this uniqueness led anthropologist Marvin Harris to remonstrate against scholars' obsession with "racially prejudiced sexuality."[5] Twenty years later, Barbara Fields seconded Harris's objection, arguing that concern with the physiological results of sexual mixing and miscegenation obscures the ideological construction of race.[6]

Fields's observation is particularly relevant to Brazil in the 1920s and 1930s, when interracial sexual relations and resulting miscegenation formed the foundation of a racialized ideology of national identity. In analyses by a wide range of intellectuals, professionals, and politicians, the miscegenation that had previously been understood as the result of the natural immorality and promiscuity of women of color became instead evidence of a tradition of interracial intimacy, a "soft" form of slavery, and a legacy of racial harmony. The notion that these traditions had precluded the formation of a racist society, although not entirely new, became a consecrated fact in prevailing interpretations of Brazilian history. Racist attitudes, including a vocabulary that sexualized women of color, did not disappear. Rather, to paraphrase Fields, these logically incompatible attitudes happily cohabited.[7]

Brazilians' supposed tolerance, or even predilection, for interracial sexual relations was central to the theory that Brazil was a racial democracy as well as to the theory that the population was "improving" because of the "whitening" effect of miscegenation. These contradictory ideas became pillars of nationalist ideologies of left and right in the 1920s and integral elements of the corporatist authoritarianism that eventually prevailed in state policy in the late 1930s. Although revisionist scholarship beginning in the 1950s discredited the claims of racial democracy by documenting the persistence of racial distinctions, extensive discrimination against Brazilians of color, and widespread racial prejudice—particularly among the urban middle and upper classes—scholars have not systematically explored the ideological influence of the long-held views concerning racial democracy and miscegenation on social practices or attitudes of the nation's lower-class majority. The ways that state ideologies concerning race were or were not put into practice by individual state officials has also received scant attention.

This omission is glaring, since intellectuals and politicians of the 1920s and 1930s based their theories about Brazilian national identity on their observation of this racially mixed social group—generally referred to as the "popular classes" or "popular mass" (*classes populares* or simply *populares*). According to the unofficial government organ *O paiz* in 1920, the *populares* whom Albert and Elisabeth would encounter on the streets of Rio de Janeiro included "*mestiços* of various races that are not ashamed to be so, nor even have any idea that they could be ashamed."[8] Over the following two decades, the popular classes were also a major target audience for Vargas and other populist politicians who invoked Brazil's racial harmony as a crucial element in the nation's homogeneous identity and common political mission. Revisionist intellectuals writing after the 1950s, for their part, tended to assume that the lower classes were less prejudiced and more accepting of interracial unions than more economically privileged Brazilians. For these scholars, the "myth of racial democracy," disseminated from above, had become a powerful ideology that undermined efforts to combat the nation's entrenched racism.[9]

Court records of sexual crimes provide a particularly interesting perspective on popular attitudes about race. On one hand, abundant circumstantial evidence, backed by direct evidence in a few cases, indicates that the victims, accused men, and witnesses who testified in these cases recognized color hierarchies and racial stereotypes and favored color endogamy. On the other hand, the near silence on race in court testimony suggests that deponents shared with nationalist intellectuals and public officials an aversion to explicit manifestations of racial prejudice. Deponents rarely mentioned race or color in testimony, and in the scattered cases in which they did, the significance of a person's color was contingent on factors such as her or his personal qualities, economic status, and insertion into particular social networks. Social contacts and even intimate relationships among people of different colors seemed to diminish the rigidity of color hierarchies in the testimony of working-class deponents.

Although the jurists involved in the same trials and investigations also avoided explicit reference to race and were unable to establish fixed criteria for racial classification, their judgments tended to reinforce racial stereotypes and color hierarchies. More significantly, notwithstanding the absence of racism in Brazilian law, judges, prosecutors, and the police could use their "interpretive power" in judgments of sexual honor in ways that allowed them to espouse, and perhaps even believe in, racial democracy while practicing racial discrimination.

The Ideological Construction of the Brazilian Race

The 1920s and 1930s saw the consolidation of a remarkably homogeneous discourse of race and national identity among Brazilian intellectuals and public officials. As the disadvantages of Brazil's export-led economy, dependent on European markets, became painfully evident and as Europe was attacked as imperialistic, immoral, and barbaric by rebels in some of its colonies and by its own intellectual vanguard, Brazilian intellectuals rejected the inferiority complex that some of their predecessors had projected onto the nation. Earlier veneration of European culture and pessimism about Brazil's racial composition, fueled by the scientific racism best exemplified in Nina Rodrigues's anthropological studies in the final decades of the nineteenth century, gave way to a faith in the eugenic improvement of the newly constructed "Brazilian race" after World War I.[10]

The mainstay of most of this thinking about Brazil's "race problem" in the post–World War I period was that it would be resolved through sexual selection, which would "whiten" the population.[11] The means by which this whitening would occur and the relative value of diverse ethnic groups were subjects of intense debate. Renato Kehl, the father of the Brazilian eugenics movement of the 1920s and 1930s, energetically (but unsuccessfully) lobbied for increased immigration of "Aryan" individuals and campaigned against miscegenation, which he believed resulted in degeneracy, disorder, crime, and vice.[12]

Equally racist Francisco de Oliveira Viana took a different view—and was much more successful in shaping diverse political and intellectual projects.[13] Following his mentor, the jurist and authoritarian nationalist Alberto Torres, Viana believed that the Brazilian population was incapable of self-government and poorly adapted to republican liberal institutions.[14] As Torres had argued, geographical dispersal and political and economic history were partly responsible for these deficiencies, but for Viana, the major problem was the nation's ethnic composition. Although the white man had produced superior, "eugenic" agents of civilization since colonization, the black and Indian "races" formed a "passive and anti-progressive mass" that had slowed the civilizing mission.[15] Notwithstanding this unfortunate racial heritage, however, the situation was not hopeless, for the population was rapidly whitening through natural selection and European immigration.[16] Viana's belief that "inferior races" could improve by "mixing with whites" reproduced the conclusions of another of his mentors, Sílvio Romero, but while Romero believed that whitening would take centuries, Viana argued that the process, already well under way, would accelerate in subsequent decades. This argument was apparently attractive to state officials, for they invited Viana to write the preface to the 1920 national census.[17]

Viana's optimism regarding miscegenation made his analysis more palatable than Kehl's, but his conclusions on the biological limitations of Africans and Indians provoked intense controversy.[18] Manoel Bonfim, a physician and leftist intellectual whose writings had attacked the reigning scientific racism and Eurocentrism since the turn of the century, published the most categorical refutation of Viana's thesis. In O Brasil na América (1929), Bonfim reiterated his earlier argument that theories of racial superiority and inferiority had no basis in science, but served as a powerful pretext for political domination. For Bonfim, cross-racial sexual relations were the key to progressive biological evolution, and the nation's racial and cultural mixture was thus its greatest strength.[19] There was no glory in whiteness, and in any case, Brazil was essentially, inevitably, a mestizo nation. The concerns of "Aryanist sociologists" such as Viana with racial "whitening" were thus both ridiculous and unpatriotic.[20]

Few among Bonfim's contemporaries were so sure that there were no naturally superior or inferior racial groups, and fewer still echoed his call for a radical popular revolution. Yet leading professional and intellectual elites were eager to reject the extremist conclusions of Nina Rodrigues, Renato Kehl, or Oliveira Viana. Anthropologists Artur Ramos and Roquette Pinto; public health specialists such as Levi Carneiro and Belisário Pena; journalists and publishers such as Monteiro Lobato; educators, including proponents of sex education such as José de Albuquerque; and other scientists, some of whom were involved in the eugenics movement organized by Kehl in Rio, studied what they saw as the degeneracy of the population and concluded that "racial improvement" would be achieved not by controlling reproduction, but by reducing endemic diseases and by improving public education. These ideas dovetailed with major trends in juridical scholarship. As we have seen, positivist school jurists had already favored social and cultural explanations over simple racial determinism at the turn of the century, and their ideas inspired the energetic social reformism of the next generation of jurists.[21] Unlike Bonfim, most of these intellectuals and professional elites of the 1920s and 1930s saw no contradiction in their appreciation of Afro-Brazilian contributions to Brazilian culture and their belief that the "Brazilian race" was improving through an evolutionary process of biological and cultural "whitening."

The nationalist desire to celebrate Brazil's diverse racial heritage without destroying existing social and racial hierarchies was satisfied in the work of social theorist Gilberto Freyre beginning in the early 1930s. His *Casa grande e senzala*, published in 1933 (later in English as *The Masters and the Slaves*) was an immediate sensation.[22] Looking to the cultural history of the colonial plantation's extended household for an explanation of the formation of Brazilian society, Freyre reevaluated the contributions of Indians, Africans, and the Portuguese. Although Freyre agreed with Viana that the Portuguese colonists had provided the civilizing impulse, he argued that the other two races had participated actively in their mission, providing labor as well as crucial material and cultural elements. Cultural and biological amalgamation of the three races had made possible the Europeans' adaptation to the new environment, and hence the implantation of civilization in the tropics.[23]

Freyre opposed Viana on another crucial point: slavery and syphilis, not racial inferiority, had resulted in moral degeneracy and indolence that characterized colonial society.[24] Freyre was fascinated by the sexuality of colonial masters and slave, for here, he believed, was the key to the Brazilian character and the nation's organic social and cultural structures. White men's promiscuous sexual domination of obliging black women not only expanded the mulatto population but evolved into culturally institutionalized social and sexual relationships among successive generations of Brazilians.[25]

The political implications of Freyre's historical analysis were optimistic and, ironically, strikingly similar to those of Viana's work. Racial discrimination and discord had been avoided through social and biological evolution, as racial diversity was gradually erased through progressive whitening. The patron-client relations that continued to predominate in national and local politics could be interpreted as authentically Brazilian traditions of intimacy and social harmony that were incompatible with impersonal politics of capitalist liberalism. Personalism and authoritarianism could be cast as humane, if hierarchical, and preferable to the ugly results of individualistic competition and racial hatred Freyre had observed while studying in the United States.[26]

Viana and Freyre were among the most consecrated intellectual figures of their time, and both inspired the nationalist political regimes headed by Getúlio Vargas after 1930. As Viana boasted in 1938, his call for centralized state authority, the subordination of local to national power, corporate social organization, and progressive ethnic and moral homogenization was answered by Vargas's political organization and social policies, particularly under the dictatorial *Estado Novo*; Viana himself, as juridical consultant and cabinet minister, helped to implement these policies.[27] Freyre's more laudatory vision of Brazil's racial roots and social harmony colored state rhetoric, intellectual projects, and cultural policies, even though Freyre opposed the Vargas governments.[28]

Under Vargas, the state encouraged study of Brazil's African and Indian heritage as nationalist folklore while encouraging whitening and repressing ethnic diversity through immigration and educational policies.[29] At the same time, it continued to project the image of Brazil as a socially advanced nation that had solved its "race problem" through miscegenation and had achieved racial democracy, an area where more powerful nations had failed. The editors of the state-sponsored journal *Cultura política* spelled this out in its first issue, in a passage reminiscent of the reports published in *O paiz* on the occasion of the 1920 royal visit:

> One of the most characteristic features of Brazil's democratic nature is the absence of racial prejudice among us. The [Estado Novo], seeking to follow our popular traditions . . . conserved this feature—inseparable from our soul and our tropical culture. . . . Brazilian nationalism does not nourish racial prejudice; if it did, it would not be Brazilian. Our racial melting pot has been, perhaps, our greatest human experience.[30]

In a similar vein, 1940 Census Bureau officials bragged that they "remained faithful to the most honorable tradition of modern Brazilian civilization, that of racial equality," and resisted the "racist aberrations" that were "spreading throughout the world."[31]

This claim was ironic, given the anti-Semitic and racist xenophobia that was especially evident in *Estado Novo* rhetoric and immigration policies.[32] Yet according to historian George Reid Andrews, the nationalist language of racial homogeneity, including some of its xenophobic manifestations, was attractive to many who identified themselves as black Brazilians. Some of the most prominent black social and political movements in São Paulo, for example, promoted the idea that Brazil was a racial democracy, blaming immigrants for persistent racial discrimination.[33]

Studies hailing Brazil's racial democracy, often citing Freyre's thesis of relatively humane relations under slavery, multiplied in the immediate post–World War II period, with Brazil's return to political democracy. Many of these studies were carried out by U.S. scholars eager to learn from Brazil's apparent success.[34] In the 1950s, at the request of Artur Ramos, UNESCO sponsored a group of Brazilian and foreign scholars in a project to study race relations in hopes of discovering solutions to ethnic discord erupting elsewhere in the world. Unfortunately for Brazil's international image, these studies found both evidence of racial prejudice among white middle-class Brazilians and severe disparities in income, employment, education, and housing between whites and people of color.[35]

A wave of revisionist scholarship followed, attacking the thesis of racial democracy as a false ideology that undermined struggles against racism. Sociologists such as Roger Bastide and Luis Costa Pinto took a new look at interracial sexual relations, concluding that these relations remained an expression of white male dominance that subjugated and humiliated women of color. Observing that most interracial sexual relations occurred outside formal marriage, Bastide argued that these relations "effectively reduce[d] a whole race to the level of prostitutes."[36] His and other studies concluded that middle- and upper-class white men saw black and especially mulatto women as sensual and easily accessible, in contrast to the chaste white women they would marry.[37] Revisionist scholars produced surprisingly little data on working-class views and practices, but many assumed working-class Brazilians were less prejudiced and more likely to accept interracial mixing and even marriage. Revisionists also tended to imply that members of Brazil's racially mixed popular mass were deceived by the myth of racial democracy disseminated from above.[38]

More recent research on racial attitudes among lower-class Brazilians suggests an alternative explanation for the persistence of the myth of racial democracy, one that might help explain why Brazilians of color were drawn to Vargas's rhetoric of national harmony. In separate local studies, set a century apart and in different regions of Rio de Janeiro state, anthropologists Robin Sheriff and Peter Fry and historian Hebe Castro reach a similar conclusion: Brazil's racial democracy was not simply a myth disseminated from above, but also an ideal shared by some members of the racially mixed lower classes.[39] Residents of an urban slum in Rio de Janeiro in the early 1990s consistently repudiated racist attitudes, explaining to Sheriff, often with ironic humor, that there are no "pure" races in Brazil. Racism, in the words of one informant, was therefore "a foolish prejudice" that "makes no sense."[40] As Sheriff concludes, this discourse inverts Gilberto Freyre's thesis, invoking racial mixture "not to argue that Brazilians are not or can not be racist, but to assert that this *mestiçagem* is precisely the reason why they *should* not be racist."[41] Peter Fry, citing these attitudes along with other evidence of everyday social practice in the 1990s, likewise rejects the thesis that the reality of racism proves that the ideal of racial democracy is an illusion. He insists, instead, that the two coexist in Rio de Janeiro, and that it is not always possible to predict which will prevail at any given moment.[42]

Hebe Castro's research on Campos, a rural county of Rio de Janeiro, suggests that an ideal of racial equality emerged among poor Brazilians alongside attempts by elites to reinforce racial hierarchies after abolition in 1888. Poor Brazilians of color did not convert a shared history of slavery into a "black" identity. Instead, they drew upon a long history of freedom that, even before abolition, had been constructed as "essentially nonracial." Castro does not argue that persistent racial discrimination went unnoticed by its victims, but that they continued to insist that it was not legitimate. Elite racial ideology during the First Republic, Castro argues, inverted the significance that former slaves gave to liberal discourses of equality and freedom by casting the bulk of the Brazilian population as an undifferentiated mass marked by racial inferiority and a history of enslavement.[43]

If Castro's hypothesis could be extended to urban Rio de Janeiro in the twentieth century, the popularity of Gilberto Freyre's theory of Brazil's racial harmony in the 1930s could be explained in part by its articulation with the historical demands by Brazilians of color for freedom from the mark of slavery. The racial ideals as well as the persistent racism described by Sheriff and Fry for contemporary Rio de Janeiro thus might have developed through social and intellectual interaction rather than a one-way dissemination of elite ideology. It is clear, as Castro points out, that the theory of racial democracy reached mythical proportions after World War I, when intellectuals and politicians replaced older strategies of exclusion with new ways of including what they perceived as a racially mixed popular mass in their conception of the national body. Could these thinkers have been influenced by an ideal that also circulated among this popular mass in the city of Rio de Janeiro? A related question is how the discourse of racial democracy coexisted with racist practices. For example, how could state institutions or individual state officials simultaneously disseminate the myth of racial democracy and practice discrimination? Were, as Emília Viotti da Costa suggests, blacks and whites of all social classes blind to racial discrimination?[44] Finally, how might popular attitudes toward interracial sexual relations have influenced, reflected, or challenged racial and national ideologies that emphasized Brazil's unique biological mixing?

Analysis of the significance of race in the sexual conflicts that resulted in police investigations and trials in the 1920s and 1930s provides an especially interesting perspective from which to address these questions. As we have seen, nearly all of the cases involved working-class victims and defendants, most of whom had been romantically involved with each other before the girl's loss of virginity prompted her parents to take her suitor to court, often with the hope that the authorities would pressure or force him to marry her. We can therefore assume that in most, though not all of these cases, the young woman's family considered the accused young man an appropriate, or at least conceivable, marriage partner for her, whereas the man might not have felt the same way about his accuser. The stories of courtship recounted in testimony of defendants, victims, and witnesses in these cases provide evidence of various ways that race or color could influence these attitudes about appropriate sexual and marriage partnerships. At the same time, the intervention of state prosecutors and judges in these relationships demonstrates the complex relationship between racial ideologies and discriminatory practices of individual juridical officials, specifically in cases of interracial courtship.

Color Classification in Records of Sexual Crime

A color label was almost always attributed to offended women in cases of sexual crime (by legal-medical specialists in the obligatory gynecological examination), but less systematically for defendants and almost never for witnesses. According to Hebe Castro, color, which had been systematically recorded in official documents in the early nineteenth century, disappeared from these documents by the 1890s.[45] In the Federal District, this was reversed again in the 1930s, when attempts to improve the police's ability to identify individuals included systematic recording of color for suspects and, later, even witnesses.[46] This explains why, of the court cases consulted, 80 percent of those from 1930 to 1941 but only 55 percent of those from 1918 to 1929 recorded the color of the defendant. Color was recorded as black, white, or *parda*, a color category considered to be between black and white.[47] Other groups, such as Asians, did not fit into the official color scheme and were given a racial identity corresponding to national origin, as in the case of a Chinese defendant in the sample. Most of the defendants and offended women were classified as Brazilian (83 percent and 94 percent of the total sample, respectively), with Portuguese a distant second (13 percent and 5 percent) and were given a color classification separate from their nationality.

The *parda* category included a variety of "types" recognized by Brazilians as mixtures of people of African, indigenous, and European descent who were not considered by officials to be white or black. The most commonly used but nonofficial categories found in the documents were *mulata* or *mulato*, *morena* or *moreno*, and *mestiça* or *mestiço*. Even legal-medical specialists, despite their training in juridical terminology, sometimes slipped and recorded *morena*, *mulata*, or *mestiça* for a patient's color.[48] It is not possible to define any of these categories with precision, since they were always subjectively determined, but a *mulato* was generally considered to have a greater number of African features and darker skin than a *moreno*. A person who was partially of indigenous descent was more likely to be called *mestiço*, although this category could also include those identified as having various mixtures of African, European, and Indian descent.

Color is a complex datum for other reasons as well. First, the three official categories do not reflect the variety of color-related terms used by Brazilians. Furthermore, determination of color usually depended on the perception of different juridical or medical officials, and did not necessarily reflect self- or peer perceptions. There were several cases in which the same person was assigned a different color by official documents and witnesses. The young woman's parents, for example, often classified her in a lighter category than legal-medical examiners. The young women's birth certificates, which usually recorded the color stated by parents, also frequently recorded a lighter color than the deflowering examinations, in which legal-medical experts were expected to use their ethnological training to determine color.[49] In one particularly complex case, Elvira Ferreira, who was called *preta* by legal-medical examiners, stated that her alleged rapist/deflowerer, who was Chinese, had referred to her as *negra*. Ferreira insisted that her assailant had impregnated her, and assured the police that when the child was born, "they would see that she was not lying." After the birth of the child, while the investigation was still underway, a neighbor testified that "the child is not black [*preta*] like the offended woman, but light-skinned [*de cor clara*]" and had "Chinese features." Ferreira's father insisted that "the child born to his daughter is white, whereas his daughter is *parda*."[50]

The complexity of color could create problems for a legal system bent on establishing fixed scientific criteria for identifying individuals. In a 1933 case, Ilka Fernandes was classified as *parda* in her deflowering examination and white in a separate medical examination done to determine her age.[51] The medical documents were prepared by Dr. Raul Santiago Bergalo, who worked with a different partner in each of the two examinations. The defense lawyer, Medeiros Jansen, argued that two different girls must have been examined and the medical evidence was therefore inadmissible.

The case demonstrates both that color or race was a subjectively determined trait and that scientific training was supposed to identify objective racial categories. Jansen, the lawyer, admitted the possibility that divergent assessments of a person's color could be simply "a question of differing points of view." He was aware that this hypothesis would provide a reasonable explanation for the discrepancies in the girl's medical documents, and that his defense therefore rested on shaky ground, for he spent considerable energy disproving the hypothesis. First, he questioned whether the same person could be legally classified into two different color groups. He then pointed out that one of the doctors was present at both examinations. Finally, and most emphatically, he insisted that "two doctors, of recognized competence, specialists in legal-medicine" could not possibly "mistake" a person's color. Significantly, he conceded that "if the records had been signed by laymen, it could be said that it was an error of appraisal."

The presiding judge requested clarification and new examinations from the same legal-medical teams. The doctors explained their confusion as follows in a new deflowering examination done on June 26, 1934:

> The offended minor represents a type of *mestiçagem* [racial mixture], already very diluted, and approximates the white race. Thus, her complexion is light, her hair black and curly, lips relatively fine and nose approximating the Aryan type, while her mother represents a type of *mestiçagem*, evidenced as much by her pigmentation as by her features and hair. According to [the daughter's] certificate of age, her father is Portuguese. In that certificate, she is identified as *morena*. These data, which demonstrate that the ethnological classification of the patient can provoke much doubt, explain the divergence in her identification in the two documents.

Still unsatisfied, Jansen demanded a new age examination as well. Performed on September 19, 1934, this examination identified the young woman as "of light *parda* color, accompanied by her mother who is frankly *parda*." Witnesses, however, responding to the defense lawyer's questions, identified the young woman as *branquinha*. The diminutive *inho/a* was often used to soften the edges of sharp race categories, used most commonly with the terms for "black," thus *preto* became *pretinho* and *negro* became *neginho;* both were often terms of endearment. *Branquinha* may have implied "a (cute) white girl" or "a whitish girl."

Despite problems like these in establishing objective criteria for the ethnological classification of individuals, or perhaps because of them, comparison of individual victims and defendants by their official color grouping reveals interesting similarities and differences among the three groups. To maximize consistency (though only relatively, since, as we have seen, officials were not always successful in their attempts to create a consistent classification system) and because color is mentioned infre-

Table 1   Color of Offended Women and Accused Men

Color	Offended Women		Accused Men		1940 Census (Percent)	
	Number	Percent	Number	Percent	Women	Men
White	181	42	165	54	69	73
Parda/o	167	38	89	29	18	17
Black	86	20	49	16	13	10
Total	434	100	303	99	100	100

Sources: Arquivo Nacional, 450 criminal cases consulted; Recenseamento Geral do Brasil (1 de setembro de 1940), part 16, Distrito Federal (Rio de Janeiro: Instituto Brasileiro de Geografia e Estatística, 1951).

Note: Excludes 16 cases with color of offended woman unknown; 147 cases with color of accused man unknown. Percentages in all tables are rounded to nearest whole numbers.

quently in testimony, the classification in medical examinations is used below to group the offended women. For the accused men, the racial classification corresponds to that recorded by police. The aggregate numbers in each category are shown in table 1, along with the proportions of each color category by gender in the 1940 census data for the Federal District as a whole.

In the absence of data on Rio de Janeiro's racial composition until the final year of the period (1940), it is difficult to determine the extent to which the color groupings of the individuals in the selected criminal records reflect those of the general population. Table 1 shows a higher proportion of individuals in the parda and black categories in the deflowering data than in the 1940 census of the Federal District—58 percent of the women and 45 percent of the men in the criminal records, compared to 31 and 27 percent in the census. This probably reflects the predominance of people considered to be black or pardo in the lower socioeconomic groups who tended to bring sexual conflicts to the police. However, Census Bureau officials cautioned that the 1940 racial data showed inflated numbers of whites; since clear racial lines did not exist, Brazilians tended to categorize themselves as lighter than "objective criteria" would warrant.[52] As was clear in the case of Ilka Fernandes, police and legal-medical officials were expected to rely on objective criteria, not subjects' declarations, to determine the "ethnological classification" recorded in judicial documents.

Although most defendants and victims were working-class, and few were either professionals or indigents, there were proportional differences among the types of jobs individuals in each color group held. The per-

Table 2   Occupations of Offended Women by Color

	White		Parda	
	Number	Percent	Number	Percent
Doméstica[a]	86	48	63	38
Domestic servant	45	25	72	43
Factory worker	19	10	13	8
Seamstress	12	7	8	5
Employed in commerce	6	3	1	1
Other	11	6	5	3
Unknown	2	1	5	3
Total	181	100	167	101

Source: Arquivo Nacional, 450 criminal cases consulted.

Note: Excludes 16 cases with color of offended woman unknown.

[a] *Doméstica* was given as the woman's occupation when she did not work outside the home,

sistence of economic disparities by race after the abolition of slavery was one of the major points of consensus among revisionist scholars who contested the ideas of Freyre's generation. It is not surprising, then, that those classified as white in the criminal records generally held the highest-status positions (see tables 2 and 3).

In all but two cases, the police certified that the victim's families were "impoverished" (*miserável*), which made the state responsible for prosecuting their cases.[53] Seventy-six percent of the young women's occupations were classified as "domestic." In 25 percent of the cases of women classified as white, this meant that they were employed as domestic servants, compared to 42 percent in the *parda* and 52 percent in the black groups. This differentiation is consistent with the color composition of domestic servants in the city as a whole.[54]

It is more difficult to compare the more varied occupations of the defendants, although a few trends are clear. First, regardless of color, most of these men apparently held good, steady jobs, which was likely to have made them attractive marriage candidates in the eyes of the deflowering victims or their parents. Some of the men in the sales/services/technical grouping might be classified as lower middle class or even middle class. There are only a few cases in which the socioeconomic positions of defendant and victim diverge sharply, however, and those are all cases of male employers or their sons and female servants. In most cases, the man seemed to be of an equal or slightly higher social position than the victim.

The correlation between ascribed color and occupation among the defendants and victims illustrates the kind of discrimination that appeared

Black		Total	
Number	Percent	Number	Percent
21	24	170	39
45	52	162	37
10	12	42	10
5	6	25	6
0	0	7	2
4	5	20	5
1	1	8	2
86	100	434	101

but it could also mean that she worked as a domestic servant or laundress or performed other remunerated activities. In this table, the category includes women who were apparently not employed.

in census data and was denounced by social scientists some decades later.[55] Men considered black were much more likely to be employed as laborers than those in the *pardo* or white categories; those considered white were more likely to hold white-collar or technical positions. Among those "employed in commerce," usually as salespeople or clerks, there were only eight considered *pardos* and one black, as compared to thirty-seven white men and women. The few liberal professionals, including a dentist, a journalist, an Air Force lieutenant, and two medical students, were classified as white, as were nine of the eleven small businessmen; the six domestic servants were in the black or *pardo* categories.

For a later period, Nelson do Valle Silva has demonstrated that as a general trend, individuals of color were not able to overcome discrimination, even if they could obtain higher levels of skills or education.[56] In any case, it was generally difficult for them to obtain these skills. Among the defendants and victims in the records consulted, whites were more likely to be literate than *pardos* or blacks (see tables 4 and 5). The differences in literacy rates were similar to those reported for the city's population in the 1940 census, although the rates for black women and men were slightly higher in the deflowering cases than in the census, while those for white women were slightly lower. This probably reflects the absence of both the extremely poor (most of whom would be black and illiterate) and wealthy women (most of whom white and literate) among the individuals who appear in these criminal records.

Like the occupations and literacy rates, the composition of the victims' families varied by color, but only slightly. Across the three color

Table 3 Occupations of Accused Men by Color

	White		Pardo	
	Number	Percent	Number	Percent
Small-business owner/ professional/student[a]	16	10	2	2
Sales/services/technical[b]	66	40	18	20
Trades[c]	13	8	11	12
Skilled or unskilled labor[d]	42	25	41	46
Enlisted military	17	10	10	11
Other[e]	11	7	7	8
Total	165	100	89	99

Source: Arquivo Nacional, 450 criminal cases consulted. Percentages are rounded to nearest whole number.

Note: Excludes 147 cases with color of accused man unknown.

[a] Includes: 5 shopkeepers; 3 medical students; 2 bakery owners; 2 small factory owners; butcher shop owner; naval academy student; student; dentist; fish-stand owner; air force lieutenant.

[b] Includes: 41 men "employed in commerce"; 13 chauffeurs; 5 barbers; 4 butchers; 2 typographers; 2 street vendors; typesetter; newspaper vendor; bank clerk; electric company comptroller; advertising agent; mailman; laboratory technician; nightclub cashier; document expediter; electrical technician; private secretary; scribe; railway company employee; publishing house employee; court official; radio operator; telegraph operator; courier; stockroom supervisor.

groups, the victims' mothers appeared more frequently than their fathers in these cases. Most of these mothers were not legally married and probably headed their households. The proportion of victims represented by mothers was five percentage points lower among the white young women than among the *parda* or black groups.[57] In cases of orphans or girls who had left their parents to work in the city, most were accompanied in the police stations by other family members or fictive kin; again, there was only slight variation among the three color groups, with the black group more likely to be orphaned.[58]

Further evidence of shared family experiences among the deflowering victims across the three color groups arose in testimony that revealed common standards of moral behavior, concern for a young woman's virtue and special vigilance over virgins, regardless of the young women's color classification. For example, a widely accepted custom among all three groups allowed adolescent girls to talk to boys at the gate of their or their employers' homes or apartment buildings. There were cases, however, of parents of both black and white young women who did not allow this kind of courting. More frequently, parents of domestic servants of all colors

Black		Total	
Number	Percent	Number	Percent
0	0	18	6
2	4	86	28
4	8	28	9
37	76	120	40
6	12	33	11
0	0	18	6
49	100	303	100

c Includes: 6 electricians; 5 mechanics; 5 shoemakers; 4 carpenters; 3 tailors; 2 cabinet makers; 2 plumbers; marble layer.

d Includes: 41 factory workers; 18 masons; 12 manual laborers; 6 domestic servants; 6 painters; 6 rural laborers; 4 train conductors; 4 dock workers; 3 cooks; 3 railway workers; 3 mason's assistants; 2 doormen; 2 bakers; truck driver's assistant; chauffeur's assistant; coach driver's assistant; chef's assistant; nurse's assistant; workshop assistant; fireman; warehouse worker; security guard; car washer.

e Includes: 8 unknown; 3 public functionaries; 2 soccer players; maritime institution assistant; farmer; cyclist; fisherman; pharmaceutical apprentice.

insisted that a young woman's employer not allow her to leave the house unaccompanied except to go home on her fortnightly Sunday off.[59] Finally, there are indications dispersed through the testimony of common leisure activities—white girls participating in Carnival; black girls going to "dancings" where they danced the tango and the waltz; young people of all colors having romantic and sexual encounters in the same public places.

Racial Ideologies in Love's Embrace

Although there is no evidence that moral values and leisure activities varied according to the color of the people involved in deflowering cases, perceptions of color difference did seem to affect young people's choice of romantic or sexual partners. In table 6, the color ascribed to the offended women is cross-tabulated with that attributed to the defendants in the 295 cases in which color is recorded for both parties. In 60 percent of the cases, the offended woman and the defendant were classified in the same color category. Most strikingly, 82 percent of the white women accused white men of deflowering them. Most (97, or 82 percent) of the cases in

Table 4   Offended Women's Literacy by Color and Compared to Women's
Literacy in 1920 and 1940 Federal District Censuses

	White			Parda		
	No.	Percent	1940 Census percent	No.	Percent	1940 Census percent
Literate	123	68	81	104	62	64
Illiterate	55	30	18	62	37	34
Unknown	3	2	1	1	1	2
Total	181	100	100	167	100	100

Sources: Arquivo Nacional, 450 criminal cases consulted; *Recenseamento Geral do Brasil (1 de
setembro de 1940),* part 16, *Distrito Federal* (Rio de Janeiro: Instituto Brasileiro de Geografia e
Estatística, 1951); *Recenseamento do Brasil realizado em 1 de setembro de 1920. População do
Rio de Janeiro (Districto Federal),* vol. 2 (Rio de Janeiro: Impresa Nacional, 1923), cv–cviii.

which the accused man's color differed from the young woman's involved
one *pardo* partner. There were only three cases involving a black man and
a white woman.

   In contrast to the insistence of many intellectuals of the period that
widespread racial mixing was a Brazilian characteristic, color endogamy
for the general Brazilian population was probably even higher than that of
the "couples" that appear in records of sexual crime. There is no consistent data on interracial unions in Brazil or in Rio before the 1970s. By
examining older age cohorts in studies of censuses and domestic surveys
since then, sociologists and demographers have concluded that color endogamy, which characterized more than 80 percent of marriages in 1980
and increased with educational level, had been even higher in earlier
decades.[60]

   Jurists frequently warned that many young women "used" the courts
to achieve an advantageous marriage through a deflowering trial. There are
several cases in which the defendant seems to be of a higher social status
than the victim—and social status was related to color category. There is
little evidence, however, that young women or their families systematically attempted to use the court as a means of whitening their stock.
Although 67 percent of the mixed-color cases involved men whose color
classification was lighter than his accuser's, the total number of mixed-
color cases was small, and a sizable minority (33 percent) of women
brought claims against darker men. Judging from evidence in testimony,
moreover, it is likely that a commonly cited attitude among white men
that black and mulatto women were good for sex but not marriage would

	Black			Total		
No.	Percent	1940 Census percent	No.	Percent	1940 Census percent	1920 Census percent
44	51	44	271	62	73	56
41	48	54	158	36	25	44
1	1	2	5	1	2	—
86	100	100	434	99	100	100

Note: Numbers are rounded to nearest whole number. Excludes 16 cases with color of offended woman unknown. The 1920 census did not provide data for color.

make men more inclined to seduce, and more reluctant to marry, darker women. This probably helps to explain why their relationships with darker women would end up at police stations more frequently than others.

For Brazil as a whole, across socioeconomic groups and throughout the twentieth century, men have been more likely to marry lighter than darker women. Carl Degler, reviewing various studies on interracial marriage rates, believed that the explanation for this phenomenon was self-evident: "Of course," he observed in a parenthesis, "since both partners cannot be satisfied [in their desire to marry someone whiter than themselves], men more often marry lighter than women."[61] The assumption is that men, rather than women, choose partners. According to Oracy Nogueira, this is true because individual men of color have had much greater opportunity for upward mobility than women of color. As professionals, if they marry within their elevated socioeconomic group or even slightly below it, their choices are largely limited to white women.[62] Either way, it would be men of color, rather than women of color, for whom social mobility was feasible and who "married up" to whiter social status. Muriel Nazzari, in a study of colonial São Paulo, finds that men, regardless of color, almost never "married down," economically or racially, although they did maintain various sorts of relationships and partnerships with women of lower economic or racial status.[63] Nazzari believes that this was an economic strategy common to the colonial São Paulo elite that persisted as a social pattern after the nineteenth century.

Unfortunately, demographic studies of racial selection in marriages

Table 5   Accused Men's Literacy by Color and Compared to Men's Literacy
in 1920 and 1940 Federal District Censuses

	White			Pardo		
	No.	Percent	1940 Census percent	No.	Percent	1940 Census percent
Literate	142	86	86	67	75	76
Illiterate	20	12	13	20	22	22
Unknown	3	2	1	2	2	2
Total	165	100	100	89	99	100

Sources: Arquivo Nacional, 450 criminal cases consulted; *Recenseamento Geral do Brasil (1 de setembro de 1940)*, part 16, *Distrito Federal* (Rio de Janeiro: Instituto Brasileiro de Geografia e Estatística, 1951); *Recenseamento do Brasil realizado em 1 de setembro de 1920. População do Rio de Janeiro (Districto Federal)*, vol. 2 (Rio de Janeiro: Impresa Nacional, 1923), cv–cviii.

do not distinguish among types of marriage (legal or consensual) and there are no clear data on sexual relations outside marriage. The preference by white men for women of color as sexual partners, but not marriage partners, however, was commonly acknowledged not only by contemporaries of Gilberto Freyre in the 1920s and 1930s but also by the subsequent generation of social scientists who contested Freyre's theories. Sociologist Luís Costa Pinto, for example, whose 1950 study concluded that middle-class whites in Rio de Janeiro held a strong aversion to interracial marriage, repeated Freyre's assertion that Brazilian men prized the *mulata* for her "special sexual prowess." While Freyre used "Brazilian men" as a generic term, Pinto specified that mulatto women were preferred sexual partners, but not marriage partners, for white middle-class men.[64] Since white middle-class women were expected to remain virgins until marriage, according to Pinto, they did not engage in interracial sexual relations.

Surprisingly, given the fervor of intellectual debates on miscegenation and abundant evidence that color was a significant factor in courtship and marriage, people involved in deflowering disputes rarely mentioned race or color at all. Most surprisingly, none of the defendants mentioned the woman's color or race as a reason for resisting marriage to her.

The stereotype of the *mulata* as a particularly sensual and easily obtainable sexual partner, and of the black woman as suited for labor or prostitution, did emerge in the documents, though not in ways that corresponded exactly to the presumptions of contemporary social scientists. The aphorism "white women are for marrying, *mulatas* for fornicating, black women for work," recorded by Freyre in the early 1930s and repeated

Black			Total			
No.	Percent	1940 Census percent	No.	Percent	1940 Census percent	1920 Census percent
33	67	59	242	80	81	66
15	31	39	55	18	17	33
1	2	2	6	2	2	—
49	100	100	303	100	100	99

Note: Numbers are rounded to nearest whole number. Excludes 147 cases with color of accused man unknown. The 1920 census did not provide data for color.

in the revisionist literature as a popular saying, was related to a widespread belief that white men and boys commonly had sexual relations with their domestic servants, who were usually mulatto or black and thought to be generally acquiescent or easily seduced.[65] Another related presumption was that most prostitutes were once domestic servants, often forced into prostitution after being deflowered by their employer.

There is some evidence in court records of common recognition that black and *parda* domestic servants were particularly susceptible to sexual insults—and that this kind of racism was offensive. There is one explicit example in the above-cited case of Elvira Ferreira, a sixteen-year-old domestic servant classified as black (*preta*) by legal-medical examiners and by one of her witnesses. When Ferreira accused her Chinese employer of raping her, she said that when his wife discovered what had happened, the employer replied "that it was not important because [the maid] was black [*negra*] and with money he would settle things with her father."[66] Whether or not the employer actually made this statement, Ferreira's accusation implies that this attitude was both familiar and reprehensible. The defense lawyer also recognized that the racist statement Ferreira attributed to his client was abhorrent, so much so that Ferreira's muted response to it would in itself demonstrate her lack of honor: "Elvira, hearing these words from the accused and not protesting the profound insult and his attitude toward her race, demonstrated that she was stripped of any trace of emotion and self-respect, inherent in any individual, whether cultured or not."[67]

The case of Elvira Ferreira is significant in its singularity. Perhaps as a

Table 6   Color of Offended Women by Color of Accused Men

Accused Men's Color	Offended Women's Color						Total
	White		Parda		Black		
	Number	Percent	Number	Percent	Number	Percent	Number
White	95	82	47	40	19	31	161
Pardo	18	16	53	45	14	23	85
Black	3	3	18	15	28	46	49
Total	116	101	118	100	61	100	295

Source: Arquivo Nacional, 450 criminal cases consulted.
Note: Excludes 155 cases with color for either or both parties unknown.

result of a common tendency to avoid explicit expressions of racist attitudes, evidence of the specific sexual vulnerability of black or *parda* domestic servants is difficult to discern in court records. Not only did deponents seldom discuss the issue of race, but few domestic servants brought employers to court. Of the 450 cases consulted, male employers or their sons were accused in only 19, and only 5 fit the model of a white employer victimizing a black or *parda* employee.

The scarcity of cases of sexual abuse by employers in the records has a few probable explanations. First, it is possible that black women's complaints of abuse by white employers were simply not recorded by police, as Boris Fausto believes occurred in São Paulo during the period he studied (1880–1924).[68] Maids also may not have gone to the police to complain of abuse by an employer because they thought they would not stand a chance—which was probably true. We might recall that in 1898, Viveiros de Castro instructed judges to discount domestic servants' accusations of employers in deflowering cases.[69] His observations point to a contradiction between legal theory and practice that persisted in subsequent generations. "In a democratic society such as ours," he insisted, "I do not consider color or class inequality to be a serious obstacle to marriage."[70] Nonetheless, he argued that it would be ludicrous for a domestic servant to believe the promise of marriage by an employer "of elevated social position," and only the prospect of marriage could convince an honest woman to give up her virginity.[71] Since social position was determined by color as well as wealth—and most domestic servants in Rio de Janeiro were women of color—his observations revealed that the absence of class and racial distinctions in Brazil's democracy represented a theoretical ideal, not a social reality. In a 1931 case, a police delegate recognized this reality explicitly when he argued that the white medical student accused of deflowering his family's servant "would never have courted a *parda* maid."[72] Although in the 1930s jurists began to accept new conceptions of seduction that did not necessarily involve a marriage promise, the long-standing precedent against prosecuting employers of domestic servants was rarely challenged before the 1940s.[73] In the records consulted, none of the nineteen employers accused of sexual crimes against their employees was convicted.[74]

Given the dim prospects for an advantageous outcome for the victim in court cases of this type, it is possible that the families of many domestic servants negotiated with employers for out-of-court settlements, as was implied by the comment that Elvira Ferreira attributed to her employer. More direct evidence of this kind of negotiation appeared in a 1923 case involving the deflowering of fourteen-year-old white Maria Almeida. Maria, who worked in the home of appeals court justice Francisco Rego de Oliveira Guedes, became pregnant and told her mother that the justice's nineteen-year-old son Fritz was responsible. Maria's mother, Esmeralda Almeida, immediately appealed to Fritz's family for a private solution to the problem. Esmeralda later told the police that Fritz's father "refused to straighten things out, and told her that if she thought Fritz was guilty, then she should take her complaint to the police." Fritz, for his part, did seek to straighten things out, working with police to bring in a horde of witnesses acquainted with Maria to testify that she was "loose" and had been deflowered by someone else. The prosecutor assigned to the case produced an uncommonly loquacious statement, detailing evidence of Maria's dishonesty and concluding that her mother's complaint was an attempt to exploit "one of the city's most distinguished" families. Not surprisingly, the judge did not indict Fritz, but ordered the case closed.[75]

Although the drama in the Guedes household represents what was commonly considered a typical scenario, it is unique among the court documents examined. Most deflowering cases do not illustrate the dynamics of sexual relations between employers and employees. They demonstrate, instead, that a great many domestic servants, most of whom were classified as black or *parda*, did not routinely engage in such relations, even though they might face both employers' advances and the suspicions of their peers. In 1934, for example, Aurora de Jesus, a fifteen-year-old *parda* domestic servant, ran away from the family that employed her because of the father's sexual advances. Three years later, when she explained to police that she had allowed her boyfriend, a twenty-five-year-old *pardo* soldier, to deflower her, it was clear that the incident with the employer had left its mark. Perhaps her boyfriend had insinuated that the abusive employer had deflowered her, or perhaps she was still trauma-

168

tized and defensive about the incident. In any case, she brought it up in her accusation, insisting that she had gotten away from the employer "without his having abused her honesty."[76]

Although deflowering cases provide some evidence that the homes of "honest families" may well have been dangerous territory for working-class young women, they also show that many black or *parda* domestic servants such as Aurora de Jesus made their own choices about their sexuality, generally choosing men of their own color and class for sexual relationships. As for the idea that employers frequently forced their domestic servants into prostitution because of their deflowering, a survey taken of prostitutes registered with police in Rio de Janeiro in the 1950s—the majority of whom were classified as black or *parda*—confirmed that a large number had indeed formerly worked as domestic servants, but none reported having been deflowered by employers. Rather, they stated that boyfriends, acquaintances, or fiancés had deflowered them.[77]

Although the data on the racial dynamics of sexual relationships between domestic servants and their employers are sparse, there is scattered evidence in court testimony throughout the period that images of the sensual *mulata* and prostituted black woman, fit for sexual relations but not marriage, were recognized by at least some men in a variety of circumstances. In a 1938 case, for example, in which both complainant and defendant were *parda*, a witness testified that the defendant "must not have been Edneia's deflowerer, because she had other boyfriends, including a white young man who couldn't marry her."[78] Jaime de Souza, a white construction worker, denied having courted the woman who accused him of deflowering her, explaining that he had always considered her an "ugly black."[79] In a few other cases, the defense drew upon negative images of *mulata* and black women in attempts to portray the offended women as dishonest. One of the witnesses Fritz Guedes rounded up in 1923 accused Maria Almeida of hanging out with "a black woman, Argentina, who had a bad reputation"; in a case that began in 1918, the white defendant, a salesclerk, testified that his accuser, a *parda* domestic servant, "kept company with a black woman who led a dishonest life."[80] José Soares Gonçalves, a *pardo* fireman, went further, claiming that he had identified his accuser as a prostitute in the street: "taking a walk through the garden of the Passeio Público, he encountered a *mulatinha* [little mulatto girl] who was walking alone in the same garden" and "in view of the actions of the *mulatinha* [these included smoking a cigarette and mentioning her lack of money] he was convinced that she was a prostitute."[81] Finally, Virgílio Pereira met "a *parda* girl" seated in front of him on a train from São Paulo to Rio de Janeiro, whom he believed was not a virgin because she was traveling alone, dressed extravagantly, conversed with first a "fat mulatto" and then with a soldier, both of whom got off at an earlier stop, and because she accepted "without hesitation" the defendant's invitation to sleep with him in a hotel in Rio. The same woman, classified as *parda* by legal-medical examiners, was described as black (*preta*) in testimony of three male defense witnesses, all of whom were certain that she was a prostitute because of her extravagant clothing and makeup and the fact that she went out after midnight with various men.[82]

What is evident in these examples is that the association between dark skin and moral laxity was not immediate, but had to be qualified. This is related to the absence of discussion of race in testimony as a whole. The word "race," in fact, was not ever mentioned. As is clear in the above examples, color was mentioned as a descriptive device, used when the speaker referred to the first encounter with someone with whom she or he was not acquainted. This does not mean that color was neutral. To the contrary, color descriptions were usually associated with particular moral or social characteristics and vice versa. A woman's behavior, attire, or multiple boyfriends or seatmates, and a man's social standing or employment, combined with color to define social position and moral character.

These factors could be cited as the basis of elders' opposition to a young woman's suitor. Parents never admitted that they opposed their daughters' suitors because of race or color difference, but a few of the deflowered daughters claimed that this was the case. For example, in 1939, when seventeen-year-old, white, literate Izalinda de Lourdes Carames began a romance with twenty-six-year-old, literate Lupércio de Oliveira Cahe, her father and her grandmother objected to the match because Lupércio "was of mixed [*mestiça*] color and without a steady job" (according to Izalinda's testimony). The grandmother's testimony omitted the reference to Lupércio's color, emphasizing only that he "did not have [a professional] position [*estava sem colocação*]."[83] Lupércio's work booklet (*carteira profissional*), which police found in the possession of his former employer and annexed to the case, confirmed his professional instability: he had held six different jobs in five years, all of which were unskilled and low-paid, and he had apparently lasted no longer than ten months in any of them. From his photograph it is possible to detect features that might be identified as mestizo or mulatto, confirming the descriptions by Izalinda and by two different witnesses (Izalinda's neighbor and Lupércio's former employer). On the same page as the photograph, however, the work booklet described him as white.

Despite the opposition to Lupércio on racial and profession grounds, when Izalinda became pregnant and confessed to her grandmother that she had been deflowered, her grandmother and father did what they could to get Lupércio to marry Izalinda, going to the police when it became clear that he was reneging on his promise to do so. For them, it was more important for Izalinda to have support from her deflowerer than for the family to uphold its social and racial standing by rejecting the marriage.

As for the young women, they were usually influenced by other factors, in addition to socioeconomic position and color category, in their choice of a partner. The attractiveness of a young man might be affected by his color, but not absolutely determined. This was clear in a case opened in 1935 by Manoel Alves, an illiterate Portuguese factory worker.[84] Alves brought his daughter Aracy, a sixteen-year-old white textile worker, into the police station because she had run away from home, to be found five days later at her boyfriend's mother's house. Alves dragged Aracy in because he wanted her to undergo a medical examination to verify whether she had been deflowered by the boyfriend, Antônio Sodré. When interrogated by her father, Aracy at first denied the charge, but later admitted to it. At the police station, she explained that "sometimes when Sodré brought her home from dances, at the door of her shack [barracão] he kissed and embraced her . . . and sought to excite her . . . ; that due to these acts she felt captivated and enchanted by Antônio, in spite of the fact that he was black."

Aracy told police that she was aware that Antônio was married and separated from his wife, which meant he could not remarry. Instead, she explained, "he had always promised to live maritally with her." Aracy also told police that she had pursued Antônio by writing him a note asking him to meet her on the night of her deflowering. She knew she had won his heart when he vowed that "if the police found out about [the deflowering], he would serve the sentence that was given him and when he was freed [from prison] they would be united."

When Aracy testified before the judge three months later, she was living with Antônio. She insisted that "in September of last year, without any prompting from the accused, she sought him in order to give herself to him. On that occasion, the accused deflowered the declarant." She concluded her testimony with a deliberate affirmation of her feelings for her boyfriend: "the declarant fell in love [ficou apaixonada] with the accused, for whom she continues to feel love." This adamant statement stands out among the testimony, for the use of the terms "to fall in love" and "love" (amor) is rare. Aracy might have been expressing righteous indignation about the impediments to her union with Antônio, including his previous marriage and his color. Certainly, she placed her amorous sentiments above other, perhaps more expedient, considerations of social and economic advantages she might have enjoyed as a white woman had she married a white man.

This case is interesting for another reason. It demonstrates that people of different colors could live in very close contact, in fact, in the same tenement, where each family had separate rooms but shared a courtyard and sanitary facilities. Aracy's father described his relationship with his black neighbors (Antônio's family) as "intimate" enough that he allowed his daughter to frequent nighttime dances with them. Although the witnesses are not identified by color, Maria Santos, the one Portuguese (therefore probably considered white) witness, testified as an intimate friend of the black defendant. She had taken Aracy in, at Antônio's request, before Aracy moved in with Antônio.

It is also interesting that neither Aracy's father nor any of the neighbors called in to testify mentioned color when reporting on the moral character of either Aracy or Antônio. Instead, in response to the prosecutor's questions, neighbors systematically reported that they had not witnessed any "immorality" in Antônio's behavior toward Aracy, observing only that the couple courted. Apparently, they did not consider interracial courtship necessarily immoral.

It is possible that Aracy and Antônio's neighbors did not consider color a significant issue in the case. But given the favoring of color endogamy by Rio's general population, and Aracy's recognition that Antônio's blackness would have presented an obstacle to their courtship had she not felt such deep attraction to him, it is more likely that her father and neighbors felt it improper to bring up the delicate issue of color difference. The only mention of color in testimony, besides Aracy's declaration that she was fascinated by Antônio in spite of the fact that he was black, was Maria Santos's explanation that Antônio had appeared at her shack "accompanied by a white girl." Since Santos lived in Mangueira, a favela already considered "black" in the 1930s, the color reference may have been simply a convenient means of distinguishing Aracy from most of Santos's neighbors.

On the whole, deflowering disputes provide evidence that color prejudice was disseminated among the working-class population and that whiteness was valued positively, particularly when it came time to select a marriage partner. Yet they also reveal a correlation between ascribed color and socioeconomic position, a relatively high degree of interracial social mixing and shared moral values among working-class people, and a general reluctance on the part of witnesses to mention color when describing someone's moral character. The silence on color might be explained by a tacit recognition among deponents that color difference was not a legitimate impediment to courtship or marriage, even if it was a de facto one.

Both assumptions emerged in a deflowering dispute that made it to the police through a circuitous route in 1943. In a letter to Brazilian president Getúlio Vargas, Maria José Pinto, describing herself as "a humble Brazilian . . . , an inexperienced country girl" complained that she had been deceived six years earlier by the marriage promises of Italian immigrant Luigi Procopio. "I even pointed out to him the color difference," Pinto wrote, presumably in an effort to preempt the charge that it was not credible that a white man would take a woman of a different color as his wife. "He responded," the letter continued, "that [the color difference] did not have anything to do with marriage, since he had taken a liking to me."[85] This attitude convinced Pinto of Procopio's good intentions, and she agreed to wait until Procopio finished building their house and paying off his new plot of land. In the meantime, she began sleeping with him regularly, "in the house she considered hers," and "considered him her husband." During all these years, she later testified, she declined any pecuniary aid from Luigi, "telling him instead to save the money for their future together," and she felt that she had thus contributed to their household expenses and the furnishings he purchased. When the house was finally finished and the land paid off, Luigi was forty-two years old and ready for marriage. To Maria José's desperation, he did not choose her.[86]

Interrogated at the local police station a few months after the date on the letter, Luigi Procopio confirmed the six-year sexual relationship with Maria José Pinto, whom he described as *parda*. He denied that he had ever promised her marriage, but claimed instead that since she "was constantly barraging him with declarations of love," he had "invited her to live with him as though they were married." According to Procopio, Maria José "rejected this proposal, saying that what she wanted was to marry him," but eventually consented to sleeping with him nightly. Although Luigi insisted that he never intended to marry Maria José, it seems that he did not necessarily want to give her up, either—and he may not have had to. According to Maria José, "that scoundrel tried to deceive [her] in every way," lying to her repeatedly and refusing to "let her see the truth." Yet Maria José also testified that even after she discovered his engagement to another woman and complained to President Vargas, she continued to have sexual relations with Procopio. "I love this man very much," she explained, according to the police investigator (perhaps after the investigator threatened to rough up Luigi) "and I don't want you to do anything to hurt him."[87] She need not have worried, for her complaint was a lost cause from the start. By her own account, she was already thirty-two years old when Luigi deflowered her, well beyond the maximum age for a deflowering victim.

It is reasonable to conjecture that Luigi Procopio saw Maria José Pinto as an appropriate partner for sex and cohabitation but not marriage because of her low status, determined by her color, her family's poverty, and her own autonomy and assertiveness. Luigi's new fiancée, according to the police investigator, was "a neighboring girl from a very good family." She may have been an Italian immigrant like Procopio (and thus would have been considered white); Maria José had initially believed Luigi when he told her the girl was his cousin.

Luigi Procopio's behavior toward Maria José Pinto, like several other cases mentioned above, seems to illustrate widely held assumptions about darker-skinned women. These cases help explain why men tended to be the darker-skinned partner in interracial marriages and why women seemed more likely to bring lighter-skinned than darker-skinned men to court over broken marriage promises.

The complex attitudes found in the same cases, however, might also reasonably lead us to suppose that Procopio may indeed have declared, six years earlier, that his affection for Maria José Pinto made "the color difference" unimportant; that he may have been sincere at the time; and that either way, it would not have been at all preposterous for Pinto to have believed him. For although racist ideologies might, as Roger Bastide claims, "extend their conflicts even into love's embrace," these conflicts were often mediated, sometimes with the help of antiracist ideologies.[88] Or, to paraphrase Peter Fry's observation for the 1990s, each particular situation determined—sometimes predictably, sometimes not—whether racism or racial democracy would prevail.[89] Consideration of how racial categorization affected people's experiences with the justice system provides even stronger evidence to support this observation.

The Significance of Color in Judges' Verdicts

In the discourses of jurists, like those of witnesses, there is little overt mention of race, in keeping with the ostensible absence of institutional racism in Brazil. Yet analysis of the outcomes of the cases shows that racial discrimination could work against both the accused and the accusers. Apparently, discrimination began at the police station. Table 7 shows the proportions of men in each color category in the police investigations that did not result in indictments and in the trials (trials resulted from police investigations that *did* result in indictment). The higher pro-

174

Table 7 Color of Accused Men in Trials and Police Investigations

| | White | | Pardo | | Black | | |
	Number	Percent	Number	Percent	Number	Percent	Total
Trials	79	49	49	30	33	20	161
Police investigations	86	61	40	28	16	11	142

Source: Arquivo Nacional, 450 criminal cases consulted.
Note: Excludes 64 trials with color of accused unknown; 83 police investigations with color of accused unknown.

portions of "black" men in the trial records and of "white" men in the police investigations suggest that black defendants were more likely to be indicted than whites. Among the men who were indicted, however, conviction and acquittal rates varied only slightly among the color groups (the rates were 29 and 53 percent overall, respectively; 16 percent married before sentences were passed and 2 percent had unknown outcomes).[90]

The absence of a consistently simple, direct relationship between color and outcome in convictions is not surprising for two reasons. First, if racial discrimination existed, the victim's and defendant's colors might influence the outcome in opposite ways. Second, since socioeconomic status and perception of color were integrally related, variables such as profession and literacy might influence outcome as well. By using a statistical technique known as logit regression, it is possible to observe the interaction of these variables, and to control for others (such as whether the man confessed and whether he was married).[91] The variables and multivariate models are described in Appendices B and C. Logit estimates are presented in Appendix D.

The logit estimates show clear relationships between outcome and color of both accused and accuser: as the defendant's color got darker, the likelihood of indictment increased; as the victim's color got darker, the likelihood of indictment as well as conviction decreased. Socioeconomic status, estimated by victims' literacy and men's professions, also affected the outcome of the cases.[92] Women's literacy showed the strongest relationship to outcome, with literate women much more likely to see their complaints result in indictments and convictions. The probability of conviction decreased as the men's job category improved, although this relationship was weaker. Since we have seen that these trials generally hinged on proving whether the young woman was honest, it is not surprising that overall, markers of the woman's status (color and literacy) seemed to bear the greatest effect on the outcome.

Calculating hypothetical probabilities, based on the logit estimates, helps illustrate the results more clearly.[93] Table 8 shows the relative probabilities of indictment for each color grouping of defendants and victims. These numbers can be read as percentages, hence, a white man accused by a black woman had a 35 percent chance of being indicted; if he was accused by a white woman, the probability rose to 57 percent. Both defendant's and victim's color affect the relative probabilities, but the most significant factor was the relationship between the victim's and defendant's color: men accused by women darker than themselves were the least likely to be indicted; men accused by lighter women were the most likely. The same pattern emerges in an analysis of the relative probability of conviction among the color groupings (table 9). These results suggest that the color prejudices of judicial officials worked to punish darker men who offended the honor of lighter women, while reinforcing the longstanding pattern by which white men engaged in sexual relationships

Table 8 Probability of Indictment by Color of Accused Man and Offended Woman

	Accused Man's Color		
	White	Pardo	Black
Offended woman's color			
White	57	69	78
Parda	46	58	69
Black	35	46	58

Source: Arquivo Nacional, 450 cases of sexual crime consulted.

First Difference Values: Offended woman's color = 1, 2, 3; Defendant's color = 1, 2, 3; Defendant's job = 2; Offended woman literate = 1; Defendant confess = 0; Dating? = 1; Defendant married = 0

Note: Excludes 180 cases with missing data for offended woman's or defendant's color, literacy, occupation, whether there was a confession, whether the couple had dated, and whether the defendant was married (thus n = 270). The analysis in tables 8 to 11 illustrates the relationship among color groups in this population. Because the analysis considers multiple significant variables, probabilities are based on a hypothetical individual: a worker who was not married, did not confess and had dated the victim, and the victim was literate. Thus, the probabilities should not be read as relevant for the entire population in the cases. Probabilities were calculated for different hypothetical individuals as well (men with different professions, etc.) Although numbers varied, the direction of the results was constant, i.e., indictment and conviction was less likely if the victim was darker and defendant lighter and if the defendant's job was lower status. To compensate for possible sample bias in the ratio of trials to investigations (see note 91), two random subsamples were created through random element sampling. The equation for probability of indictment was re-estimated using the subsamples. Results mirrored the findings here, suggesting that the results are robust to potential sample bias.

Table 9   Probability of Conviction by Color of Accused Man and
Offended Woman[a]

	Accused Man's Color		
	White	Mixed	Black
Offended woman's color			
Defendant confessed			
White	28	32	36
Mixed	19	22	26
Black	13	15	18
Defendant did not confess			
White	22	25	28
Mixed	15	17	20
Black	10	11	13

Source: Arquivo Nacional, 450 cases of sexual crime consulted.

First Difference Values: Offended woman's color = 1, 2, 3; Defendant's color = 1, 2, 3; Defendant's job = 2; Offended woman literate = 1; Defendant confess = 0; Dating? = 1; Defendant married = 0

Note: Probabilities are computed from regression results described in appendixes B–D. Excludes 187 cases with missing data for outcome, offended woman's or defendant's color, literacy, occupation, and whether there was a confession, the couple had dated, and if the defendant was married (thus n = 263). See Table 8's note about how probabilities should be understood.

[a] Because a confession by the defendant influenced conviction rates substantially, the cases with and without confessions were compared in Table 9. Confessions were frequently obtained by police during early stages of the investigation and later denied by defendants once they contracted lawyers.

with darker, lower-status women with impunity. Either way, the results do not reveal a celebration or encouragement by jurists of Brazil's supposedly generalized miscegenation.

Finally, tables 10 and 11 suggest that the likelihood that the man would "repair the damages" of a sexual crime through marriage may have increased as the women's color "lightened," regardless of the man's color. These results are not as clear as those regarding conviction or indictment because some men seemed to have wanted to marry the young women all along. Not surprisingly, the variable that most influenced the probability of marriage was the prior existence of courtship.[94] Thus, while we may suspect that the relationship between color and probability of indictment and conviction reflects the prejudices of judges, prosecutors, and police investigators, the decision to marry was certainly more complex.

Of course, statistical relationships do not reveal nuances or motivations, nor do they show how prejudices creep into juridical theories that were supposed to be neutral. Evidence from individual cases, such as the two cases of interracial courtship discussed above, illustrate the complex and contradictory ways that color and class prejudices could influence verdicts.

In the case of Aracy Alves and Antônio Sodré, the judge found Antônio guilty and the higher court denied Antônio's appeal. Antônio served two years and four months, thus living out his declaration to Aracy that he was willing to pay the price of a jail sentence in order to be "united with her." The case was archived after Antônio's release from prison, leaving us to wonder whether he and Aracy were then finally united.

Antônio Sodré's conviction was based on a newly expanded conception of seduction. The prosecutor argued that since Aracy Alves "was not poorly behaved nor a carrier of morbid anomalies, it cannot be believed that she would give herself to the accused . . . if she had not been induced by him to allow him to deflower her." He concluded that Sodré had "awakened her natural voluptuousness, corrupting her consent with a long-standing practice of libertinage."[95] The judge, Francisco de Paula Rocha Lagoa Filho, disagreed that the deflowering had been a result of seduction, convicting Sodré instead of "corruption of a minor," which carried a longer maximum prison term than deflowering (one to six years rather than one to four).

The guilty verdict in this case is surprising in the light of Aracy's insistence that she, not Antônio, had pursued their romance and her own deflowering. It seems likely that the prosecution's recourse to an inter-

Table 10 Probability of Marriage (Among Police Investigations)

	Accused Man's Color		
	White	Pardo	Black
Offended woman's color			
White	63	61	59
Parda	59	57	55
Black	55	53	51

Source: Archivo Nacional, 450 cases of sexual crime consulted.

First Difference Values: Offended woman's color = 1, 2, 3; Defendant's color = 1, 2, 3; Defendant's job = 2; Offended woman literate = 1; Defendant confess = 0; Trial? = 0; Dating? = 1; Defendant married = 0

Note: Probabilities are computed from regression results described in appendixes B–D. Excludes 187 cases with missing data for outcome, offended woman or defendant's color, literacy, occupation, and whether there was a confession, the couple had dated, and if the defendant was married (thus n = 263). See Table 8's note for a discussion on probabilities.

Table 11   Probability of Marriage (Among Trials)

	Accused Man's Color		
	White	Pardo	Black
Offended woman's color			
White	24	22	21
Parda	21	20	18
Black	18	17	16

Source: Archivo Nacional, 450 cases of sexual crime consulted.

First Difference Values: Offended woman's color = 1, 2, 3; Defendant's color = 1, 2, 3; Defendant's job = 2; Offended woman literate = 1; Defendant confess = 0; Trial = 1; Dating? = 1; Defendant married = 0

Note: Probabilities are computed from regression results described in appendixes B–D. Excludes 187 cases with missing data for outcome, offended woman or defendant's color, literacy, occupation, whether there was a confession, whether the couple had dated, and whether the defendant was married (thus n = 263). See Table 8's note for a discussion on probabilities.

pretation of seduction that was selectively employed in court was influenced by Antônio's color. The notion that the criminal means of seduction could be physical excitation, rather than the traditional promise of marriage, was a novelty in the 1920s. Not even the most ardent defenders of this "vulgar" understanding of seduction had contemplated invoking it in defense of assertive young women who openly admitted that they had been the ones to request defloration in full knowledge of their deflowerer's inability to marry them. Moreover, although many jurists argued theoretically that seduction could apply to cases in which women had sex when the motive was a promise of "concubinage," in practice these cases were almost always summarily dismissed, or the defendant was easily acquitted. Thus, although none of the legal officials involved in the case—police delegate, prosecutor, and judge—mentioned race or color at any time in the documents, it is difficult not to suspect that this verdict was influenced by a racialized conception of honor, applied to both Aracy and Antônio.

Lupércio de Oliveira Cahe's trial for the deflowering of Izalinda de Lourdes Carames demonstrates more clearly the ways judges' attitudes toward cross-color sexual relations could influence the outcome of a trial in favor of a defendant they perceived as inferior to the victim. It also provides a rare example of explicit acknowledgment by judicial officials—in this case, justices of the appeals court—of the influence of both class and color on their verdict.[96]

When the trial went to court and Izalinda explained once again that her family had objected to her boyfriend because he was "of inferior color and social position," Judge Eduardo Espinola Filho asked her why she had consented to being deflowered by such an individual. Izalinda responded with a dramatic new version of the events: her boyfriend had pulled out a knife and threatened to kill her if she resisted. It is likely that she was drawing upon an image of lower-class male violence that she thought the judge would find credible. The judge, however, was not convinced. He acquitted Lupércio on the grounds that the story Izalinda told in court contradicted her previous testimony.

The two prosecutors assigned to the case appealed the decision, insisting that the judge had intimidated Izalinda, provoking her to invent the threat of violence. The final verdict of the appeals court justices, however, left no doubt that they believed that a woman who consented to having sex with a man of lower status lacked virtue and honesty. Although the justices acknowledged that the evidence proved that Lupércio had deflowered Izalinda (and, implicitly, that he was the father of the child she bore before the trial took place), they unanimously confirmed Lupércio's acquittal, arguing the following:

> The very circumstance of the difference of color and social condition, the motive of the family's opposition, serves to prove the absence of seduction, since it is incomprehensible that an honest and virtuous [pudorosa] girl, with good intentions and proud [ciosa] of her family's position, against her family's will, would persist in a courtship with an individual of different color and social condition than her own. Even more frightening is that she would give herself sexually to this individual.

The attitude of the justices in this 1939 verdict seems oddly anachronistic. The colonial legislation that had allowed parents to obstruct their children's marriage in cases of "inequality" between bride and groom had been overturned by the liberal legal codes passed at the outset of the First Republic, which eliminated class and racial distinctions among Brazilian citizens. But this verdict illustrates one way that the concept of sexual honor could work to preserve these distinctions. The justices were certainly aware of the nationalist discourses of Brazil's racial mixture and whitening that were vigorously disseminated through state propaganda in the late 1930s. Clearly, however, they did not consider white women the appropriate vehicles for racial homogenization through miscegenation, particularly if the women chose partners of "inferior social condition."

Both Lupércio Cahe and Antônio Sodré's sentences also shed light on jurists' fears of the independent modern woman who had appeared with increasing frequency in juridical literature in the 1920s and 1930s. Independent women such as Izalinda de Lourdes Carames and Aracy Alves were not only subverting the legal function of sexual honor as a mechanism of gender discipline, but they were simultaneously subverting its function as a means of class and racial differentiation. This was often true symbolically, even in cases in which racial difference was not an issue, or at least not explicitly so. Because differentiation among individuals was symbolically established through the category of gender in legal codes that had eliminated previous distinctions of race and class, the reconfiguration of gender norms seemed an ominous sign of social disintegration and impending chaos. Modern women, casting aside the female modesty and inhibition (*pudor*) that, in Nelson Hungria's words, "civilized the sexual instinct," were thus held responsible for cultural retrogression and racial degeneracy.

These kinds of symbolic associations between gender, class, and racial discipline were also at work in Judge Eurico Cruz's imagination when he described the kind of virginity "that devirginifies itself" in his famous 1926 deflowering verdict:

> What virginity is this that devirginifies itself? It is the virginity that rocks and sways to the indolent rhythm of the slave quarters, in the dance schools—it is a virginity spent in spasms, betrayed by the dulled gaze, the wanton swaying of the body, in the contact of faces . . . and of everything else . . . beneath clothing that is carefully donned yet recklessly stripped.[97]

We have seen that Judge Cruz was concerned about the immorality of modern times and nostalgic for days past. He was also concerned about racial degeneracy. In a fascinating argument, he equated "the modern environment," in which (to his horror) "the sexes face one another, in the ambience that generated the present case, as equals" to the barbarism of "inferior people":

> When people dance in public places, what one notes is what the missionary Holden already noted among an inferior people: "As far as I could observe, perfection consisted in both partners being capable of putting into motion at the same time all parts of the body. . . . Marriage promises born in such scenarios, marriage being the base of the constitution of the family, mean nothing; they are merely the banal entanglement from which flow other liaisons: outings in automobiles, escapes to the brothels.[98]

For Cruz, the erosion of male sexual dominance by women's assuming "gestures and attitudes that are peculiar only to the unashamed and innate boldness of the male" (recall that his outrage was provoked by a young woman's description of a sexual position in which she was on top) signaled generalized moral degeneracy and the blurring of boundaries between civilized and primitive peoples. Evidence from cases tried over the following fifteen years, in which Cruz's sentence was frequently cited, suggests that this image continued to disturb jurists through the regime changes that institutionalized new discourses of racial pride and modernization in the 1930s.

The racial implications of Cruz's sentence are clear. In a nation whose major social theorists and politicians had long stressed the need to civilize and whiten its population, the international success and national space Afro-Brazilian culture was gaining could only be viewed with, at best, ambivalence. Samba, probably the "music of the *senzala*" that perturbed Cruz, presented a problem similar to that of the tango in Argentina.[99] For Cruz, this cultural universe, by producing sexual equality, corrupted women and destroyed virginity.

The discomfort of men like Cruz with broadened acceptance of Afro-Brazilian music, considered together with jurists' tendency to look disparagingly upon interracial courtship, places many jurists beside other public authorities in their desire to project to the world a vision of Brazil as a modern, civilized nation that had left its non-European roots behind, or had relegated those roots to the folklore of an imagined past. These modern men looked to women to uphold a moral order that would preserve traditional social hierarchies during this period of change.

Conclusion

Despite the elaboration in the 1920s and 1930s of official ideologies celebrating Brazil's history of cultural advancement through miscegenation and racial democracy, records of sexual crimes illustrate the ways racial attitudes could encourage color endogamy, even though these attitudes were rarely made explicit, and even though "color" was subjectively determined and difficult to pin down. The concept of sexual honor could be interpreted in ways that maintained color and class distinctions that had been ostensibly eliminated from republican law. Jurists interpreted honor in ways compatible with long-standing notions of appropriate racial and class divisions. Although racial attitudes could affect the outcome of the cases in contradictory ways, judicial officials tended to sustain an understanding among men considered lighter that their relationships with darker women were not binding. They also placed the responsibility for the maintenance of endogamy in the hands of lighter women. This explains the stigmatization of women who chose darker partners or who, in the words of Judge Cruz, "swayed to the indolent rhythm of the slave quarters," regardless of their phenotype. The enforcement of the "family values" embodied in concepts of sexual honor gave jurists the interpretive space in which to practice this kind of discrimination, while perceiving themselves as impartial defenders of abstract cultural values, or even a natural social order. In short, sexual honor was an instrument that allowed jurists to espouse racial democracy while practicing discrimination.

Color also seems to have mattered to the common people who took their sexual conflicts to court. Although they never cited color as the sole determinant of honor or social status, they discerned color differences, and these differences influenced their choices of partners for sex or for marriage. Not everyone agreed on the significance of color differences, however, and color was only one among various attributes that made someone a desirable partner. Moreover, the general silence on color in testimony, broken in rare instances, may suggest a recognition among deponents that it was not legitimate criteria for determining moral character or social worth. These values did not directly contradict those of state officials such as jurists, but while everyday social contacts among common people could sometimes work to diminish racial differences, jurists' discourses seemed to accentuate them. Although it is impossible to determine whether juridical officials succeeded in influencing popular conceptions of color (or vice versa), it is likely that in many cases, working-class people's experiences with the justice system reinforced their recognition of the disadvantages of dark skin.

Epilogue

When Maria José Pinto wrote to President Getúlio Vargas in 1943 to complain that her companion of six years had left her for another woman, she testified to the very literal ways the paternalist discourse of the dictatorial Estado Novo could be interpreted by a "humble Brazilian." Lacking the "courage" to trouble her parents, who had given her "a strict upbringing" and who were old, poor, and in failing health back in the rural town she had left twelve years earlier, she appealed to the president who called himself "the father of the poor":

> Although I am of legal age and not having parents here but in [neighboring state] Minas and wanting to avoid upsetting them as I said, I beg you Mr. President as though you were my Judge, my father and protector, after God and Jesus, [there is] thou for me, because in the state I find myself expecting this man's child in the next few months, and not having anywhere to go, I cannot go to my parents' home in this condition and I also cannot remain with my relatives where I am now, they are poor and cannot support me while I am unable to work.[1]

Maria José knew well that her age (thirty-eight) made her ineligible for legal recourse. She appealed nonetheless for the "justice" that a father and protector could grant. Her letter almost certainly was produced by someone else, for a typewriter was beyond the means of most domestic servants, and her name was signed in the unsteady hand of someone with little writing practice. She may have dictated the text, for its tone matched that of her later testimony at the police station. There, Pinto reiterated her faith that "the father of us all, the President of the Republic, will surely arrange for the harm to her to be repaired."

President Vargas's secretary sent Maria José Pinto's letter to the new minister of Justice and Internal Affairs, Alexandre Marcondes Filho, who sent it to the new chief of police, Alcides Gonçalves Etchegoyen, who ordered an inquiry by Affonso Gentil da Silva Morais, the police delegate in Marechal Hermes, Pinto's suburban neighborhood.

Morais found that Luigi Procopio was an honest, skilled worker held in high regard by reputable neighbors. "Around the area where he resides," the delegate reported, "I spoke to various business owners and neighbors, who were unanimous in affirming that his background and previous behavior were those of a perfectly normal, morally upstanding man . . . there was not one discrediting remark about his conduct." Even Maria José Pinto testified as to Procopio's good character, calling him "a hardworking, honest man" who "fulfills his obligations, having failed only in relation to his sentiments for her."

Morais did not open a formal criminal investigation of Procopio and thus did not request an identity check from the Identification Institute. He nonetheless filled in the subjective information he gathered with hard data that Procopio himself could immediately supply with his immigration and labor ministry documents:

I-Luigi Procopio . . . came to Brazil on 5 July 1921, having disembarked in the port of Rio de Janeiro. He fought in 1914 against the Germans. . . . In our country he has never become involved in political conflicts, living from his honest work, and concerning himself exclusively with the same. . . .

II-Luigi Procopio is registered in the Immigration Service [S.R.E.] . . . , he has revalidated his registration card each year, and is perfectly legal in the country.

III-Luigi Procopio is a metalworker, and has worked [regularly until 1936 when he was injured on the job] and is currently undergoing treatment through the insurance agency. He holds worker identification booklet [carteira de trabalho] no. 22.031.

Morais was less sympathetic to Maria José Pinto. He described her as a domestic servant who was overtaken by "a profound passion for the accused, which is the reason she wants to marry him." Morais noted that her complaint that Procopio had seduced her with a marriage promise was invalid, since "the promises of a cheap conqueror" should not have deceived someone of her maturity. More serious was her claim, in the letter to President Vargas, that Luigi Procopio had used her money to furnish their future home. Questioning her on this, however, Morais learned that she had not given Procopio money "earned from her own work." Rather, she had refused his gifts and offers of financial help, insisting that he save the money instead for their marriage and life together. Finally, the delegate found that Maria José had miscarried, and was thus no longer carrying Luigi's child.

Morais sent his report to Chief of Police Etchegoyen, who found Procopio's behavior "quite reproachable" but agreed with Morais that Procopio had committed no crime. Etchegoyen included the file with his own report to Justice Minister Marcondes Filho, who in turn sent it, with his own report, back to President Vargas. It is likely that Vargas's staff drafted a letter to Pinto explaining the outcome of her petition, for this was the routine response to the hundreds of letters Vargas received each month from poor citizens like Pinto. The response, however, was not attached to her case, which was eventually filed in the National Archives.[2]

Neither the story of Maria José Pinto's relationship with Luigi Procopio nor the outcome of the investigation into her complaint seems surprising. We have seen that men of diverse social classes often felt free of their commitments to their lovers when these were women of inferior social status, and we have seen that Maria José Pinto's honor, in relation to Luigi Procopio's, was blemished by her poverty, her independence, and her color. Even if her status had been equal to Luigi's, her legal case against him would be null since she was too old to claim criminal seduction.

Yet three aspects of the case are striking: Pinto's skillful, literal use of the paternalistic rhetoric that is perhaps the most characteristic mark of the Estado Novo; the attention her letter received from top-ranking state officials; and the bureaucratic resources that were immediately available to Luigi Procopio for establishing his identity as an honorable worker. These aspects make the case a good starting point for exploring some of the political and legal changes that affected how women and men could interpret honor in their dealings with state institutions under the Estado Novo. Maria José Pinto's letter to President Vargas thus provides a fitting epilogue to the preceding two decades of debate over how to define and defend honor in the nation's capital.

Maria José Pinto had certainly heard and understood the Vargas regime's promise of paternal protection for "the Brazilian people," particularly the formerly neglected, even disdained, mixed-race and impoverished masses. This promise was the ideological cornerstone of the dictatorial Estado Novo, which Vargas created in 1937 in reaction to what he considered the "excessive liberalism" of republican state institutions and the "opportunism" of political factions that emerged under democracy. In place of regional, factional, or class divisions, Vargas envisioned a society organized on corporatist principles and "organic hierarchy." An idealized patriarchal family was the basic unit of this "natural" social order and the model for the organization of the state. The "Brazilian family" thus became the central metaphor for social order. Paternal authority symbolized state power, incarnated in Getúlio Vargas himself.

Since Vargas came to rely increasingly on mass support as one of the pillars of his regime in the 1940s, he made substantial investments in publicity that would reach the working class. The elaborate system of state propaganda coordinated by the Department of Press and Publicity (*Departamento de Imprensa e Propaganda;* DIP), created in 1939, did more than familiarize the population with state policy. Working through the press and especially the radio, Vargas's propagandists aimed to deify Vargas, inspire gratitude among workers for the social legislation he created, and "construct the Brazilian people" politically, physically, and morally.[3]

Of course, this social engineering had a brutally coercive element. Even before Vargas created the Estado Novo, police agents led by Nazi-sympathizer Police Chief Filinto Müller (1933–1942) took advantage of successive states of siege to erect the apparatus of a virtual police state. There was a tradition of police authoritarianism in the First Republic, and many opponents of this tradition had initially been among Vargas's strongest supporters in Rio de Janeiro. The victory of the military authoritarians over the progressive populists of the early Vargas coalition was clear by 1936, however, when Müller imprisoned Rio de Janeiro's mayor, Pedro Ernesto, for his supposed Communist loyalties. Finally freed of civilian interference, police and secret agents systematized and "perfected" previous moralization campaigns by repressing or eliminating political opponents and anyone else they considered social marginals.[4] The element of Estado Novo politics that reached people such as Maria José Pinto, however, was its rhetoric of inclusion and reciprocity, which included a pledge to protect the honor of "humble Brazilians." This was particularly true after 1942, when Filinto Müller and Justice Minister Francisco Campos, two of the figures most solidly associated with the repression, were replaced by the more conciliatory and paternalistic Etchegoyen and Marcondes Filho.

While Etchegoyen loosened some of Müller's more draconian moralization measures in Rio de Janeiro, such as the extralegal confinement of prostitutes, and worked to make the police more accessible to "popular sectors," Marcondes Filho designed the rhetorical strategy for building the Estado Novo's corporatist society. In addition to heading the Justice and Internal Affairs Ministry (1942–1945), Marcondes Filho was, from 1941 to 1945, the labor minister most responsible for incorporating "honorable workers" into the Estado Novo without threatening the nation's most powerful industrialists.[5] He did this by strengthening official labor unions and social welfare legislation and, perhaps more important in terms of the numbers of people affected, by disseminating an inclusionist ideology. His weekly radio broadcasts, "Speaking to the Brazilian Workers," played an important part in creating what historian Angela de Castro Gomes describes as a social contract between the state, personified by Vargas, and the working class. This was not a contract based on the Rousseauistic tension between individual interest and common good. Rather, the contract was based on personalized bonds of reciprocity: fatherly love inspired Vargas to bequeath social legislation and protection to "his" people; "the people" were supposed to reciprocate, not by fulfilling civic duty, but with passionate displays of obedience, discipline, and reverence.[6]

Gomes demonstrates that Marcondes and the DIP worked to cement the people's personal, emotional commitment to Vargas by disseminating a remarkably coherent historical narrative and set of images. When he spoke to Brazilian workers over the radio, Marcondes portrayed Vargas as a clairvoyant who foresaw the bankruptcy of the laissez-faire state and the deficiency of liberal democracy well before these failures were made manifest by the outbreak of World War II. Erasing the recent history of struggles for social reform and worker's rights, Marcondes explained that Vargas had personally handed down progressive social legislation (state-led unionism, worker's compensation, social security, minimum wage and maximum workweek, paid vacation, pension) before the workers were forced to defend their interests in bloody battles against the bourgeoisie.[7] By replacing liberal democracy with *trabalhismo* ("laborism"), Vargas's trademark set of political and social policies that began with his entry into power in 1930 and culminated in the Estado Novo, Vargas gave birth to the true Brazilian nation, a nation that incorporated all in its familial embrace.

The Vargas regime used the rhetoric of family values in an attempt to lend moral legitimacy to Brazil's entrenched social hierarchy and personalistic patron-client relations—a technique the regime borrowed from Mussolini's Italy and adapted to Brazil.[8] Vargas's attempts to centralize national political power and modernize the national economy did not wipe away the older system whereby the state granted favors to regional oligarchies in return for their loyalty. The Estado Novo's innovation was to integrate new political actors into the system by establishing patron-client relations between urban workers and the state. By elevating the status of at least some working men and extending to them the means to head honorable families, the regime sought to neutralize the potential threat that the mobilized masses presented to older relations of dominance.

Vargas, Marcondes Filho proclaimed, defended not only workers' material interests, but their honor. Under the slogan "make the people advance" (fazer o povo progredir), he pledged to lift the Brazilian worker out of misery, ignorance, and ignominy. Railing against the favoring of white immigrant labor by previous regimes, Marcondes Filho and other Estado Novo officials extolled the quality of the Brazilian worker and the honor of the "Brazilian race." African heritage, miscegenation, and "racial democracy" became the basis of "authentic" national culture. Of course, these themes were hardly new. Different elements of these themes had already been articulated by critics ranging from popular musicians to mainstream journalists when King Albert visited Rio in 1920, and they enjoyed a great deal of legitimacy over the two decades that followed Albert's visit, even as racism continued to permeate Brazilian society. By the early 1940s, Vargas had converted these themes into another slogan for the Estado Novo. DIP agents, and even Vargas himself, worked with popular musicians to "sanitize" popular cultural manifestations, particularly samba, and incorporate them into nationalist campaigns for moral and cultural uplift. Meanwhile, new laws in the 1930s reserved jobs for Brazilians, established immigration quotas, and placed immigrants under the vigilance of the police and the Immigration Service, which weeded out those suspected of spreading "exotic" and pernicious ideologies.[9]

Gomes points out that honor and citizenship under the Estado Novo were not defined by autonomy and political rights, but by the rights to social benefits earned through disciplined work and loyalty to the state. These "social rights" were limited to holders of a carteira de trabalho (worker identification booklet, created in 1933). In a text that is still printed in the booklets themselves, Marcondes Filho explained that the carteira documented not only the worker's "civil identification and professional qualification," but also his or her "life history," as told by the comments each employer wrote on its pages: "The booklet configures a life history. Whoever examines it will see immediately whether the holder is of an even or versatile temperament; . . . whether he went from factory to factory like a bee or stayed in the same establishment, moving up through the ranks. It can be a badge of honor. It can be a warning."[10]

Luigi Procopio's carteira was a badge of honor. It showed that he had worked steadily and earned the right to the compensation that had supported him since his injury six years earlier. His compliance with annual registration at the Immigration Service further confirmed his status as honest worker by showing that he refrained from political activism. In spite of his Italian birth, Luigi Procopio was precisely the kind of worker who benefited most from trabalhismo. His ability to make a decent living, even after an injury, and to earn the esteem of reputable neighbors and state officials allowed him to achieve a dream that Estado Novo propaganda held before all honorable workers: to marry an honest girl, head an honest family, and own the family home.[11]

Maria José Pinto could aspire to a similar dream of security and upward mobility only by earning the protection of a man like Luigi Procopio, which helps explain her desperate feeling of injustice when she lost him. Even if she were younger and still a virgin, finding someone of Procopio's status would not be easy. He was among a minority of workers who had access to benefits and skilled employment in the industrial sector. Rural workers and those in the informal sector, which included Pinto and most other working women, did not have *carteiras* and were excluded from the social legislation and labor unions that the Vargas regime created for public employees and industrial labor. The Estado Novo's construction of the honorable worker did not uplift the poorest and most unprotected sectors of society, but reinforced the stratification and layers of dependence already in place decades earlier.

In particular, and quite consciously, interventionist social policies reinforced women's dependence on men. The patriarchal family was not only a metaphor for the organic nation, but the basic "cell" of society, where each member learned his or her place. The Constitutions of both 1934 and 1937 placed "the family, constituted by indissoluble marriage" under "the special protection of the State."[12] This guarantee, as well as subsequent legislation that defined the state's "organization and protection of the family," make it clear that by the early 1940s, the Catholic right had won the upper hand in earlier debates over family, honor, and morality. Indeed, church-state relations were stronger than they had been since Brazil's independence in 1822. The 1937 Constitution closed "the divorce question" tightly; it would not be reopened for decades. Catholic calls for broad censorship of the "moral content" of the media, especially movies, were answered. Feminist gains of the early 1930s—including the right to vote, female control over family and social policies, equal pay, and equal access to public jobs—were lost with the end of democracy. Worse, the "protective" legislation for mothers and women workers became grounds for restricting women's employment and reinforcing their subordination to men.[13] After 1937, Minister of Education Gustavo Capanema purged local and national school systems of secular progressives such as the director of the Federal District Department of Education, Anísio Teixeira, who had led the "New School" movement for educational reform in the early 1930s. Religious lessons, traditional discipline, and rote learning methods, favored by the Catholic opposition to Teixeira, were reinstated along with differentiated curricula for boys and girls.

None of these policies, however, were implemented without a great deal of conflict, even among the principle Estado Novo ideologues themselves, as is illustrated by Simon Schwartzman's study of the history of the 1941 law regulating "the organization and protection of the family." Minister of Education Gustavo Capanema produced a draft of the statute in 1939 that was modeled on recommendations of key Catholic militants. Capanema's document stipulated that state efforts should "bolster the authority of the [male] head of the family" and "progressively restrict women's employment in the private and public sector to jobs appropriate to feminine nature, and strictly limited to those that serve the good of the family." Educational policies would guarantee women's compliance: "Men shall be educated to become fully qualified for the responsibility of head of the family. Women shall be given an education that makes them yearn for marriage and desire maternity." The state would "protect . . . the development, security, and honor of the family" by encouraging marriage, financing diverse family assistance programs, imposing moral censorship of cultural, intellectual, and artistic production, and otherwise creating "a moral climate that fosters the formation, duration, fecundity, and prestige of families."[14]

Capanema's draft statute was applauded by key Catholic spokesmen, but it was rejected in favor of what the state Commission for the Protection of the Family considered a more practical decree two years later.[15] As Schwartzman demonstrates, the new decree responded to the criticism of other government ministers and consultants, who argued that Capanema's draft recapitulated already existing censorship and educational policies and made unrealistic promises of state assistance. More important, the commission—which included prominent conservatives such as Oliveira Viana and Catholic Action leader Stela de Faro—eliminated restrictions on women's labor because they believed that increasing production, not reducing the labor force, would promote the Brazilian family. The opinions of conservative feminists such as journalist and diplomat Rosalina Lisboa were clearly influential as well. In correspondence with government ministers in 1939, Lisboa argued that Capanema's statute would reverse the moral gains Vargas had achieved through earlier legislation that protected women's right to honest work.[16] Disagreements over women's work were far from resolved with the 1941 decree; other laws, consolidated in 1945, would attempt a compromise by allowing married women to work only with their husbands' permission.[17] Yet the most controversial issue surrounding the 1941 decree did not involve women's work, but a clause that extended paternity benefits to fathers whose children were illegitimate. This clause provoked angry protests by the major organizations of the Catholic Right—precisely the groups the regime aimed to appease through its family policy.[18]

Although it is inarguable that the influence of authoritarian thinkers and Catholic militants expanded under the Estado Novo, when many progressive reformers were silenced or exiled, these debates over the legal defense of the Brazilian family demonstrate that conservatives did not always agree on moral issues and that they could not reverse the gains women had made in the labor market since World War I. Moreover, the social-reformist professionals who had struggled for prominence under the First Republic and in the early 1930s did not disappear. Some criticized state suppression of civil liberties, but, as in the earlier period, worked with more conservative colleagues to shape important aspects of interventionist state policy. The best example of this is the work of the Juridical Commission that wrote the penal code of 1940, a document that reflected persistent tensions between different legal philosophies as well as persistent contradictions regarding the definition and punishment of moral and sexual offenses.

Some of the code's most dramatic and controversial changes involved honor, sexual crimes, and crimes against the family. In part, these changes responded to feminist demands for women's legal equality and widespread criticism of barbaric aspects of Brazil's patriarchal traditions by urban professionals. In an attempt to guarantee punishment for wife murderers, the code stipulated that emotion or passion did not abrogate criminal responsibility. More significantly, family honor disappeared. Crimes that had been classified as "Crimes against the security of honor and honesty of families" in the 1890 code were separated into two sections. "Crimes against families" included bigamy, child neglect or abandonment, marital fraud, and adultery—the latter now carrying equal punishment for both spouses (six months to one year of imprisonment). Sexual crimes—rape, indecent assault, seduction, corruption of a minor, and abduction—were redefined as "crimes against customs." "Rape" was defined as forcing a woman to have intercourse, regardless of her civil status, profession, or "honesty." "Seduction" replaced "deflowering" and was defined as achieving a "carnal conjunction" with a virgin by "taking advantage of her inexperience or justifiable trust." The maximum age for the victim was lowered from twenty to seventeen. This put an end to the technical confusion over cases of complacent hymens and allowed judges a wider margin for deciding which girls deserved the protection of the courts. It also shifted the focus of the law more firmly away from the concern with women's virtue and toward the protection of minors.[19]

Patriarchal gender norms, however, continued to guide penal law.

Although passion did not abrogate responsibility, it still attenuated it. Men convicted of sexual crimes were still pardoned if they married their victims, and punishment could still include payment of a dowry, regulated by civil law. The law continued to protect physiological virginity, recognizing it as an important prerequisite for marriage. More significant, although sexual crimes were no longer considered offenses against family honor, neither were they offenses against individual citizens. Like the positivist-inspired jurists who established republican legal science at the turn of the century, the men who wrote the 1940 code defined women's sexual honesty and physical integrity as a collective social good, now emphasizing that the state, rather than individual patriarchs, was responsible for defending it.[20]

The new penal code was considered a compromise solution for the debates between proponents of classical and positivist doctrines, represented on the Juridical Commission by Judge Nelson Hungria and Prosecutor Roberto Lira, respectively. Through the innovation of "security measures," it divided criminals into those whose medical and psychological profile determined that they were dangerous, and those who were considered "occasional criminals." The former were subject to internment or imprisonment at the discretion of the judge.[21]

According to Lira, contemporary commentators immediately "speculated" that the 1940 code represented the victory of his reformist position over Hungria's more conservative classical orientation. Lira himself, however, denied that the five-man commission was divided along lines of theoretical or political "dogma."[22] Rather, he claimed that the commission followed "the force of justice, utility, and truth." Lira, who opposed Vargas and the Estado Novo, also insisted that Justice Minister Campos did not subject the commission to political constraints or censorship. Because he and his colleagues worked "not for the State, old or new, but for the Nation, the people, and science," the code followed Brazil's "liberal legal traditions" and was more committed to "social justice" than legislation passed under any of Brazil's democratic regimes.[23] By "social justice," Lira meant that judges could take social, cultural, and biological factors into account in sentencing and that a variety of institutions for rehabilitation were contemplated.

By granting greater interpretive power to legal and medical authorities, the 1940 code allowed for a more subjective application of justice. Given the authoritarian political climate of the Estado Novo and the regime's desire to create a hegemonic moral order, it is not surprising that penal law, along with state investments in criminal science, resulted in a more systematic criminalization of individuals who did not conform to moral ideals defined by legal and medical officials.[24]

It is also not surprising that in a climate of intense promotion of traditional family values by religious and state authorities, the concern with sexual honor that progressive jurists and other professionals considered a mark of the nation's backwardness continued unabated. While discourses of honor—personal, family, and national—proliferated in state propaganda, debates over its meaning in civil and penal law seemed even further from resolution. Deflowering complaints—now called seduction—continued to pour into local police stations, although the reduction of the victims' maximum age meant that fewer would result in investigations and trials. Their adjudication nonetheless generated a wide array of jurisprudential opinions about honest and dishonest women.

Jurists and the general public also continued to argue over whether cuckolded men who "washed their honor in blood" should be forgiven. Since the 1940 code stipulated that "intense passion" no longer abrogated "criminal responsibility," lawyers invented the "legitimate defense of honor" strategy, arguing that killing to defend one's honor was an act of self-defense (legítima defesa is analogous to "self-defense" in Anglo-American law).[25] Debates over the issue were reinvigorated, but the defense survived for another half century. As late as 1975, São Paulo appeals court judge and law professor Edgard Bittencourt wrote that husbands who assaulted and battered adulterous wives were acquitted "in most trials," while murderous husbands received reduced sentences, a state of affairs the author and most other jurists found legally sound.[26] Although apparently less frequently, juries sometimes acquitted murders on the "defense of honor" grounds as well, according to Bittencourt. Not until feminists led a campaign to publicize the issue in the early 1980s—which caught the attention of the national and international news media, including the U.S. news program 60 Minutes—was the defense effectively challenged. As late as 1991, however, the Brazilian Federal Supreme Court reiterated the position that the nation's elite jurists had defended since the early decades of the century: acquittal on the grounds of "legitimate defense of honor" was illegal, for honor was "a personal attribute that can not be projected onto another person."[27]

The victory of conservative authoritarians in 1937 thus did not put an end to debates over the nation's moral ideals. To the contrary, the margin for interpreting morality widened as the growing state bureaucracy and new social legislation generated new claims for the rights of honorable citizens. Despite the constitutional stipulation that the state would protect families bound by "indissoluble marriage," for example, many of the labor laws of the 1930s and 1940s provided guarantees of benefits and pensions to the illegitimate children and common-law wives of honest workers.[28] Constant appeals by women who lived in "free unions" eventually led jurists to recognize these women's rights to benefit from virtually all national social legislation. Although Catholic intellectuals and lay militants continued to object vociferously to the recognition of concubines, women not legally married to their partners made steady legal gains over the course of the 1940s and 1950s. By the late 1960s, Brazilian jurists could cite a substantial body of jurisprudence regarding concubinage and consider it "among the most progressive legislation in the world."[29] Already in the 1950s, concubines no longer had to prove that they had cohabited with their partners to claim social benefits or prove their children's rights to paternal recognition.[30] Jurists came to insist on the distinction between the "honest concubine" (previously inconceivable) and the "dishonest concubine."[31] They determined that "the family" was defined by bonds of affection and support, not legal documents or even necessarily a shared household. Correspondingly, jurists came to agree by the 1950s that young women who gave up their virginity for a promise of concubinage could successfully sue their deflowerers in court.[32]

Despite the predictions, hopes, or fears of diverse observers in the 1920s and early 1930s, it is clear that the patriarchal family and the concept of sexual honor survived the transformations that Rio de Janeiro underwent as diverse actors competed to shape the nation's "modernization." In fact, Estado Novo policies worked to increase women's dependence on men and bolster notions of sexual honor. Yet as they designed policies to promote family values, Estado Novo officials and their successors were obliged to recognize both the changes in gender norms that had occurred over the previous two decades and the traditions that defined the meaning of morality, honor, and family for most of the city's population.

Appendix A
Description of Criminal Records Consulted

Investigations of sexual crime in early-twentieth-century Rio de Janeiro were initiated by a private complaint at a local police station, usually filed by the victim's parent or guardian (the same is true today). Not all complaints resulted in a full investigation; many were only recorded in police logbooks, either because police did not consider them sufficiently credible, the complainant decided not to pursue prosecution, or the conflict was resolved with the help of police intervention. Once a complaint was converted into an investigation, police were required to gather the relevant evidence: testimony by the victim, defendant, and at least three witnesses; medical examination performed at the Institute of Legal Medicine; declaration of victim's "impoverishment," which justified the intervention of the public prosecutor's office; and a report by the police delegate. The file was then submitted to the public prosecutor, who either wrote an official accusation or requested that the case be archived without a trial.

From the prosecutor's office, the file was sent to Federal District criminal courts, where it was distributed among one of eight *varas criminais* (criminal courts, a system created in 1923), each headed by a single judge. The distribution among the varas was done centrally to insure an even workload; thus, each vara received cases randomly from all of the city's police stations, with the exception of the jury tribunal (the sixth vara), which, after 1911, tried only the most grievous offenses (murder, attempted murder, and treason). On the basis of the written report and the prosecutor's opinion, the judge decided whether to indict. Frequently, the marriage of victim and accused intervened, in which case the judge ordered the case closed.

If the accused was indicted, the investigation became part of the trial proceedings. Defendant and prosecutors were permitted time to collect additional evidence, and a date was set for the trial, during which arguments and witnesses were heard by the same judge (or, often, his substitute).

Analysis of sexual crime records in this book is based on a selection of 250 police investigations that did not result in an indictment and 250 court trials, all initiated between 1918 and 1941. I recorded key data from all of these records and transcribed 200 of them in full. Throughout the book, names of victims, defendants, and witnesses have been changed to protect the privacy of individuals who might still be living.

The cases were drawn from the records of the first, fifth, seventh, and eighth varas, held by the Arquivo Nacional in Rio de Janeiro. Fifty cases were excluded in order to balance the selections from different years and varas; thus, numeric comparative data in chapters 4 and 5 are drawn from 225 investigations and 225 trials. It was not possible to select cases evenly from all of the varas, because the Arquivo Nacional holdings are incomplete for the period studied (1918–1941), and records from each vara are not catalogued consistently. Thus, most of the cases were taken from the archives of the first and eighth varas (150 from each), for which records and archival guides were available for the entire period. One hundred cases were subsequently located for the seventh vara, also spanning the period; fifty additional cases came from the fifth vara. Twenty-five of the pre-1923 records that are filed with the eighth vara holdings were adjudicated in what was formerly the fourth vara. Although a single judge held responsibility for each vara, turnover and substitutions were frequent, even within the same case, so comparison of various judges' decisions is possible. Prosecutors rotated among the varas, and frequently more than one appeared at different points in each case. The cases originated from all thirty of the city's local police stations, although fewer came from the more remote suburban areas than the downtown districts. The rates of acquittals, convictions, marriages, and decisions not to indict did not vary significantly among the cases selected for each of the varas. Overall, 57 percent of the trials ended in acquittals, 27 percent in convictions, and 16 percent in marriage. Of the police investigations that did not result in indictment, 38 percent were resolved by marriage and 62 percent of the men were freed of any charges.

Cases were initially selected randomly, but the few cases that involved more than one defendant or violence against small children were excluded. The youngest victims in these records are twelve years old (four cases); most are between the ages of sixteen and twenty (396 cases); all are female. The records include 336 cases of deflowering a minor through seduction, deceit, or fraud (art. 267); eighty-nine rape cases (art. 268); and twenty-five cases of indecent assault of a minor (art. 266). The relative proportions of each crime roughly match the proportions found in scattered criminal statistics for the period. Only thirty of the rape cases clearly involved the use of force; only twenty-one involved women older than fifteen. The remainder involved girls younger than sixteen who were considered incapable of consent. The young women accused men of threatening or using violence in some of the deflowering cases (10 percent); many more describe some level of coercion or force. However, with few exceptions, they describe at the same time romance, seduction, and courtship. Rape or deflowering by someone other than the young woman's beau is an exception rather than the rule in criminal records: by the young women's account, they had been dating the accused men in 80 percent of the cases (90 percent of deflowering cases; 55 percent of rape; 50 percent of indecent assault).

Criminal statistics are sparse and unreliable for the Federal District between

1918 and 1942, as police and judicial officials often complained. It is clear, however, that after various categories of physical assault, deflowering consistently vied with robbery as the most frequent crime brought before the courts through the first half of the century and made up about 75 percent of the three major sexual crimes (arts. 266, 267, 268). Available statistics suggest that up until 1940, the numbers of deflowering cases rose with the growing population from an approximate average of 210 per year between 1908 and 1918; 449 in 1927 and 502 in 1928; and an approximate average of 530 from 1937–1940. These numbers dropped by half after 1942, when the crime name was changed to "seduction" and the maximum age of victims was lowered from twenty-one to seventeen. From 1942 to 1961, the numbers of sexual crimes remained relatively steady, while the number of all other crimes more than doubled. See *Estatística policial e criminal de 1912* (Rio de Janeiro: Gabinete de Identificação e de Estatística, 1918), 6; *Anuário estatístico da polícia da Capital Federal, 1917* (Rio de Janeiro: Imprensa Nacional, 1927), 3; Coriolano de Araújo Góes Filho, *Relatório apresentado ao Ministro da Justiça e Negócios Interiores Dr. Augusto de Viana de Castello pelo Chefe de Polícia do Distrito Federal, Dr. Coriolano de Araújo Goes Filho* (Rio de Janeiro: Imprensa Nacional, 1928), 123–24; and *Relatório apresentado ao Ministro da Justiça e Negócios Interiores Dr. Augusto de Viana de Castello pelo Chefe de Polícia do Distrito Federal, Dr. Coriolano de Araújo Goes Filho* (Rio de Janeiro: Imprensa Nacional, 1929), 123–24; José Filadelfo de Barros e Azevedo, *Relatório apresentado ao Sr. Ministro da Justiça e Negócios Interiores pelo Procurador Geral do Distrito Federal* (Rio de Janeiro: Imprensa Nacional, 1936), 17–19; and "Relatório da Procurador Geral," AN, Ministério da Justiça e Negócios Interiores, caixa 595 (1939); *Anuário estatístico do Brasil* (Rio de Janeiro: Instituto Brasileiro de Geografia e Estatística, 1939–1940), 1169–71. After 1942, see the annual reports titled *Crimes e contravenções (Distrito Federal)* (Estado da Guanabara after 1960), published by the Instituto Brasileiro de Geografia e Estatística. The city's population rose from 811,000 in 1906 to 1,158,000 in 1920 and 1,764,000 in 1940 (*Recenseamento Geral do Brasil (1 de Setembro de 1940): Pt. 16, Distrito Federal* [Rio de Janeiro: Instituto Brasileiro de Geografia e Estatística, 1951], xxi).

Appendix B
List of Variables

Variable	Variable Name	Coding
Dependent		
Was the defendant indicted?	Indictment	Yes (trial) = 1;
		No (police investigation) = 0
Outcome of all cases (investigations and trials)	Outcome	Case merely archived = 1
		Defendant acquitted = 1
		Marriage = 2
		Conviction = 3
Defendant was acquitted	Acquit	Yes = 1; No = 0
Defandant married offended woman	Marry	Yes = 1; No = 0
Defendant was convicted	Convict	Yes = 1; No = 0
Independent		
Defendant's occupation	Def_Job	Enlisted military = 1
		Worker = 2
		Tradesman = 3
		Sales/Service/Technical = 4
		Businessman = 4
		Student/Professional = 5
		Other/Unknown is considered missing
Offended woman's occupation	Vic_Job	Domestic servant = 1
		Seamstress = 2
		Factory worker = 3
		Employed in commerce = 4
		Other/Unknown is considered missing

Variable	Variable Name	Coding
Defendant's color	Def_Col	White (branca/o) = 1
		Mixed (parda/o) = 2
		Black (preta/o) = 3
Offended woman's color	Vic_Col	White (branca/o) = 1
		Mixed (parda/o) = 2
		Black (preta/o) = 3
Offended woman is literate	Vic_Read	Yes = 1; No = 0
Defendant confessed	Confess	Yes = 1; No = 0
Defendant and offended woman dating?	Dating	Yes = 1; No = 0
Is defendant married?	Def_Mar	Yes = 1; No = 0
Offended woman's nationality	Vicnatio	Brazilian = 1; Other = 0

Data was recorded by the author for 450 cases of sexual crime consulted at the Arquivo Nacional, Rio de Janeiro, Brazil, and coded by Irfan Nooruddin, Francisco Sanchez, and Harwood McClerking in consultation with the author.

Appendix C
Multivariate Models

Models were designed by Irfan Nooruddin in consultation with the author.

Model I: INDICTMENT (Did the case go to trial?)

$$\text{\ss}_0 + \text{\ss}_1 \text{ VIC\_COL} + \text{\ss}_2 \text{DEF\_COL} + \text{\ss}_3 \text{DEF\_JOB} + \text{\ss}_4 \text{VIC\_READ} + \text{\ss}_5 \text{CONFESS} + \text{\ss}_7 \text{DATING} + \text{\ss}_8 \text{DEF\_MAR} + \epsilon$$

Model II: ACQUIT (Was the defendant acquitted?)

$$\text{\ss}_0 + \text{\ss}_1 \text{ VIC\_COL} + \text{\ss}_2 \text{DEF\_COL} + \text{\ss}_3 \text{DEF\_JOB} + \text{\ss}_4 \text{VIC\_READ} + \text{\ss}_5 \text{CONFESS} + \text{\ss}_6 \text{INDICTMENT} + \text{\ss}_7 \text{DATING} + \text{\ss}_8 \text{DEF\_MAR} + \epsilon$$

Model III: MARRY (Did the defendant marry the offended woman?)

$$\text{\ss}_0 + \text{\ss}_1 \text{ VIC\_COL} + \text{\ss}_2 \text{DEF\_COL} + \text{\ss}_3 \text{DEF\_JOB} + \text{\ss}_4 \text{VIC\_READ} + \text{\ss}_5 \text{CONFESS} + \text{\ss}_6 \text{INDICTMENT} + \text{\ss}_7 \text{DATING} + \text{\ss}_8 \text{DEF\_MAR} + \epsilon$$

Model IV: CONVICT (Was the defendant convicted?)[1]

$$\text{\ss}_0 + \text{\ss}_1 \text{ VIC\_COL} + \text{\ss}_2 \text{DEF\_COL} + \text{\ss}_3 \text{DEF\_JOB} + \text{\ss}_4 \text{VIC\_READ} + \text{\ss}_5 \text{CONFESS} + \text{\ss}_7 \text{DATING} + \text{\ss}_8 \text{DEF\_MAR} + \epsilon$$

where,		
	VIC_COL	= Offended woman's color
	DEF_COL	= Defendant's color
	DEF_JOB	= Defendant's job
	VIC_READ	= Was offended woman literate?
	CONFESS	= Did the defendant confess?
	DATING	= Were the defendant and offended woman dating?
	DEF_MAR	= Was the defendant married?

[1] Trial variable not included because convictions could result only from trials.

Appendix D
Logit Estimates for Each Model

Since all four dependent variables are dichotomous, logit regression is the most appropriate statistical method. The data were also tested using the OLS technique, with very similar results. All initial analysis was performed by Irfan Nooruddin in consultation with the author.

| | Dependent Variable | | | |
	Indictment	Acquittal	Marriage	Conviction
Independent Variables				
Offended woman's color	−0.464***	0.175	−0.161	−0.472***
	(0.203)	(0.254)	(0.258)	(0.228)
Defendant's color	0.479***	0.219	−0.082	0.177
	(0.204)	(0.259)	(0.289)	(0.223)
Defendant's job	−0.226**	0.059	−0.028	−0.167*
	(0.119)	(0.147)	(0.163)	(0.136)
Offended woman literate?	0.628***	−0.514*	0.558*	0.784***
	(0.266)	(0.349)	(0.353)	(0.358)
Defendant confess?	−0.606***	−1.299***	1.702***	0.343
	(0.289)	(0.410)	(0.377)	(0.368)
Indictment		3.165***	−1.701***	
		(0.560)	(0.364)	
Dating?	−0.115	−0.458	1.109***	−0.594*
	(0.329)	(0.483)	(0.422)	(0.460)
Defendant married	−0.353	−0.347	−2.003***	0.229
	(0.362)	(0.415)	(0.750)	(0.424)
Constant	0.805	−3.128***	−0.825	−1.022*
	(0.632)	0.959	(0.856)	(0.792)

| | Indictment | Dependent Variable | | Conviction |
		Acquittal	Marriage	
N	273	265	265	265
Log-Likelihood	−176.84508	−113.05563	−110.44856	−122.74154

Robust Standard Errors are in parentheses.

***Statistically significant at 0.05

** Statistically significant at 0.10

* Statistically significant at 0.20

Notes

Introduction

1 Arquivo Nacional, Rio de Janeiro, Brazil, Ministério da Justiça e Negócios Interiores, Processos Criminais, vara 8, caixa 1807 no. 430 (1923). Criminal records,
cited hereafter as AN, followed by the *vara* (court), *caixa* (box), and record numbers, are all taken from this collection. The names of all deponents have been
changed. See Appendix A for a description of the records selected for this study.
[Readers of Portuguese will appreciate the original language of the letter's crucial passage: "Mas casar só pela pulicia [*sic*]! Em 7 de setembro principiei a amar
outra, até que breve a vou deixar. Em 12 de outubro de 922 [*sic*] principiei a amar
outra imagina fez hotem 130 dias quer diser [*sic*] 4 meses e dez dias pois Lucrecio peco-te que nunca confesses nada a ninguem, mas tirei os trez vintens
dela! Aqui aplica-se o nome de cabaço."]
2 "To deflower a minor woman through seduction, deceit or fraud" was a crime
under art. 267 of the 1890 penal code. Jorge Severiano, *Código penal da República dos Estados Unidos do Brasil* (Rio de Janeiro: Jacinto Ribeiro dos
Santos, 1923), 393.
3 See appendix A.
4 See Appendix A. Beginning in 1911, by Decree 9263 of December 28, sexual
crimes were tried before individual judges (they had previously been tried before juries). Firm statistics are not available, but in a comparison of a small
sample of cases from the turn of the century and from the 1920s and 1930s,
Martha de Abreu Esteves and I found that the earlier jury trials seemed even
more likely to result in an acquittal than the later cases, tried by individual
judges. See Sueann Caulfield and Martha de Abreu Esteves, "Fifty Years of
Virginity in Rio de Janeiro: Sexual Politics and Gender Roles in Juridical and
Popular Discourse, 1890–1940," *Luso-Brazilian Review* 30, 1 (summer 1993):
51, 73, table 1.
5 Evidence of such illegal practices is obviously not recorded by the police themselves, and is therefore sparse. Among cases consulted, there were many in

which the accused young man claimed before a judge that his prior confession at the police station had been coerced. See for example AN, vara 8, caixa 2718 no. 73 (1926); AN, vara 1, caixa 1738 no. 2242 (1927); AN, vara 8, caixa 2772 no. 1191 (1936); AN, vara 1, caixa 1837 no. 1534 (1937); AN, vara 1, caixa 1813 no. 1998 (1938). In one case, a mother testified that police had obtained information about her daughter's whereabouts by beating the daughter's boyfriend. In this case, the casual attitude of the mother and other witnesses about this police action suggested that they did not find this unusual. AN, vara 8, caixa 2770 no. 1361 (1936).

6 I focus on the capital city, Rio de Janeiro, for a number of reasons. Rio had been the center of Brazil's political and cultural life since the late colonial period, and it had been the focus of federally funded renovations that aimed to make it a showcase of modern civilization under the Republic. Although in terms of industrial development and political base the city of São Paulo outshined Rio by World War I, many of the cultural references that came to represent Brazil during these decades, the most obvious being samba music, were associated with the capital. Rio also developed, in the first half of the century, a reputation for pleasure and sensuality, partly a result of the development of the leisure and tourist industries. Finally, the capital attracted a disproportionate number of professional leaders, particularly in the field of law, whose writings reflected their observations in the city.

7 I have found Joan Scott's definition of gender as "a primary way of signifying relations of power" extremely helpful. See "Gender: A Useful Category of Historical Analysis," in her *Gender and the Politics of History* (New York: Columbia University Press, 1988), 28–50. I analyze the usefulness and limitations of Scott's theoretical approach for analyzing historical documents and writing feminist history in "Getting into Trouble: Dishonest Women, Modern Girls, and Women-Men in the Conceptual Language of *Vida policial*, 1925–1927," *Signs* 19, 1 (fall 1993): 146–76.

8 For a brief outline of legal definitions of sexual crimes in Roman and canon law, see Milton Duarte Segurado, *Sedução* (Curitiba: Juruá, 1977), 23–25, 28–29. For an interesting discussion of lawsuits over stolen virginity and broken marriage promises under canon law in Italy, see Sandra Cavallo and Simona Cerutti, "Female Honor and the Social Control of Reproduction in Piedmont between 1600 and 1800," in *Sex and Gender in Historical Perspective*, ed. Edward Muir and Guido Ruggiero (Baltimore: Johns Hopkins University Press, 1990), 73–109. For France in the *ancien régime*, see Claude Grimmer, *La femme et le bâtard: Amours illégitimes et sécrets dans l'ancienne France* (Paris: Renaissance, 1983). Brazilian studies of these kinds of cases include Donald Ramos, "Marriage and Family in Colonial Vila Rica," *Hispanic American Historical Review* 55, 2 (1975): 200–225; Mary del Priore, *Ao sul do corpo: Condição feminina, maternidades e mentalidades no Brasil colônia* (Rio de Janeiro: José Olympio, 1993), 68–80; Maria Beatriz Nizza da Silva, *História da família no Brasil colonial* (Rio de Janeiro: Nova Fronteira, 1998), 196–97; Sheila de Castro

Farias, *A colônia em movimento: Fortuna e família no cotidiano colonial* (Rio de Janeiro: Nova Fronteira, 1998), 67; Dain Borges, *The Family in Bahia, Brazil, 1870–1945* (Stanford: Stanford University Press, 1992), 106–7, 205–8; Celeste Zenha, "As práticas da justiça no cotidiano da pobreza" (master's thesis, Universidade Federal Fluminense, 1984); Boris Fausto, *Crime e cotidiano: A criminalidade em São Paulo, 1880–1924* (São Paulo: Brasiliense, 1984); Cristina Donza Cancela, "Adoráveis e dissimuladas: As relações amorosas das mulheres das camadas populares na Belém do final do século XIX e início do XX" (master's diss., Universidade Estadual de Campinas, 1997); Karla Adriana Martins Bessa, "O crime de sedução e as relações de gênero," *Cadernos Pagu* 2 (1994): 175–96; Martha de Abreu Esteves, *Meninas perdidas: Os populares e o cotidiano do amor no Rio de Janeiro da belle époque* (Rio de Janeiro: Paz e Terra, 1989). For statistics of criminal cases in Rio de Janeiro, see Appendix A.

9 See Stuart B. Schwartz, "Pecar en colonias: Mentalidades populares, inquisición y actitudes hacia la fornicación simple en España, Portugal, y las colonias americanas," *Cuadernos de historia moderna* 18 (1997): 51–68; José María García Fuentes, *Inquisición en Granada en el siglo XVI: Fuentes para su estudio* (Granada: Departamento de Historia de la Universidad de Granada, 1981); Sara T. Nalle, *God in La Mancha: Religious Reform and the People of Cuenca, 1500–1650* (Baltimore: Johns Hopkins University Press, 1992); Henry Kamen, *The Phoenix and the Flame: Catalonia and the Counter Reformation* (New Haven: Yale University Press, 1993). There are no similar studies for Portugal, but this attitude was expressed by the Portuguese who testified before the Brazilian Holy Tribunal. See esp. Ronaldo Vainfas, *Trópico dos pecados: Moral, sexualidade e inquisição no Brasil* (Rio de Janeiro: Campus, 1989), 53.

10 Schwartz, "Pecar"; Solange Alberro, "La sexualidad manipulada en Nueva España: Modalidades de recuperación y de adaptación frente a los tribunales eclesiásticos," in *Familia y sexualidad en Nueva España* (Mexico City: Fondo de Cultura Económica, 1982), 238–57; Vainfas, *Trópico dos pecados*, 64.

11 Asunción Lavrin, "Introduction: The Scenario, the Actors and the Issues," in *Sexuality and Marriage in Colonial Latin America*, ed. Lavrin (Lincoln: University of Nebraska Press, 1989), 1–43; Sergio Ortega, ed., *De la santidad a la perversión o de por qué no se cumplía la ley de Dios en la sociedad novohispana* (Mexico City: Grijalbo, 1985). Ronaldo Vainfas demonstrates the relative leniency of the Inquisition in colonial Brazil in "A teia da intriga," in *História e sexualidade no Brasil*, ed. Vainfas (Rio de Janeiro: Graal, 1986), 41–66, and in *Trópico dos pecados*. See also Laura de Mello e Souza, *O diabo e a terra de Santa Cruz* (São Paulo: Companhia das Letras, 1987); Luciano Raposo de Almeida Figueiredo, *Barrocas famílias: Vida familiar em Minas Gerais no século XVIII* (São Paulo: Hucitec, 1997); Fernando Torres Londoño, "El concubinato y la iglesia en el Brasil colonial," *Estudos CEDHAL* (Centro de Estudos de Demografia Histórica da América Latina, Universidade de São Paulo), 1988; Eduardo Hoornaert, "A cristianidade durante a primeira época colonial," in *História da Igreja no Brasil*, ed. Hoornaert et al. (Petrópolis: Vozes, 1979), 2:

248–49; Elizabeth Anne Kuznesof provides summaries of the conclusions of the historical literature on church vigilance of colonial morality in "Sexual Politics, Race and Bastard-Bearing in Nineteenth-Century Brazil: A Question of Culture or Power?" *Journal of Family History* 16, 3 (1991): 241–60, esp. 242, 244–45; and in "Sexuality, Gender and the Family in Colonial Brazil," *Luso-Brazilian Review* 30, 1 (summer 1993): 119–132, esp. 121–22.

12 See Vainfas, *Trópico dos pecados*, 93–101; Faria, *Colônia em movimento*, esp. 49–67, 312–42; Robert Slenes, *Na senzala uma flor: As esperanças e as recordações na formação da família escrava* (Rio de Janeiro: Nova Fronteira, 1999). For the nineteenth century, Eni de Mesquita Samara, *As mulheres, o poder e a família, São Paulo, Século XIX* (São Paulo: Ed. Marco Zero, 1989), 39–44, 87; Elizabeth Anne Kuznesof, *Household Economy and Urban Development: São Paulo, 1765–1836* (Denver: Westview Press, 1986), 153–171.

13 Verena Martínez-Alier, *Marriage, Class, and Colour in Nineteenth-Century Cuba*, 2d ed. (Ann Arbor: University of Michigan Press, 1989).

14 This point is elaborated most fully by Patricia Seed, *To Love, Honor, and Obey in Colonial Mexico: Conflicts over Marriage Choice, 1574–1821* (Stanford: Stanford University Press, 1988), 65–67.

15 Muriel Nazzari, *Disappearance of the Dowry: Women, Families, and Social Change in São Paulo, Brazil, 1600–1900* (Stanford: Stanford University Press, 1991); Asunción Lavrin and Edith Couturier, "Dowries and Wills: A View of Women's Socioeconomic Role in Colonial Guadalajara and Puebla, 1640–1790," *Hispanic American Historical Review* 59, 2 (1970): 280–304.

16 This honor/shame complex grants men broad sexual license but requires women's sexual chastity and submission to male authority. A woman has no honor, only shame; a man's honor depends largely on his ability to command authority and to defend the sexual honesty of the women in his family. The model was built in the anthropological literature on the Mediterranean produced mostly in the 1960s and 1970s. The work is generally based on participant-observation among nonelite men; much of this literature discusses the ways these values differ by social class. See the seminal collection by J. G. Peristiany, ed., *Honor and Shame: The Values of Mediterranean Society* (Chicago: University of Chicago Press, 1966); Julian Pitt-Rivers, *The Fate of Shechem, or the Politics of Sex: Essays in the Anthropology of the Mediterranean* (Cambridge: Cambridge University Press, 1977); Jane Schneider, "Of Vigilance and Virgins: Honor, Shame and Access to Resources in Mediterranean Societies," *Ethnology* 10, 1 (January 1971): 1–24; Anton Blok, "Rams and Billy-Goats: A Key to the Mediterranean Code of Honour," *Man*, n.s. (1981): 16: 427–40; Julian Pitt-Rivers, "Honor," in *International Encyclopedia of the Social Sciences* (New York: Macmillan, 1968), 6: 503–11. More recent anthropological work, focusing on women's lives in so-called honor/shame cultures, has challenged the rigidity of the model by demonstrating that women interpret their own lives and worlds in dynamic and diverse ways, and their sense of virtue cannot be summed up as "shame." See esp. Lila Abu-Lughod, *Veiled Sentiments: Honor and Poetry in a*

Bedouin Society (Berkeley and Los Angeles: University of California Press, 1986) and *Writing Women's Worlds: Bedouin Stories* (Berkeley and Los Angeles: University of California Press, 1993); Unni Wikan, "Shame and Honour: A Contestable Pair," *Man*, n.s., 19 (1984): 635–52. For Latin America, studies of honor and shame have focused almost exclusively on historical analyses of the colonial period and the nineteenth century, and concur that "honor" and "honesty" were determined by varying combinations of an individual's behavior, wealth, nobility, family precedence, race or ethnicity, physical traits, and other criteria. For Brazil, see esp. Vainfas, *Trópico dos pecados;* Mello e Souza, *O diabo;* Figueiredo, *Barrocas famílias;* Leila Mezan Algranti, *Honradas e devotas: Mulheres da colônia* (Rio de Janeiro: José Olympio, 1993); Priore, *Ao sul do corpo;* Esteves, *Meninas perdidas;* Rachel Soihet, *Condição feminina e formas de violência: Mulheres pobres e ordem urbana, 1890–1920* (Rio de Janeiro: Forense, 1989); Celeste Zenha, "As práticas da justiça"; Sandra Lauderdale Graham, *House and Street: The Domestic World of Servants and Masters in Nineteenth-Century Rio de Janeiro* (New York: Cambridge University Press, 1989); Peter Beattie, "The House, the Street, and the Barracks: Reform and Honorable Masculine Social Space in Brazil, 1864–1945," *Hispanic American Historical Review* 76, 3 (1996): 439–73. For other Latin American regions, see Martínez-Alier, *Marriage;* Ramón Gutiérrez, *When Jesus Came, the Corn Mothers Went Away: Marriage, Sexuality, and Power in New Mexico, 1500–1846* (Stanford: Stanford University Press, 1991); Seed, *To Love, Honor, and Obey;* Steve Stern, *The Secret History of Gender: Women, Men and Power in Late Colonial Mexico* (Chapel Hill: University of North Carolina Press, 1995), esp. 13–18; and two outstanding collections of articles: Lavrin, ed., *Sexuality and Marriage;* Lyman Johnson and Sonia Lipsett-Rivera, *The Faces of Honor: Sex, Shame, and Violence in Colonial Latin America* (Albuquerque: University of New Mexico Press, 1998).

17 In addition to works cited above, see Mariza Corrêa, "Repensando a família patriarcal brasileira," in *Colcha de retalhos: Estudos sobre a família no Brasil* (São Paulo: Brasiliense, 1982), 13–38; and historiographical reviews by Kuznesof, "Sexuality," 119–21; Borges, *The Family in Bahia*, 1–7; and Sheila de Castro Faria, "História da família e demografia histórica," in *Domínios da história: Ensaios de teoria e metodologia*, ed. Ciro Flamarion Cardoso and Ronaldo Vainfas (Rio de Janeiro: Campus, 1997), 241–58. On elite women's transgressions, see esp. Muriel Nazzari, "An Urgent Need to Conceal," in *The Faces of Honor: Sex, Shame, and Violence in Colonial Latin America*, ed. Lyman Johnson and Sonia Lipsett-Rivera (Albuquerque: University of New Mexico Press, 1998), 103–26; Maria Beatriz Nizza da Silva, "A imagem da concubina no Brasil colonial," in *Rebeldia e submissão*, ed. Albertina de Oliveira Costa and Cristina Bruschini (São Paulo: Vértice, 1989), 17–60.

18 See for example Priori, *Ao sul do corpo;* Figueiredo, *Barrocas famílias;* Eliana Maria Rea Goldschmidt, "Virtude e pecado: Sexualidade em São Paulo colonial" in *Entre a virtude e o pecado,* ed. Albertina de Oliveira Costa and

Cristina Bruschini (São Paulo: Rosa dos Tempos and Fundação Carlos Chagas, 1992), 15–36; Del Priore, *Ao sul do corpo*, 68–80. Del Priore argues that colonial women "used" church morality to gain the security that marriage offered for raising children and thus sees women's complaints of seduction and other sexual crimes as forms of resistance to patriarchal oppression. For the nineteenth and early twentieth centuries, Maria Odila Leite da Silva Dias, *Quotidiano e poder em São Paulo no século XIX: Ana Gertrudes de Jesus* (São Paulo: Brasiliense, 1984); Soihet, *Condição feminina*; Esteves, *Meninas perdidas*.

19   Vainfas argues that the Catholic Church succeeded in instilling guilt in the colonial "collective conscience," and in "superimposing Catholic morality over colonial moralities," in "A teia da intriga," 65–66. This argument is developed further in *Trópico dos pecados*; see esp. p. 111.

20   Faria, *A colônia em movimento*, esp. 67. Faria believes that virginity was an important prerequisite for marriage among elites, but not slave and free poor families.

21   Lavrin, "Introduction," 7. Stern, reviewing the literature on the colonial "honor/shame complex of values" in Spanish America remarks that a major scholarly advance has been the awareness of "a dialectic of women's active conformity to and deviance from" a gendered code of honor. See *The Secret History*, 17, 386 nn. 21, 22.

22   Susan M. Socolow, "Acceptable Partners: Marriage Choice in Colonial Argentina, 1778–1810," in *Sexuality and Marriage*, ed. Lavrin, 212. The first to study the complex and shifting royal edicts regarding parental rights over children's marriage choices and marriages among social "unequals" is Martínez-Alier, *Marriage*. Patricia Seed sees this legislation and its effects as evidence that parental control over marriage choices increased in the late colonial period, but other scholars argue the opposite. See Seed, *To Love, Honor, and Obey*; Gutiérrez, *When Jesus Came*, 298–336; Stern, *The Secret History*, 384–85 n. 13; Lavrin, "Introduction," 17; Nazzari, *Disappearance*, 130–40.

23   Socolow, "Acceptable Partners."

24   Borges, *The Family in Bahia*, 1; Gutiérrez, *When Jesus Came*, 327–36.

25   Nazzari, *Disappearance*. The transformation, as Nazzari recognizes, was a relative one, as wealthy families continued, and continue, to form business and political partnerships through marriages well into the twentieth century, particularly in the Northeast, but also in São Paulo. See also Susan K. Besse, *Restructuring Patriarchy: The Modernization of Gender Inequality in Brazil, 1914–1940* (Chapel Hill: University of North Carolina Press, 1996), 51–53. For the Northeast, see Linda Lewin, *Politics and Parentela e Paraíba: A Case Study of Family-Based Oligarchy in Brazil* (Princeton: Princeton University Press, 1987).

26   Doris Sommer, *Foundational Fictions* (Berkeley and Los Angeles: University of California Press, 1991), esp. introduction. See also Jean Franco, *Plotting Women: Gender and Representation in Mexico* (New York: Columbia University Press, 1989), chap. 4. Campaigns to control prostitution in the late nine-

teenth century make the link between nation-building and sexual morality particularly clear, as Donna Guy argues in *Sex and Danger in Buenos Aires: Prostitution, Family and Nation in Argentina* (Lincoln: University of Nebraska Press, 1991). Prostitution control and other "moral hygiene" campaigns in nineteenth- and early twentieth-century Rio de Janeiro are discussed in chaps. 2 and 3.

27 Roberto da Matta, *A casa e a rua: Espaço, cidadania, mulher e morte no Brasil* (São Paulo: Brasiliense, 1985); *Carnivals, Rogues, and Heroes: An Interpretation of the Brazilian Dilemma*, trans. John Drury (Notre Dame: University of Notre Dame Press, 1991), 61–90.

28 Beattie, "The House, the Street, and the Barracks."

29 Sidney Chalhoub, *Trabalho, lar e botequim: O cotidiano dos trabalhadores no Rio de Janeiro da belle époque* (São Paulo: Brasiliense, 1986); Esteves, *Meninas perdidas*, pt. 2; Soihet, *Condição feminina*; S. Graham, *House and Street*.

30 Richard Graham, *Patronage and Politics in Nineteenth-Century Brazil* (Stanford: Stanford University Press, 1990), 7.

31 Esteves, *Meninas perdidas*, esp. 15–16, 19–34. For Foucault's hypothesis for Western Europe, see Michel Foucault, *A History of Sexuality*, vol. 1 (New York: Vintage, 1980).

32 Interesting parallels can be drawn in very different contexts, such as prerevolutionary Russia and interwar Japan. Laura Engelstein argues that Russian professional elites welcomed Western "modernity," but distrusted what they considered the excesses of liberal individualism, particularly in regard to women's autonomy. See Engelstein, *The Keys to Happiness: Sex and the Search for Modernity in Fin-de-Siècle Russia* (Ithaca: Cornell University Press, 1992), esp. 4–8. Japanese observers of the "modern woman" in the 1920s were torn between admiration for Western modernity and preoccupation with the loss of tradition. See Laurel Rasplica Rodd, "Yosano Akiko and the Taisho Debate over the 'New Woman,' " and Miriam Silverberg, "The Modern Girl as Militant," in *Recreating Japanese Women, 1600–1945* ed. Gail Lee Bernstein (Berkeley and Los Angeles: University of California Press, 1991), 175–98, 239–66. This ambiguity about imported modernity surfaced at the center of Western Europe as well. Mary Nolan finds that Germans who were "infatuated" with modern industry in the United States were also preoccupied about the effects of modernity on women and the family. Nolan, *Visions of Modernity: American Business and the Modernization of Germany* (Oxford: Oxford University Press, 1994), 108–130.

33 See appendix A.

34 Chalhoub, *Trabalho, lar e botequim*; Esteves, *Meninas perdidas*; Caulfield and Esteves, "Fifty Years of Virginity."

35 Sidney Chalhoub, *Visões da liberdade: Uma história das últimas décadas da escravidão na corte* (São Paulo: Companhia das Letras, 1990), 18–19. Martha de Abreu Esteves has also revised her understanding of the breach between

210

popular and official cultures. See Martha Abreu (formerly Martha de Abreu Esteves), "O império do divino: Festas religiosas e cultura popular no Rio de Janeiro, século XIX" (Ph.D. diss., Universidade Estadual de Campinas, 1996).

36 Judith Butler, *Gender Trouble: Feminism and the Subversion of Identity* (New York: Routledge, 1990). See also Caulfield, "Getting into Trouble." My understanding of culture follows the recent trend in anthropology that defines culture as a contested process of social change rather than a system. I have found Lila Abu-Lughod's work on culture and honor particularly useful. Abu-Lughod warns that culture is a "dangerous fiction" that essentializes differences among cultures as it denies the differences within them. Her strategy is to "write against culture" by relating stories that illustrate how individuals experience, give meaning to, and use cultural systems such as honor and shame. Individuals rarely reject the norms that hold these systems together, but nonetheless continually reshape them. Abu-Lughod, *Writing Women's Worlds*, esp. 1–42; *Veiled Sentiments*; and "Writing against Culture," in *Recapturing Anthropology*, ed. Richard Fox (Santa Fe: School of American Research Press, 1991), 137–62.

37 Other changes included lowering the maximum age of potential deflowering victims from twenty to seventeen and stipulating that the crime involved taking advantage of a minor's "inexperience" or "justifiable trust." See Tiago Ribeiro Pontes, *Código penal brasileiro comentado* (Rio de Janeiro: Freitas Bastos, 1977), 339.

Chapter 1 Sexual Honor and Republican Law

1 Afrânio Peixoto, *Sexologia forense* (Rio de Janeiro: Guanabara, 1934), 58–59. See also Nina Rodrigues, "Des formes de l'hymen et de leur rôle dans la rupture de cette membrane," *Annales d'hygiene publique et de médécine légale* (June 1900); Agostinho J. de Souza Lima, *Tratado de medicina legal*, 5th ed. (Rio de Janeiro: Freitas Bastos, 1933 [1st ed. 1905]), 513–581; Miguel Sales, *Hymens complacentes* (Rio de Janeiro: Imprensa Nacional, 1912); Nascimento Silva, "Defloramento," *Revista siniátrica*, 6, 6 (June 1923); Oscar Freire, "Conceito do crime de defloramento—'ruptura hymenal incompleta,'" *Revista dos tribunais*, 44 (1922): 695–710; J. P. Porto-Carrero, preface to A. Lima, *Tratado*. Dissatisfied with the absence of a precise vocabulary for forensic description, Rodrigues, Silva, Peixoto, and Freire each developed original systems for classifying different types of hymens. In 1933, the Portuguese legal-medical specialist Asdrubal Antônio de Aguiar published a compendium of what he considered the eighteen best hymenal classification systems, including the work of Rodrigues, Silva, and Peixoto. See Aguiar, *Ciência sexual: Contribuições para o seu estudo* (Lisbon, 1933). For a brief outline of Freire's system, see Flamínio Favero, "Classificação de Oscar Freire para as formas himenais," *Arquivos do Instituto Médico-Legal e do Gabinete de Identidade* (July 1932): 77–79.

2 French specialists were cited most frequently, particularly Charcot, Voisin, Devergie, Tourdes, Ambroise Tardieu, Lacassagne, Legrande du Saulle, L. Thoinot, Vibert, Brouardel, Balthazar, Lutaud, Parent-Duchalet, and Coutagne. Italians such as Lombroso also appeared frequently in Brazilian texts, as did the German specialist Hofmann and the Russian Maschka.

3 Of greatest significance was the debate over the *hímen complacente* ("complacent" or "yielding" hymen). The French forensic expert Legrande du Saulle coined the phrase in the mid-nineteenth century to describe a highly elastic hymen that did not necessarily rupture during sexual intercourse, a phenomenon most European specialists writing up until the early decades of the twentieth century considered extremely rare.

4 Peixoto, *Sexologia*, 84–85.

5 See L. Thoinot, *Medicolegal Aspects of Moral Offenses*, trans. Arthur W. Weysse (Philadelphia: F. A. Davis, 1919), for a discussion of sexual crime in the French penal code and the obligatory legal-medical examination, including information on the previous state of the victim's hymen.

6 Miguel Sales, "A perícia médico-legal nos crimes sexuais," *Revista de criminologia e medicina legal* 2, 3–4 (September–October 1928): 59–62, esp. 59.

7 Peixoto, *Sexologia*, 85. The demographic imbalance of men to women was primarily attributable to the heavy influx of single male immigrants beginning in the late nineteenth century. As foreign immigration dropped in the second decade of the twentieth century and women made up greater proportions of those who did immigrate, males as a percentage of the total population of the Federal District declined in census data from 58 percent in 1872 to 52 percent in 1920 and 50 percent in 1940. See *Recenseamento geral do Brasil (1 de setembro de 1940)*, pt. 16, *Distrito Federal* (Rio de Janeiro: 1951), 5.

8 Peixoto, *Sexologia*, 85.

9 Sales, "A perícia médico-legal," 59.

10 Martha de Abreu Esteves, *Meninas perdidas: Os populares e o cotidiano do amor no Rio de Janeiro da belle époque* (Rio de Janeiro: Paz e Terra, 1989), esp. pt. 2; Sueann Caulfield and Martha de Abreu Esteves, "Fifty Years of Virginity in Rio de Janeiro: Sexual Politics and Gender Roles in Juridical and Popular Discourse, 1890–1940," *Luso-Brazilian Review* 30, 1 (summer 1993): 47–74.

11 Studies of conjugal conflicts in colonial Latin America have come to this conclusion as well. Women find allies first among their families of origin, kin, and neighbors, then higher authorities when their male partners break what Richard Boyer calls a "patriarchal contract"; or the unwritten agreement between women and men on gender roles, prerogatives, and responsibilities. Boyer, "Women, *La Mala Vida*, and the Politics of Marriage," in *Sexuality and Marriage in Colonial Latin America*, ed. Asunción Lavrin (Lincoln: University of Nebraska Press, 1989), 252–86; Stern, *The Secret History of Gender: Women, Men and Power in Late Colonial Mexico* (Chapel Hill: University of North Carolina Press, 1995), esp. 82–88, 97–114, 269–84, 313–23. Women might also take recourse against men through witchcraft and networks of

female allies. See for example Ruth Behar, "Sexual Witchcraft, Colonialism, and Women's Powers: Views from the Mexican Inquisition," in *Sexuality and Marriage,* ed. Lavrin, 178–208.

12 "Hymenolatria" is the title of ch. 4 of Peixoto's *Sexologia forense.* He also published an article that summarizes his position with the same title in *Arquivos de medicina legal e identificação* 4, 9 (July 1934): 105–17.

13 Peixoto, "Hymenolatria," 117. Peixoto's analysis has a contemporary echo in the work of Bernardo Elias Lahdo, who declared that hymenolatry was a sign of underdevelopment in *O defloramento da mulher, ignorado pelo marido, é causa de anulação de casamento?* (Rio de Janeiro: n.p., 1981), 22.

14 Francisco José Viveiros de Castro, *Os delitos contra a honra da mulher,* 2d ed. (Rio de Janeiro: Freitas Bastos, 1932), 11, cited in Caulfield and Esteves, "Fifty Years of Virginity," 48.

15 Esteves, *Meninas perdidas,* esp. pt. 1; Caulfield and Esteves, "Fifty Years of Virginity," 48–49. The quotes are from Francisco José Viveiros de Castro, *Atentados ao pudor,* 3d ed. (Rio de Janeiro: Freitas Bastos, 1934), xiii, cited in Caulfield and Esteves, "Fifty Years of Virginity," 49.

16 Esteves, *Meninas perdidas,* introduction and pt. 1, esp. 25–32.

17 For the decline in jurists' political influence after the establishment of the Federal Republic see Boris Fausto, "Society and Politics," in *Brazil: Empire and Republic, 1822–1930,* ed. Leslie Bethell (Cambridge: Cambridge University Press, 1989), 265–66. On the homogeneity and political influence of nineteenth-century law school graduates, especially magistrates, who were trained in Coimbra until the Olinda (later Recife) and São Paulo law schools opened in 1827–1828, see Thomas Flory, *Judge and Jury in Imperial Brazil, 1808–1871* (Austin: University of Texas Press, 1981); José Murilo de Carvalho, *A construção da ordem: A elite política imperial* (Rio de Janeiro: Campus, 1980); Fernando Azevedo, *Brazilian Culture: An Introduction to the Study of Culture in Brazil,* trans. William Rex Crawford (New York: Macmillan, 1950), 177–91; Kátia de Queiros Mattoso, "Os baianos no governo central: Origem social e formação," in *Bahia, século XIX: Uma província no Império* (Rio de Janeiro: Nova Fronteira, 1985), 279–80; Alberto Venâncio Filho, *Das arcadas ao bacharelismo,* 2d ed. (São Paulo: Perspectiva, 1982); Sérgio Adorno, *Os aprendizes do poder* (Rio de Janeiro: Paz e Terra, 1988). Magistrates had also occupied the top rungs of the colonial administration.

18 João Luiz Alves, *Código civil da República dos Estados Unidos do Brasil,* 2d ed. (Rio de Janeiro: F. Briguiet, 1923), xxi, xxv–xxvi. See also Clóvis Bevilaqua's description of the criticism of his proposal for the civil code, particularly that of conservative nationalist Andrade Figueira in *Código civil dos Estados Unidos do Brasil comentado por Clóvis Bevilaqua,* 9th ed. (Rio de Janeiro: Livraria Francisco Alves, 1951), vol. 1:29–55, esp. 38.

19 F. Castro, *Atentados ao pudor,* xi.

20 The term "classical law," or the "classical school," was used in mid– to late-nineteenth-century Europe to refer to a range of Enlightenment thought, in-

cluding that of Italian jurist Cesare Beccaria (1738–1794) as well as Montesquieu, Rousseau, Kant, Hegel, and Bentham. Despite crucial differences among these thinkers, they shared a set of principles including notions of equality, free will, moral responsibility, and just, "proportional" punishment for each criminal act. See esp. Cesare Beccaria, *On Crimes and Punishments* (1764; Indianapolis: Hackett, 1986). For discussion of the classical school in France, see Gordon Wright, *Between the Guillotine and Liberty: Two Centuries of the Crime Problem in France* (New York: Oxford University Press, 1983), 111; for Germany, Richard Friedrich Wetzell, "Criminal Law Reform in Imperial Germany" (Ph.D. diss., Stanford University, 1991). Brazilian jurists generally associated classical law with Beccaria and especially his nineteenth-century follower, Francesco Carrara (1805–1888); the work most often cited was Carrara, *Programma del corso di diritto criminale*, 10th ed. (1865; Florence: Fratelli Cammelli, 1907). Enlightenment philosophers were discussed by only a few turn-of-the-century legal theorists in Brazil, leading Pedro Lessa to complain in 1912 that ignorance of the philosophical principles of law was to blame for grave defects in Brazil's legal system (*Estudos de filosofia de direito*, 2d ed. [1912; Rio de Janeiro: Francisco Alves, 1916], 7–11).

21 As was the case in many former Spanish colonies, nineteenth-century state politics came to be dominated by two parties: Conservative and Liberal. It became increasingly difficult to discern the differences between them after the initial post-Independence Liberal idealism gave way to class solidarity and pragmatism among the political elites affiliated with each party, and as liberal principles were increasingly disassociated from democratic principles. Nonetheless, Roberto Schwartz's argument that liberalism was an imported ideology, out of sync with Brazil's authoritarian and patriarchal political reality, has been discredited by scholars who argue that Brazilian thinkers developed eclectic forms of liberalism that were compatible with limited citizenship rights, social inequality and even slavery. See Adorno, *Os aprendizes*, esp. 235–40; Emília Viotti da Costa, *The Brazilian Empire: Myths and Histories* (Chicago: University of Chicago Press, 1985), 63–70; J. Carvalho, *A construção da ordem*; Maria Sylvia de Carvalho Franco, "As idéias estão no lugar," *Caderno de debates* 1 (1976): 61–64; Alfredo Bosi, *Dialética da colonização* (São Paulo: Companhia das Letras, 1992); Paulo Mercadante, *A consciência conservadora no Brasil* (Rio de Janeiro: Nova Fronteira, 1985). For a synopsis of some of the major positions in this debate, see Keila Grinberg, *Liberata: a lei da ambigüidade: As ações de liberdade da Corte de Apelação do Rio de Janeiro no século XIX* (Rio de Janeiro: Relume-Dumará, 1994), 53–57; for a more in-depth analysis, see Roberto Ventura, *Estilo tropical: História cultural e polêmicas literárias no Brasil* (São Paulo: Companhia das Letras, 1991). For Schwartz's argument, see "As idéias fora do lugar," *Estudos Cebrap* 3 (1973): 151–61.

22 Araújo Filgueiras Júnior, *Código criminal do Império do Brasil*, 2d ed. (Rio de Janeiro: Laemmert, 1876). Liberal attempts to decentralize and democratize

the judicial system through a second document, the 1832 Procedural Code, had a more significant immediate impact on imperial politics. Procedural innovations such as the jury trial and popularly elected local justices of the peace (created in 1827) threatened the authority of the central state and its cadre of elite professional bureaucrats, most of whom were magistrates. Conservative Party legislators mounted a successful campaign to reverse these effects by rewriting the Procedural Code in 1841. Flory, *Judge and Jury*, 15–16, 50–108, 111–115, 172–73. See also Américo Jacobina Lacombe, "A cultura jurídica," in *História geral da civilização brasileira*, ed. Sérgio Buarque de Holanda (São Paulo: Difusão Européia do Livro, 1967), vol. 2, pt. 3, 356–68. Brazil shared with the rest of Latin America and most of Europe the civil law tradition, rooted in Roman and canon law, as well as the drive to codify civil, commercial, and penal law in the nineteenth century. For an excellent, succinct overview of civil law, see John Henry Merryman, *The Civil Law Tradition: An Introduction to the Legal Systems of Western Europe and Latin America* (Stanford: Stanford University Press, 1969).

23 Cândido Mendes de Almeida, *Código filipino ou ordenações do Reino de Portugal*, 14th ed. (Rio de Janeiro: Tipografia do Instituto filomático, 1870).

24 Flory, *Judge and Jury*, 50–108, 172–73.

25 See João Vieira de Araújo, *O código penal interpretado: Parte especial* (Rio de Janeiro: Imprensa Nacional, 1902), 1: vii; Alves, *Código civil*, xvii; C. J. de Assis Ribeiro, *Contribuição ao conhecimento do código criminal brasileiro de 1830: A revolução francesa e suas conseqüências jurídico-penais* (Rio de Janeiro: Fundação Getúlio Vargas, 1946); Basileu Garcia, *Instituições de direito penal* (São Paulo: Grijalbo, 1967), 122–123; Lacombe, "A cultura jurídica," 357.

26 Lacombe, "A cultura jurídica," 357.

27 See Ribeiro, *Contribuição*; Flory, *Judge and Jury*, 109–11. For a discussion of these concerns in Beccaria, see Wetzell, "Criminal Law Reform," ch. 1; Wright, *Between the Guillotine*, ch. 1.

28 The Marquês de Pombal, for example, nullified state enforcement of Council of Trent mandates after expelling the Jesuits in 1759. See Almeida, *Código filipino*, 503, n. 2. In the annexes to this work, Almeida reprints the most important civil and criminal laws that modified the Philippine Ordenances. See also J. M. Correa Telles, "Comentário crítico à Lei da Boa Razão," in *Auxiliar jurídico servindo de apêndice a décima quarta edição do código filipino*, ed. Cândido Mendes de Almeida (Rio de Janeiro: Tipografia do Instituto Filomático, 1869); and F. K. Juenger, "The Legal Heritage of the Americas," in *Law and Legal Systems of the Commonwealth Caribbean States* (Washington, D.C., OAS, 1986), 57, 63, cited in Thomas H. Reynolds and Arturo A. Flores, *Foreign Law: Current Sources of Codes and Basic Legislation in Jurisdictions of the World* (Littleton, Colo.: Fred B. Rothman, 1989), 1: 3.

29 Like their European contemporaries, Brazilian jurists modified the rigid classical conception of equal responsibility and made exceptions for minors, the

insane, those acting in self-defense, and others. They also specified attenuating and aggravating circumstances that would modify sentencing (Arts. 3, 14–20, Filgueras Junior, *Codigo criminal*, 6, 15–23).

30 For a description of each of these efforts see "Preliminares" in Bevilaqua, *Código civil*, 1: 9–20.

31 See n. 28.

32 Bk. 5, title 38, Almeida, *Código filipino*, 1188.

33 Bk. 5, title 6, par. 8; title 7; title 49, pars. 1, 2, 5; title 50, Almeida, *Código filipino*, 1154, 1158, 1197–1201.

34 On regulation of titles and clothing, see Silvia Lara, "The Signs of Color: Women's Dress and Racial Relations in Salvador and Rio de Janeiro, ca. 1750–1815," *Colonial Latin American Review* 6, 2 (1997): 205–24. For laws punishing dueling, insults, and gossip see Bk. 5, titles 42, 43, 84, 85, Almeida, *Ordenaçoes filipinas*, 1192–93; 1232–33.

35 Sodomy, for example, was considered equivalent to *lesa magestad*; sleeping with infidels, nuns, or married women were capital offenses; different laws punished entering private homes or convents with the intention "to do something illicit"; and a man who married an honest woman under twenty-five against her guardian's wishes lost his property to the guardian among other punishments (the woman could be disinherited under Bk. 4, title 88), unless the marriage raised the woman's status (Bk. 5, titles 13–16, 22, Almeida, *Código filipino*, 1162–64, 1172).

36 The code separated "public crimes," or crimes against the state (part 2), from "private crimes," or those against individuals (part 3); the latter included "Crimes against the security of honor" (title 2, ch. 2). Sexual crimes (arts. 219–228) included defloration of a virgin or seduction of an honest woman younger than seventeen; incestuous rape; rape of an honest woman; rape of a prostitute, and abduction of a woman for libidinous purposes with or without violence. Arts. 229–246 punished diverse insults (Filgueiras Júnior, *Código criminal*, 241–55).

37 "Response to insult or dishonor" was an attenuating circumstance under Art. 18, par. 4, Filgueiras Júnior, *Código criminal*, 21. Almeida explains that this referred to female adultery (Almeida, *Código filipino*, 1188, n. 6).

38 Bk. 5, title 25, Almeida, *Código filipino*, 1174. As Michel Foucault has argued, the most extreme corporal punishments in medieval law were seldom applied, but served to instill terror and respect for royal power (Foucault, *Discipline and Punish: The Birth of the Prison*, 2d ed. [New York: Vintage, 1995]). Ronaldo Vainfas and others have shown that this was particularly true in Brazil. See esp. Vainfas, *Trópico dos pecados*, 285–339. Muriel Nazzari finds that in eighteenth-century São Paulo, extreme penalties for sexual transgressions were attenuated by subterfuge, aided even by the Church, which instructed clergy to conceal women's sexual sins in order to preserve their honor and protect them from male violence. See Muriel Nazzari, "An Urgent Need to Conceal," in *The Faces of Honor: Sex, Shame, and Violence in Colonial Latin*

216

America, ed. Lyman Johnson and Sonia Lipsett-Rivera (Albuquerque: University of New Mexico Press, 1998), 103–26. For adultery laws in the 1830 code, see Arts. 250–251, Filgueiras Júnior, *Código criminal*, 268. However reminiscent of the Ordinances, these laws were among the most advanced of their time. Nineteenth-century French and Italian legislation also punished adulterous women and was even more lenient to husbands than Brazilian law: adulterers were punished only if they kept a concubine "notoriously" or "in the conjugal home" (F. Castro, *Os delitos*, 40–54).

39 This age limit had been established by royal decree in 1784. See Galdino Siqueira, *Direito penal brasileiro* (Rio de Janeiro: Jacinto R. dos Santos, 1924), 436.

40 Arts. 219–228, Filgueiras Júnior, *Código criminal*, 241–47; Bk. 5, titles 16, 18, 23, Almeida, *Código filipino*, 1166, 1168–70, 1172–74.

41 The Philippine Ordinances included slaves as possible rape victims; the 1830 code did not mention rape of slaves. In an 1884 Supreme Court case uncovered by Robert Conrad, the rape of a thirteen-year-old slave by her master generated substantial juridical debate. The court acquitted the master, even though it acknowledged that he had raped the girl (Conrad, *Children of God's Fire: A Documentary History of Black Slavery in Brazil* [University Park: Pennsylvania State University Press, 1994], 273–80). Grinberg, in *Liberata*, analyzes an equally complicated case of rape of a slave by her master in which the court decided in favor of the slave. On the controversy over forced prostitution of slaves see Sandra Lauderdale Graham, "Slavery's Impasse: Slave Prostitutes, Small-Time Mistresses, and the Brazilian Law of 1871," *Comparative Studies in Society and History* 33, 4 (October 1991): 669–94.

42 Esteves, *Meninas perdidas*, 43–54. Sandra Lauderdale Graham, in *House and Street: The Domestic World of Servants and Masters in Nineteenth-Century Rio de Janeiro* (New York: Cambridge University Press, 1989), finds that domestic servants who worked in the street were generally assumed to not be virgins; employers were expected to protect the honor of their virgin servants by keeping them indoors.

43 See, for example, João Vieira de Araújo, *O código penal interpretado* (1896; Rio de Janeiro, 1890), 307–73.

44 The three major obstacles to the codification of civil law were slavery and conflicts regarding the relationships between church and state and between commercial and civil law. Scholars such as Paulo Mercadante, Eduardo Spiller Pena, Pedro Dutra, and Keila Grinberg have argued that the incompatibility between slavery and liberal ideals was the major, insuperable problem. See Mercadante, *A consciência conservadora*; Pena, "Um romanista entre a escravidão e a liberdade," *Afro-Ásia* 18 (1996): 33–75; Dutra, *Literatura jurídica no império* (Rio de Janeiro: Topbooks, 1992), esp. 103–11; Grinberg, "Slavery, Liberalism, and Civil Law: The Definition of Status and Citizenship in Memorials Regarding the Elaboration of the Brazilian Civil Code, 1855–1916" (paper presented at the "Status, Honor, and Law in Modern Latin America" con-

ference, University of Michigan, December 5, 1998). Cited with the author's permission.

45   The best account of this criticism of liberal legislation is Flory, *Judge and Jury*, 20–30, 131–56. The most contentious issue initially was not the penal code itself, but the organization of the judicial system (creating the popular jury and strengthening the local justices of the peace) through the procedural code of 1832.

46   See "Lei de 10 de Junho de 1835," in Filgueiras Júnior, *Código criminal*, 321–33; B. Garcia, *Instituições*, 122–23; Flory, *Judge and Jury*, 131–56; Francisco Iglesias, *Historia política de Brasil, 1500–1964* (Madrid: Mapfre, 1992), 178–90; João José Reis, *Slave Rebellion in Brazil: The Muslim Uprising of 1835 in Bahia* (Baltimore: Johns Hopkins University Press, 1993), 189–230.

47   Grinberg, *Liberata*, 49–57, 71–78.

48   Cristiana Schettini Pereira, *Nas barbas de momo: Os sentidos da presença feminina no carnaval das "grandes sociedades" nos últimos anos do século XIX* (Campinas: IFCH/UNICAMP, 1995), 94; June Hahner, *Emancipating the Female Sex: The Struggle for Women's Rights in Brazil, 1850–1940* (Durham: Duke University Press, 1990), 75. For discussion of the female suffrage movement up to the 1930s, see Branca Moreira Alves, *Ideologia e feminismo: A luta pelo voto no Brasil* (Petrópolis: Vozes, 1980); Susan K. Besse, *Restructuring Patriarchy: The Modernization of Gender Inequality in Brazil, 1914–1940* (Chapel Hill: University of North Carolina Press, 1996), 164–92; Hahner, *Emancipating*, 121–80.

49   Hahner, *Emancipating*, 73–75.

50   Ibid., 75; *As constituições do Brasil*, ed. Floriano de Aguiar Dias (Rio de Janeiro: Liber Juris, 1975): 392–97.

51   Alves, *Código civil*, xvii–xxvii. Bevilaqua was associated with the "Recife school" of legal thought, which challenged elements of classical law with "scientific" and positivist-inspired criticism of liberal notions of free will and responsibility. See Roberto Lira, *Novo Direito Penal* (Rio de Janeiro: Editor Borsoi, 1972), 2: 32–54; Clóvis Bevilaqua *História da Faculdade de Direito do Recife, 11 de agosto de 1827, 11 de agosto de 1927* (Rio de Janeiro: F. Alves, 1927). Bevilaqua's opponents were not necessarily classical law enthusiasts; some were conservative nationalist politicians who rejected innovations, particularly innovations inspired by radical European thought. For the opinions of a range of contemporary politicians and jurists who were invited to comment on a preliminary draft, see *Projeto do Código Civil brasileiro: Trabalhos da Comissão Especial da Câmara dos Deputados*, 8 vols. (Rio de Janeiro: Imprensa Nacional, 1902) (hereafter *Projeto*); and *Código civil brasileiro: Trabalhos relativos à sua elaboração*, 3 vols. (Rio de Janeiro: Imprensa Nacional, 1917, 1918, 1919) (hereafter *Trabalhos*); and Bevilaqua's summary of the revision process and public debates in *Código civil*, 1: 20–59. Bevilaqua's most colorful critics were the jurisconsult Andrade Figueira, who objected to many of Bevilaqua's "innovations" on religious and moral grounds, and Senator Rui

Barbosa, who wrote copious volumes attacking Bevilaqua on philological grounds, delaying passage of the code for years. Barbosa was an important critic of some of the extreme postulates of the reformist criminologists, but, as San Tiago Dantas argues, Barbosa's intervention was motivated more by political and personal than philosophical interests (Dantas, *Dois momentos de Rui Barbosa* [Rio de Janeiro: Casa de Rui Barbosa, 1951]). See also Sílvio Meira, *O código civil de 1917: o projeto Bevilaqua*, special ed. of *Studi in Onore di Cesare Sanfilippo* (Milan: Giuffré eds., 1982); Rui Barbosa, *Réplica de Rui Barbosa: Às defesas da redação do projecto de código civil brasileiro na Câmara dos Deputados, 1904* (Rio de Janeiro: Fundação Casa de Rui Barbosa, 1980).

52 Bevilaqua, *Código Civil*, 1: 26–27.

53 See Bevilaqua's explanation for why he gave family law precedence over other sections of civil law and his comments regarding Art. 6 (Bevilaqua, *Código Civil*, 1: 84–89, 199–200).

54 Bevilaqua, *Código Civil*, 1: 200; *Projeto*, 4: 113.

55 Art. 2, Bevilaqua, *Código Civil*, 1: 179–81.

56 Arts. 6, 233, 242, 379–80, Bevilaqua, *Código Civil*, 1: 196–205, 2: 110–11, 127–28, 356–60. Against Bevilaqua's recommendation, Art. 6 retained the wording of the Philippine Ordinances (Bk. 4, tit. 103), in declaring "prodigals," or those who squandered their patrimony, incompetent; over time, this had come to mean the insane. Indians were incompetent because they were placed under special state protection until they could be "assimilated" into Republican society.

57 Bevilaqua, *Código Civil*, 1: 199–200. Art. 235 stipulated that husbands must have their wives' permission for important financial transactions; 247 authorized women to make domestic expenditures without their husbands' permission (ibid., 2: 115, 141–42).

58 See Besse, *Restructuring Patriarchy*, 169; for more general discussions of women's struggles for civil rights, see Hahner, *Emancipating*, Alves, *Ideologia e feminismo*.

59 Bk. 2, title 47, bk. 4, titles 46–48, 50, Almeida, *Código filipino*, 631, 832–57. The 1916 code allowed married couples to opt for separation of property, a premarital contract, or the older dowry system, but communal property marriage was the norm (Arts. 256, 258, 269, 276, 278, Bevilaqua, *Código Civil*, 2: 159–203). Muriel Nazzari, in "Widows as Obstacles to Business: British Objections to Brazilian Marriage and Inheritance Laws," *Comparative Studies in Society and History* 17, 4 (October 1995): 781–802, shows that women's superior position in Brazilian inheritance law provoked conflicts over the prerogatives of British men who took Brazilian wives in the nineteenth century. On British law, see Lee Holcombe, *Wives and Property: Reform of the Married Women's Property Laws in Nineteenth-Century England* (Toronto: University of Toronto Press, 1983); Eileen Spring, *Law, Land, and Family: Aristocratic Inheritance in England 1300–1800* (Chapel Hill: University of North Carolina

Press, 1993). See also Linda Lewin, "Natural and Spurious Children in Brazilian Inheritance Law from Colony to Empire: A Methodological Essay,"
Americas 48, 3 (January 1992): 351–96, esp. 357–59.

60 Nazzari, *Disappearance*, 168; Arts. 233, 240, Bevilaqua, *Código civil*, 110–13,
123. Nazzari argues that these changes came about in large part because the
rise of commerce, capital markets, individualism, and urban professions made
it possible for men to make a living without acquiring the means of production
through their wives' dowries.

61 Bevilaqua, *Código civil*, 2: 113.

62 Wives could also seek annulment if they had made an essential error about
their husband's identity, or if he proved to be impotent. On the debate over
annulment because of women's defloration, see "Preliminares" and Art. 219,
Bevilaqua, *Código civil*, 1: 30, 2: 84–90.

63 The Philippine Ordinances disinherited daughters younger than twenty-five
who "slept with any man" or married without parental consent, unless the
marriage elevated the daughter's social status (Bk. 4, title 88). Nineteenth-
century jurists debated whether to interpret "slept with any man" literally, or
whether it meant a woman who prostituted herself. Disinheritance of dishonest women of any age was an innovation of the 1916 code, although some
nineteenth-century jurists had interpreted earlier laws regarding minors to
include mature women as well. The 1916 civil code allowed parents to annul a
minor child's marriage, but not to disinherit the child (Almeida, *Código filipino*, 927–28; Art. 1595, 1744, Bevilaqua, *Código civil*, 6: 45, 183–84.

64 The Republican regime had secularized marriage by Decree 181 of January 24,
1890. The 1830 penal code prohibited clergy from celebrating marriages of
minors without their parents' consent, but imperial policy discouraged arranged marriages. The republican civil code maintained parent's rights to oppose minor children's marriage choices, but allowed the courts to override
"unjust" parental opposition; the code also stipulated that all marriages must
be based on free will. See Arts. 185, 188, 194, 197, Bevilaqua, *Código civil*, 28,
32, 45, 51; Nazzari, *Disappearance*, 130–40. A number of scholars have shown
that the Tridentine doctrine of free will versus parental rights to determine
children's marriage partners frequently pitted church against state in the
Spanish and Portuguese empires until the early nineteenth century. See, for
example, Verena Martinez-Alier, *Marriage, Class, and Colour in Nineteenth-
Century Cuba*, 2d ed. (Ann Arbor: University of Michigan Press, 1989); Lavrin,
"Introduction: The Scenario, the Actors, and the Issues," and Susan Socolow,
"Acceptable Partners: Marriage Choice in Colonial Argentina, 1778–1810,"
in *Sexuality and Marriage*, ed. Lavrin, 17–19, 209–46, esp. 235–36; Patricia
Seed, *To Love, Honor, and Obey in Colonial Mexico: Conflicts over Marriage
Choice, 1574–1821* (Stanford: Stanford University Press, 1988); Ramón Gu-
tiérrez, *When Jesus Came, the Corn Mothers Went Away: Marriage, Sexuality,
and Power in New Mexico, 1500–1846* (Stanford: Stanford University Press,
1991), 315–18.

65 See Hahner, *Emancipating*, 118; Besse, *Restructuring Patriarchy*, 43, 66–67.

66 For the debates over divorce, see Bevilaqua, *Código civil*, 1: 39; *Projeto*, 5: 3–81. The key marital separation and alimony laws are Arts. 317, 320, Bevilaqua, *Código civil*, 2: 272, 280.

67 In a 1929 case of a man who tried to rescind his wife's right to alimony and custody of their children by accusing her of adultery after their separation, the attorney general intervened, inveighing against judges who accepted suits of this sort. Although subsequent modifications in separation agreements were not permitted by law, the fact that this attorney general wrote a thesis attacking this practice attests to its frequency. See Arquivo Nacional, Tribunal de Justiça (hereafter AN-TJ), caixa 571 no. 4336 (1929). See also AN-TJ, caixa 571 no. 579 (1928), in which the husband won custody of his children because he encountered his estranged wife with another man in the street, and AN-TJ, caixa 01745 n. 5 (1923), in which a man won custody of his daughter after leaving her mother, his "concubine" of seven years, by arguing that the mother "behaved dishonestly" after their separation. "Amicable separations" could also include contracts that required the woman to "live honestly" in exchange for alimony and child custody; see, for example, AN-TJ caixa 5378 no. 565.

68 Bk. 2, title 3, art. 1, title 35, art. 12; bk. 4, titles 92–93, Almeida, *Código filipino*, 423, 457–62, 939–47. There was controversy over whether legitimized spurious children could share rights to forced inheritance or merely testamentary inheritance (the latter could comprise only one-third of an estate). Legitimization certificates did not always grant succession rights, and late-eighteenth-century inheritance legislation favored legitimate and natural children (if plebeian) over legitimized children. See Lewin, "Natural and Spurious Children," esp. 357, 367; Astolpho Rezende, "As mães solteiras: Sua protecção e dignidade. Pesquisa da paternidade. Penalidade pecuniária na fecundação extra-legal," *Revista de jurisprudência brasileira* 4 (June 1929): 207–18; J. Alves, *Código civil*, 305.

69 See Andrade Figueira's opinions in *Trabalhos*, 5; and Perdigão Malheiro, "Commentario á lei sobre sucessão dos filhos naturaes"; both cited in Rezende, "As mães solteiras," 212–13. Brazilian legislators followed French law, which rescinded illegitimate children's rights to demand paternal recognition after the French Revolution. French law allowed paternity suits only after 1912. See Rezende, "As mães solteiras," 211–14.

70 Bevilaqua refers especially to Figueira (*Código civil*, 2: 329).

71 Arts. 352–67, Bevilaqua, *Código civil*, 2: 317–45. Illegitimate children could sue for paternal recognition if they were conceived while the father was living in concubinage with the mother, had abducted her, or had "sexual relations with her" (Art. 363). The latter condition, as civil magistrates would later complain, was excessively broad, and abduction was rare.

72 See the epilogue.

73 Similar legislation existed in contemporary Argentina, Uruguay, and Mexico. Roman law allowed natural children to sue for maternal recognition, but not

spurious. Bevilaqua compares these laws and comments on the rarity of maternity suits in his comments on Art. 364, Bevilaqua, *Código civil*, 2: 341–42.

74 See Nazzari, "An Urgent Need to Conceal." It was apparently common for elite women to give their illegitimate children to families who raised them; sometimes the mother herself or her own family members raised the child as a foundling. Another option was to leave their children anonymously at convents or other state or religious institutions. Scattered studies of different regions and periods, including Nazzari's, have found that white women abandoned illegitimate children more frequently than women of color. Evaluating the historical literature, Maria Beatriz Nizza da Silva concludes that the motive for abandonment was more often family honor than economic hardship, which concurs with Nazzari's hypothesis (Silva, *História da família no Brasil colonial* [Rio de Janeiro: Nova Fronteira, 1998], 208).

75 Bevilaqua, *Código civil*, 2: 342.

76 Francisco Campos, "Exposição de motivos," in Brazil, *Leis penais* (Rio de Janeiro: Imprensa Nacional, 1949), 5–48. Campos's essay opens by noting that "the desire to reform the [1890] Penal Code was born with the code itself." See also Galdino Siqueira, *Código penal brasileiro* (Rio de Janeiro: Jacinto, 1941), 11–18.

77 Viveiros de Castro links his admiration for August Comte to his enthusiasm for legal positivism in *Atentados ao pudor*, vii, but positivist political philosophy was never as influential in the law or in medical schools as it was in military and technical training; this provoked important rifts between graduates of each. See Francisco de Oliveira Viana, *O ocaso do Império*, 2d ed. (São Paulo: Melhoramentos, 1933), 122–26, 135–41; Miguel Reale, "Pedro Lessa e a filosofia positiva em São Paulo," in *Juristas brasileiros*, ed. Instituto Histórico e Geográfico de São Paulo (São Paulo: IHGSP, 1960), 55–90; F. Azevedo, *Brazilian Culture*, 177–91; Celso Castro, *Os militares e a República: Um estudo sobre cultura e ação política* (Rio de Janeiro: Jorge Zahar, 1995), 52–68. Beginning in the 1870s, the Recife law school led a movement to renovate legal studies; by the 1890s, Recife graduates, including Castro, were major disseminators of the new "scientific" legal theory. The São Paulo law school was slower to renovate legal training, but Adorno shows that the new theories circulated among its students outside the classroom (Adorno, *Os aprendizes*, 157–234). Major works of Brazilian proponents of positive legal theory include L. Pereira Barreto, *As três filosofias*, pt. 1, *Filosofia teológica* (Rio de Janeiro, 1874), lxxv; Tobias Barreto, *Estudos alemães* (Rio de Janeiro: Laemert, 1892) and *Menores e loucos e fundamentos do direito de punir* (1884; Rio de Janeiro: Paulo Pongetti, 1926); Francisco José Viveiros de Castro, *A nova escola penal*, 2d ed. (1894; Rio de Janeiro: Jacinto Ribeiro dos Santos, 1913), Antônio Moniz Sodré de Aragão, *As três escolas penais: Clássica, antropológica e crítica*, 3d ed. (1907; São Paulo: Saraiva, 1928); Araújo, *O código penal*; Aurelino Leal, *Germens do crime* (Salvador: Magalhães, 1896; Lessa, *Estudos de filosofia*; Evaristo de Morais, *Criminalidade passional: O homicídio e o homicídio-

suicídio por amor em face da psicologia criminal e penalística (São Paulo: Saraiva, 1933) and *Ensaios de patologia social* (Rio de Janeiro: Leite Ribeiro and Maurillo, 1921). The best study of Brazilian legal positivism is Marcos César Alvarez, "Bacharéis, criminologistas e juristas: Saber jurídico e nova escola penal no Brasil (1889–1930)" (Ph.D. diss., Universidade de São Paulo, 1996). See also Peter Fry, "Direito positivo versus direito clássico: A psicologização do crime no pensamento de Heitor Carrilho" in *Cultura da psicanálise,* ed. Sérvulo Figueira (São Paulo: Brasiliense, 1985), 117–41; Peter Fry and Sérgio Carrara, "As vicissitudes do liberalismo no direito penal brasileiro," *Revista brasileira de ciências sociais* 2, 1 (1986), 48–54; Clóvis de Carvalho Júnior, "Escola positiva penal," *Ciência penal* 2, 4 (1975): 99–128; Mariza Corrêa, *Os crimes da paixão* (Rio de Janeiro: Graal, 1983); Carlos Antônio Costa Ribeiro, "Clássicos e positivistas no moderno direito pena brasileiro: Uma interpretação sociológica" in *Invenção do Brasil moderno: medicina, educação e engenharia nos anos 20–30,* ed. Michael Herschman and Carlos Alberto Messeder Pereira (Rio de Janeiro: Rocco, 1994): 130–46.

78 See Robert A. Nye, "Heredity or Milieu: The Foundations of Modern European Criminological Theory," *Isis* 67 (1976): 335–55; Nye, *Crime, Madness, and Politics in Modern France: The Medical Concept of National Decline* (Princeton: Princeton University Press, 1984), 97–131; Ruth Harris, *Murders and Madness: Medicine, Law, and Society in the* Fin de Siècle (New York: Oxford University Press, 1989), 80–98; Wright, *Between the Guillotine,* chap. 5; Pierre Darmon, *Médecins et assassins de la belle époque* (Paris: Seuil, 1989). For the United States, see Thomas A. Green, "Freedom and Criminal Responsibility in the Age of Pound: An Essay on Criminal Justice," *Michigan Law Review* 93, 7 (June 1995): 1915–2053.

79 The term "positivist" here refers to those whom Brazilian jurists labeled as belonging to the "positive school," although some of these European criminologists would not have accepted this label. Most European jurists espoused modified versions of classical legal philosophy by the mid–nineteenth century, frequently referred to in retrospect as the neoclassical school. Some writers, however, use this term to refer to later tendencies that combined classical and positivist thought; the terminology varies from country to country. See Wright, *Between the Guillotine,* 114–15, 240 n. 12. Brazilian jurists seldom used the term "neoclassical," preferring to simplify by positioning "classical" against "positive" law. An exception is Pedro Lessa, who recognized the compatibility of determinism, associated with the positive school, and criminal responsibility, associated with free will and the classical school (*Estudos de filosofia,* 161–339, esp. 231). For European debates regarding classical and positivist law, see sources in n. 75.

80 The most adamant defenders of the notion that law should reflect national culture and traditions were political conservatives such as Andrade Figueira. Others, most notably João Luiz Alves, Galdino Siqueira, Pedro Lessa, Oscar de Macedo Soares, and liberal nationalist Rui Barbosa, believed that law should

reflect cultural values, but not to the detriment of the advance of modern civilization and universal moral principles. See Bevilaqua, *Código civil*, 38; Alves, *Código civil*, xxi, xxvii; *Projeto*, 4: 5–6, 6: 252–53; Lessa, *Estudos de filosofia*, 34–35; 377–414.

81 See Alvarez, *Bacharéis*, 74–82, for Brazilian responses to contemporary European debates and reception of Brazilian work by European criminologists.

82 F. Castro, *Atentados ao pudor*, xi–xii.

83 Nina Rodrigues, *As raças humanas e a responsabilidade penal no Brasil*, 3d ed. (1894; São Paulo: Editora Nacional, 1938).

84 Alvarez, in *Bacharéis*, 81, argues that the prominence of Lombroso in Brazilian studies demonstrates that biological determinism was predominant among Brazilian authors, especially Viveiros de Castro, Araújo, Aragão, Soares, and Cândido Mota. Unlike Lombroso, however, Brazilian jurists almost never cited biology alone, and the few scientific studies of racial determinants proved inconclusive. Roberto Lira, a member of the next generation of scientific legal theorists, provides a genealogy of Brazilian theories of social causes of crime in which Tobias Barreto, Alberto Torres, Sílvio Romero, and Galdino Siqueira figure prominently (Lira, *Novo direito penal*, 32–55).

85 See Olívia Gomes, "1933: Um ano em que fizemos contatos," *Revista USP/Dossiê Povo Negro—300 Anos* (December–February 1996): 142–63; Carvalho Júnior, "Escola positiva"; Fry, "Direito positivo"; Fry and Carrara, "As vicissitudes"; C. A. C. Ribeiro, "Clássicos e positivistas." Alvarez, in *Bacharéis*, 145–61, shows that Castro, Cândido Mota, Paulo Egídio, and Aurelino Leal undertook empirical studies of criminal trends, but the absence of reliable statistics made it impossible for them to sustain credible conclusions.

86 See chap. 5. Studies focusing on the racist conclusions of medical and psychiatric campaigns to improve the physical health and social hygiene of Brazil's population include Jurandir Freire Costa, *Ordem médica e norma familiar* (Rio de Janeiro: Graal, 1979); Roberto Machado et al., *Danação da norma: Medicina social e constituição da psiquiatria no Brasil* (Rio de Janeiro: Graal, 1978); Sidney Chalhoub, *Cidade febril: Cortiços e epidemias na corte imperial* (São Paulo: Companhia das Letras, 1996) and "The Politics of Disease Control: Yellow Fever and Race in Nineteenth Century Rio de Janeiro," *Journal of Latin American Studies* 25 (1993): 441–63; Dain Borges, " 'Puffy, Ugly, Slothful and Inert': Degeneration in Brazilian Social Thought, 1880–1940," *Journal of Latin American Studies* 25 (1993): 235–56; Nancy Stepan, *The Hour of Eugenics": Race, Gender, and Nation in Latin America* (Ithaca: Cornell University Press, 1991).

87 This is evident in the numerous volumes of annotated penal codes in which the authors compare each article to previous legislation and to European and sometimes other Latin American laws, commenting on jurisprudence, legal theory and the views of Brazilian and European scholars. See, for example, Araújo, *O código penal*; Oscar de Macedo Soares, *Código penal da República dos Estados Unidos do Brasil comentado*, 5th ed. (Rio de Janeiro: Garnier,

1910); Siqueira, *Direito penal brasileiro.* Alvarez shows that Brazilian jurists borrowed eclectically from diverse, sometimes opposing criminological theories, but he does not analyze other influences on their work (*Bacharéis,* 75–82).

88 There were a few exceptions, most notably Evaristo de Morais.

89 For Barbosa's criticism of legal positivism, see Alvarez, *Bacharéis,* 127–28. Just before the empire was overthrown, the legislature had commissioned João Vieira de Araújo to elaborate a revision of the 1830 code that would eliminate references to slaves. The Vieira proposal was rejected by a juridical review commission headed by the liberal jurist Batista Pereira on the grounds that an entirely new code was needed. Almost immediately after the proclamation of the republic, Pereira himself was chosen to write the new code; his proposal, influenced strongly by the Italian code of 1889, was passed after a few modifications. See Siqueira, *Código penal brasileiro,* 11–15.

90 Title 11, Arts. 315–25, Severiano, *Código penal,* 475–83. See comments in O. Soares, *Código Penal,* 640–42; and Siqueira, *Direito penal brasileiro,* 635–42.

91 "Dos crimes contra a segurança da honra e honestidade das familias e do ultraje público ao pudor," title 8, arts. 266–282, Jorge Severiano, *Código penal da República dos Estados Unidos do Brasil* (Rio de Janeiro: Jacinto Ribeiro dos Santos, 1923), 391–422. Crimes include corruption of a minor, deflowering, rape, abduction, pandering, adultery, and public indecency.

92 Tropical girls "became women" as early as eight years old, according to a 1904 manuscript by Judge Antônio Cardoso de Gusmão, though most specialists agreed with Miguel Sales that "in our climate . . . a girl is already a woman . . . at around fourteen," a few years younger than in European nations (A. Gusmão, "Delitos sexuais," in *Arquivos do Departmento Federal de São Paulo* 4 [1948]: 43; Sales, "A perícia médico-legal," 59; Crisólito de Gusmão, *Dos crimes sexuais: Estupro, atentado ao pudor, defloramento e corrupção de menores* [Rio de Janeiro: Briguiet, 1921], 172–76). Esteves finds that turn-of-the-century lawyers defending men accused of sexual crimes routinely argued that black and especially mulatto women were innately sensual and that Brazil's tropical climate awakened their sexuality. See Esteves, *Meninas perdidas,* 59. Several prominent jurists, however, supported keeping the age of majority at twenty-one, as stipulated in civil law, and argued for raising the age for voluntary consent. See F. Castro, *Delitos,* 63–74; Araújo, *O código penal,* 335; A. Lima, *Tratado,* 526–28.

93 See O. Soares, *Código penal,* 549.

94 F. Castro, *Os delitos,* 69–74; see the discussion in Esteves, *Meninas perdidas,* 93–94.

95 Bk. 5, title 23, Almeida, *Código filipino,* 1172–74; Siqueira, *Direito penal brasileiro,* 436; Milton Duarte Segurado, *Sedução* (Curitiba: Jurua, 1977), 23–25, 28–29.

96 Araújo, *O código penal*, 331–33; Gusmão, *Dos crimes sexuais*, 230–41; Si-
    queira, *Direito penal brasileiro*, 435–36.

97 Siqueira, *Direito penal brasileiro*, 437. Although Siqueira published this vol-
    ume in 1924, it is based on earlier scholarship and is representative of the
    work he produced in earlier decades, including a proposal for a new penal
    code in 1912.

98 A. Lima, *Tratado*, 542. "Seduction of an honest woman" was proposed as a
    replacement for deflowering in proposals for a new penal code presented to
    Congress in 1893 and 1899. See Araújo, *O código penal*, 331; F. Castro, *Os
    delitos*, 62.

99 Araújo, *O código penal*, 330–35; F. Castro, *Os delitos*, 59–61; O. Soares, *Có-
    digo penal*, 537–38; Gusmão, *Dos crimes sexuais*, 242–48.

100 Siqueira discusses legal-medical training in the nineteenth century in *Di-
    reito penal brasileiro*, 441–42; cited in Caulfield and Esteves," Fifty Years of
    Virginity," 51.

101 A. Lima, *Tratado*, 542–80; Esteves, *Meninas perdidas*, 61–67.

102 Barbosa, *Réplica*, cited in Segurado, *Sedução*, 22.

103 F. Castro, *Os delitos*, 61.

104 Ibid., 63.

105 Arts. 266, 282, Severiano, *Código penal*, 391, 421.

106 Esteves, *Meninas perdidas*, 76–82. I found similar discourses on male honor
    in the cases from 1918 to 1940 that I read; see ch. 4. See also Mariza Corrêa,
    Morte em família: Representações jurídicas de papéis sexuais (Rio de Ja-
    neiro: Graal, 1983).

107 Francisco José Viveiros de Castro, *Jurisprudência criminal* (Rio de Janeiro:
    H. Garnier, 1900), 257.

108 F. Castro, *Os delitos*, 91; *Jurisprudência criminal*, 88, cited in Esteves, *Me-
    ninas perdidas*, 68.

109 F. Castro, *Os delitos*, 77.

110 Ibid., 78.

111 The most vehement opponent of the marriage promise as the sole means of
    seduction was Galdino Siqueira. See *Direito penal brasileiro*, 446–49.

112 A. Lima, *Tratado*, 530–31; F. Castro, *Delitos*, 63.

113 This definition developed in Catholic thinking in the writings of St. Jerome
    in the fourth century. See James A. Brundage, *Law, Sex, and Christian So-
    ciety in Medieval Europe* (Chicago: University of Chicago Press, 1987), 248.
    For Augustine's views, see Brundage, *Law*, 106.

114 Donna Guy, *Sex and Danger in Buenos Aires: Prostitution, Family, and Na-
    tion in Argentina* (Lincoln: University of Nebraska Press, 1991), 12–14.

115 On the attempts by police or physicians to control prostitution in the nine-
    teenth century, see Arquivo Geral da Cidade do Rio de Janeiro, Coleção Séries
    Documentais: Prostituição no Rio de Janeiro; S. Graham, "Slavery's Im-
    passe," esp. 684–85; Magali Engel, *Meretrizes e doutores: O saber médico e a*

prostituição na cidade do Rio de Janeiro, 1845–1890 (São Paulo: Brasiliense, 1990); Luís Carlos Soares, *Rameiras, ilhoas, polacas . . . prostituição no Rio de Janeiro do século XIX* (São Paulo: Ática, 1992). Lená Medeiros de Menezes, *Os estrangeiros e o comércio do prazer nas ruas do Rio, 1890–1930* (Rio de Janeiro: Arquivo Nacional, 1992), describes the deportation of foreigners accused of procurement during the First Republic. Police Chief Aurelino de Araújo Leal outlines the city's legislation on prostitution from the nineteenth century to 1917 in "Tese III: I—A Prostituição, II—Localização," in *Anais da conferência judiciária-policial*, ed. Leal (Rio de Janeiro: Imprensa Nacional, 1918), 1: 403–24; see the attack on Leal's conclusions and on police abuses of prostitutes by Evaristo de Morais, *Ensaios de patologia social* (Rio de Janeiro: Leite Ribeiro e Maurillo, 1926), 257–87. For discussion of attempts by police chiefs to clarify municipal laws on prostitution since the early nineteenth century, see Leonídio Ribeiro Filho, "Os problemas médico-legais em face da reforma da polícia," speech reprinted in *Gazeta policial*, June 16, 1931. On the position of public health physicians in the early twentieth century, see Ribeiro Filho, "Os problemas"; Morais, *Ensaios*, 285–87; Teófilo de Almeida, "Syphilis e prostituição no Rio de Janeiro," *Arquivos da Fundação Gaffrée-Guinle* 2 (1929): 21–52; Hélio Gomes, "O problema da prostituição sob o ponto de vista sanitário e jurídico," in *Anais da Primeira Conferência Nacional de Defesa Contra a Sífilis* (Rio de Janeiro: Imprensa Nacional, 1941), 423–35; Manoel Odorico de Morais, "Estado atual da prostituição no Rio de Janeiro," *A folha médica* 23, 12 (July 1942): 148–52. See also Sueann Caulfield, "The Birth of Mangue: Race, Nation, and the Politics of Prostitution in Rio de Janeiro, 1850–1942," in *Sex and Sexuality in Latin America*, ed. Daniel Balderston and Donna Guy (New York: New York University Press, 1997), 86–100.

116 The penal code punished pimping with one to two years' imprisonment (Arts. 277, 278, Severiano, *Código penal*, 415–17). Subsequently, decree 1034 A of 1892 reiterated a series of imperial laws that gave the chief of police the power to "keep prostitutes under severe vigilance, taking actions against them, under the law, when they publicly offend morality and good customs." Leal, "These III," 403–4.

117 Arts. 278, 279, modified by law 2.992 of Setembro 25, 1915. Severiano, *Código penal*, 415–17; and Vicente Piragibe, *Dicionário de jurisprudência penal* (Rio de Janeiro: Freitas Bastos, 1938), 529–83. Legislative decree 1641 of January 7, 1907, mandated deportation of foreign pimps and others who "threatened national security or public tranquility"; this law was used to legitimize summary deportation of labor activists. See *Coleção de leis* (Rio de Janeiro: Imprensa Nacional, 1908), 1: 24–25; Eduardo E. A. Espinola, "O 'habeas-corpus' e a expulsão do estrangeiro," in *Pandectas brasileiras* (Rio de Janeiro: Casa Gráfica, 1929), 210–21; Menezes, *Os estrangeiros*, 74–75.

118 Morais, *Ensaios*, 257–87.

119 Leal, *Germens do crime;* and "Ata da primeira reunião da terceira seção da Conferência Judiciária-Policial," in *Anais,* ed. Leal, 2: 265–67. Prostitution was one of a variety of issues relating to social order addressed at this conference. The major aim of the conference was to encourage collaboration of justice and police officials in repressing labor mobilization.

120 A. Lima, *Tratado,* 529; F. Castro, *Delitos,* 123–24.

121 Siqueira, *Direito penal brasileira,* 460–61. The Philippine Ordinances suggested, however, that the Crown might attenuate punishment in cases of prostitute rape (Bk. 5, title 18, Almeida, *Código filipino,* 1168).

122 See Gusmão, *Dos crimes,* 192–93; O. Soares, *Código penal,* 540.

123 See esp. A. Lima, *Tratado,* 518–20.

124 A. Lima, *Tratado,* 523–24. The law on reparation of damages (dowry payment and marriage) is Art. 276, Severiano, *Código penal,* 413.

125 Siqueira, *Direito penal brasileiro,* 483; Gusmão, *Dos crimes sexuais,* 409.

126 See opinions and jurisprudence cited in Araújo, *O código penal,* 371–72; F. Castro, *Os delitos,* 194–95; Siqueira, *Direito penal brasileiro,* 482–85; Gusmão, *Dos crimes sexuais,* 409. Marriage of deflowered women was so important that a judge could lower the legal minimum age for marriage (from sixteen for women and eighteen for men) in such cases (Art. 1548, Bevilaqua, *Código civil,* 5: 254–55). Aggravating circumstances included those that prohibited marriage, such as close kinship or the man's marriage to someone else (Art. 273, Severiano, *Código penal,* 410–11).

127 A. Lima, *Tratado,* 520.

128 F. Castro, *Os delitos,* 240–43; Araújo, *O código penal,* 367–69; Gusmão, *Dos crimes sexuais,* 403, Siqueira, *Direito penal brasileiro,* 480–82.

129 F. Castro, *Os delitos,* 199–243.

130 Siqueira, *Direito penal brasileiro,* 426, 456. Women shared the "conjugal right" to sex and could demand a marriage annulment in cases of husbands' impotence, but by definition could not commit rape.

131 Arts. 279–281, Severiano, *Código penal,* 419–20. For opposition to adultery laws and support of divorce, see F. Castro, *Os delitos,* 54; Araújo, *O código,* 392, O. Soares, *Código penal,* 504–8.

132 Punishment was lowered for mothers who acted to defend their honor by one-third for abortion, which carried a one to five years' prison term, and from six to twenty-four to three to nine years' imprisonment for infanticide. Punishment for homicide was six to thirty years (Arts. 294, 298, 301, Severiano, *Código penal,* 433–34, 447, 454). See discussion in O. Soares, *Código penal,* 614; Siqueira, *Direito penal brasileiro,* 588–91; F. Castro, *Jurisprudência criminal,* 291–95; Agostinho J. de Souza Lima, "Figura do aborto," *Revista de jurisprudência* (July 1898), 251; Eduardo Durão, "Infanticídio" in *Direito* (June 1891): 184–92.

133 Morais, *Criminalidade passional* and *Reminiscências de um rábula criminalista* (Belo Horizonte: F. Briguiet, 1989), 157–69; Enrico Ferri, *O delito*

passional na civilização contemporânea, trans. and intro. Roberto Lira (São
Paulo: Saraiva, 1934).

134 Ferri, *O delito passional*, 59–60; Morais, *Criminalidade passional*, 47–70.
For refutation of Morais's arguments, see Roberto Lira, *O amor e a responsabilidade criminal* (São Paulo: Saraiva, 1932), 11; Lira, *Novo direito penal*,
1: 22–63. Mariza Corrêa provides an excellent overview and analysis of these
debates in *Os crimes da paixão*.

135 Morais, *Criminalidade passional*, 65. For the most vehement attacks on the
jury, see F. Castro, *A nova escola*, 243; Leal, *Germens do crime*.

136 Morais, *Criminalidade passional*, 65, 70.

137 Ferri, *O delito passional*, 57–58.

138 Titulo 3, art. 27, par. 4, Severiano, *Código penal*, 62.

139 Ferri, *O delito passional*, esp. 70–74; for France, see R. Harris, *Murders and
Madness*.

140 This campaign is discussed in chap. 2. See also Susan K. Besse, "Crimes of
Passion: The Campaign against Wife Killing in Brazil, 1910–1940," *Journal of
Social History* 22, 4 (summer 1989): 653–66.

141 Julian Pitt-Rivers, "Honor," in *International Encyclopedia of Social Science*
6 (1968): 507.

142 Lira, *Novo direito penal*, 36.

143 Decree 2457 of February 8, 1897, art. 2, cited in Dr. Almachio Diniz, "Conceito Legal da Miserabilidade," *Revista de direito* 39 (1916): 482–83.

144 Almost all the cases of sexual crime encountered by Esteves (1900–1911) and
by Boris Fausto in São Paulo (1880–1924) were prosecuted by the public
prosecutor because of the victim's poverty, as were all but three of the 450
cases I consulted. Attorney Almachio Diniz complained about the fact that
virtually all victims of sexual crimes were considered impoverished in 1916;
see Diniz, "Conceito," 481–87; Esteves, *Meninas perdidas*, 90; Fausto, *Crime
e Cotidiano: A criminalidade em São Paulo, 1880–1924* (São Paulo: Brasiliense, 1984).

145 Esteves, *Meninas perdidas*, 83–114.

146 Gusmão, *Os crimes sexuais*, 358, cited in Esteves, *Meninas perdidas*, 88.

147 F. Castro, *Atentados ao pudor*, xiii, cited in Esteves, *Meninas perdidas*, 25.

148 F. Castro, *Os delitos*, 11; O. Soares, *Código penal*, 533; Gusmão, *Dos crimes
sexuais*, 18–20, 45–95, esp. 95; Siqueira, *Direito penal brasileiro*, 419.

149 See, for example, F. Castro, *Os delitos*, 16–18; O. Soares, *Código penal*, 533;
Gusmão, *Dos crimes sexuais*, 109–15; Siqueira, *Direito penal brasileiro*, 419.

150 F. Castro, *Os delitos*, 16–19.

151 O. Soares, *Código penal*, 533.

152 Gusmão, *Dos crimes sexuais*, 109–15.

153 Ibid., 102, 109–10, 113, 114.

154 F. Castro, *Jurisprudência*, 290.

155 Esteves, *Meninas perdidas*, esp. chaps. 1, 2.

Chapter 2 National Honor, the Family, and the Construction of the Marvelous City

1   "Visita de reis: A actividade official e a falta de braços," *A noite*, May 14, 1920.

2   "À Bélgica e ao seu rei," *Revista da semana* 21, 33 (Special issue; *A visita do Rei Alberto*) September 18, 1920.

3   "A viagem do rei da Bélgica ao Brasil," *O jornal*, May 15, 1920, 2; "Invencionices perversas," *O paiz*, July 20, 1920.

4   "A recepção do Rei Alberto: Cem mil contos para melhoramentos," *O jornal*, June 16, 1920, 2. See also "Reparações na área do porto e calçamento da Avenida do Mangue," *O jornal*, June 11, 1920, 2; "A viagem do Rei Alberto pela Central: Os carros construídos em São Paulo," *O jornal*, July 29, 1920, 3; "A real visita dos soberanos belgas—como o congresso deve receber Alberto I," *A noite*, September 6, 1920; "O couraçado " 'São Paulo,' a cujo bordo viajam os reis da Bélgica: Os brilhantes preparativos para a sua visita (o caso dos tapetes do Monroe)," *Correio da manhã*, September 18, 1920, 1; "Para a visita do rei-herói—Para o Rei Alberto ver," *A noite*, July 2, 1920; "A visita do rei-herói—O caso do camarote no Municipal—Um boato desfeito," *A noite*, June 10, 1920.

5   Built in 1906 and named for U.S. statesman James Monroe, author of the Monroe Doctrine.

6   "O Rei Alberto da Bélgica: Os preparativos para a recepção no Palácio Guanabara," *O paiz*, April 23, 1920, 2; "Ainda a brilhante recepção dos reis da Bélgica: A iluminação na Rua Paisandú," *Correio da manhã*, September 20, 1920, 2; "Para a visita do rei: A terminação da Avenida Niemeyer—Rápidas impressões de um passeio," *A noite*, May 29, 1920; "O rei voltou hontem a Tijuca, inaurando [sic] a Avenida Niemeyer" *Correio da manhã*, September 28, 1920, 1.

7   "O couraçado 'São Paulo,' " 1.

8   "Alberto I chega hoje ao Rio de Janeiro," *Correio da manhã*, September 19, 1920, 1.

9   "Os soberanos belgas chegaram hontem ao Rio de Janeiro: Alberto I e a Rainha Elisabeth tiveram uma recepção imponente que assumiu proporções de verdadeira apotheose," *Correio da manhã*, September 20, 1920, 1.

10   Ibid.

11   Ibid.

12   Ibid.

13   "A avenida à noite," *Correio da manhã*, September 23, 1920, 4.

14   Only thirty years earlier, Brazil had its own monarchs. The lavish republican reception for European royalty is one indication that the monarchist threat, which was a major issue in the 1890s, had evaporated by 1920. An even stronger indication was the decree allowing for the repatriation of the remains of the deposed monarch, Pedro II. On its way back from taking the Belgian monarchs home, the *São Paulo* picked up the remains in Lisbon and delivered them to Rio.

15 "Alberto I, rei dos belgas," *Jornal do comércio*, September 19, 1920, 1.
16 "Alberto I chega hoje," 1.
17 "Alberto I, rei dos belgas," 1.
18 "À Bélgica e ao seu rei."
19 The comment was made in a welcoming dinner toast by President Pessoa and in a letter by Rui Barbosa. Reported in "Le voyage de nos souverains au Brésil," *Soir*, September 22, 1920.
20 "À Belgica e ao seu rei."
21 "Os soberanos belgas chegaram hontem," 1.
22 The terms used in Portuguese are *a massa popular* or simply *os populares*, or *o povo*.
23 Determining the shape and size of relevant socioeconomic categories is difficult. The renowned educational reformer Anísio Teixeira constructed a social model for Brazil as a whole that estimated the "elite" at about 5 percent of the total population, the "classes," including salaried professionals and white-collar workers, at about 15 percent, and the "masses," or everyone else, at about 80 percent. See Michael Conniff, "Rio de Janeiro during the Great Depression, 1928–1937: Social Reform and the Emergence of Populism in Brazil" (Ph.D. diss., Stanford University, 1976). Jeffrey Needell estimates that the "elite," or the tightly knit group of economically privileged families that controlled the key republican political, social, and intellectual institutions, made up about 0.58 percent of the total urban population at the turn of the century. Needell, *A Tropical Belle Époque*, The Elite Culture of Turn-of-the-Century Rio de Janeiro (New York: Cambridge University Press, 1987), 237–42.
24 "Os soberanos belgas chegaram hontem," 1.
25 Sidney Chalhoub, "Medo branco de almas negras: Escravos, libertos e republicanos na cidade do Rio," *Revista brasileira de história* 8, 16 (1988): 87.
26 Ibid.
27 Ibid., 91.
28 Despite the existence of a race-based slave system, there was no discrimination on the basis of race alone in Brazilian law. Historian Hebe Castro's current research on nineteenth-century politicians suggests that racial exclusion from middle and upper-class society was looser in the early nineteenth century and became more rigidly enforced as slavery drew to an end. Personal communication with Hebe Castro, October 12, 1996. It was always possible, though not common, for individuals of notably mixed African and European descent to occupy elevated social positions, and the lower classes were composed of individuals of diverse ethnic origin. For commentary on elite inclusion of individuals of color, see Emília Viotti da Costa. *The Brazilian Empire: Myths and Histories* (Chicago: University of Chicago Press, 1985), chap. 8. For a discussion of cross-ethnic solidarity and ethnic conflict among lower-class Cariocas in the early republican period, see Sidney Chalhoub, *Trabalho, lar e botequim: O cotidiano dos trabalhadores no Rio de Janeiro da belle époque* (São Paulo: Brasiliense, 1986); and for the late Empire, Chalhoub, *Visões da*

liberdade: Uma história das últimas dé cadas da escravidão na corte (São Paulo: Companhia das Letras, 1990), 212–48.

29 Chalhoub, *Visões da liberdade,* 212–248, and Teresa Meade, *"Civilizing" Rio Reform and Resistance in a Brazilian City, 1889–1930* (University Park: Pennsylvania State University, 1997), 34–36, discuss elite panic over the proximity of various racial and social categories, especially after abolition. Magali Engel, *Meretrizes e doutores: O saber médico e a prostituição na cidade do Rio de Janeiro, 1845–1890* (São Paulo: Brasiliense, 1990), finds a strikingly similar rhetoric in the work of physicians concerned with prostitution.

30 On the imposition of moral norms through medical intervention in elite families in the nineteenth century, see Jurandir Freire Costa, *Ordem médica e norma familiar* (Rio de Janeiro: Graal, 1979); Roberto Machado et al., *Danação da norma: Medicina social e constituição da psiquiatria no Brasil* (Rio de Janeiro: Graal, 1978); Sandra Lauderdale Graham, *House and Street: The Domestic World of Servants and Masters in Nineteenth-Century Rio de Janeiro* (New York: Cambridge University Press, 1989), esp. chap. 5. On campaigns to clean up the downtown by controlling prostitution, see S. Graham, "Slavery's Impasse: Slave Prostitutes, Small-Time Mistresses, and the Brazilian Law of 1871," *Comparative Studies in Society and History* 33, 4 (October 1991): 669–94; Engel, *Meretrizes e doutores;* Luís Carlos Soares, *Rameiras, ilhoas, polacas . . . A prostituição no Rio de Janeiro do século XIX* (São Paulo: Ática, 1992). On the authoritarian implementation of public health and moralization policies, the class and racial prejudices of these polices, and the responses of poor residents, see S. Graham, *House and Street;* Sidney Chalhoub, *Cidade febril: Cortiços e epidemias na corte imperial* (São Paulo: Companhia das Letras, 1996); and for the republican period, Martha de Abreu Esteves, *Meninas perdidas: Os populares e o cotidiano do amor no Rio de Janeiro da belle époque* (Rio de Janeiro: Paz e Terra, 1989); Meade, *"Civilizing" Rio;* José Murilo de Carvalho, *Os bestializados: O Rio de Janeiro e a república que não foi* (São Paulo: Companhia das Letras, 1989); Needell, *A Tropical Belle Époque;* Chalhoub, *Trabalho, lar e botequim;* Jaime Larry Benchimol, *Pereira Passos.* On the organization of the police forces and their role in implementing various policies of social control, see Thomas Holloway, *Policing Rio de Janeiro: Repression and Resistance in a Nineteenth-Century City* (Stanford: Stanford University Press, 1993); Marcos Bretas, *A guerra das ruas: Povo e polícia na cidade do Rio de Janeiro* (Rio de Janeiro: Arquivo Nacional, 1997); Bretas, *Ordem na cidade: O exercício cotidiano da autoridade policial no Rio de Janeiro: 1907–1930* (Rio de Janeiro: Rocco, 1997); Eugênio Soares, *A negregada instituição: Os capoeiras no Rio de Janeiro* (Rio de Janeiro: Secretaria Municipal de Cultura, Departamento Geral de Documentação e Informação Cultural, 1994); José Luiz Werneck da Silva, Gizlete Neder, and Nancy Naro, *A polícia na corte e no Distrito Federal, 1831–1930* (Rio de Janeiro: Pontifícia Universidade Católica, 1981).

31 J. F. Costa, *Ordem médica;* Machado et al., *Danação da norma.*

32 S. Graham, *House and Street*, ch. 2.

33 Esteves, *Meninas perdidas*, 43–54.

34 S. Graham, *House and Street*, 18. For a discussion of poor women and street life in nineteenth-century São Paulo, see Maria Odila Leite da Silva Dias, *Quotidiano e poder em São Paulo no século XIX: Ana Gertrudes de Jesus* (São Paulo: Brasiliense, 1984).

35 Esteves, *Meninas perdidas*, 43–54.

36 The city's population jumped from 275,000 in 1872 to 523,000 in 1890 and 811,000 in 1906. It jumped again to 1,158,000 in 1920 and 1,764,000 in 1940 (figures rounded). *Recenseamento geral do Brasil (1 de setembro de 1940)*, pt. 16, *Distrito Federal* (Rio de Janeiro: Instituto Brasileiro de Geografia e Estatística, 1951), xxi.

37 Meade, "Civilizing Rio," 50–51, 66–70; Samuel C. Adamo, "The Broken Promise: Race, Health, and Justice in Rio de Janeiro, 1890–1940" (Ph.D. diss., University of New Mexico, 1983), 40–42, 73–76, 122–47; Lia de Aquino Carvalho, *Contribuição ao estudo das habitações populares, Rio de Janeiro, 1886–1906*, 2d ed. (Rio de Janeiro: Prefeitura da Cidade do Rio de Janeiro, Secretaria Municipal de Cultura, 1995); Lilian Fessler Vaz, "Contribuição ao estudo da produção e transformação do espaço da habitação popular: As habitações coletivas no Rio antigo" (master's thesis, Universidade Federal do Rio de Janeiro, 1985). For contemporary descriptions of working-class residences, see Aluísio Azevedo's famous novel *O cortiço*, translated as *A Brazilian Tenement* (New York: McBride, 1926); Luís Edmundo, *O Rio de Janeiro do meu tempo* (Rio de Janeiro: Imprensa Nacional, 1938); and Everardo Backheuser, *Habitações populares: Relatório apresentado ao Exmo. Sr. Dr. J. J. Seabra, ministro da Justiça e Negócios Interiores* (Rio de Janeiro: Imprensa Nacional, 1906).

38 On occupations of working-class men and women, see "População classificada segundo as profissões," *Recenseamento geral da República dos Estados Unidos do Brasil em 31 de dezembro de 1890, Distrito Federal* (Rio de Janeiro: Imprensa Nacional, 1895), 408–21; and "Profissões," *Recenseamento do Rio de Janeiro realisado em 20 de setembro de 1906* (Rio de Janeiro: Imprensa Nacional, 1895), 180–389; Meade, "Civilizing Rio, 67 nn. 50, 51, 121–50; Eulália Maria Lahmeyer Lobo, *História do Rio de Janeiro (do capital comercial ao capital industrial e financeiro)*, 2 vols. (Rio de Janeiro: Instituto Brasileiro de Mercado de Capitais, 1978), 1: 227–23; Benchimol, *Pereira Passos*, chaps. 4, 7, 10; Jeffrey D. Needell, "The *Revolta contra vacina* of 1904: The Revolt against 'modernization' in Belle Époque Rio de Janeiro," *Hispanic American Historical Review* 67, 2 (1989): 249; on women's work specifically, see Meade, "Civilizing" Rio, 67, 164–65; S. Graham, *House and Street*; for women's work in urban Brazil generally, June Hahner, *Emancipating the Female Sex: The Struggle for Women's Rights in Brazil, 1850–1940* (Durham: Duke University Press, 1990), 90–113.

39 See, for example, José Ricardo Pires de Almeida, *Higiene moral* (Rio de Janeiro:

Laemmert, 1906), 41–73, cited in Needell, *A Tropical Belle Époque*, 289 n. 24; Vivaldo Coaracy, *Memorias da cidade do Rio de Janeiro* (Rio de Janeiro: José Olympio, 1955), 136–39; and Meade's discussion of Coaracy in *"Civilizing" Rio*, 37–43. As Meade points out, there is a tension between Coaracy's nostalgia for Rio's colorful and varied late-nineteenth-century prostitution market and his moralizing tone; Coaracy, writing from the perspective of a later generation, echoes many of the earlier observers analyzed by Needell. See also Engel, *Meretrizes e doutores*; L. Soares, *Rameiras*; Needell, *A Tropical Belle Époque*, chap. 5; Sueann Caulfield, "The Birth of Mangue: Race, Nation, and the Politics of Prostitution in Rio de Janeiro, 1850–1942," in *Sex and Sexuality in Latin America*, ed. Daniel Balderston and Donna Guy (New York: New York University Press, 1997), 86–100. For similar tensions in turn-of-the-century São Paulo, see Margareth Rago, *Os prazeres da noite: Prostituição e códigos da sexualidade feminina em São Paulo, 1890–1930* (Rio de Janeiro: Paz e Terra, 1991).

40   See esp. S. Graham, "Slavery's Impasse."

41   Gilberto Freyre, *Order and Progress: Brazil from Monarchy to Republic*, trans. Rod W. Horton (New York: Knopf, 1970), 57–59, 65; Needell, *A Tropical Belle Époque*, 173–75. Several of Needell's informants confirm Freyre's observation. See Ibid., 291 n. 70.

42   For analysis of the elite consumption of French "luxury" prostitutes, see Needell, *A Tropical Belle Époque*, 171–75. The best accounts by contemporaries are Almeida, *Higiene moral*, 48–50, 70–72; E. Mattoso, *Coisas do meu tempo* (Bordeaux: Gounouilhou, 1916), 272–73, cited in Needell, *A Tropical Belle Époque*, 175, 289 n. 24, 291 n. 69. See also Coaracy, *Memorias*, 136–37; Meade, *"Civilizing" Rio*, 37–38.

43   See, for example, the petition sent to the Municipal Council in 1879, signed by 759 citizens, requesting the removal of prostitutes from central streets on the grounds of their "offense of morality and prejudice to established businessmen who find themselves obliged to move because of the rise in rents produced by the greater demand of those who deal in the exploitation of prostitutes imported from Europe" (Arquivo Geral da Cidade do Rio de Janeiro, Coleção Séries Documentais: Prostituição no Rio de Janeiro [hereafter AGCRJ/CSD/PRJ], cod. 48-4-63. For a discussion of lower-class prostitution and the "white slave trade" based on memoirs and other writings by contemporaries, see Needell, *A Tropical Belle Époque*, 172, 290–91 nn. 54–56. For studies based on criminal records and other archival sources, see Beatriz Kushnir, *Baile de máscaras: Mulheres judias e prostituição* (Rio de Janeiro: Imago, 1996); Lená Medeiros de Menezes, *Os estrangeiros e o comércio do prazer nas ruas do Rio, 1890–1930* (Rio de Janeiro: Arquivo Nacional, 1992); Rago, *Os prazeres da noite*, chap. 5. For a fictional account of the trade in Eastern European Jewish prostitutes, see Esther Largman, *Jovens polacas* (Rio de Janeiro: Rosa dos Tempos, 1993). Donna Guy describes the white slave traffic to Latin America focusing on its "mecca," Buenos Aires, in *Sex and Danger in Buenos Aires*:

234

Prostitution, Family, and Nation in Argentina (Lincoln: University of Nebraska Press, 1991), 5–35.

44 Engel, *Meretrizes e doutores,* 103–36; Soares, *Rameiras,* 102–9. Caulfield, "The Birth of Mangue," 90–92.

45 AGCRJ/CSD/PRJ, cod. 48-3-59.

46 Imperial law dating from 1849 had charged the chief of police with surveillance of prostitutes, along with vagrants, beggars, drunks, and others "who disturb public tranquillity." See Aurelino de Araújo Leal, "These III: I—A prostituição, II—Localização," in *Anais da conferência judiciária-policial,* ed. Leal (Rio de Janeiro: Imprensa Nacional, 1918), 1: 403–24. This decree reiterated executive decree 1,034-A of September 1, 1892, art. 22, no. 21, which in turn reaffirmed regulations dating from 1841, when responsibility for controlling prostitution was passed from justices of the peace to the police chief (law 261, December 3, 1841).

47 AGCRJ/CSD/PRJ, cod. 43-3-59 (1879).

48 See the documents collected in AGCRJ/CSD/PRJ, dated from 1853 to 1910, which include correspondence between chiefs of police and the minister of justice, the mayor, the Municipal Council, and public health officials. Rio's police chiefs, unhappy with the absence of a legal basis for actions against prostitution, repeatedly submitted formal proposals for regulatory measures to the Municipal Council, but these proposals were consistently rejected. See, for example, AGCRJ/CSD/PRJ, cod. 48-4-54 (1853); cod. 48-4-58 (1853); cod. 48-4-63 (1883); cod. 48-4-61 (1888); cod. 48-4-62 (1900); and cod. 61-4-5 (1910).

49 A 1917 conference of police and judicial authorities organized by police chief Aurelino de Araújo Leal reveals that these issues had become the major concerns of law enforcement agencies, particularly the police. See Leal, "These III," 1: 403–24. See also Engel, *Meretrizes e doutores;* Meade, *"Civilizing" Rio,* 36–44.

50 Alberto Torres, *A organização nacional* (1914), cited in Francisco de Oliveira Viana, *Problemas da política objetiva* (São Paulo: Editora Nacional, 1930), 244.

51 The Federal District chief of police, named by the president, was responsible for law enforcement in the district as well as counter insurgency and federal investigations. See Bretas, *Ordem na cidade,* 39–60.

52 Nicolau Sevcenko, *Literatura como missão: Tensões sociais e criação cultural na Primeira República* (São Paulo: Brasiliense, 1983), 30; Needell, *A Tropical Belle Époque,* chap. 1, esp. 33–34; Needell, "The *Revolta contra vacina,*" 243–44; Needell, "Making the Carioca Belle Époque Concrete: The Urban Reforms of Rio de Janeiro under Pereira Passos," *Journal of Urban History* 10, 4 (August 1984): 383–422, esp. 400–401. See also Maurício de A. Abreu, *Evolução urbana do Rio de Janeiro* (Rio de Janeiro: IPLANRIO/ZAHAR, 1988), 59–68; Benchimol, *Pereira Passos;* Oswaldo Porto Rocha, *A era das demolições: Cidade do Rio de Janeiro, 1870–1920,* 2d ed. (Rio de Janeiro: Secretaria Municipal de Cultura, 1995). The best studies of the responses by the urban and suburban poor to these and earlier reforms are Meade, *"Civilizing" Rio;* Sidney

Chalhoub, *Cidade febril*, and "A guerra contra os cortiços: Cidade do Rio, 1850–1906," *Primeira versão* 9 (Campinas, São Paulo: IFCH/UNICAMP, 1990); S. Graham, *House and Street*. See also José Murilo de Carvalho, *Os bestializados: O Rio de Janeiro e a República que não foi* (São Paulo: Companhia das Letras, 1989).

53   See Caulfield, "The Birth of Mangue," 86–89.

54   Nicolau Sevcenko, *A revolta da vacina: Mentes insanas em corpos rebeldes* (São Paulo: Brasiliense, 1984); J. Carvalho, *Os bestializados*, 66–91; Teresa Meade, " 'Civilizing Rio de Janeiro': The Public Health Campaign and the Riot of 1904," *Journal of Social History* 20, 2 (winter 1986): 301–22; Needell, "The *Revolta contra vacina*"; Robert G. Nachman, "Positivism and Revolution in Brazil's First Republic: The 1904 Revolt," *Americas* 34, 1 (1977): 3–23. Sidney Chalhoub argues that African and Afro-Brazilian beliefs and experiences with disease control influenced popular responses to vaccination in Chalhoub, "The Politics of Disease Control: Yellow Fever and Race in Nineteenth Century Rio de Janeiro," *Journal of Latin American Studies* 25 (1993): 441–63.

55   Evaristo de Morais attacks police "moralization campaigns" in *Ensaios de patologia social* (Rio de Janeiro: Leite Ribeiro e Maurilo, 1921). Teresa Meade, *"Civilizing" Rio*, is the most comprehensive study of popular urban and suburban strategies for protesting faulty public services and urban policies. See Chalhoub, "A guerra contra os cortiços," 37–41, for a description of the often quixotic resistance to eviction by downtown tenement dwellers. For discussion of working-class resentment of the police, see Chalhoub, *Trabalho, lar e botequim*, 172–204, esp. 195–96. Eduardo Silva, studying letters to the editor in a major daily, finds that the majority of complaints focus on police abuses of power or inefficiency. Silva, *As queixas do povo* (Rio de Janeiro: Paz e Terra, 1988).

56   Morais, *Ensaios*, 257–87.

57   The most complete discussion of the influence of the Haussmann reforms on the turn-of-the-century engineers who implemented Rio's reforms is Needell, *A Tropical Belle Époque*, 39–44, esp. 36. See also M. de A. Abreu, *Evolução urbana*, 59–68; Benchimol, *Pereira Passos*, 192–194; and Rocha, *A era das demolições*, 63–64.

58   "No Guanabara," *O Paiz*, September 23, 1920; *Correio da manhã*, September 22, 1920; "Os inimigos do protocolo," *Correio da manhã*, September 27, 1920.

59   Laurita Pessoa Raja Gabaglia, *Epitácio Pessoa, 1865–1942* (São Paulo: José Olympio, 1941), 394.

60   "Os soberanos belgas no Rio: Realisa-se hoje, na Quinta da Boa Vista, grande parada em honra aos soberanos belgas," *Correio da manhã*, September 22, 1920, 3.

61   With post–World War I decolonization movements shaking Europe, it was not surprising that Albert glorified colonial domination.

62   The speech is reprinted in full in "O dia dos soberanos belgas," *Correio da manhã*, September 21, 1920, 3.

63 Ibid.

64 "Nos Soverains au Brésil," *Etole belge*, September 30, 1920.

65 The need to "moralize Brazilian political customs," was the battle cry of Rui Barbosa's *civilista* movement. Barbosa was the most important opposition presidential candidate in 1910 and 1919. See Marieta de Moraes Ferreira, *Conflito regional e crise política: A reação republicana no Rio de Janeiro* (Rio de Janeiro: Centro de Pesquisa e Documentação de História Contemporânea do Brasil, 1988); Anita Leocádia Prestes, *Os militares e a reação republicana* (Petrópolis: Vozes, 1993).

66 The article was published on November 6, 1920, and reprinted in Morais, *Ensaios*, 279–84.

67 Ibid., 279–280.

68 Ibid., 280.

69 Ibid.

70 Ibid.

71 Ibid.

72 "Para o rei não ver," *O imparcial*, September 14, 1920.

73 Mayor Sampaio tried to use the occasion of the royal visit to reinitiate a controversial project to raze Castelo Hill, which had been delayed decades earlier by popular opposition and lack of funds. The hill, argued Sampaio's supporters in the press, with its precarious tenements and other "wretched and disorderly buildings," was "an obstacle to the progress" represented by Rio Branco Avenue, a block away. "Até que em fim?" *Revista da semana*, August 14, 1920.

74 Conniff, *Urban Politics*, chap. 1; Meade, *"Civilizing" Rio*, esp. chap. 3. Meade shows that urban services and development preceded the population in the expensive South Zone, while the North Zone was left with severe sanitation and transportation deficiencies.

75 "Os soberanos da Bélgica no Brasil: A renda da Central augmentou consideravelmente," *Correio da manhã*, September 24, 1924, 3.

76 Favela dwellings had already multiplied many times since the first shacks were erected on Favela Hill in the late nineteenth century. In the 1920s, the number of favela shacks sextupled; by 1933, they housed some seventy thousand persons. Conniff, *Urban Politics*, 32.

77 Geminiano da Franca, "Serviço policial," in *Relatório apresentado ao Presidente da República dos Estados Unidos do Brasil pelo Ministro da Justiça e Negócios Interiores*, Dr. Alfredo Pinto Vieira de Mello (Rio de Janeiro: Imprensa Nacional, 1920), 75.

78 For a discussion of Brazilian modernists' responses to Parisian cultural trends, see Nicolau Sevcenko, *Orfeu extático na metrópole: São Paulo, sociedade e cultura nos frementes anos 20* (São Paulo: Companhia das Letras, 1992), esp. 277–302.

79 For an account of this process, see Hermano Vianna, *O mistério do samba*, 2d

ed. (Rio de Janeiro: Jorge Zahar, 1995). See also John Charles Chasteen, "The Prehistory of Samba: Carnival Dancing in Rio de Janeiro, 1840–1917," *Journal of Latin American Studies* 28 (1996): 29–47.

80   H. Vianna, *O mistério do samba*, 117–18.

81   See Chasteen, "The Prehistory of Samba," 30–31; Alison Raphael, "Samba and Social Control: Popular Culture and Racial Democracy in Rio de Janeiro" (Ph.D. diss., Columbia University, 1981); Maria Isaura Pereira de Queiroz, *Carnaval brasileiro: O vivido e o mito* (São Paulo: Brasiliense, 1992); Dulce Tupi, *Carnivais de guerra: O nacionalismo no samba* (Rio de Janeiro: ASB Arte Gráfica e Editora, 1985), 96–115; Ana Maria Rodrigues, *Samba negro, espoliação branca* (São Paulo: Hucitec, 1984). The classic text for the evolution of Brazilian popular music and the development of samba as "the most authentically Carioca" music form is José Ramos Tinhorão, *Pequena história da música popular: Da modinha à lambada*, 6th ed. (São Paulo: Art Editora, 1991), esp. 119–31, 169–82.

82   The *cateretê* is reprinted in Sérgio Cabral, *Pixinguinha: Vida e obra* (Rio de Janeiro: Lumiar, 1997), 60. Cabral also mentions the samba "Para o Rei Alberto ver" by Lourival de Carvalho. See also the samba score by Antônio P. Velho, "Para o Rei Alberto ver" (Rio de Janeiro: Casa Bevilaqua, 1920), held by the Biblioteca de Música, Rio de Janeiro.

83   Advertisement cited in Cabral, *Pixinguinha*, 61.

84   Cabral, *Pixinguinha*, 63.

85   Letter by Catulo da Paixão Cearense published in the *Gazeta de notícias*, cited in Cabral, *Pixinguinha*, 61.

86   "A visita do rei-herói: Uma festa carnavalesca no mar," *A noite*, July 24, 1920; "A próxima visita do rei Alberto," *O imparcial*, July 25, 1920.

87   Luís Martins, *Noturno da Lapa* (Rio de Janeiro: Civilização Brasileira, 1964), 23, 25.

88   See Teófilo de Almeida, "Sífilis e prostituição no Rio de Janeiro," *Arquivos da Fundação Gaffrée-Guinle* 2 (1929): 21–52, esp. chart on 48; Nelson Hungria, "Relação das mulheres que exercem o meretrício em zona do 12 distrito policial," Arquivo Nacional, Ministério da Justiça e Negócios Interiores, caixa 6C751A; Franklin Galvão, "Mapa discriminativo das meretrizes moradoras sob a jurisdição do 9 districto," Arquivo Nacional, Ministério da Justiça e Negócios Interiores, caixa 6C751A. I am greatly indebted to Cláudio Batalha and Marcos Brettas for drawing my attention to the police documents and making copies available to me. For further discussion of the racial and national makeup of the two zones, see Caulfield, "The Birth of Mangue."

89   Nelson Werneck Sodré, *Do tenentismo ao Estado Novo: Memórias de um soldado* (Petrópolis: Vozes, 1986), 52.

90   "Polícia Civil: Relatório de 4-11-30 a 4-11-31," Arquivo Nacional IJ6-401 (1932).

91   In the late 1930s, for example, public health officials estimated the number of

prostitutes in the city at 20,000 to 30,000, of which only 1,462 were registered in 1942. Manoel Odorico de Morais, "Estado atual da prostituição no Rio de Janeiro," *A folha médica* 23, 12 (July 1942): 148–52, 148.

92 Martins, *Noturno da Lapa*, 109.

93 Ibid., 141.

94 "O homem e a mulher," *Revista feminina*, January, 1923, cited in Rago, *Os prazeres da noite*, 74.

95 See Susan K. Besse, *Restructuring Patriarchy: The Modernization of Gender Inequality in Brazil 1914–1940* (Chapel Hill: North Carolina University Press, 1996); Míriam Lifchitz Moreira Leite, *Outra face do feminismo: Maria Lacerda de Moura* (São Paulo: Ática, 1984).

96 "O feminismo no parlamento: A poetisa Gilka Machado entende que onde o homem entra a mulher pode entrar também," *O jornal*, January 4, 1920.

97 Martins, *Noturno da Lapa*, 130.

98 Besse, *Restructuring, Patriarchy*, 21–22, 28–29; for São Paulo, *Rago, Os prazeres da noite*, 58–67; G. Freyre, *Order and Progress*, 65.

99 The development of similar spaces of heterosocial leisure happened earlier in industrialized cities such as New York. See Kathy Peiss, *Cheap Amusements: Working Women and Leisure in Turn-of-the-Century New York* (Philadelphia: Temple University Press, 1986).

100 "O feminismo no parlamento."

101 See Maria Fernanda Baptista Bicalho, "The Art of Seduction: Representation of Women in Brazilian Silent Cinema," *Luso-Brazilian Review* 30, 1 (summer 1993): 21–33.

102 *Vida policial*, July 24, 1926.

103 Raphael, "Samba and Social Control," 86–88.

104 See Appendix A and introduction, n. 1.

105 AN, vara 8, caixa 1807 no. 430 (1923).

106 AN, vara 1, caixa 1775 no. 2265 (1927).

107 AN, vara 1, caixa 1775 no. 1974 (1930).

108 AN, vara 1, caixa 1731 no. 1282 (1936).

109 AN, vara 5, caixa 1843 no. 380 (1933).

110 Of the 450 cases analyzed, 24 percent of the deflowerings occurred in these kinds of public places, compared to 15 percent at the woman's home, 12 percent at her gate or in her yard, 5 percent at her workplace, 21 percent at the man's home (often a rented room), 10 percent in a hotel or pension, and 6 percent at the home of a friend or relative, (7 percent unknown).

Chapter 3 "What Virginity Is This?": Judging the Honor of the Modern Woman

1 Francisco Viveiros de Castro, *Os delitos contra a honra da mulher*, 2d ed. (Rio de Janeiro: Freitas Bastos, 1932), 21.

2   Nelson Hungria, "Crimes sexuais," in *Revista forense* 70 (April–May 1937): 216–27, esp. 220.

3   Ibid., 220.

4   Ibid.

5   Michael Herzfeld, "Semantic Slippage and Moral Fall: The Rhetoric of Chastity in Rural Greece," *Journal of Modern Greek Studies* 1 (1983): 161.

6   Urbanization and the move from the household-based economy toward commercial and industrial capitalism was a long term and uneven process. For analysis of this process in Rio de Janeiro, see Eulália Maria Lahmeyer Lobo, *História do Rio de Janeiro (do capital comercial ao capital industrial e financeiro)*, 2 vols. (Rio de Janeiro: Instituto Brasileiro de Mercado de Capitais, 1978). Studies of its effects on gender and family strategies in the eighteenth and nineteenth centuries have focused especially on the state of São Paulo. See Muriel Nazzari, *Disappearance of the Dowry: Women, Families, and Social Change in São Paulo, Brazil, 1600–1900* (Stanford: Stanford University Press, 1991); Elizabeth Anne Kuznesof, *Household Economy and Urban Development: São Paulo, 1765–1836* (Denver: Westview Press, 1986). For effects of urbanization on gender in the twentieth century, see Susan K. Besse, *Restructuring Patriarchy: The Modernization of Gender Inequality in Brazil, 1914–1940* (Chapel Hill: University of North Carolina Press, 1996); June Hahner, *Emancipating the Female Sex: The Struggle for Women's Rights in Brazil, 1850–1940* (Durham: Duke University Press, 1990), 77–120. For Bahia, see Dain Borges, *The Family in Bahia, Brazil, 1870–1945* (Stanford: Stanford University Press, 1992).

7   On post–World War I technological and cultural transformations, see Nicolau Sevcenko, "A capital irradiate: Técnica, ritmos e ritos do Rio," in *História da vida privada no Brasil*, ed. Fernando A. Novais (São Paulo: Companhia das Letras, 1998), 3: 513–620.

8   See Besse, *Restructuring Patriarchy*, 19–37; Margareth Rago, *Os prazeres da noite: Prostituição e códigos da sexualidade feminina em São Paulo, 1890–1930* (Rio de Janeiro: Paz e Terra, 1991). Studies of anxieties about the modern woman in Western Europe include Mary Louise Roberts, *Civilization without Sexes: Reconstructing Gender in Postwar France, 1917–1927* (Chicago: University of Chicago Press, 1994); Beth Irwin Lewis, "*Lustmord:* Inside the Windows of the Metropolis," in *Berlin: Culture and Metropolis*, ed. Charles W. Haxthausen and Heidrun Suhr (Minneapolis: University of Minnesota Press, 1990); and Bonnie Smith, *Changing Lives: Women in European History since 1700* (Lexington, Mass.: D. C. Heath, 1989), chap. 10. For the United States, see Rayna Rapp and Ellen Ross, "The Twenties: Feminism, Consumerism, and Political Backlash in the United States," in *Women in Culture and Politics: A Century of Change*, ed. Judith Friedlander (Bloomington: Indiana University Press, 1986), 55. These debates were even more complex outside the industrialized nations. See, for example, Laura Engelstein, *The Keys to Happiness: Sex and the Search*

for Modernity in Fin-de-Siècle Russia (Ithaca: Cornell University Press, 1992); Laurel Rasplica Rodd, "Yosano Akiko and the Taisho Debate over the 'New Woman'"; and Miriam Silverberg, "The Modern Girl as Militant," in *Recreating Japanese Women, 1600–1945*, ed. Gail Lee Bernstein (Berkeley and Los Angeles: University of California Press, 1991), 175–98, 239–66.

9 Jurists drew from the growing literature on sexology produced by Brazilian medical and psychological professionals in the first half of the twentieth century. For analysis of this literature, see Talisman Ford, "Passion Is in the Eye of the Beholder: Sexuality as Seen by Brazilian Sexologists, 1900–1940" (Ph.D. diss., Vanderbilt University, 1995). Homosexuality would become an important focus of sexologists, especially after the dissemination of legal-medical specialist Leonídio Ribeiro's work in the 1930s. See Ford, "Passion," chap. 5; James Green, "Beyond Carnival: Homosexuality in Twentieth-Century Brazil" (Ph.D. diss., University of California, Los Angeles, 1996), chap. 4.

10 Hungria, "Crimes sexuais," 217. For a discussion of the various meanings of *pudor*, see chap. 1.

11 For discussion of ideas of free sex and challenges to the bourgeois family among anarchist intellectuals, see Margareth Rago, *Do cabaré ao lar: A utopia da cidade disciplinar, Brasil, 1890–1930* (Rio de Janeiro: Paz e Terra, 1985).

12 See Barbara Weinstein, *For Social Peace in Brazil: Industrialists and the Remaking of the Working Class in São Paulo, 1920–1964* (Chapel Hill: University of North Carolina Press, 1996), 20–27, 51–58, for the complex political positions of São Paulo industrialists and merchants and their influence in state politics in the 1920s.

13 Pedro Ernesto was the nonelected administrator, or Interventor, of Rio from 1931 to 1935; he was elected mayor from 1935 to 1936. See Paulo Brandi and Dora Flaksman, "Ernesto, Pedro," in *Dicionário histórico-biográfico brasileiro*, ed. Israel Beloch and Alzira Alves de Abreu (Rio de Janeiro: Forense Universitária, 1984), 2: 1176–80.

14 See Michael Conniff, *Urban Politics in Brazil: The Rise of Populism, 1925–1945* (Pittsburgh: University of Pittsburgh Press, 1981). For a discussion of professional efforts to intervene in family relations in Rio de Janeiro, see Susan K. Besse, "Crimes of Passion: The Campaign against Wife Killing in Brazil, 1910–1940," *Journal of Social History* 22, 4 (summer 1989): 653–66. An influential group of modernizing industrialists developed similar ideas about the need for social reform and created agencies that provided various worker training and social assistance programs. For a discussion of the work of these industrialists from the 1920s to the 1960s in São Paulo, where they were most important, see Weinstein, *For Social Peace*, esp. 114–279.

15 Conniff, *Urban Politics*; John Charles Chasteen, "The Prehistory of Samba: Carnival Dancing in Rio de Janeiro, 1840–1917," *Journal of Latin American Studies* 28 (1996): 30–31; Alison Raphael, "Samba and Social Control: Popular Culture and Racial Democracy in Rio de Janeiro" (Ph.D. diss., Columbia University, 1981).

16   For analysis of the complex and changing political alliances in power during
     this period, see Luciano Martins, "Estado Novo," in *Dicionário histórico-
     biográfico*, 2: 1195–1201; Thomas Skidmore, *Politics in Brazil, 1930–1964:
     An Experiment in Democracy* (New York: Oxford University Press, 1980), 3–
     21; Boris Fausto, *A revolução de 1930: Historiografia e história* (São Paulo:
     Brasiliense, 1986), 29–30.

17   See Hans Henze, "O Centro D. Vital: Igreja, sociedade sivil e sociedade política
     no Brasil, 1930–1945" (master's thesis, Universidade Federal Fluminense,
     1995).

18   Brandi and Flaksman, "Ernesto, Pedro" and Renato Lemos and César Benja-
     min, "Müller, Felinto," in *Dicionário histórico-biográfico*, 2: 1176–80; 2342–
     46. See also Paulo Sérgio de M. S. Pinheiro, *Estratégias da ilusão: A revolução
     mundial e o Brasil, 1922–1935* (São Paulo: Companhia das Letras, 1991). Fer-
     nando Morais's biography of the German wife of Brazilian Communist leader
     Luís Carlos Prestes vividly illustrates Müller's ties to Nazi Germany and the
     brutal role he played in repressing opposition (Morais, *Olga* [São Paulo: Com-
     panhia das Letras, 1984], 123–80).

19   Roberto Lira, *Frutos verdes* (Rio de Janeiro: Brasileira Lux, 1925), 17.

20   See, for example, Nelson Hungria, in "Do lenocínio e do tráfico de mulheres,"
     Arquivos do Departamento Federal de Seguranca Pública 3, 7 (January–
     March 1946): 19–20, in which he criticizes the attempt to end the traditional
     police regulation in Mangue in 1942. See Lira, *Novo direito penal*, 120–26, for
     an opposing view of the same event.

21   Roberto Lira, *Novo direito penal* (Rio de Janeiro: Editor Borsoi, 1972), 110.

22   Donna Guy, *Sex and Danger in Buenos Aires: Prostitution, Family, and Na-
     tion in Argentina* (Lincoln: University of Nebraska Press, 1991), 95–104.

23   There are repeated complaints about police interference in physicians' reports
     on their efforts to fight syphilis in the *Anais da Fundação Gaffrée-Guinle*
     from 1927 to 1935 and in the *Anais da Primeira Conferência Nacional de
     Defesa Contra a Sífilis* in 1941. See also Leonídio Ribeiro Filho, "Os problemas
     médico-legais em face da reforma da policia," speech reprinted in *Gazeta Poli-
     cial*, June 16, 1931. For the diplomatic representation of Brazil's prostitution
     policy, and conflicts and faulty communication between diplomats and Rio's
     police on the issue, see Ministério das Relações Exteriores, "Papeis sobre o
     tráfico de mulheres e crianças," in Arquivo Nacional, Ministério de Justiça e
     Negócios Interiores (MJNI), caixa 537. The papers include correspondence
     between the Justice and Foreign ministries between 1921 and 1939 regarding
     local and international efforts to combat the white slave trade. Diplomats
     were frustrated, for example, that the Justice Ministry did not make a specific
     official responsible for monitoring foreign prostitution, as required by the
     1904 anti-traffic treaty, until the mid-1930s.

24   Jeffrey Lesser, *Welcoming the Undesirables: Brazil and the Jewish Question*
     (Berkeley and Los Angeles: University of California Press, 1995), 36.

25   For Jewish prostitution networks in Rio de Janeiro and the mobilization of

Brazilian Jews against prostitution see Lesser, *Welcoming the Undesirables*, 33–39; Beatriz Kushnir, *Baile de máscaras: Mulheres judias e prostituição* (Rio de Janeiro: Imago, 1996).

26 Lesser, *Welcoming the Undesirables*, 37–38.

27 Lira, *Novo direito penal*, 110.

28 Ibid. On the absence of empirical data on pimping and prostitution, see Carlos Sussekind de Mendonça, "Preface" to Anísio Frota Aguiar, *O lenocínio como problema social no Brasil* (Rio de Janeiro: n.p., 1940), 5.

29 Ribeiro Filho, "Os problemas médico-legais."

30 See Sueann Caulfield, "The Birth of Mangue: Race, Nation, and the Politics of Prostitution in Rio de Janeiro, 1850–1942," in *Sex and Sexuality in Latin America*, ed. Daniel Balderston and Donna Guy (New York: New York University Press, 1997), 95–96.

31 See Aguiar, *O lenocínio*, for the delegate's own account of the campaign. Several memorialists complained that this campaign brought the deterioration of the picturesque bohemian nightlife of Lapa and Mangue of the early decades of the century. See, for example, Luís Martins, *Nocturno da Lapa* (Rio de Janeiro: Civilização Brasileira, 1964), 204–27; Hernani de Irajá, *Adeus Lapa!* (Rio de Janeiro: Gráfica Record, 1967). Muza Clara Chaves Velasques analyzes these and other memoirs focusing on Lapa in "A Lapa boêmia: Um estudo da identidade carioca" (master's thesis, Universidade Federal Fluminense, 1994).

32 See Eurico Cruz's discussion of police zoning policies in his verdict of June 6, 1927, reprinted in Eduardo Espinola, "O 'habeas-corpus' e a expulsão do estrangeiro: Prática do lenocínio," *Pandectas Brasileiras* (Rio de Janeiro: Casa Gráfica, 1929), 210–21. Several of Cruz's sentences are published along with appeals court decisions supporting them in Vicente Piragibe, *Dicionário de jurisprudência penal do Brasil* (Rio de Janeiro: Freitas Bastos, 1938), 1: 529–83.

33 Aurelino de Araujo Leal, "Tese III: I—A prostituição II—Localização," in *Anais da conferência judiciria-policial*, ed. Leal (Rio de Janeiro: Imprensa Nacional, 1918), 1: 403–24.

34 Mendonça, "Preface," 8; Lira, *Novo direito penal*, 110, 120–26.

35 For their respective positions on divorce, see Roberto Lira, *Polícia e justiça para o amor!* (Rio de Janeiro: S. A. A. Noite, 1939), 57–58; Nelson Hungria, *Compêndio de direito penal*, pt. 2, cited in Nelson Hungria and Ramão Cortes de Lacerda, *Comentários ao código penal* (Rio de Janeiro, Revista Forense, 1947), 8: 318–21 n. 2.

36 Lira, *Polícia e justiça*, 24. See also Besse, "Crimes of Passion."

37 See chap. 1, 42–44.

38 In addition to defending prostitutes, Morais had campaigned for abolition and the rights of Afro-Brazilians, workers, and women; in the last decades before his death in 1939, he struggled against the ban against black immigrants and defended Jews against rising anti-Semitism. See the biographical introduction by Morais's son, Evaristo de Morais Filho, in Evaristo de Morais, *Reminiscências de um rábula criminalista* (Rio de Janeiro: Briguiet, 1989), 9–48.

39   See chap. 4.

40   Carlos Sussekind de Mendonça, "Os crimes passionais: A sua repetição, entre nós—algumas das suas causas," *Revista criminal* 5, 9 (November 1927).

41   Lira, *Polícia e justiça*, 57–58, 190.

42   Besse, "Crimes of Passion," 653.

43   Ibid.

44   Besse, *Restructuring Patriarchy*, 23–27, 225.

45   Ibid., 210 n. 49. Prandi, José R., "Catolicismo e família," Cadernos CEBRAP 21 (1975): 29–35.

46   Carolina Pereira, "Os assassinos de mulheres," *Revista feminina* 7, 70 (March 1920).

47   Anna Rita Malheiros, "Junho," *Revista feminina* 7, 73 (June 1920).

48   Ruy Castro, *O anjo pornográfico: A vida de Nelson Rodrigues* (São Paulo: Companhia das Letras, 1992). Female sympathy for women who killed men in defense of their honor, was echoed in a celebrated case in Caracas, Venezuela, in 1941. See Judith Ewell, "Ligia Parra Jahn: The Blonde with the Revolver," in *The Human Tradition in Latin America: The Twentieth Century*, ed. William H. Beezley and Judith Ewell (Wilmington, Del.: Scholarly Resources, 1987).

49   Cecília Bandeira de Melo Rebelo de Vasconcelos (pseud. Chrysantheme), *Minha terra e sua gente* (Rio de Janeiro, 1929), 22–29, quoted in Besse, "Crimes of Passion," 654.

50   Lira, *Polícia e justiça*, 35–40.

51   Ibid.

52   Mendonça, "Os crimes passionais."

53   Lira, *Frutos verdes*, 33. Besse and Mariza Corrêa both mention the antifeminist attitudes of Lira as well as other critics of passionate criminals such as writers Lima Barreto and João do Rio. See Besse, "Crimes of Passion," 657 n. 22; Corrêa, *Os crimes da paixão* (São Paulo: Brasiliense, 1981), 37–40.

54   Lira, *Frutos verdes*, 32. In an illogical afterthought, Lira excluded factory workers from this generalization, "because they are isolated in their own life, in a separate society." Perhaps his socialist affiliation restrained him from making derogatory statements about factory workers. Lower-middle-class or upwardly mobile clerks, secretaries, and public employees were apparently fair game.

55   Ibid., 17.

56   Besse, "Crimes of Passion."

57   On the nineteenth-century conflicts over the jury, see Thomas Flory, *Judge and Jury in Imperial Brazil, 1808–1871* (Austin: University of Texas Press, 1981), 20–30, 131–56; on the controversy over the jury during the First National Juridical Congress in 1933 and the Constitutional Assembly in 1934, see Antônio Eugênio Magarinos Torres, *Processo penal do juri no Brasil* (Rio de Janeiro: Jacinto, 1939), 43; and Torres, *Dialogos sobre o juri* (Rio de Janeiro: Jacinto, 1933), 21–22.

58 See Torres, *Processo penal;* Torres, *Diálogos,* esp. 19–20; Roberto Lira, *O juri sob todos os aspetos* (Rio de Janeiro: Saraiva, 1950); Lira, *O Ministério Público e o juri* (Rio de Janeiro: Jacinto, 1933); Evaristo de Morais, *Criminalidade passional: O homicidio e o homicidio-suicidio por amor* (São Paulo: Saraiva, 1933), 65; Morais, *Reminiscências,* 54 n. 1, 158–59.

59 See interview of Evaristo de Morais on women in juries, *A noite,* September 22, 1932, reprinted in Torres, *Processo penal,* 86–87; Anônio Eugênio Magarinos Torres, *A mulher e o juri* (Rio de Janeiro: Jacinto, 1934). On the jury tribunal conviction rates, see Torres, "Crónica do juri," *Revista de direito penal* 11, 1–2 (October–November 1935): 149; Torres, *Diálogos,* 5; Lira, *Polícia e justiça,* 24.

60 Chap. 2, arts. 8–9 of decree 16,273 of December 20, 1923, determined that jury members must be literate and possess a minimum annual income and should be drawn from high-level public servants and professionals (*Coleção das leis da República dos Estados Unidos do Brasil de 1923* (Rio de Janeiro: Imprensa Nacional, 1924), 388. For Peixoto's refusal to serve, see Anônio Eugênio Magarinos Torres, "Um caso original de rebeldia ao serviço do juri," *Revista de direito penal* 11, 1–2 (October–November, 1935): 150–58.

61 See the summary of the positions of Lira, Hungria, Peixoto, and Torres in Carlos de Araújo Lima, *O júri: Sua atualização e crescente democratização* (Rio de Janeiro: n.p., 1966), 6–16.

62 Arts. 94–96 of decree 167 of January 5, 1938 (*Coleção das leis da República dos Estados Unidos do Brasil de 1923* [Rio de Janeiro: Imprensa Nacional, 1939], 20). On the protests over the law, see Flora Ferraz Veloso, *Sobre a instituição do juri* (Rio de Janeiro: n.p., 1959), 4.

63 Mendonça, "Os crimes passionais."

64 Quoted in Célio Loureiro, "Conferência na Radio Sociedade," in *Sensacionalismo,* ed. Carlos Sussekind de Mendonça (Rio de Janeiro: Casa do Estudante do Brasil, 1933), 133.

65 Ibid.

66 Fernando Castro Rebelo, "Conferência," in *Sensacionalismo,* 173.

67 Loureiro, "Conferência na Rádio Sociedad," 136.

68 Roberto Lira, "Psicanálise do sensacionalismo," in *Sensacionalismo,* 40.

69 Mendonça, "Os crimes passionais."

70 Lira, "Psicanálise," 27–28.

71 Lira, *Polícia e justiça,* 32.

72 Ibid., 28.

73 Afrânio Peixoto, *Sexologia forense* (Rio de Janeiro: Guanabara, 1934), esp. 54–60, 119–42; Agostinho J. de Souza Lima, *Tratado de medicina legal,* 5th ed. (1905; Rio de Janeiro: Freitas Bastos, 1933), 515. See also chap. 1, 35–36.

74 Among 450 criminal records of sexual crime consulted (from 1918 to 1940), "flaccidity" was not mentioned in any of the medical examinations. Thirty percent of these examinations reported complacent hymens. This is a significantly higher proportion than that reported by Peixoto for 1907–1915 (12.5–18

percent), but lower than the 33 percent reported by Miguel Sales in the 1930s. See Peixoto, *Sexologia forense*, 85. Sales's figure is quoted in Hungria, "Crimes sexuais," 2.

75 Peixoto, *Sexologia forense*, 140.

76 Judging from the examples of the vignettes Peixoto chose to illustrate these tragedies, including a case from his home state (Bahia) more than half a century earlier (a physician who returned his bride to her family in 1871 after giving her a self-styled virginity examination), the frequency of the more dramatic scenes was probably not high. Peixoto, *Sexologia forense*, 95–96. This famous case, known as "the Braga Affair," is described in Borges, *The Family in Bahia*, 205–8.

77 Peixoto, *Sexologia forense*, 30.

78 Ibid., 55.

79 Ibid.

80 Ibid., 123.

81 Ibid., 140.

82 Ibid., 57, 79–80, 85.

83 Ibid., 130–31.

84 Galdino Siqueira, *Código penal* (Rio de Janeiro: Livraria Jacinto, 1941), 12. Anderson Perdigão Nogueira, "Jurisprudência—defloramento," *Revista de direito penal* 16 (1937): 206–25, esp. 223.

85 Mário Gameiro, "O crime de sedução na exegese de quatro juizes modernos," *Revista criminal* 8, 3 (December 1934): 689–90.

86 Peixoto, *Sexologia forense*, 131.

87 Cited in Hungria, "Crimes sexuais," 221.

88 F. Castro, *Os delitos*, 25.

89 Peixoto, *Sexologia forense*, 131.

90 C. A. Lúcio Bitencourt, "Comentário," in *Revista de direito penal* 12 (1936): 105–14, esp. 113.

91 Aldovando Fleury, "Doutrina: Defloramento," *Revista dos tribunais* 69 (1929): 441–43, esp. 443.

92 Fleury, "Doutrina," 443.

93 See the jurisprudence cited in Peixoto, *Sexologia forense*, 130–40; Gameiro, "O crime de sedução"; Piragibe, *Dicionário*, 234–38.

94 Quoted in Darcy Campos de Medeiros and Aroldo Moreira, *Do crime de sedução* (Rio de Janeiro: Freitas Bastos, 1967), 90. See also Gameiro, "O crime de sedução."

95 Hungria, "Crimes sexuais," 219.

96 Francisco Campos, "Exposição de motivos," in Siqueira, *Código penal brasileiro*, 146–236, 222.

97 See, for example, "Crime de estupro—cópula carnal com menor de 16 anos, prostituta—inteligência do art. 272 do código penal," *Revista de direito* 91 (1929): 49–52; "Acórdão de 7 de junho de 1935," *Revista Forense* 65 (1935): 197; "Acórdão da Primeira Câmara do Tribunal de Apelação de São Paulo,"

reprinted in *Revista de crítica judiciária* 29 (1939): 175–77; "Acordão do Tribunal de Apelação de São Paulo," *Revista forense* 77 (1940): 173; "Razões do Sr. Promotor Público de Ouro Fino dr. J. D. Almeida Magalhães," *Revista de direito penal* 32 (1941): 197–204. Nelson Hungria led the minority that opposed this interpretation. See Hungria, "Crimes sexuais," 222.

98 "Women-men" was the term used to ridicule mannish fashions of the modern woman in the 1920s as well as women cross-dressers, of which there were various reports in the first decades of the century. Several of these women, according to journalistic accounts, disguised as men to escape the constrictions of their gender. See Sueann Caulfield, "Getting into Trouble: Dishonest Women, Modern Girls, and Women-Men in the Conceptual Language of *Vida policial, 1925–1927*," *Signs* 19, 1 (fall 1993): 146–76; Rago, *Os prazeres da noite*, 15–16.

99 Eurico Cruz, "Sentença do juiz da 2a vara criminal, de 8 de setembro de 1926," in Vicente Piragibe, *Dicionário de jurisprudência penal do Brasil* (Rio de Janeiro: Freitas Bastos, 1938), 1: 234–35. The sentence is cited by lawyers and judges in several criminal records consulted as well as in the major juridical works on sexual crime. See, for example, Peixoto, *Sexologia forense*, 132; Hungria, "Crimes sexuais," 221; Medeiros and Moreira, *Do crime da sedução*, 52–53.

100 Oscar Freire, "Organs genitais femininos—sua insensibilidade; influência nos atos sexuais," in *Exames e pareceres médico-legais* (São Paulo: Saraiva, 1926), 43.

101 J. P. Porto-Carrero, "Sexo e cultura," *Arquivos brasileiros de higiene mental* 3, 5 (May 1930): 157.

102 Other judges also cited unconventional sexual positions for the "first coitus" as evidence that women were "already corrupted." See Piragibe, *Dicionário*, 236; A. Nogueira, "Jurisprudência," 221.

103 Cruz, "Sentença," 234.

104 Ibid.

105 F. Castro, *Os delitos*, 105.

106 "Alegações finais pelo reu," statement by defense lawyers Francisco de Lasses Manheiros and Mário de Andrade Neves Meyrelles (AN, vara 7, caixa 10869 no. 59 [1932]).

107 Cruz, "Sentença," 235.

Chapter 4 *Single Mothers, Modern Daughters, and the Changing Politics of Freedom and Virginity*

1 See Appendix A. According to Judge Atugasmin Medici Filho, deflowering remained "one of the most common crimes" after it was renamed "seduction" in 1940 even though the absolute numbers seem to have dropped. Medici characterized seduction as a crime committed by "normal people," unlike most crimes, which he argued were committed by the mentally disturbed

(Médici Filho, "O crime de sedução no novo código penal," *Revista dos tribunais,* 134 [1941]: 399–416, esp. 412, 416.

2 These observations are based on a comparison of eighty-eight cases analyzed by Esteves from 1900 to 1911 with 450 cases from 1918 to 1941 that I read, all found in the Arquivo Nacional (hereafter AN) criminal records collections. See Martha de Abreu Esteves, *Meninas perdidas: Os populares e o cotidiano do amor no Rio de Janeiro da belle époque* (Rio de Janeiro: Paz e Terra, 1989). For an early comparison of our data, based on a subset of the cases I consulted, see Sueann Caulfield and Martha de Abreu Esteves, "Fifty Years of Virginity in Rio de Janeiro: Sexual Politics and Gender Roles in Juridical and Popular Discourse, 1890–1940," *Luso-Brazilian Review* 30, 1 (summer 1993): 47–74.

3 See ch. 5, table 2.

4 Arquivo Nacional, Rio de Janeiro (hereafter AN, vara 7, caixa 10842 no. 269 (1930). Although at least one attorney argued in 1916 that "the concept of impoverishment" was routinely abused in the Federal District, where police indiscriminately provided "verification of poverty" to all complainants in deflowering cases, there was no discernible support over the following decades for his campaign to end this practice. Almachio Diniz, "Conceito legal da miserabilidade," *Revista de direito* 39 (1916): 481–87.

5 Ch. 5, table 3.

6 See chap. 5, tables 1, 4, 5. The tables exclude cases for which no color was recorded for victim or defendant. The proportions of men and women in each job category do not change significantly if all 450 cases are compared. Defendants' literacy (including all 450 cases) was 78 percent, slightly lower than the 1940 census data (81 percent) but still 12 percentage points higher than the 1920 census data (66 percent). The defendant's rates overall are proportionally higher than the victim's literacy, which was closer to the (lower) 1920 literacy rate for women. In the tables in chap. 5, defendants' color and literacy rates are slightly skewed toward the post-1930 cases, since more of the earlier cases were excluded because of missing color data for defendants. We shall see that color classification in these records was not based on fixed phenotypical criteria and did not always coincide with self-identification. In the present chapter, color classifications and occupations of victims and accused are provided, when these data are available, as a very rough indication of their social backgrounds.

7 See, for example, AN, vara 1, caixa 1776 no. 419 (1918); AN, vara 4, caixa 10813 no. 62 (1919); AN, vara 1, caixa 1926 no. 493 (1923); AN, vara 8, caixa 2702 no. 484 (1925); AN, vara 1, caixa 1775 no. 2265 (1927); AN, vara 7, caixa 10869 no. 59 (1932); AN, vara 1, caixa 1733 no. 1117 (1935); AN, vara 1, caixa 1731 no. 1057 (1935); AN, vara 7, caixa 2734 no. 1183 (1935); AN, vara 8, caixa 2734 no. 1183 (1935); AN, vara 8, caixa 2997 no. 1230 (1935); AN, vara 1, caixa 1770 no. 1214 (1936); AN, vara 7, caixa 10849 no. 1459 (1936); AN, vara 8, caixa 2734 no. 1270 (1936); AN, vara 8, caixa 2775 no. 1233 (1936); AN, vara 1, caixa 1837 no. 1534 (1937); AN, vara 1, caixa 1779 no. 1723 (1937); AN, vara 7, caixa 2780 no. 1647 (1937); AN, vara 8, caixa 2775 no. 1608 (1937); AN, vara 8, caixa 2778

248

no. 1630 (1937); AN, vara 1, caixa 1771 no. 1956 (1938); AN, vara 1, caixa 1771
no. 2104 (1939); AN, vara 1, caixa 1813 no. 2410 (1940); AN, vara 8, caixa 2795
no. 237 (1940).

8 AN, vara 1, caixa 1837 no. 1459 (1936).

9 AN, vara 7, caixa 10842 no. 104 (1931).

10 AN, vara 7, caixa 10869 no. 77 (1931); AN, vara 7, caixa 10869 no. 59 (1932);
AN, vara 1, caixa 1779 no. 1723 (1937).

11 AN, vara 7, caixa 10869 no. 77 (1931).

12 AN, vara 1, caixa 1772 no. 1429 (1936). For similar comments by defense
lawyers about the victim's mother, see AN, vara 7, caixa 10869 no. 77 (1931);
AN, vara 1, caixa 1731 no. 1057 (1935); AN, vara 1 caixa 1837 no. 1459 (1936).

13 AN, vara 1, caixa 1926 no. 493 (1923).

14 Ibid.

15 AN, vara 1, caixa 1770 no. 1214 (1936).

16 AN, vara 1, caixa 1813 no. 8 (1927); AN, vara 1, caixa 1837, no. 1575 (1937).

17 AN, vara 7, caixa 10869 no. 77 (1931).

18 See for example AN, vara 5, caixa 1728 no. 165 (1919); AN, vara 1, caixa 1807
no. 83 (1929); AN, vara 1, caixa 1772 no. 240 (1930); AN, vara 5, caixa 1776
no. 262 (1930); AN, vara 8, caixa 2770 no. 1276 (1936); AN, vara 8, caixa 2730
no. 2174 (1939).

19 Lila Abu-Lughod has demonstrated a somewhat similar association of male
honor with autonomy and female modesty (hasham) with deference to the
men who protected her in Bedouin society. See Abu-Lughod, *Veiled Sentiments: Honor and Poetry in a Bedouin Society* (Berkeley and Los Angeles:
University of California Press, 1986).

20 See, for example, AN, vara 1, caixa 1776 no. 419 (1918); AN, vara 5, caixa 1728
no. 165 (1919); AN, vara 1, caixa 312 no. 7029 (1920); AN, vara 5, caixa 10817
no. 340 (1921); AN, vara 1, caixa 1926 no. 493 (1923); AN, vara 1, caixa 1926
no. 537 (1923); AN, vara 1, caixa 1813 no. 8 (1927); AN, vara 5, caixa 1776
no. 262 (1930); AN, vara 7, caixa 10869 no. 77 (1931); AN, vara 1, caixa 1770
no. 1182 (1935); AN, vara 5, caixa 1731 no. 1057 (1935); AN, vara 8, caixa 2770
no. 1726 (1936); AN, vara 1, caixa 1837 no. 1575 (1937); AN, vara 1, caixa 1779
no. 1723 (1937); AN, vara 1, caixa 1771 no. 2053 (1938); AN, vara 8, caixa 2815
no. 1838 (1938).

21 AN, vara 1, caixa 1813 no. 2082 (1939).

22 AN, vara 1, caixa 1769 no. 1976 (1927).

23 AN, vara 1, caixa 1776 no. 205 (1929).

24 AN, vara 1, caixa 1776 no. 406 (1933).

25 It is highly likely that legal-medical and other professional men, like the
mostly working-class subjects they studied, placed a high premium on the
virginity of women of their own class, even if they ridiculed working-class
hymenolatry. Retired Institute of Legal Medicine official Carlos Henrique de
Andrade Gomide and two former colleagues, all of whom were at the institute
a little more than a decade after Peixoto published *Sexologia forense* (1934),

chuckled at the absurdity of their predominantly working-class patients' concern with virginity, but admitted that they, too, had demanded virginity of their own brides (interview with the author, February 20, 1992).

26 AN, vara 1, caixa 1813 no. 1077 (1935).

27 AN, vara 1, caixa 1771 no. 2146 (1939).

28 AN, vara 1, caixa 1813 no. 1553 (1937).

29 AN, vara 1, caixa 1772 no. 1080 (1935).

30 AN, vara 1, caixa 1772 no. 240 (1930).

31 AN, vara 1, caixa 1738 no. 2240 (1927).

32 AN, vara 7, caixa 10817 no. 265 (1921). Other cases of men who cited this kind of "material" evidence as proof of the woman's prior defloration include AN, vara 7, caixa 10811 no. 50 (1919); AN, vara 7, caixa 10811 no. 234 (1920); AN, vara 7, caixa 10817 no. 265 (1921); AN, vara 7, caixa 10806 no. 113 (1924); AN, vara 1, caixa 1772 no. 1252 (1925); AN, vara 1, caixa 1738 no. 2240 (1927); AN, vara 1, caixa 1773 no. 159 (1930); AN, vara 1, caixa 1772 no. 240 (1930); AN, vara 1, caixa 1735 no. 259 (1932); AN, vara 1, caixa 1813 no. 2082 (1939); AN, vara 1, caixa 1841 no. 150 (1922); AN, vara 8, caixa 2667 no. 161 (1923); AN, vara 1, caixa 1838 no. 1593 (1923); AN, vara 8, caixa 2822 no. 1617 (1937).

33 AN, vara 8, caixa 2730 no. 2174 (1939).

34 AN, vara 1, caixa 1771 no. 1956 (1938). Other cases in which the defendant claimed he had sex with his fiancée after her confession and broke the engagement because of the confession include AN, vara 7, caixa 10806 no. 48 (1919); AN, vara 7, caixa 10613 no. 145 (1922); AN, vara 7, caixa 10811 no. 201 (1923); AN, vara 5, caixa 1744 no. 815 (1924); AN, vara 1, caixa 1837 no. 1459 (1936); AN, vara 1, caixa 1771 no. 2189 (1939); AN, vara 1, caixa 1771 no. 2219 (1939); AN, vara 1, caixa 1772 no. 1429 (1936); AN, vara 1, caixa 1813 no. 2410 (1940).

35 Art. 355, 363 in Clóvis Bevilaqua, *Código Civil dos Estados Unidos do Brasil comentado por Clóvis Bevilaqua* (Rio de Janeiro: Livraria Francisco Alves, 1952), 2: 323, 334–35.

36 AN, vara 1, caixa 1775 no. 2265 (1927).

37 Testimony of Antônio Pimenta, ibid.

38 See introduction, n. 5.

39 AN, vara 1, caixa 1775 no. 2265 (1927).

40 AN, vara 4, caixa 10811 no. 67 (1918).

41 AN, vara 7, caixa 10806 no. 48 (1919).

42 AN, vara 1, caixa 1837 no. 1534 (1937).

43 AN, vara 1, caixa 1772 no. 1961 (1938). For similar statements relating the victim's honor to her work habits, see AN, vara 8, caixa 2837 no. 32 (1927); AN, vara 1, caixa 1735 no. 671 (1934); AN, vara 1, caixa 1813 no. 1553 (1937); AN, vara 1, caixa 1772 no. 1961 (1938).

44 AN, vara 5, caixa 1731 no. 1057 (1935).

45 AN, vara 7, caixa 10806 no. 113 (1924).

46 AN, vara 1, caixa 1807 no. 301 (1928).

47 Thirty-five of the victims' mothers stated that they were "living maritally"

with men who were not their legal husbands. Many of those who declared themselves to be married, single, or widowed were likely to have had informal unions as well.

48 According to a report by Attorney General Segadas Viana in 1940, the high number of "so-called illegal unions" was due to "the great difficulty and above all the high cost of the documents necessary for civil marriage." Cited in Edgard de Moura Bittencourt, *O concubinato no direito*, 2d ed. (Rio de Janeiro: Biblioteca Jurídica, 1969), 1: 39.

49 AN, vara 8, caixa 2815 no. 2155 (1939).

50 In response to the lawyer's questioning, the witness stated "*que a sua profissão é de tratador de papéis, não só nas delegacias como no foro em geral*" (AN, vara 1, caixa 1813 no. 1998 [1938]).

51 Ibid.

52 José Filadelpho de Barros e Azevedo, *Relatório apresentado ao Sr. Ministro da Justiça e Negócios Interiores pelo Procurador Geral do Distrito Federal relativo aos trabalhos judiciários do ano de 1935* (Rio de Janeiro: Imprensa Nacional, 1936), 8.

53 AN, vara 1, caixa 1772 no. 1961 (1938).

54 See, for example, AN, vara 7, caixa 10817 no. 347 (1921); AN, vara 1, caixa 1926 no. 537 (1923).

55 See AN, vara 1, caixa 1737 no. 2333 (1927); AN, vara 5, caixa 1731 no. 542 (1933); AN, vara 1, caixa 1772 no. 1155 (1935).

56 AN, vara 1, caixa 1776 no. 406 (1933).

57 AN, vara 7, caixa 10806 no. 113 (1924).

58 AN, vara 8, caixa 2734 no. 1183 (1935).

59 AN, vara 8, caixa 2738 no. 1212 (1936).

60 AN, vara 7, caixa 10811 no. 50 (1919).

61 AN, vara 7, caixa 10842 no. 40 (1930).

62 Margaret Eleanor Greene, "The Importance of Being Married: Marriage Choice and Its Consequences in Brazil" (Ph.D. diss., University of Pennsylvania, 1991).

63 See AN, vara 7, caixa 10817 no. 347 (1921); AN, vara 1, caixa 1807 no. 1439 (1925); AN, vara 1, caixa 1807 no. 1436 (1927); AN, vara 1, caixa 1737 no. 93 (1928); AN, vara 8, caixa 2708 no. 372 (1933); AN, vara 1, caixa 1776 no. 406 (1933); AN, vara 1, caixa 1731 no. 542 (1933); AN, vara 1, caixa 1772 no. 1155 (1935); AN, vara 1, caixa 1733 no. 2079 (1939).

64 AN, vara 1, caixa 1807 no. 1439 (1925).

65 AN, vara 1, caixa 1733 no. 2079 (1939).

66 See E. Bittencourt, *O concubinato no direito*. According to more recent analyses of census data from the 1940s to the present, women in consensual unions were more likely to consider themselves married than men. See Greene, "The Importance of Being Married."

67 AN, vara 7, caixa 1084, no. 293 (1931). See also E. Bittencourt, *O concubinato no direito*.

68 AN, vara 1, caixa 1926 no. 537 (1923).

69 Paulino José Soares de Souza Neto, "Repressão à fraude nas anulações de casamento," in *Anais do Primeiro Congresso Nacional do Ministério Público* (Rio de Janeiro: Imprensa Nacional, 1942), 9: 123–32, esp. 126.

70 Asunción Lavrin, "Introduction: The Scenario, the Actors and the Issues," in *Sexuality and Marriage in Colonial Latin America,* ed. Lavrin (Lincoln: University of Nebraska Press, 1989), 1–43, esp. 5–6; Elizabeth Anne Kuznesof, "Sexual Politics, Race and Bastard-Bearing in Nineteenth-Century Brazil: A Question of Culture or Power?" *Journal of Family History* 16, 3 (1991): 243; Maria Beatriz Nizza da Silva, *Sistema de casamento no Brasil colonial* (São Paulo: T. A. Queiroz, 1984), iii.

71 See esp. Sheila de Castro Faria, *A colônia em movimento: Fortuna e família no cotidiano colonial* (Rio de Janeiro: Nova Fronteira, 1998), 52–58. Faria points out that local studies of eighteenth-century rural areas in the Center-South show that a vigorous regional economy was accompanied by high legitimacy rates, even among slaves. Her conclusions draw from her own work in notarial archives as well as studies by Renato Pinto Venâncio of parish records in Rio de Janeiro and São Paulo, "Nos limites da sagrada família: Illegitimidade e casamento no Brasil colonial," in *História e sexualidade no Brasil,* ed. Ronaldo Vainfas (Rio de Janeiro: Graal, 1986), 107–24; and Maria Luiza Marcílio's work in Minas Gerais, *Caiçara: Terra e população* (São Paulo: CEDHAL, 1986). In contrast, Kátia de Queiróz Mattoso found that 52 percent of couples lived in consensual unions in the city of Salvador, Bahia, according to an 1855 census. As Kuznesof notes, this was probably an undercount, since many couples would have reported marriages when their unions were informal. See Mattoso, *Família e sociedade na Bahia do século XIX* (São Paulo: Corrupio, 1988), 82; Kuznesof also finds rising illegitimacy in nineteenth-century São Paulo (Kuznesof, "Sexual Politics," 246, and *Household Economy and Urban Development: São Paulo, 1765–1836* (Boulder: Westview Press, 1986, 153–71).

72 According to census data, proportions of married people in Rio de Janeiro rose from 23 to 42 percent of the population older than fifteen between 1872 and 1920 and to 46 percent in 1940 (*Recenseamento do Brasil realizado em 1 de setembro de 1920: População do Rio de Janeiro,* pt. 1 [*Distrito Federal*] [Rio de Janeiro: Directoria Geral de Estatística], 2: 414–15; *Recenseamento geral do Brasil [1 de setembro de 1940],* pt. 16, *Distrito Federal* [Rio de Janeiro: Instituto Brasileiro de Geografia e Estatística, 1951], 1, 6–7). Most of the rise had occurred between 1872 and 1906, when 40 percent of the population older than fifteen was married. As Sandra Lauderdale Graham suggests, the change from religious to civil marriage in 1890 probably explains a good deal of this increase, especially since religious officials had charged for their services. See also Lauderdale Graham's calculations of marriage rates for domestic servants and for the general population in the 1872, 1890, and 1906 censuses in *House and Street: The Domestic World of Servants and Masters in Nineteenth-*

Century Rio de Janeiro (New York: Cambridge University Press, 1989), 74, 191–92. Despite this rise in marriage rates, state and public health officials expressed concern that marriage rates remained very low and single motherhood high. See Décio Parreiras, *Atividades de hygiene pública no Rio de Janeiro, 1939–1940* (Rio de Janeiro: Imprensa Nacional, 1941), 28–29; *Estudo sobre a fecundidade da mulher no Brasil, segundo o estado conjugal* (Rio de Janeiro: Instituto Brasileiro de Geografia e Estatística, 1949), 33; Germano Gonçalves Jardim, "Os recenseamentos e a estatística do estado conjugal," *Revista brasileira de estastística* 15, 57 (January–March 1954): 166; Giorgio Mortara, "As mães solteiras no Brasil," *Revista brasileira de estatística* 85 (January–June 1961): 1–32, and the introduction to the 1920 census, *Recenseamento . . . 1920*, 2: lxxx. According to a 1960 government publication, marriage rates in Rio de Janeiro decreased in the decade of the 1950s and remained much lower than in other major Brazilian cities. See Instituto Brasileiro de Geografia e Estatística, *Flagrantes brasileiros* 16 (March 1960).

73 Mortara, "As mães solteiras," 2; Ovídio de Andrade Júnior, "Classificação da população brasileira segundo o estado conjugal," *Revista brasileira de estatística* 14, 57 (January–March, 1954), 176.

74 Mortara, "As mães solteiras," 3; Andrade Júnior, "Classificação da população," 172; Jardim, "Os recenseamentos," 166–67.

75 *Estudo sobre a fecundidade*, 25.

76 AN, vara 1, caixa 1737 no. 93 (1928). Deflowering examinations were among the most frequently performed examinations at the institute throughout the period of the 1890 penal code. Statistics of the examinations performed at the Medical-Legal Institute between 1913 and 1918 were published in the *Anuário estatístico da polícia da capital federal* and averaged 363 per year; for 1926 to 1930, they were published in the chief of police reports included in the annual *Relatório do Ministro de Justiça e Negócios Exteriores* (Rio de Janeiro: Imprensa Nacional) and averaged 522 per year. For 1937 to 1941, they were published in Manoel Odorico de Morais, "Estado atual da prostituição no Rio de Janeiro," *A folha médica* 23, 13 (July 1942): 149, and averaged 663. In all of the Institute of Legal Medicine statistics, deflowering exams were outnumbered only by corpus delicti exams.

77 According to Carlos Henrique de Andrade Gomide, an examiner at the Institute of Legal Medicine from the 1940s to 1982, the institute provided private deflowering examinations in addition to those ordered by police from early in the century up through the 1960s. The quantity of deflowering exams, both private and public, far outnumbered exams for rape or other sexual crimes up until the mid-1970s, when the proportions began to reverse. Dr. Gomide attributes this to the declining valorization of virginity as well as to feminist activism of the 1970s that encouraged women to prosecute rapists. Interview with the author, February 20, 1992. The institute's archive has been relocated to the state archive in Niterói, and was not available for consultation

for this study. The annual reports of the institute do not provide information on the "private" examinations.

78 AN, vara 1, caixa 1831 no. 2159 (1939).

79 AN, vara 1, caixa 1775 no. 1974 (1927).

80 AN, vara 8, caixa 1807 no. 430 (1923); AN, vara 8, caixa 2658 no. 433 (1924); AN vara 1, caixa 1775 no. 1264 (1925); AN, vara 8, caixa 2660 no. 574 (1925); AN, vara 8, caixa 2664 no. 656 (1925); AN, vara 8, caixa 2664 no. 924 (1926); AN, vara 1, caixa 1743 no. 342 (1927); AN, vara 1, caixa 1743 no. 249 (1927); AN, vara 8, caixa 2673 no. 567 (1928); AN, vara 8, caixa 2703 no. 261 (1930); AN, vara 8, caixa 2703 no. 254 (1930); AN, vara 8, caixa 2718 no. 115 (1931); AN, vara 8, caixa 2714 no. 452 (1933); AN, vara 8, caixa 1735 no. 734 (1934); AN, vara 8, caixa 2774 no. 1541 (1937); AN, vara 8, caixa 2774 no. 1541 (1938); AN, vara 1, caixa 1771 no. 2189 (1939).

81 AN, vara 1, caixa 1926 no. 698 (1923); AN, vara 7, caixa 10806 no. 455 (1924); AN, vara 1, caixa 1807 no. 2021 (1927); AN, vara 1, caixa 1737 no. 2154 (1927); AN, vara 1, caixa 1807 no. 2346 (1927).

82 For discussion of debates in the early years of the Republic over the classification of sexual crime as "public" or "private," see Esteves, *Meninas perdidas*, 83–114.

83 AN, vara 1, caixa 1807 no. 2021 (1927).

84 AN, vara 1, caixa 1926 no. 537 (1923).

85 See ch. 1, 36–38.

86 AN, vara 1, 1779 no. 1723 (1937).

87 See Esteves, *Meninas perdidas*, 171–74.

88 AN, vara 1, caixa 1813 no. 1115 (1935); AN, vara 7, caixa 10806 no. 164 (1922); AN, vara 1, caixa 1737 no. 2161 (1927).

89 AN, vara 7, caixa 10842 no. 104 (1931).

90 AN, vara 7, caixa 10869 no. 59 (1932). The case, initiated in 1932, was tried in 1934.

91 In the remaining seventy-two cases, the hymen was found to be "intact" (33); there was no examination (20); or results were uncertain (19).

92 AN, vara 1, caixa 1926 no. 1409 (1925); AN, vara 1, caixa 312 no. 7049 (1940).

93 AN, vara 1, caixa 1770 no. 1570 (1926); AN, vara 1, caixa 1807 no. 1936 (1927); AN, vara 1, caixa 1767 no. 1969 (1927).

94 AN, vara 1, caixa 1807 no. 324 (1926).

95 AN, vara 8, caixa 2734 no. 1183 (1935).

96 Cited in Caulfield and Esteves, "Fifty Years of Virginity," 56.

97 AN, vara 1, caixa 1813 no. 2082 (1939).

98 AN, vara 1 caixa 1807 no. 1936 (1927).

99 AN, vara 8, caixa 2770 no. 1276 (1936); AN, vara 1, caixa 1926 no. 326 (1922).

100 AN, vara 1, caixa 1813 no. 2350 (1927). See also AN, vara 7, caixa 10806 no. 164 (1922); AN, vara 1, caixa 1743 no. 249 (1927).

101 See AN, vara 7, caixa 10869 nos. 59 and 136 (1932).

102 See Vicente Piragibe, *Dicionário de jurisprudência penal do Brasil* (Rio de Janeiro: Freitas Bastos, 1938), 1: 226–230.

103 See AN, vara 1, caixa 1843 no. 380 (1933); AN, vara 1, caixa 1813 no. 746 (1939); AN, vara 1, caixa 1813 no. 1113 (1929).

104 See, for example, AN, vara 1, caixa 1807 no. 746 (1923); AN, vara 1, caixa 1843 no. 380 (1933); AN, vara 1, caixa 1813 no. 1113 (1929).

105 AN, vara 1, caixa 1813 no. 2410 (1940).

106 The woman was quoted in the published decision of the Supreme Court in 1924. See Apelação Crime no. 7.087, Acórdão in *Revista do Supremo Tribunal* (Rio de Janeiro) 76 (1924): 49–54.

107 AN, vara 1, caixa 1772 no. 1155 (1935).

108 AN, vara 8, caixa 2770 no. 1936 (1936). For similar statements about young girls seeing movies, see vara 1, caixa 1926 no. 1409 (1925); vara 1, caixa 1743 no. 249 (1927); AN, vara 7, caixa 10869 no. 59 (1932).

109 Martha de Abreu Esteves's evidence included deflowering victims' descriptions of nudity, caresses, and repeated sexual contacts. See Esteves, *Meninas perdidas*, 171–79.

110 AN, vara 1, caixa 312 no. 7019 (1940); AN, vara 1, caixa 1733 no. 28 (1932).

111 The eight cases are: AN, vara 7, caixa 10613 no. 168 (1922); AN, vara 7, caixa 10806 no. 124 (1924); AN, vara 1, caixa 1767 no. 2143 (1927); AN, vara 8, caixa 2708 no. 11a (1932); AN, vara 1, caixa 1770 no. 1182 (1935); AN, vara 1, caixa 1837 no. 1454 (1936); AN, vara 1, caixa 1813 no. 2410 (1940); and AN, vara 1, caixa 312 no. 7063 (1940).

112 See ch. 3; Caulfield and Esteves, "Fifty Years of Virginity," 49–53.

113 AN, vara 1, caixa 1737 no. 2276 (1927).

114 This strategy was commonly employed among diverse social classes all over Latin America during the colonial period. The church was often involved on the side of children in litigation to determine the legitimacy of parental opposition to marriage on the grounds of "inequality" of bride and groom. See, for example, Verena Martinez-Alier, *Marriage, Class, and Colour in Nineteenth-Century Cuba*, 2d ed. (Ann Arbor: University of Michigan Press, 1989); Patricia Seed, *To Love, Honor, and Obey in Colonial Mexico: Conflicts over Marriage Choice, 1574–1821* (Stanford: Stanford University Press, 1988); Ramón Gutiérrez, *When Jesus Came, the Corn Mothers Went Away: Marriage, Sexuality, and Power in New Mexico, 1500–1846* (Stanford: Stanford University Press, 1991); Susan Socolow, "Acceptable Partners: Marriage Choice in Colonial Argentina, 1778–1810," in *Sexuality and Marriage in Colonial Latin America*, ed. Asunción Lavrin (Nebraska: University of Nebraska Press, 1989), 209–51. For the Portuguese crown's reaction against this strategy, see Muriel Nazarri, *Disappearance of the Dowry: Women, Families, and Social Change in São Paulo, Brazil, 1600–1900* (Stanford: Stanford University Press, 1991), 130–38. Republican legislation in Brazil eliminated the possibility of this kind of litigation by removing marriages from church juris-

diction, eliminating parents' power to intervene in marriages of children over twenty-one, and making parental opposition incontestable for minor children. See chap. 1 nn. 63, 64. It seems that in any case parents were no longer inclined to formally oppose children's marriage choices through the courts. Although legislators retained the criminalization of abduction as a means of discouraging elopement, according to available criminal statistics, this crime was very rarely reported.

115 AN, vara I, caixa 1837 no. 1459 (1936).

116 The tenement was a *cortiço*, a type of lower-class housing unit that characterized the squalid living conditions of turn-of-the-century downtown Rio de Janeiro. Marquês Filho used the term *cabeça de porco* to describe the family's home, making reference to a downtown tenement condemned as unsanitary and immoral and demolished in a violent spectacle in 1906. See Sidney Chalhoub, "A guerra contra os cortiços: cidade de Rio, 1850–1906," *Primeira versão* (Campinas, São Paulo: IFCH/UNICAMP, 1990). For a discussion of the reputation of military recruits in Brazil, see Peter Beattie, "Transforming Enlisted Army Service in Brazil" (Ph.D. diss., University of Miami, 1994).

117 AN, vara I, caixa 1837 no. 1459 (1936). I have translated the term *cabeça do casal* as "head of the family," since "head of the couple" sounds awkward in English, however, the Portuguese term evokes the subordination of the woman to the man more explicitly.

118 Ibid.

119 Forty-six percent of the complaints were filed by mothers, 27 percent by fathers, 12 percent by the offended girls themselves (who were sometimes provided a guardian for the purpose of legal representation), 11 percent by relatives or fictive kin, 2 percent by employers, and 2 percent by others.

120 *Estudo sobre a fecundidade,* 66.

121 See n. 74.

122 Scattered studies of cases of verbal insult cases in Latin America suggest that women are more apt to take complaints to the authorities, while men are expected to defend their honor personally, often through violence. See the papers presented at the Conference on Honor, Status, and Law in Modern Latin America, University of Michigan, Ann Arbor, December 4–6, 1998, by Lara Putnam, "Sex and Standing in the Streets of Port Limón, Costa Rica, 1890–1935"; Laura Gotkowitz, "El castigo de la mala lengua: Verbal Violence, Honor, and Citizenship in Early Twentieth-Century Bolivia"; and Brodwyn Fischer, "Slandering Citizens: Insults, Class, and Social Legitimacy in Rio de Janeiro's Criminal Courts," cited with authors' permission. Unlike some Caribbean and Andean nations, there were very few insult cases filed in early-twentieth-century Rio de Janeiro (fewer than fifty per year in the 1930s), and since the archival holdings for these kinds of cases are incomplete and uncatalogued, it is very difficult to uncover them; quantitative comparisons must therefore be done cautiously. Based on a sample of fifteen cases

from 1928 to 1933 and criminal statistics available for later decades, Brodwyn Fischer found that as in Costa Rica and Bolivia, complainants and the accused are more likely to be female than in other types of crimes.

123 The trials are held by the Arquivo Judiciário in Rio de Janeiro, where they are filed chronologically by tribunal, packet (maço), and record number.

124 Arquivo Judiciário, 1st jury tribunal, maço 245 no. 3068 (appeals court no. 2601); A Notícia, January 12, 1921.

125 AN, Tribunal de Justiça, Corte de Apelação Civil, caixa 598 no. 6390.

126 AN, vara 1, caixa 1771 no. 2140 (1939). The 16 cases are AN, vara 5, caixa 1940 no. 97 (1919); AN, vara 5, caixa 1849 no. 243 (1919); AN, vara 5, caixa 1728 no. 165 (1919); AN, vara 5, caixa 9144 no. 166 (1920); AN, vara 5, caixa 1730 no. 134 (1920); AN, vara 1, caixa 1946 no. 1252 (1921); AN, vara 8, caixa 2666 no. 158 (1922); AN, vara 8, caixa 2673 no. 519 (1928); AN, vara 8, caixa 2670 no. 21 (1928); AN, vara 8, caixa 2708 no. 478 (1933); AN, vara 8, caixa 2997 no. 985 (1935); AN, vara 8, caixa 2730 no. 1431 (1936); AN, vara 8, caixa 2733 no. 16216 (1937); AN, vara 8, caixa 2772 no. 1463 (1937); AN, vara 1, caixa 7139 no. 2972 (1940); AN, vara 8, caixa 2975 no. 195 (1941). In another 10 cases, it was unclear whether the mother's husband was the girl's father; of these, 7 mothers filed the complaints: AN, vara 1, caixa 1841 no. 1194 (1925); AN, vara 8, caixa 2666 no. 854 (1925); AN, vara 8, caixa 2666 no. 829 (1926); AN, vara 8, caixa 2666 no. 25 (1926); AN, vara 1, caixa 1737 no. 2333 (1927); AN, vara 1, caixa 1772 no. 240 (1930); AN, vara 1, caixa 1795 no. 893 (1934).

127 AN, vara 7, caixa 10806 no. 455 (1924); AN, vara 1, caixa 1926 no. 1409 (1925); AN, vara 8, caixa 2664 no. 656 (1925); AN, vara 1, caixa 1737 no. 2145 (1927); AN, vara 1, caixa 1737 no. 2276 (1927); AN, vara 8, caixa 2679 no. 73-A (1932); AN, vara 1, caixa 1735 no. 715 (1934); AN, vara 8, caixa 2822 no. 1122 (1935); AN, vara 1, caixa 1837 no. 1459 (1936); AN, vara 8, caixa 2774 no. 1460 (1937); AN, vara 1, caixa 1772 no. 1921 (1938).

128 Art. 380, Bevilaqua, Código civil, 2: 358–359.

129 AN, vara 1, caixa 1807 no. 83 (1929).

130 AN, vara 1, caixa 1831 no. 2159 (1939).

131 AN, vara 1, caixa 1737 no. 2216 (1927).

132 AN, vara 1, caixa 1770 no. 1214 (1936).

133 AN, vara 1, caixa 1733 no. 1117 (1935).

134 Ibid.

135 Ibid.

136 "Jurisprudência: Defloramento—Conceito de Sedução (Acórdão da 1a Câmara da Corte de Apelação do Distrito Federal e Comentário de C. A. Lúcio Bitencourt)," Revista de direito penal 12 (1936): 103–14, esp. 103.

137 Francisco Viveiros de Castro, Os delitos contra a honra da mulher, 2d ed. (Rio de Janeiro: Freitas Bastos, 1932), 78.

138 Ibid., 79.

139 These jurists were Virgílio de Sá Pereira, Evaristo de Morais, Mário Bulhões Pedreira, C. A. Lúcio Bitencourt, and Alcântara Machado.

140 The two proposals were named for their major collaborators: Sá Pereira (1933) and Alcântara Machado (1938). See Virgílio de Sá Pereira, Evaristo de Morais, and Mário Bulhões Pedreira, *Projeto do código criminal* (Rio de Janeiro: Imprensa Nacional, 1933), 66; Tiago Ribeiro Pontes, *Código penal brasileiro comentado* (Rio de Janeiro: Freitas Bastos, 1977), 341.

141 Pontes, *Código penal*, 341.

142 Ibid.

143 Anderson Perdigão Nogueira, "Doutrina: Defloramento," in *Revista de direito* 123 (1937): 52.

144 Quoted in Pontes, *Código penal*, 341. The statements were in response to a paper presented at the first Brazilian Conference on Criminology by Lúcio Bittencourt, who supported the concept of seduction as requiring a prior formal, public, and notorious engagement, as was "crystalized in the Sá Pereira proposal."

145 "Our code, by distinguishing seduction, deceit, and fraud, made it clear that it did not interpret these terms in the usage expounded by Carrara, unless it fell into the vice of redundancy, which we cannot accept as good hermeneutics," *Direito penal brasileiro*, special pt., 446. Quoted in Francisco Pereira de Bulhões Carvalho, "Conceito de estupro e de sedução," *Revista de direito penal* 4 (1934): 230–31.

146 Siqueira, *Direito penal brasileiro*, 447–8.

147 See Siqueira, *Direito penal brasileiro*, 447–48, cited in Caulfield and Esteves, "Fifty Years of Virginity," 51. Crisólito de Gusmão was the leader of an opposing tendency, which, following Viveiros de Castro's teachings, maintained the "promise of marriage" as essential for the configuration of the crime. See Crisólito de Gusmão, *Dos crimes sexuais*, 5th ed. (Rio de Janeiro: Freitas Bastos, 1981), 278–82.

148 Several Federal District Court of Criminal Appeals decisions that employ this definition, generally verbatim, are cited in F. Carvalho, "Conceito de estupro," 228–232; and in the Federal District Court of Criminal Appeals decision of January 27, 1936, cited in n. 136, p. 105.

149 Nelson Hungria, "Crimes sexuais," *Revista forense* 70 (April 1937): 219.

150 Cited in Pontes, *Código penal*, 327.

151 Nelson Hungria, "Em torno de um parecer," *Revista de crítica judiciária* 21, 2–3 (1935): 81–84, esp. 82.

152 Ibid., 83.

153 Maria Valéria Junho Pena points out that labor legislation of the 1930s and 1940s also aimed at protecting maternity and was less concerned with women themselves. See Pena, *Mulheres e trabalhadoras: Presença feminina na constituição do sistema fabril* (Rio de Janeiro: Paz e Terra, 1981), 150–69.

154 Piragibe, *Dicionário*, 1: 229.

155 Nelson Hungria, "Em torno do ante-projeto," *Revista forense* 77 (1940): 423, cited in Médici Filho, "O crime de sedução," 412.

156 Jurists continued to debate the difference between moral and physiological

virginity; confusion over the complacent hymen was no longer a problem, for jurists were well versed in the legal-medical literature on this. For ongoing debates, see, for example, Médici Filho, "O crime de sedução," 400; A. de Almeida Júnior, "Crimes contra os costumes—contribuição da medicina legal," *Revista forense* 94 (1943): 236.

157 Nelson Hungria and Romão Côrtes de Lacerda, *Comentários ao código penal* (Rio de Janeiro: Revista Forense, 1947), 8: 80.

158 Nelson Hungria, *Revista forense* 86 (1935): 51, quoted in Médici Filho, "O crime de sedução," 405.

159 Hélio Gomes, *Medicina legal* (Rio de Janeiro: Forense, 1945), 468.

160 See, for example, Almeida Júnior, "Crimes contra os costumes," 236.

161 See, for example, Hélio Gomes, "O problema da prostituição sob o ponto de vista sanitário e jurídico," *Anais da Primeira Conferência Nacional de Defesa Contra a Sífilis* (Rio de Janeiro: Imprensa Nacional, 1941), 427; Morais, "Estado atual da prostituição," 148.

162 Hungria, "Crimes sexuais," 220.

163 Quoted in Hungria and Lacerda, *Comentários,* 8: 321.

164 Nogueira, "Doutrina: Defloramento," 67.

Chapter 5 Honorable Partnerships: The Importance of Color in Sex and Marriage

1 Francisco José Viveiros de Castro, *Atentados ao pudor,* 3d ed. (Rio de Janeiro: Freitas Bastos 1934) xiii, cited in Martha de Abreu Esteves, *Meninas perdidas: Os populares e o cotidiano do amor no Rio de Janeiro da belle époque* (Rio de Janeiro: Paz e Terra, 1989), 25.

2 "A vinda do Rei Alberto," *O paiz,* June 14, 1920, which proclaimed that Brazil had overcome the racism "that the United States preserves and perpetuates, demonstrating the moral inferiority of its people."

3 "Invencionices perversas," *O paiz,* July 20, 1920; "A viagem do rei da Bélgica ao Brasil," *O jornal,* May 15, 1920.

4 "Invencionices perversas."

5 Marvin Harris, *Patterns of Race in the Americas* (New York: Walker, 1964), 68–69, cited in Barbara Fields, "Ideology and Race in American History," in *Region, Race and Reconstruction: Essays in Honor of C. Vann Woodward,* ed. J. Morgan Kousser and James M. McPherson (Oxford: Oxford University Press, 1982), 150.

6 Fields, "Ideology and Race," 150.

7 Ibid., 155.

8 "A vinda do Rei Alberto."

9 See the syntheses of the revisionist literature of the 1950s and 1960s in Abdias do Nascimento, *Brazil: Mixture or Massacre? Essays in the Genocide of a Black People,* 2d ed. (Dover, Mass.: Majority Press, 1989); Carl Degler, *Neither Black nor White: Slavery and Race Relations in Brazil and the*

United States (Madison: University of Wisconsin Press, 1986); Emília Viotti da Costa, "The Myth of Racial Democracy," in *The Brazilian Empire: Myths and Histories* (Chicago: University of Chicago Press, 1985), 234–35, 276 n. 3. Costa lists the most important of the revisionists; she herself should be added to the list. For a sample of the most influential works, see Florestan Fernandes and Roger Bastide, *Relações raciais entre brancos e negros em São Paulo* (São Paulo, Companhia Editora Nacional, 1955); Fernandes, *A integração do negro na sociedade de classes* (São Paulo: Dominus, Universidade de São Paulo, 1965); Fernando Henrique Cardoso and Octóvio Ianni, *Cor e mobilidade social em Florianópolis: Aspectos das relações entre negros e brancos numa comunidade do Brasil meridional* (São Paulo: Companhia Editora Nacional, 1960); Luis A. Costa Pinto, *O negro no Rio de Janeiro: relações de raça numa sociedade em mudança* (São Paulo: Companhia Editora Nacional, 1953); Octávio Ianni, *Raças e classes sociais no Brasil* (Rio de Janeiro: Civilização Brasileira, 1966); Guerreiro Ramos, *Introdução crítica à sociologia brasileira* (Rio de Janeiro, Editorial Andes, 1957); and Thales de Azevedo, *Cultura e situação racial no Brasil* (Rio de Janeiro: Civilização Brasileira, 1966).

10   Raymundo Nina Rodrigues has been classified by many as a mulatto. His racism, and particularly his belief that miscegenation caused degeneracy, has therefore been seen as self-hatred. Thomas Skidmore argues that Rodrigues excluded himself from the "degenerate" mixed category by claiming that superior individuals of mixed race existed, even though the majority were inferior or degenerate. See Skidmore, *Black into White: Race and Nationality in Brazilian Thought* (New York: Oxford University Press, 1974), 57–59. Evidence that Rodrigues's color was problematic—if not for him, then for his followers—can be found in a book written for a U.S. audience by Artur Ramos in 1939. Ramos made a point of stating that Rodrigues was white in a bibliographical essay that does not mention the color of any of the other authors except Martiniano de Bomfim, whom Ramos described as "an aged Negro professor with great influence among the blacks of Bahia." See Ramos, *The Negro in Brazil* (Philadelphia: Porcupine Press, 1983), 178. On the broad shifts in early-twentieth-century racial thought, see Skidmore, *Black into White*; E. Costa, "The Myth of Racial Democracy"; Nancy Stepan, *"The Hour of Eugenics": Race, Gender and Nation in Latin America* (Ithaca: Cornell University Press, 1991).

11   As Skidmore notes, this idea was first expressed by nineteenth-century abolitionists; it influenced the state-subsidized European policies of the early Republic. The decline of this immigration after World War I contributed to the shifts in racial thinking. Skidmore, *Black into White*, 21–27.

12   Renato Ferraz Kehl, *Aparas eugénicas: Sexo e civilização* (Rio de Janeiro: Francisco Alves, 1933), esp. 18, 44; *Porque eu sou eugenista: Vinte anos de campanha eugênica, 1917–1937* (Rio de Janeiro: Francisco Alves, n.d.), 24–65; *Lições de eugenia*, 2d ed. (Rio de Janeiro: F. Alves, 1935). For a discussion of

Kehl and the eugenics movement in Brazil and Latin America, see Stepan, *"The Hour of Eugenics."* Stepan shows that Lamarkian theory stressing inheritance of acquired characteristics was favored by Latin American eugenicists, for this theory allowed for eugenic "improvement" through the intervention of social hygiene and other environmental factors. Kehl's work mixed medical/environmental solutions such as combating syphilis with recommendations for controlling reproduction of "inferior" types.

13 Viana's direct influence on state policy and legislation reached its height after 1930, just as his racial analyses came under attack by cultural analysts such as Gilberto Freyre and Artur Ramos. As Jeffrey Needell points out, Viana's conclusions regarding race were central to all of his work in the areas of political organization and law. See Needell, "History, Race, and State in Oliveira Viana," *Hispanic American Historical Review* 75, 1 (1995): 1–30, 12. Viana's most important works on race and society are Francisco de Oliveira Viana, *Populações meridionais: Pequenos estudos de psicologia social* (São Paulo: Monteiro Lobato, 1921); *Evolução do povo brasileiro*, 3d ed. (São Paulo, Editora Nacional, 1938 [1st ed. 1923]); and *Raça e assimilação* (São Paulo: Editora Nacional, 1932). Specifically political analyses include *O ocaso do Império*, 2d ed. (1926; São Paulo: Melhoramentos, 1933) and *Problemas de política objectiva* (São Paulo: Editora Nacional, 1930). For an analysis of the intellectual genesis and impact of Viana's thought see Needell, "History." See also José Murilo de Carvalho, "A utopia de Oliveira Viana," and Angela de Castro Gomes, "A práxis corporativa de Oliveira Viana," in *O pensamento de Oliveira Viana*, ed. Elide Rugai Bastos and João Quartim de Moraes (Campinas: Editora da Unicamp, 1993), 13–42, 43–62. Like Needell, I diverge from Carvalho and Gomes on the issue of Viana's racism, which these authors believe is possible to separate from his political thought. Significantly, the Bastos and Moraes volume does not include a study of Viana's racial thought.

14 These themes run through all of Viana's major works. See, for example, *Populações meridionais*, chap. 9, 12, 14–16; *Evolução do povo*, 45–53; *Problemas da política*, 29–30, 39–40, and chap. 5.

15 Viana, *Problemas de política*, 178; *Evolução do povo*, 160.

16 Viana, *Problemas de política*, 179; *Evolução do povo*, 160. Following Torres, Viana argued that Brazil's population could be "improved" through "culture and education," but the level of improvement depended on the "quantity [and] quality of the racial elements that compose it" (Viana, *Problemas de política*, 242–44; *Raça e assimilação*, 49; for Torres's original argument, see Alberto Torres, *O problema nacional brasileiro* [Rio de Janeiro: Editora Nacional, 1914]). Viana consolidated his commitment to biological racism after reviewing European and U.S. studies on race in the early 1930s. He rejected the "absolute" racism of German writers as well as theories of racial equality, embracing instead U.S. studies of racial "propensities." See *Raça e assimilação*, esp. pt. 1.

17 The census introduction is included in Viana, *Evolução do povo*. In his intro-

duction to the third (1938) edition, Viana claimed that "aryanization" persisted and had even accelerated since 1923. The 1940 census provided evidence for this claim, showing that the proportion of white individuals rose from 38 to 65 percent from 1872 to 1940. The census bureau itself, however, warned that the numbers did not reflect an objective reality, but rather widespread racial prejudices and different criteria used for recording color in the different censuses. The bureau concluded that the white population had, in fact, expanded, but to a lesser degree than the census numbers suggested. See *Estudos sobre a composição da população do Brasil segundo a cor* (Rio de Janeiro: Instituto Brasileiro de Geografia e Estatística, 1950), 7–51.

18 See Viana's response to criticism of his racism in *Raça e assimilação*, 274–85. For analysis of this debate see Needell, "History," 13–14, 13 n. 37.

19 Manoel Bonfim, *O Brasil na América: Caracterização da formação brasileira*, 2d ed. (1929; Rio de Janeiro: Topbooks, 1997), 170–74, 196. Bonfim's argument is based on Darwinian evolutionism: cross-racial sex expanded human variation, creating greater potential for natural selection and more vigorous progeny. Similarly, the merging of different cultural traditions was essential to social progress. For Bonfim's earlier repudiation of racism, see Manoel Bonfim, *A América Latina: Males de origem* (Rio de Janeiro: Garnier, 1905); Flora Sussekind and Roberto Ventura, "Uma teoria biológica da mais-valia? Análise da obra de Manoel Bonfim," in *História e dependência: Cultura e sociedade em Manoel Bonfim* (São Paulo: Moderna, 1984), 1–35.

20 Bonfim, *O Brasil na América*, 194, 206.

21 Already in the 1900s and 1910s, jurists such as Pedro Lessa and Viana's mentor, the nationalist authoritarian thinker Alberto Torres, had adamantly rejected simple biological theories of racial inferiority in favor of arguments stressing the need for better education or political organization. Turn-of-the-century jurists such as Viveiros de Castro, João Vieira de Araújo, and Oscar de Macedo Soares also rejected extremist biological racism, although they were generally less sure about the relative weight of racial, cultural, and social causes of criminality. See chap. 1, 32–33, 45–46; Marcos César Alvarez, "Bacharéis, criminologistas e juristas: Saber jurídico e nova escola penal no Brasil (1889–1930)" (Ph.D. diss., Universidade de São Paulo, 1996, esp. 145–49); Needell, "History," 10–13. Although I agree with Needell that scientific racist ideas such as those of Viana were not obsolete in the 1930s, I do not agree that these ideas were dominant. Instead, I see the coexistence of racist attitudes and policies with social and cultural explanations of inferiority as characteristic of Brazilian racial thought well before the 1920s.

22 Gilberto Freyre, *Casa grande e senzala*, 14th ed. (Recife: Imprensa Oficial, 1966).

23 See Freyre, *Casa grande*, 12–18, on the capacity of Portuguese civilizers to adapt to tropical climates and cultures, which Freyre argues is superior to the capacity of northern Europeans; for Indian contributions, see esp. chap. 2; for African contributions and miscegenation, see esp. chaps. 4–5. The influence

of anthropologist Franz Boas on *Casa grande* is discussed in Jeffrey Needell, "Identity, Race, Gender, and Modernity in the Origins of Gilberto Freyre's Oeuvre," *American Historical Review* 100, 1 (February 1995): 51–75, esp. 67. Freyre refutes the biological racism of Viana, whom he calls "the biggest mystic of aryanism to emerge among us" in *Casa grande*, 328–29, 346; the passage on page 346 is reprinted in *Tempo morto e outros tempos* (Rio de Janeiro, 1944), 358–59, cited in Needell, "Identity," 70 n. 67. For Viana's response to Freyre's criticism, see Needell, "History," 13 n. 37. As Needell notes, Viana avoided criticizing Freyre publicly. Viana did criticize the spread of Franz Boas' "culturalism" in Brazil in the late 1930s, however, arguing that it set back the scientific studies of race upon which public policy should be based (Oliveira Vianna, "Raça e cultura (fragmentos de um ensaio)," in Viana, *Ensaios inéditos* (Campinas: Editora da UNICAMP, 1991), 65–68.

24 Bonfim, in *O Brasil na América*, 194, had also blamed slavery, along with parasitic Portuguese domination, for moral degeneracy. Freyre explains that this "moral dissolution" originated in fifteenth-century Portugal as a result of slavery and other characteristics of imperialism such as social mobility, economic instability, and contacts with polygamous societies. In Brazil, the tropical climate, prior contacts with North African polygamy, and slavery resulted in precocious sexuality, polygamous concubinage, and other "sexual irregularities"; slavery resulted in masters' indolence as well (Freyre, *Casa grande*, 275–78, 465–66. For his discussion of the effects of syphilis and sado-masochism of sexual and social relations between masters and slaves, see esp. *Casa grande*, 50–56, 340–46. See Dain Borges, 'Puffy, Ugly, Slothful and Inert': Degeneration in Brazilian Social Thought, 1880–1940," *Journal of Latin American Studies* 25 (1993): 253, for discussion of Freyre's portrayal of the sexual degeneracy of white slave owners.

25 Freyre, *Casa grande*, esp. 55–56. Needell, in "Identity," 69–71, argues that these conclusions about the relationship between sexual domination, race relations, and nationality were influenced by Freyre's personal childhood and sexual experiences.

26 In *Sobrados e mucambos* (São Paulo: Companhia Editora Nacional, 1936), a sequel to *Casa grande*, Freyre blames Jewish commercial values for the rise of "modernizing" urban professionals who since the nineteenth century were distorting Brazil's organic patriarchal social relations, replacing them with alien liberal institutions and class conflict. See Needell's analysis in "Identity," 73–77. Freyre elaborated his conclusions regarding Brazil's "racial democracy" and whitening more explicitly a decade later, in a series of lectures given in the United States and published as *Brazil: An Interpretation* (New York: Knopf, 1945); see Costa's summary in "The Myth of Racial Democracy," 284. Needell, in "Identity," 58 n. 24, 59, 63–68, analyzes the importance of Freyre's experience in the United States, where he was particularly horrified by a lynching (Freyre, *Tempo morto*, 32–33, cited in Needell, "Identity," 58 n. 24).

27 Viana, *Evolução do povo*, 13. See Needell, "History," 2, for a synopsis of Viana's political and intellectual career. For discussion of political rhetoric of the Vargas regime and its principal ideologues see Alcir Lenharo, *Sacralização da política* (Campinas: Papirus, 1986).

28 See Needell, "Identity," 62–63, for Freyre's response to the Republic's overthrow in 1930.

29 See Jeffrey Lesser, *Welcoming the Undesirables: Brazil and the Jewish Question* (Berkeley and Los Angeles: University of California Press, 1995); Lenharo, *Sacralização da política*, esp. chaps. 3 and 4; Stepan, *"The Hour of Eugenics,"* 164–67.

30 "A igualdade," *Cultura política* 1, 1 (March 1941). These images were also promoted through the Department of Press and Publicity (Departamento de Imprensa e Propaganda; DIP), which censored the news and cultural media and produced films, radio programs, and various types of publications.

31 This document explains, however, that the apparent tremendous proportional expansion of the white population since 1872 was greatly exaggerated because people tended to classify themselves in a lighter category than "objective criteria" would warrant, partly because of the influence of "the contagion of racist prejudice" of Nazi Europe (*Estudos sobre a composicao da populacao*, 8, 28).

32 Lenharo, *Sacralização da política*, esp. 120, 129–31; Lesser, *Welcoming the Undesirables*; Maria Luiza Tucci Carneiro, *O anti-semitismo na era Vargas* (São Paulo: Brasiliense, 1988). For more on immigration debates centering on the need to integrate the nation and improve the race in the 1930s, see Flávio Venâncio Luizetto, *Os constituintes em face da imigração* (master's diss., Universidade de São Paulo, 1975); N. Jahr Garcia, *Estado Novo: Ideologia e propaganda política* (São Paulo: Loyola, 1982); L. Oliveira Lippi, *Estado Novo: Ideologia e poder* (Rio de Janeiro: Aahar, 1982); Abdias do Nascimento, *Brazil: Mixture or Massacre? Essays in the Genocide of a Black People*, 2d ed. (Dover, Mass.: Majority Press, 1989); Skidmore, *Black into White*, 193–200.

33 See George Reid Andrews, *Blacks and Whites in São Paulo, Brazil: 1888–1988* (Madison: University of Wisconsin Press, 1991), 146–56, esp. 147.

34 Among the most influential U.S. scholars writing of Brazil's relative racial democracy were Frank Tannenbaum, *Slave and Citizen: The Negro in the Americas* (New York: Knopf, 1946); Donald Pierson, *Negroes in Brazil* (Chicago: University of Chicago Press, 1942); and Stanley Elkins, *Slavery: A Problem in American Institutional and Intellectual Life* (Chicago: University of Chicago Press, 1959).

35 See n. 9.

36 Roger Bastide, "Dusky Venus, Black Apollo," *Race* 3 (November 1961): 11, cited in Degler, *Neither Black nor White*, 190.

37 See for example Bastide, "Dusky Venus," and Pinto, *O negro no Rio de Janeiro*.

38 See discussion in Viotti, "The Myth of Racial Democracy," 236.

39 Hebe Maria Mattos Castro, *Das cores do silêncio: Os significados da liberdade no sudeste escravista—Brasil, século XIX* (Rio de Janeiro: Arquivo Na-

cional, 1995); Peter Fry, "O que a Cinderela negra tem a dizer sobre a 'política racial' no Brasil," *Revista USP* 28 (December–February 1995–1996): 122–35; Robin E. Sheriff, "Negro é um apelido que os brancos deram aos pretos: Discursos sobre cor, raça e racismo num morro carioca" (IFSS/UFRJ, 1995; mimeo). I thank Robin Sheriff for generously providing me a copy of this paper and for permission to quote it.

40 Sheriff, "Negro é um apelido," 23.

41 Ibid., 24.

42 Fry, "O que a Cinderela negra tem a dizer," 135.

43 Castro, *Das cores do silêncio*, 404.

44 Emília Viotti da Costa, "O mito da democracia racial," in *Da monarquia a república* (São Paulo: Livraria Humana Ltda., 1977), 230. Costa is less categorical in her revised English edition of this work. See "The Myth of Racial Democracy," 235.

45 Castro believes this demonstrates that color was no longer considered a fundamental marker of identity in the late nineteenth century. H. Castro, *Das cores do silêncio*.

46 For discussion of racial "types" in police identification techniques, see Olívia Gomes, "1933: Um ano em que fizemos contatos," *Revista USP/Dossiê Povo Negro—300 Anos* (December–February 1995–96): 142–63.

47 *Parda* is the feminine form of the word recorded on documents, *pardo* the masculine.

48 See, for example, the following cases: Arquivo Nacional, Rio de Janeiro (hereafter AN), vara 1, caixa 1776 no. 1348 (1926); AN, vara 5, caixa 1746 no. 41 (1926); AN, vara 1, caixa 1838 no. 230 (1930); AN, vara 1, caixa 1795 no. 239 (1931); AN, vara 7, caixa 10869 no. 93 (1932); AN, vara 8, caixa 2679 no. 327 (1933); AN, vara 8, caixa 2775 no. 233 (1936); AN, vara 1, caixa 1771 no. 2140 (1939); AN, vara 1, caixa 1771 no. 2053 (1939); AN, vara 1, caixa 312 no. 7019 (1940).

49 See for example AN, vara 7, caixa 10613 no. 145 (1922); AN, vara 4, caixa 2659 no. 159 (1923); AN, vara 5, caixa 1746 no. 61 (1926); AN, vara 1, caixa 1737 no. 2216 (1927); AN, vara 7, caixa 10842 no. 40 (1930); AN, vara 1, caixa 1831 no. 2159 (1932); AN, vara 1, caixa 1770 no. 625 (1934); AN, vara 1, caixa 1731 no. 1057 (1935); AN, vara 1, caixa 1813 no. 1279 (1936); AN, vara 1, caixa 1837 no. 1534 (1937); AN, vara 1, caixa 1840 no. 1905 (1938); AN, vara 4, caixa 2975 no. 112 (1941); AN, vara 1, caixa 1837 no. 1534 (1937); AN, vara 8, caixa 2795 no. 237 (1940).

50 AN, vara 1, caixa 1767 no. 1969 (1927).

51 AN, vara 1, caixa 1731 no. 542 (1933).

52 *Estudos sobre a composição da população*, 8–9. The 1920 census did not collect data on color and there was no census in 1930. Since the 1970s, proponents of Afro-Brazilian consciousness have complained that blacks have been systematically undercounted in national censuses. See Nascimento, *Brazil:*

Mixture or Massacre?; O. Nogueira, introduction to *Tanto preto quanto branco*. As George Reid Andrews comments, however, census figures have shown that from 1940 to 1980, "Brazil has experienced a process of not whitening, but 'browning,' in which movement from 'black' to 'parda' is common, but movement into the 'white' category is not. See Andrews, *Blacks and Whites in São Paulo*, 252–53.

53 See chap. 1, 73–74.

54 According to 1940 census, 4 percent of white women, 14 percent of pardas, and 32 percent of black women worked as domestic servants in Rio de Janeiro. See "Os empregados domésticos, em geral e segundo a cor, no Distrito Federal" and "Atividades e posições na ocupação, nos diversos grupos de cor da população do Distrito Federal," in *Pesquisa sobre os diversos grupos de cor nas populações do Estado de São Paulo e do Distrito Federal* (Rio de Janeiro: IBGE, 1951), 101, 110–18. The higher proportions of domestic servants among the deflowering victims reflects the absence of middle-class women in the cases. Most of the remaining cases of women classified as "domestic" in the deflowering data did not work outside their homes. Mothers of the victims are almost always classified as "domestic," and it is impossible to determine whether they work for wages in most cases. The fathers who appear in the records have occupations similar to those of the defendants, except that there are only two in the higher-level occupations (businessmen or professionals). Literacy rates of mothers are slightly lower than that of their daughters; those of the fathers are slightly higher.

55 See "Atividades e posições," 86–109, for analysis of the distribution of employment by race in the 1940 census of the Federal District. Black Brazilians were rarely hired for positions that required contact with the public. Employment advertisements, for example, often specified that the candidate be "of good appearance," a euphemism for "white." This mechanism, as well as more explicit means of shutting out candidates of color such as employers' instructions to employment agencies that they would accept only white applications was observed in many of the post-1950s studies of racial discrimination. See Degler's discussion based on these studies in *Neither Black nor White*, 130–42. Oracy Nogueira discusses this issue specifically in "Atitude desfavorável de alguns anunciantes de São Paulo em relação aos empregados de cor," in *Tanto preto quanto branco*, 95–122. See also Andrews, *Blacks and Whites in São Paulo*, 160–71. Pinto, *O negro no Rio de Janeiro*, 71–111.

56 Nelson do Valle Silva, "The High Cost of Not Being White in Brazil," in *Race, Class, and Power in Brazil*, ed. Pierre-Michel Fontaine (Los Angeles: Center for Afro-American Studies, University of California at Los Angeles, 1985), 42–55.

57 This is based on comparison of the proportion of complaints filed by mothers to those filed by fathers, excluding cases in which no parent appears. The proportions of complaints filed by mothers are 60, 66, and 65 percent for the white, *parda*, and black groups, respectively. Unfortunately, although the cen-

sus bureau collected data on both color and household composition, it did not publish data that would allow a comparison of the prevalence of female-headed households by color. Higher proportions of female-headed households among black or parda families are consistent with studies of black family structures in later decades. For a discussion of black family structures based on studies produced in the 1960s–1980s, see Degler, *Neither Black nor White*, 170–76. Two of the most influential of these studies are Fernandes, *A integração do negro*; and Azevedo, *Cultura e situação racial*, 121–23. See also Samuel C. Adamo, "The Broken Promise: Race, Health, and Justice in Rio de Janeiro, 1890–1940" (Ph.D. diss., University of New Mexico, 1983), 102–3.

58 Twenty-two percent of black, 19 percent of *parda*, and 14 percent of white victims were orphans. This is consistent with the higher mortality rates for the black population in the city. See Adamo, "The Broken Promise."

59 Examples can be found in the following cases: AN, vara 1, caixa 1926 no. 493 (1923); AN, vara 1, caixa 1733 no. 28 (1932); AN, vara 1, caixa 1843 no. 380 (1933); AN, vara 8, caixa 2708 no. 372 (1933); AN, vara 1, caixa 1813 no. 1115 (1935).

60 These studies do not specify precise dates, but note a decline in endogamy "in the recent past." See Elza Berquó, "Como se casam negros e brancos no Brasil?" in *Desigualdade racial no Brasil contemporâneo*, ed. A. Peggy Lovell (Belo Horizonte: CEDEPLAR-FACE/Universidade Federal de Minas Gerais," 1991), 120; Nelson do Valle Silva, "Estabilidade temporal e diferenças regionais no casamento inter-racial," *Estudos afro-asiáticos* 21 (December 1991): 49–60; Maria Celi Ramos da Cruz Scalon, "Cor e seletividade conjugal no Brasil," *Estudos afro-asiáticos* 23 (December 1992): 17–36.

61 Degler, *Neither Black nor White*, 191.

62 O. Nogueira, introduction to *Tanto preto quanto branco* 25–26. Studies of census data from the 1970s and 1980s find that women in all color categories tend to marry men of equal or slightly higher educational levels than themselves, and that this tendency remained constant over previous decades and included those in interracial marriages, whether the man was darker or lighter. See Berquó, "Como se casam negros e brancos"; Scalon, "Cor e seletividade conjugal."

63 Muriel Nazzari, "Concubinage in Colonial Brazil: The Inequalities of Race, Class, and Gender," *Journal of Family History* 21, 2 (April 1996): 107–24.

64 L. Pinto, *O negro no Rio de Janeiro*, 214–217.

65 Freyre, *Casa grande*, 341; Pinto, *O negro no Rio de Janeiro*, 214–17. Degler cites nineteenth-century traveler Hermann Burmeister as quoting the same aphorism in *Viagem ao Brazil* (São Paulo, n.d.), 247. The saying is frequently cited as a reflection of Brazilian racial and gender stereotypes in the sociological literature of both Freyre's and Fernandes's generations.

66 AN, vara 1, caixa 1767 no. 1969 (1927).

67 This is by necessity a loose translation. The original reads: "Ela, Elvira, ouvindo essas palavras do acusado, não protestando imediatamente pela ofensa grave e o conceito que o acusado fazia de sua raça, demonstrou ser despida de

qualquer resquício de sentimento e de amor próprio nato no indivíduo, cultivado ou não." Ibid.

68 Boris Fausto, *Crime e cotidiano: A criminalidade em São Paulo, 1880–1924* (São Paulo: Brasiliense, 1984).

69 Francisco José Viveiros de Castro, *Os delitos contra a honra da mulher,* 2d ed. (Rio de Janeiro: Freitas Bastos, 1932), 77.

70 Ibid., 195.

71 Ibid., 77.

72 AN, vara 8, caixa 2718 no. 84 (1931).

73 Judge Atugasmin Médici Filho mentioned an appeals decision in São Paulo in 1937 that ruled against an employer in a deflowering case, even though the employee knew he was married. It is not clear whether the case involved a domestic servant. The precedent was only possible with the new conception of seduction in its "vulgar sense"; Medici cited it as a novelty. See "O crime de sedução no novo código penal," *Revista dos tribunais* 134 (1941): 399–413.

74 In fourteen cases, the judges decided not to indict after the police investigation. One employer was convicted in a lower court and acquitted in the appeals court. The remaining four were acquitted by the lower courts.

75 AN, vara 1, caixa 1807 no. 746 (1923).

76 AN, vara 1, caixa 1813 no. 1553 (1937).

77 H. D. Barruel de Lagenest, *Lenocínio e prostituição no Brasil* (Rio de Janeiro: Agir, 1960), 23–24.

78 AN, vara 1, caixa 1813 no. 1998 (1938).

79 AN, vara 1, caixa 1776 no. 262 (1930).

80 AN, vara 1, caixa 1807 no. 746 (1923); AN, vara 7, caixa 10811 no. 67 (1918).

81 AN, vara 1, caixa 1837 no. 1249 (1920).

82 AN, vara 1, caixa 1735 no. 1290 (1936).

83 AN, vara 1, caixa 1727 no. 2663 (1940).

84 AN, vara 1, caixa 1772 no. 1155 (1935).

85 AN, Gabinete Civil da Presidência da República, Código de Fundo 35; Seção de Guarda SDE, lata 527, doc. 5.897, 1943. The names here, as in the citations of other deflowering cases, are fictitious. This letter contains typographical and grammatical errors that make it difficult to translate precisely. The phrase quoted here reads "Ainda fiz ver a ele a diferença de cor, e ele respondeu-me que nada tinha com o casa, désde que tinha simpatisado comigo." By "o casa," Pinto might have meant "o casamento" (the marriage) or "o caso" (the matter); so the phrase might translate as "he responded that it didn't have anything to do with the matter."

86 Ibid. The quotations here are taken from the testimony Pinto gave in the police investigation that was opened as a result of her letter. The investigation consists of testimony by Pinto and Luigi Procopio.

87 Ibid.

88 Bastide, "Dusky Venus," 11.

89 Fry, "O que a cinderela negra tem a dizer," 135.

90 Simple cross-tabulation comparison also shows no significant relationship be-
    tween victim's color and outcome of trials, nor between color of either accused
    men or victims and outcome (marriage or no marriage) for the investigations.

91 The results presented here are suggestive, not conclusive, because it is not
    possible to determine the exact representativeness of the sample (see Ap-
    pendix A for a description of the cases selected). Scattered statistics suggest
    that there were about 500–600 cases of sexual crime per year in Rio de Janeiro
    per year in the 1920s and 1930s, including police investigations that did not
    result in indictment and court trials, but it is not possible to determine the
    relative numbers of each. Criminal statistics published regularly after 1942,
    however, do provide these relative numbers. From 1942 to 1949, a yearly aver-
    age of 53 percent of the investigations of sexual resulted in indictments; 47
    percent were archived after the police investigation. This proportion is calcu-
    lated from the data for seduction, rape, and assault of a minor in *Crimes e
    contravenções (Distrito Federal) 1942/1946* (Rio de Janeiro: Instituto Brasi-
    leiro de Geografia e Estatística, 1950), 147; *Crimes e contravenções (Distrito
    Federal) 1947* (Rio de Janeiro: Instituto Brasileiro de Geografia e Estatística,
    1951), 36; *Crimes e contravenções (Distrito Federal) 1948* (Rio de Janeiro:
    Instituto Brasileiro de Geografia e Estatística, 1952), 36; and *Crimes e con-
    travenções (Distrito Federal) 1949* (Rio de Janeiro: Instituto Brasileiro de
    Geografia e Estatística, 1953), 36. Coincidentally, the data analyzed here for
    the two previous decades match these proportions exactly. Although equal
    numbers of trials and police investigations were collected (225 of each), color
    was recorded more frequently in the trials. The final numbers of cases ana-
    lyzed, excluding those with missing color for defendants, is 142 investigations
    and 161 trials (47 and 53 percent, respectively). It is unlikely that the propor-
    tions of investigations and trials for these kinds of cases changed dramatically
    from the 1920s to the 1940s. Thus, although the data analyzed might be
    skewed toward either investigations or trials, it is unlikely that the error
    is great.

92 Neither men's literacy nor women's occupation showed a significant relation-
    ship to outcome, probably because there was so little variation within these
    variables (literacy rates for men were very high overall; the range of women's
    occupations was very small).

93 These tables also reveal the substantive impact of particular variables on the
    results, regardless of statistical significance. Substantive significance is con-
    sidered by many to be equally or more important than statistical significance.
    For a discussion of the two in a standard text, see Christopher H. Achen,
    Interpreting and Using Regression (Beverly Hills: Sage Publications, 1982).

94 This is indicated by the numbers for the variables "dating" and "marry?" in
    Appendix D.

95 AN, vara 1, caixa 1772 no. 1155 (1935).

96 AN, vara 1, caixa 1727 no. 2663 (1940).

97 Eurico Cruz, "Sentença do juiz da 2a vara criminal, de 8 de set de 1926," in

Vicente Piragibe, *Dicionário de jurisprudência penal do Brasil* (Rio de Janeiro: Freitas Bastos, 1938), 1: 234–35.

98 Cruz, "Sentença," 235.

99 Besides the explicit mutual seduction and sexual suggestiveness of tango dancing, the tango's origin in brothels of poor, immigrant neighborhoods in Buenos Aires made it an ambiguous symbol of national culture for middle-class Argentines. For discussion of the acceptance of the tango by middle-class Argentines after it was "sanitized" in Paris and New York, see Donna Guy, *Sex and Danger in Buenos Aires: Prostitution, Family and Nation in Argentina* (Lincoln: University of Nebraska Press, 1991), chap. 5.

Epilogue

1 Arquivo Nacional, Gabinete Civil da Presidência da República, Código de Fundo 35; Seção de Guarda SDE, lata 527, doc. 5.897, 1943. The original text reads: "Embora de maior idade e não tendo paes aqui e sim em Minas e querendo evitar um desgosto a eles conforme já lhes falei, rogo-vos Snr. Presidente, como se fosse meu Juiz, meu pae e protector, depois de Deus e Jesus, vos por mim, pois no estado em que me acho esperando d'aqui ha uns mezes um bébé [*sic*] d'este homem, e sem ter um lugar paea [*sic*] ficar, não posso ir para a casa dos meus paes n'este estado e tambem não podendo ficar em casa dos meus parentes onde me acho, estes São pobres e não podem me sustentar durante o tempo que eu não possa trabalhar fora. Portanto apelo para a Vssa. Excia. com justiça no que eu tenho direito."

2 Ibid.

3 Paulo Augusto de Figueiredo, "O estado nacional e a valorização do homem brasileiro," in *Cultura política* 15 (May 1942): 26–31, cited in Angela de Castro Gomes, *A invenção do trabalhismo*, 2d ed. (Rio de Janeiro: Relume-Dumará, 1994). The following discussion of Estado Novo ideology follows Gomes's analysis in this classic book, esp. 195–248. A good, brief description of the evolution of radio programming from the first broadcast in 1922 to the Vargas period in Sônia Virgínia Moreira, *O rádio no Brasil* (Rio de Janeiro: Rio Fundo, 1991).

4 This was done under the states of siege declared in 1932 and again in 1935 on account of a civil war in São Paulo, intense worker mobilization by the opposition National Liberatory Alliance (*Aliança Nacional Libertadora*, ANL), supported by the Communist Party, and an aborted Communist revolt. Paulo Sérgio de M. S. Pinheiro, *Estratégias da ilusão: A revolução mundial e o Brasil, 1922–1935* (São Paulo: Companhia das Letras, 1991), 321–22, provides the best description of the repression that followed the revolt and the relationship between repression of political militants and common criminals. For a description of ANL mobilization among industrial workers in São Paulo, see John French, *The Brazilian Workers' ABC* (Chapel Hill: University of North Carolina Press, 1992), 62–67. On the erection of a "national security state" and

the creation of a special tribunal for political crimes after 1935, see Pinheiro, *Estratégias*, 324–325; French, *The Brazilian Workers'*, 64–72; Gomes, *A invenção*, 160–62.

5 Marcondes Filho was a lawyer with strong connections to the industrial elite in São Paulo. See Gomes, *A invenção*, 169–172. Barbara Weinstein argues that despite these connections, Marcondes Filho made an effort to "maintain some distance from his employer allies." See Weinstein, *For Social Peace in Brazil: Industrialists and the Remaking of the Working Class in São Paulo, 1920–1964* (Chapel Hill: University of North Carolina Press, 1996), 144.

6 Gomes, *A invenção*, 169–172, 195–216.

7 Ibid., 204–206.

8 Susan K. Besse has made this point regarding the Vargas regime in *Restructuring Patriarchy: The Modernization of Gender Inequality in Brazil, 1914–1940* (Chapel Hill: University of North Carolina Press, 1996), 202–3. For Italy, see Victoria de Grazia, *How Fascism Ruled Women: Italy 1922–1945* (Berkeley and Los Angeles: University of California Press, 1992).

9 In fact, Estado Novo cultural and immigration policies—the latter designed largely by Oliveira Viana—continued to be shaped by racist arguments about assimilative qualities of different ethnic types. See Lesser, *Welcoming the Undesirables: Brazil and the Jewish Question* (Berkeley and Los Angeles: University of California Press, 1995); Alcir Lenharo, *Sacralização da política* (Campinas: Papirus, 1986), 107–38.

10 Gomes, *A invenção*, 207, 218 n. 18.

11 Legislation passed in 1941 for the "organization and protection of the family" made funds available for newlyweds at low interest rates for the purchase of real estate, forgave 10 percent of the loan for each child the couple bore, and gave preference for government jobs to "married over single persons and, among married persons, those with the most children" (Decree-law n. 3,200 of April 19, 1941, *Código civil atualizado* 43d ed. (Rio de Janeiro: Aurora, n.d.), 372–87.

12 Art. 144 in the 1934 Constitution, in *As constituições dos estados e da República* (Rio de Janeiro: Imprensa Nacional, 1937), 696; Art. 124 in the 1937 Constitution, in *Constituições do Brasil* (São Paulo: Saraiva, 1967), 462.

13 See Besse, *Restructuring Patriarchy*, 174; Maria Valéria Junho Pena, "A revolução de 30, a família e o trabalho feminino," *Cadernos de pesquisa da Fundação Carlos Chagas* 37 (May 1981): 78–83; June Hahner, *Emancipating the Female Sex: The Struggle for Women's Rights in Brazil, 1850–1940* (Durham: Duke University Press, 1990), 176–79; Joel Wolfe, *Working Women, Working Men: São Paulo and the Rise of Brazil's Industrial Working Class, 1900–1955* (Chapel Hill: University of North Carolina Press, 1993), 72–73. Most of the legislation regulating labor was passed between 1932 and 1934 and "consolidated" in the 1943 labor code. For the restrictions on women's work, see *Consolidação das leis do trabalho* (Rio de Janeiro: Imprensa Nacional, 1943), 67–70.

14 Simon Schwartzman, "A Igreja e o Estado Novo: O estatuto da família," *Cadernos de pesquisa da Fundação Carlos Chagas* 37 (May 1981): 72.

15 Ibid., 72, 76. The decree and the clause modifying it are decree 3200 of April 19, 1941, and decree 3284 of May 19, 1941.

16 Centro de Pesquisa e Documentação da Fundação Getúlio Vargas, Rio de Janeiro, Arquivo Oswaldo Aranha, OA, 39.00.00/6, cited in ibid., 74.

17 *Consolidação das Leis do Trabalho*, 67–70.

18 Schwartzman, "A igreja e o Estado Novo," 73–76.

19 Arts. 24, 213–222, 235–240, Galdino Siqueira, *Código penal brasileiro* (Rio de Janeiro: Livraria Jacinto, 1941), 243, 315–17, 321–25.

20 Arts. 108, 170, ibid., 273, 277–78.

21 Arts. 75–101, ibid., 261–71.

22 In addition to Lyra and Hungria, the juridical commission included Judges Vieira Braga and Narcélio de Quieroz and worked under the direction of Justice Minister Francisco Campos.

23 Roberto Lira, *Novíssimas escolas penais* (Rio de Janeiro: Borsoi, 1956), 92, 109, 128.

24 See Olívia Gomes, "1933: um ano em que fizemos contatos." *Revista USP/ Dossiê Povo Negro—300 Anos* (December–February 1995–1996) 142–163; Peter Fry, "Direito positivo versus direito clássico: A psicologização do crime no pensamento de Heitor Carrilho," in *Cultura da psicanálise*, ed. Sérvulo Figueira (São Paulo: Brasiliense, 1985), 117–41.

25 For discussion of the evolution of this legal argument, see Mariza Corrêa, *Os crimes da paixão* (São Paulo: Brasiliense, 1981), 22–26.

26 Edgard de Moura Bitencourt, *Concubinato* (São Paulo: Livraria Editora Universitária de Direito, 1975), 422–23.

27 *Jornal do Brasil*, March 13, 1991, 6.

28 In 1919, the first law granting compensation to the families of workers killed on the job allowed for reduced compensation to "a person whose subsistence was provided by the victim" if the victim had no legal heirs. In 1931, decree 2.0465 changed the word "wife" to "woman" in social security legislation; this was increasingly interpreted by jurists to include concubines. See E. Bitencourt, *Concubinato*, 383. Social legislation of the 1930s and 1940s was increasingly straightforward about the rights of workers' companions and jurisprudence granted the "concubine" guarantees similar to those of wives. Francisco Pereira de Bulhões Carvalho, "Direito de indenização da concubina," *Revista dos tribunais* 216 (1953): 25–28.

29 Edgard de Moura Bitencourt, *O concubinato no direito*, 2d ed. (Rio de Janeiro: Biblioteca Jurídica, 1969), 305; E. Bitencourt, *Concubinato*, 39.

30 Through the 1930s, this was under debate. See Federal District Supreme Court Civil Appeal no. 1541 in *Revista de jurisprudência brasileira* 13 (1931): 55–79, which determined that concubinage must involve proven cohabitation. Deciding a paternity suit in 1942, however, the São Paulo Appeals Court held that "in the modern conception, cohabitation is not a necessary characteristic

of concubinage." See "Investigação de paternidade—Acórdão," *Revista dos tribunais* 141 (January 1943): 663. The latter decision reflected the jurisprudential trend after the 1940s. See E. Bittencourt, *Concubinato*, 68.

31 Ibid., 48–49, 54–57.

32 Ibid., 435. This question generated a great deal of disagreement in the jurisprudence; see cases Bittencourt cites on both sides.

Bibliography

Government Documents

Anuário estatístico da polícia da capital federal. Rio de Janeiro: Imprensa Nacional, 1927.

Anuário estatístico do Brasil. Rio de Janeiro: Instituto Brasileiro de Geografia e Estatística, 1940.

Código civil atualizado. 43d ed. Rio de Janeiro: Aurora, n.d.

Código civil brasileiro: Trabalhos relativos à sua elaboração. Vols. 1–3. Rio de Janeiro: Imprensa Nacional, 1917, 1918, 1919.

Consolidação das leis do trabalho. Rio de Janeiro: Imprensa Nacional, 1943.

Constituições do Brasil. São Paulo: Saraiva, 1967.

As constituições dos estados e da República. Rio de Janeiro: Imprensa Nacional, 1937.

Estudo sobre a fecundidade da mulher no Brasil, segundo o estado conjugal. Rio de Janeiro: Instituto Brasileiro de Geografia e Estatística, 1949.

Estudos sobre a composição da população do Brasil segundo a cor. Rio de Janeiro: Instituto Brasileiro de Geografia e Estatística, 1950.

Leis Penais. Rio de Janeiro: Imprensa Nacional, 1942.

Projeto do código civil brasileiro: Trabalhos da Comissão Especial da Câmara dos Deputados. Vols. 1–8. Rio de Janeiro: Imprensa Nacional, 1902.

Recenseamento Geral do Brasil realizado em 1 de setembro de 1920: População do Rio de Janeiro (Distrito Federal). Vol. 2. Rio de Janeiro: Imprensa Nacional, 1923.

Recenseamento geral do Brasil (1 de setembro de 1940). Pt. 16, Distrito Federal. Rio de Janeiro: Instituto Brasileiro de Geografia e Estatística, 1951.

Todas as constituições do Brasil. Ed. Adriano Campanhole and Hilton Lobo Campanhole. São Paulo: Editora Atlas, 1971.

Annual Reports by Police and Judicial Officials

Barros e Azevedo, José Filadelfo de. *Relatório apresentado ao Sr. Ministro da Justiça e Negócios Interiores pelo Procurador Geral do Distrito Federal relativo aos trabalhos judiciários do ano de 1935.* Rio de Janeiro: Imprensa Nacional, 1936.

Belisário F. da Silva Távora. *Relatório da polícia do Distrito Federal apresentado ao Dr. Rivadávia da Cunha Corrêa pelo Chefe de Polícia Dr. Belisário F. da Silva Távora.* Rio de Janeiro: Imprensa Nacional, 1911.

———. *Relatório da polícia do Distrito Federal apresentado pelo Chefe de Polícia Dr. Belisário F. da Silva Távora.* Rio de Janeiro: Imprensa Nacional, 1912.

———. *Relatório da polícia do Distrito Federal apresentado pelo Chefe de Polícia Dr. Belisário F. da Silva Távora.* Rio de Janeiro: Imprensa Nacional, 1914.

Carneiro da Fontoura, Manoel Lopes. "Polícia Civil." In *Relatório apresentado ao Presidente da República dos Estados Unidos do Brasil pelo Ministro da Justiça e Negócios Interiores, Dr. João Luiz Alves,* 172–192. Rio de Janeiro: Imprensa Nacional, 1923.

———. "Polícia Civil." In *Relatório apresentado ao Presidente da República dos Estados Unidos do Brasil pelo Ministro da Justiça e Negócios Interiores, Dr. João Luiz Alves,* 163–187. Rio de Janeiro: Imprensa Nacional, 1924.

Costa, Carlos da Silva. "Polícia Civil." In *Relatório apresentado ao Presidente da República dos Estados Unidos do Brasil pelo Ministro da Justiça e Negócios Interiores, Dr. Augusto Viana do Castelo,* 103–119. Rio de Janeiro: Imprensa Nacional, 1929.

Franca, Geminiano da. "Serviço policial." In *Relatório apresentado ao Presidente da República dos Estados Unidos do Brasil pelo Ministro da Justiça e Negócios Interiores, Dr. Alfredo Pinto Vieira de Melo,* 70–81. Rio de Janeiro: Imprensa Nacional, 1920.

Góes Filho, Coriolano de Araújo. *Relatório apresentado ao Ministro da Justiça e Negócios Interiores Dr. Augusto Viana do Castelo pelo Chefe de Polícia do Distrito Federal, Dr. Coriolano de Araújo Góes Filho.* Rio de Janeiro: Imprensa Nacional, 1928.

———. *Relatório apresentado ao Ministro da Justiça e Negócios Interiores Dr. Augusto Viana do Castelo pelo Chefe de Polícia do Distrito Federal, Dr. Coriolano de Araújo Góes Filho.* Rio de Janeiro: Imprensa Nacional, 1929.

———. *Relatório apresentado ao Ministro da Justiça e Negócios Interiores Dr. Augusto Viana do Castelo pelo Chefe de Polícia do Distrito Federal, Dr. Coriolano de Araújo Góes Filho.* Rio de Janeiro: Imprensa Nacional, 1930.

Melo, Alfredo Pinto Vieira de. *Relatório apresentado ao Presidente da República dos Estados Unidos do Brasil pelo Ministro da Justiça e Negócios Interiores, Dr. Alfredo Pinto Vieira de Melo.* Rio de Janeiro: Imprensa Nacional, 1921.

———. *Relatório da polícia do Distrito Federal apresentado ao Dr. Rivadávia da Cunha Corrêa pelo Chefe de Polícia, Dr. Alfredo Pinto Vieira de Mello.* Rio de Janeiro: Imprensa Nacional, 1908.

Parreiras, Décio. *Atividades de higiene pública no Rio de Janeiro, 1939–1940.* Rio de Janeiro: Imprensa Nacional, 1941.

Pereira, André de Faria. "Procuradoria Geral do Distrito Federal." In *Relatório apresentado ao Presidente da República dos Estados Unidos do Brasil pelo Minis-*

tro da Justiça e Negócios Interiores, Dr. João Luiz Alves, 20–61. Rio de Janeiro: Imprensa Nacional, 1925.

Legal and Medical Journals

Arquivos da Fundação Gaffrée-Guinle (Rio de Janeiro), 1927, 1929, 1930, 1932–1933, 1934–1935.
Arquivos de medicina legal do Instituto Médico Legal do Rio de Janeiro, 1928, 1929.
Arquivos do Departamento Federal de Segurança Pública (Rio de Janeiro), 1944–1948.
Brasil-Médico (Rio de Janeiro), 1930–1943.
A Folha Médica (Rio de Janeiro), 1920–1943.
Justitia (São Paulo), 1940–1945.
Revista de crítica judiciária (Rio de Janeiro), 1924–1945.
Revista de direito (Rio de Janeiro), 1916–1929.
Revista de direito penal (Rio de Janeiro), 1933–1945.
Revista de jurisprudência brasileira (Rio de Janeiro), 1928–1955.
Revista dos tribunais (São Paulo), 1920–1965.
Revista do Supremo Tribunal (Rio de Janeiro), 1920–1945.
Revista forense (Rio de Janeiro), 1920–1945.

Newspapers and Magazines

Correio da manhã, 1919–1922.
Cultura política
Gazeta de notícias, 1924–1925.
Gazeta policial, 1931.
O jornal, 1919–1921.
Jornal do comércio, 1919–1926.
A noite, 1917–1921.
A notícia, 1920–1930.
O paiz, 1917–1922.
Revista criminal, 1927–1930, 1934–1935.
Revista da semana, 1919–1921.
Revista de polícia, 1926–1929.
Revista feminina, 1918–1927.
Vida policial, 1925–1927.

Books, Articles, and Theses

Abreu, Martha. "O império do divino: Festas religiosas e cultura popular no Rio de Janeiro, século XIX." Ph.D. diss., Universidade Estadual de Campinas, 1996.

——. "Slave Mothers and Freed Children: Emancipation and Female Space in Debates on the 'Free Womb' Law, Rio de Janeiro, 1871." *Journal of Latin American Studies* 28 (1996): 567–580.

Abreu, Maurício de A. *Evolução urbana do Rio de Janeiro.* Rio de Janeiro: IPLANRIO/ZAHAR, 1988.

Abu-Lughod, Lila. *Veiled Sentiments: Honor and Poetry in a Bedouin Society.* Berkeley and Los Angeles: University of California Press, 1986.

——. "Writing against Culture." In *Recapturing Anthropology,* ed. Richard Fox, 137–62. Santa Fe: School of American Research Press, 1991.

——. *Writing Women's Worlds: Bedouin Stories.* Berkeley and Los Angeles: University of California Press, 1993.

Adamo, Samuel C. "The Broken Promise: Race, Health, and Justice in Rio de Janeiro, 1890–1940." Ph.D. diss., University of New Mexico, 1983.

Adorno, Sérgio. *Os aprendizes do poder.* Rio de Janeiro: Paz e Terra, 1988.

Aguiar, Anésio Frota. *Assuntos jurídico-policiais.* Rio de Janeiro: Arthur Lakschevitz, 1944.

——. *O lenocínio como problema social no Brasil.* Rio de Janeiro: Arthur Lakschevitz, 1940.

Aguiar, Asdrúbal Antônio de. *Ciência sexual: Contribuições para o seu estudo.* Lisbon, 1933.

——. *Ciência sexual—virgindade.* Lisbon: Alland e Bertrand, 1924.

Alberro, Solange. "La sexualidad manipulada en Nueva España: Modalidades de recuperación y de adaptación frente a los tribunales eclesiásticos." In *Familia y sexualidad en Nueva España,* 238–57. Fondo de Cultura Económica, Mexico City: 1982.

Albuquerque, José de. *Educação sexual pelo rádio.* Rio de Janeiro: Círculo Brasileiro de Educação Sexual, 1935.

Algranti, Leila Mezan. *Honradas e devotas: Mulheres da colônia.* Rio de Janeiro: José Olympio, 1993.

Almeida Júnior, A. de. "Crimes contra os costumes—contribuição da medicina legal." *Revista forense* 94 (1943): 235–341.

Almeida, Cândido Mendes de. *Código filipino ou Ordenações do Reino de Portugal.* 14th ed. Rio de Janeiro: Tipografia do Instituto Filomático, 1870.

Almeida, Teófilo de. "Sífilis e prostituição no Rio de Janeiro." *Arquivos da Fundação Gaffrée-Guinle* 2 (1929): 21–52.

Alvarez, Marcos César. "Bacharéis, criminologistas e juristas: Saber jurídico e nova escola penal no Brasil (1889–1930)." Ph.D. diss., Universidade de São Paulo, 1996.

Alves, Branca Moreira. *Ideologia e feminismo: A luta pelo voto no Brasil.* Petrópolis: Vozes, 1980.

Alves, João Luiz. *Código civil da República dos Estados Unidos do Brasil.* 2d ed. Rio de Janeiro: F. Briguiet, 1923.

Anais da Primeira Conferência Nacional de Defesa Contra a Sífilis. Rio de Janeiro: Imprensa Nacional, 1941.

Andrews, George Reid. *Blacks and Whites in São Paulo, Brazil, 1888–1988.* Madison: University of Wisconsin Press, 1991.

———. "Racial Inequality in Brazil and the United States: A Stastistical Comparison." *Journal of Social History* 26, 2 (winter 1992): 229–63.

Aragão, Antônio Moniz sodré de. *A três escolas penais: Clássica, antropológica e crítica.* 3d ed. São Paulo: Saraiva, 1928.

Araújo, João Vieira de. *O código penal interpretado.* 2d ed. Rio de Janeiro, 1902.

Azevedo, Aluísio de. *A Brazilian Tenement.* New York: McBride, 1926.

Azevedo, Fernando. *Brazilian Culture: An Introduction to the Study of Culture in Brazil.* Trans. William Rex Crawford. New York: Macmillan, 1950.

Azevedo, Thales de. *Cultura e situação racial no Brasil.* Rio de Janeiro: Civilização Brasileira, 1966.

Backheuser, Everardo. *Habitações populares: Relatório apresentado ao Exmo. Sr. Dr. J. J. Seabra, Ministro da Justiça e Negócios Interiores.* Rio de Janeiro: Imprensa Nacional, 1906.

Barbosa, Rui. *Réplica de Rui Barbosa: Às defesas da redação do projeto de código civil brasileiro na Câmara dos Deputados, 1904.* Rio de Janeiro: Fundação Casa de Rui Barbosa, 1980.

Barreto, Castro. *A criança é o melhor imigrante.* Rio de Janeiro: Gráfica Real Grandeza, 1938.

Barreto, L. Pereira. *As três filosofias.* Pt. 1, *Filosofia teológica.* Rio de Janeiro, 1874.

Barreto, Tobias. *Estudos alemães.* Rio de Janeiro: Laemert, 1892.

———. *Menores e loucos e fundamentos do direito de punir.* Rio de Janeiro: Pongetti, 1926.

Bastide, Roger, and Florestan Fernandes. *Brancos e negros em São Paulo.* São Paulo: Editora Nacional, 1959.

Bastos, Elide Rugai, and João Quartim de Moraes. *O pensamento de Oliveira Viana.* Campinas: Editora da UNICAMP, 1993.

Beattie, Peter. "The House, the Street, and the Barracks: Reform and Honorable Masculine Social Space in Brazil, 1864–1945." *Hispanic American Historical Review* 76, 3 (1996): 439–73.

———. "Transforming Enlisted Army Service in Brazil." Ph.D. diss., University of Miami, 1994.

Beccaria, Cesare. *On Crimes and Punishments.* Indianapolis: Hackett, 1986.

Behar, Ruth. "Sexual Witchcraft, Colonialism, and Women's Powers: Views from the Mexican Inquisition." In *Sexuality and Marriage in Colonial Latin America,* ed. Asunción Lavrin, 178–208. Lincoln: University of Nebraska Press, 1989.

Belo, José Maria. *A History of Modern Brazil, 1889–1964.* Trans. James L. Taylor. Stanford: Stanford University Press, 1966.

Beloch, Israel, and Alzira Alves de Abreu, ed. *Dicionário histórico-biográfico brasileiro.* Rio de Janeiro: Forense Universitária, 1984.

Benchimol, Jaime Larry. *Pereira Passos—Um Haussmann tropical: A renovação urbana da cidade do Rio de Janeiro no início do século XX.* Rio de Janeiro: Secretaria Municipal de Cultura, Turismo e Esportes, 1990.

278

Bentham, Jeremy. *The Rationale of Punishment*. London: R. Heward, 1830.

Berquó, Elza. "Como se casam negros e brancos no Brasil?" In *Desigualdade racial no Brasil contemporâneo*, ed. Peggy A. Lovell, 115–20. Belo Horizonte: CEDEPLAR-FACE, Universidade Federal de Minas Gerais, 1991.

Bessa, Karla Adriana Martins. "O crime de sedução e as relações de gênero." *Cadernos Pagu* 2 (1994).

Besse, Susan K. "Crimes of Passion: The Campaign against Wife Killing in Brazil, 1910–1940." *Journal of Social History* 22, 4 (summer 1989): 653–66.

———. "Freedom and Bondage: The Impact of Capitalism on Women in São Paulo, Brazil, 1917–1937." Ph.D. diss., Yale University, 1983.

———. *Restructuring Patriarchy: The Modernization of Gender Inequality in Brazil, 1914–1940*. Chapel Hill: University of North Carolina Press, 1996.

Bevilaqua, Clóvis. *Código civil dos Estados Unidos do Brasil comentado por Clovis Bevilaqua*. 9th ed. Vols. 1–6. Rio de Janeiro: Livraria Francisco Alves, 1951–1953.

———. *Direito da família*. 9th ed. Rio de Janeiro: Freitas Bastos, 1959.

———. *História da Faculdade de Direito do Recife, 11 de agosto de 1827, 11 de agosto de 1927*. Rio de Janeiro: Francisco Alves, 1927.

Bicalho, Maria Fernanda Baptista. "The Art of Seduction: Representation of Women in Brazilian Silent Cinema." *Luso-Brazilian Review* 30, 1 (summer 1993): 21–33.

———. "O belo sexo: Imprensa e identidade feminina no Rio de Janeiro em fins do século XIX e início do século XX." Master's thesis, Universidade Federal do Rio de Janeiro, 1988.

Bittencourt, C. A. Lúcio. "Comentário." *Revista de direito penal* 12 (1936): 105–14.

Bittencourt, Edgard de Moura. *Concubinato*. São Paulo: Livraria Universitária de Direito, 1975.

———. *O concubinato no direito*, 2d ed. Vols. 1–4. Rio de Janeiro: Biblioteca Jurídica, 1969.

Blok, Anton. "Rams and Billy-Goats: A Key to the Mediterranean Code of Honor." *Man*, n.s., 16 (1981): 427–40.

Bonfim, Manoel. *A América Latina: Males de origem*. Rio de Janeiro: Garnier, 1905.

———. *O Brasil na América: Caracterização da formação brasileira*. 2d ed. Rio de Janeiro: Topbooks, 1997.

Borges, Dain. *The Family in Bahia, Brazil, 1870–1945*. Stanford: Stanford University Press, 1992.

———. "'Puffy, Ugly, Slothful and Inert': Degeneration in Brazilian Social Thought, 1880–1940." *Journal of Latin American Studies* 25 (1993): 235–56.

Bosi, Alfredo. *Dialética da colonização*. São Paulo: Companhia das Letras, 1992.

Boyer, Richard. "Women, *La Mala Vida*, and the Politics of Marriage." In *Sexuality and Marriage in Colonial Latin America*, ed. Asunción Lavrin, 252–286. Lincoln: University of Nebraska Press, 1989.

Brandão, B. C. *Polícia e a força policial no Rio de Janeiro.* Rio de Janeiro: Série Estudos PUC/RJ, 1981.

Bretas, Marcos. *A guerra das ruas: Povo e polícia na cidade do Rio de Janeiro.* Rio de Janeiro: Arquivo Nacional, 1997.

———. *Ordem nacidade. O exercício cotidiano da autoridade policial no Rio de Janeiro: 1907–1930.* Rio de Janeiro: Roccó, 1997.

Brundage, James A. *Law, Sex, and Christian Society in Medieval Europe.* Chicago: University of Chicago Press, 1987.

Burns, E. Bradford. *A History of Brazil.* New York: Columbia University Press, 1980.

———. "As relações internacionais do Brasil durante a Primeira República." In *História geral da civilização brasileira,* bk. 3, vol. 2, ed. Boris Fausto, 377–400. São Paulo: Difusão Européia do Livro, 1977.

———. *The Unwritten Alliance: Rio-Branco and Brazilian-American Relations.* New York: Columbia University Press, 1966.

Butler, Judith. *Gender Trouble: Feminism and the Subversion of Identity.* New York: Routledge, 1990.

Cabral, Sérgio. *Pixinguinha: Vida e obra.* Rio de Janeiro: Lumiar, 1997.

Campos, Francisco. "Exposição de motivos." In *Leis Penais,* 5–48. Rio de Janeiro: Imprensa Nacional, 1942.

Cancela, Cristina Donza. "Adoráveis e dissimuladas: As relações amorosas das mulheres das camadas populares na Belém do final do século XIX e início do XX." Master's thesis, Universidade Estadual de Campinas, 1997.

Cardoso, Fernando Henrique, and Octávio Ianni. *Cor e mobilidade social em Florianópolis: Aspectos das relações entre negros e brancos numa comunidade do Brasil meridional.* São Paulo: Editora Nacional, 1960.

Carneiro, Maria Luiza Tucci. *O anti-semitismo na era Vargas.* São Paulo: Brasiliense, 1988.

Carrara, Francesco. *Programma del corso di diritto criminale.* 10th ed. Florence: Fratelli Cammelli, 1907.

Carvalho, Beni. *Sexualidade anômala no direito criminal.* 2d ed. Rio de Janeiro: Revista Forense, 1957.

Carvalho Júnior, Clóvis de. "Escola positiva penal." *Ciência penal* 2, 4 (1975): 99–128.

Carvalho, Francisco Pereira de Bulhões. "Conceito de estupro e de sedução." *Revista de direito penal* 4 (1934): 230–31.

———. "Conceito de estupro e de sedução." *Revista de direito penal* 4 (1934): 230–31.

———. "Direito de indenização da concubina." *Revista dos tribunais* 216 (1953): 13–31.

———. "A verdadeira população da cidade do Rio de Janeiro." Rio de Janeiro: Tipografia do Jornal do Comércio, 1901.

Carvalho, José Murilo de. *Os bestializados: O Rio de Janeiro e a república que não foi.* São Paulo: Companhia das Letras, 1989.

——. *A construção da ordem: A elite política imperial.* Rio de Janeiro: Campus, 1980.

Carvalho, José Murilo de. "A utopia de Oliveira Viana. In *O pensamento de Oliveira Viana*, ed. Elide Rugai Bastos and João Quartim de Morais, 13–42. Campinas: Editora da UNICAMP, 1993.

Carvalho, Lia de Aquino. *Contribuição ao estudo das habitações populares, Rio de Janeiro, 1886–1906.* 2d ed. Rio de Janeiro: Prefeitura da Cidade do Rio de Janeiro, Secretaria Municipal de Cultura, 1995.

Castro, Celso. *Os militares e a República: Um estudo sobre cultura e ação política.* Rio de Janeiro: Jorge Zahar, 1995.

Castro, Francisco José Viveiros de. *Atentados ao pudor: Estudo sobre as aberrações do instinto sexual.* Rio de Janeiro: Livraria Moderna, 1895.

——. *Os delitos contra a honra da mulher.* 2d ed. Rio de Janeiro: Freitas Bastos, 1932.

——. *Jurisprudência criminal.* Rio de Janeiro: H. Garnier, 1900.

——. *A nova escola penal.* 2d ed. Rio de Janeiro: Jacinto Ribeiro dos Santos, 1913.

Castro, Hebe Maria Mattos. *Ao sul da história: Lavradores pobres na crise do trabalho escravo.* São Paulo: Brasiliense, 1987.

——. *Das cores do silêncio: Os significados da liberdade no sudeste escravista— Brasil, século XIX.* Rio de Janeiro: Arquivo Nacional, 1995.

Castro, Ruy. *O anjo pornográfico: A vida de Nelson Rodrigues.* São Paulo: Companhia das Letras, 1992.

Castro, Mary Garcia. "Mulheres chefes de familias, racismo, códigos de idade e pobreza no Brasil (Bahia e São Paulo). In *Desigualdade nacial no Brasil contemporâneo*, ed. Peggy A. Lovell, 121–59. Belo Horizonte: CEDEPLAR/FACE/ Universidade Federal de Minas Gerais, 1991.

Caulfield, Sueann. "The Birth of Mangue: Race, Nation, and the Politics of Prostitution in Rio de Janeiro, 1850–1942." In *Sex and Sexuality in Latin America*, ed. Daniel Balderston and Donna Guy, 86–100. New York: New York University Press, 1997.

——. "Getting into Trouble: Dishonest Women, Modern Girls, and Women-Men in the Conceptual Language of *Vida policial*, 1925–1927." *Signs* 19, 1 (fall 1993): 146–76.

Caulfield, Sueann, and Martha de Abreu Esteves. "Fifty Years of Virginity in Rio de Janeiro: Sexual Politics and Gender Roles in Juridical and Popular Discourse, 1890–1940." *Luso-Brazilian Review* 30, 1 (summer 1993): 47–74.

Cavalcante, Berenice. "Beleza, limpeza, ordem e progresso: A questão da higiene na cidade do Rio de Janeiro no final do século XIX." *Revista do Rio de Janeiro* 1, 1 (1985).

Cavallo, Sandra, and Simona Cerutti. "Female Honor and the Social Control of Reproduction in Piedmont between 1600 and 1800." In *Sex and Gender in Historical Perspective*, ed. Edwardo Muir and Guido Ruggiero, 73–109. Baltimore: Johns Hopkins University Press, 1990.

Chalhoub, Sidney. *Cidade febril: Cortiços e epidemias na corte imperial.* São Paulo: Companhia das Letras, 1996.

——. "A guerra contra os cortiços: Cidade do Rio, 1850–1906." *Primeira versão* (Campinas, São Paulo: (UNICAMP) 9 (1990).

——. "Medo branco de almas negras: Escravos, libertos e republicanos na cidade do Rio." *Revista brasileira de história* 8, 16 (1988): 83–105.

——. "The Politics of Disease Control: Yellow Fever and Race in Nineteenth-Century Rio de Janeiro." *Journal of Latin American Studies* 25 (1993): 441–63.

——. *Trabalho, lar e botequim: O cotidiano dos trabalhadores no Rio de Janeiro da belle époque.* São Paulo: Brasiliense, 1986.

——. *Visões da liberdade: Uma história das últimas décadas da escravidão na corte.* São Paulo: Companhia das Letras, 1990.

Chasteen, John Charles. "The Prehistory of Samba: Carnival Dancing in Rio de Janeiro, 1840–1917." *Journal of Latin American Studies* 28 (1996): 29–47.

Coaracy, Vivaldo. *Memórias da cidade do Rio de Janeiro.* Rio de Janeiro: José Olympio, 1955.

Conniff, Michael. "Rio de Janeiro during the Great Depression, 1928–1937: Social Reform and the Emergence of Populism in Brazil." Ph.D. diss., Stanford University, 1976.

——. *Urban Politics in Brazil: The Rise of Populism, 1925–1945.* Pittsburgh: University of Pittsburgh Press, 1981.

Conrad, Robert Edgar. *Children of God's Fire: A Documentary History of Black Slavery in Brazil.* University Park: Pennsylvania State University Press, 1994.

Corrêa, Mariza. *Os crimes dà paixão.* São Paulo: Brasiliense, 1981.

——. *Morte em família: Representações jurídicas de papéis sexuais.* Rio de Janeiro: Graal, 1983.

——. "Repensando a família patriarchal brasileira." In *Colcha de retalhos: Estudos sobre a família no Brasil,* 13–38. São Paulo: Brasiliense, 1982.

Costa, Emília Viotti da. *The Brazilian Empire: Myths and Histories.* Chicago: University of Chicago Press, 1985.

——. "O mito da democracia racial." In *Da monarquia à república.* São Paulo: Livraria Humana, 1977.

Costa, João Cruz. "O pensamento brasileiro sob o império." In *História geral da civilização brasileira,* ed. Sérgio Buarque de Holanda, vol. 2, pt. 3, 323–42. São Paulo: Difusão Européia do Livro, 1967.

——. *Pequena história da República.* São Paulo: CNPq and Brasiliense, 1988.

Costa, Jurandir Freire. *Ordem médica e norma familiar.* Rio de Janeiro: Graal, 1979.

Costa, Luiz Edmundo da. *O Rio de Janeiro do meu tempo.* Rio de Janeiro: Conquista, 1957.

Costa, Nilson do Rosário. "Estado e políticas de saúde pública, 1889–1930." Master's thesis, Instituto Universitário de Pesquisas do Rio de Janeiro, 1983.

Couto, Miguel. *Seleção social: O perigo japones.* Rio de Janeiro: Jornal do Comércio, 1930.

Cruls, Gastão. *Aparência do Rio de Janeiro (notícia histórica e descritiva da cidade).* Rio de Janeiro: José Olympio, 1949.

Cunha, Maria Clementina Pereira. *O espelho do mundo: Juquery, a história de um asilo*. Rio de Janeiro: Paz e Terra, 1986.

Dantas, San Tiago. *Dois momentos de Rui Barbosa*. Rio de Janeiro: Casa de Rui Barbosa, 1951.

Darmon, Piérre. *Médecins et assassins de la Belle époque*. Paris: Seuil, 1989.

Degler, Carl. *Neither Black nor White: Slavery and Race Relations in Brazil and the United States*. Madison: University of Wisconsin Press, 1986.

Dias, Maria Odila Leite da Silva. *Quotidiano e poder em São Paulo no século XIX: Ana Gertrudes de Jesus*. São Paulo: Brasiliense, 1984.

Diniz, Almachio. "Conceito legal da miserabilidade." *Revista de direito* 39 (1916): 481–87.

Donzelot, Jacques. *The Policing of Families*. New York: Pantheon Books, 1977.

Dória, Álvaro. "A mãe solteira." In *Terceira semana da saúde e da raça*, ed. Sociedade Brasileira de Urologia, 387–92. Rio de Janeiro: Imprensa Nacional, 1944.

Douglas, Mary. *Purity and Danger: An Analysis of Concepts of Pollution and Taboo*. London: Routledge and Kegan Paul, 1966.

Durão, Eduardo. "Infanticídio." *Direito* (June 1891): 184–92.

Dutra, Pedro. *Literatura jurídica no império*. Rio de Janeiro: Topbooks, 1992.

Elkins, Stanley. *Slavery: A Problem in American Institutional and Intellectual Life*. Chicago: University of Chicago Press, 1959.

Engel, Magali. *Meretrizes e doutores: O saber médico e a prostituição na cidade do Rio de Janeiro, 1845–1890*. São Paulo: Brasiliense, 1990.

———. "Sexualidade feminina e alienação mental no Rio de Janeiro, 1919–1920." 1993. Typescript.

Engelstein, Laura. *The Keys to Happiness: Sex and the Search for Modernity in Fin-de-Siècle Russia*. Ithaca: Cornell University Press, 1992.

Espínola, Eduardo, E. A. "O 'habeas-corpus' e a expulsão do estrangeiro." In *Pandectas brasileiras*, ed. E. A. Eduardo Espínola, 210–21. Rio de Janeiro: Casa Gráfica, 1929.

Esteves, Martha de Abreu. *Meninas perdidas: Os populares e o cotidiano do amor no Rio de Janeiro da belle époque*. Rio de Janeiro: Paz e Terra, 1989.

Ewell, Judith. "Ligia Parra Jahn: The Blonde with the Revolver." In *The Human Tradition in Latin America: The Twentieth Century*, ed. Judith Ewell and William H. Beezley. Wilmington: Scholarly Resources, 1987.

Faria, Sheila de Castro. *Colônia em movimento: Fortuna e família no cotidiano colonial*. Rio de Janeiro: Nova Fronteira, 1998.

———. "História da família e demografia histórica." In *Domínios da História*, ed. Ciro Flamarian Cardoso e Ronaldo Vainfas, 241–258. Rio de Janeiro: Campus, 1997.

Fausto, Boris. *Crime e cotidiano: A criminalidade em São Paulo, 1880–1924*. São Paulo: Brasiliense, 1984.

———. "Society and Politics." In *Brazil: Empire and Republic, 1822–1930*, ed. Leslie Bethell, 257–307. Cambridge: Cambridge University Press, 1989.

Favero, Flamínio. "Classificação de Oscar Freire para as formas himenais." *Arquivos do instituto médico-legal e do gabinete de identidade* (July 1932): 77–79.

Fernandes, Florestan. *A integração do negro na sociedade de classes.* São Paulo: Dominus Editora, Universidade de São Paulo, 1965.

Fernandes, Florestan, and Roger Bastide. *Relações raciais entre brancos e negros em São Paulo.* São Paulo: Companhia Editora Nacional, 1955.

Ferreira, Marieta de Moraes. *Conflito regional e crise política: A reação republicana no Rio de Janeiro.* Rio de Janeiro: Centro de Pesquisa e Documentação de História Contemporânea do Brasil, 1988.

Ferri, Enrico. *O delicto passional na civilização contemporânea.* Trans. and introduction by Roberto Lira. São Paulo: Saraiva, 1934.

Fields, Barbara. "Ideology and Race in American History." In *Region, Race and Reconstruction: Essays in Honor of C. Vann Woodward,* ed. J. Morgan Kousser and James M. McPherson, 143–77. Oxford: Oxford University Press, 1982.

Figueiredo, Luciano Raposo de Almeida. *Barrocas famílias: Vida familiar em Minas Gerais no século XVIII.* São Paulo: Hucitec, 1997.

Filgueiras Júnior, Araújo. *Código criminal do Império do Brasil.* 2d ed. Rio de Janeiro: Laemmert, 1876.

Fleury, Aldovando. "Doutrina: Defloramento." *Revista dos tribunais* 69 (1929): 441–443.

Flory, Thomas. *Judge and Jury in Imperial Brazil, 1808–1871.* Austin: University of Texas Press, 1981.

Ford, Talisman. "Passion is in the Eye of the Beholder: Sexuality as Seen by Brazilian Sexologists, 1900–1940." Ph.D. diss., Vanderbilt University, 1995.

Foucault, Michel. *Discipline and Punish: The Birth of the Prison.* New York: Vintage, 1979.

———. *A History of Sexuality.* Vol. 1. New York: Vintage, 1980.

Fragoso, João Luis Ribeiro. "Comerciantes, fazendeiros e formas de acumulação numa economia escravista colonial: Rio de Janeiro, 1790–1888." Ph.D. diss., Universidade Federal Fluminense, 1990.

———. *Homens de grossa aventura: Acumulação e hierarquia na praça mercantil do Rio de Janeiro, 1790–1830.* Rio de Janeiro: Arquivo Nacional, 1992.

Franco, Afrânio de Melo. "Penitenciária para mulheres." In *Pandectas brasileiras,* ed. Eduardo E. A. Espínola, 458–60. Rio de Janeiro: Casa Gráfica, 1929.

———. *Rodrigues Alves.* Rio de Janeiro: José Olympio, 1973.

Franco, Jean. *Plotting Women: Gender and Representation in Mexico.* New York: Columbia University Press, 1989.

Franco, Maria Sylvia de Carvalho. "As idéias estão no lugar." *Caderno de debates* 1 (1976): 61–64.

Freire, Oscar. "Conceito do crime de defloramento—'ruptura himenal incompleta.' " *Revista dos tribunais* 44 (1922): 695–710.

———. "Orgãos genitais femininos—sua insensibilidade; influência nos atos sexuais." In *Exames e pareceres médico-legais,* 43. São Paulo: Saraiva, 1926.

Freire-Maia, Newton. *Brasil: Laboratório racial.* Rio de Janeiro: Vozes, 1973.

French, John. *The Brazilian Workers' ABC.* Chapel Hill: University of North Carolina Press, 1992.

Freyre, Gilberto. *Brazil: An Interpretation.* New York: Knopf, 1945.

——. *Casa grande e senzala.* 14th ed. Recife: Imprensa Oficial, 1966.

——. *Order and Progress: Brazil from Monarchy to Republic.* Trans. Rod W. Horton. New York: Knopf, 1970.

——. *Sobrados e mucambos.* São Paulo: Editora Nacional, 1936.

Fry, Peter. "Direito positivo versus direito clássico: A psicologização do crime no pensamento de Heitor Carrilho." In *Cultura da psicanálise,* ed. Sérvulo Figueira, 117–14. São Paulo: Brasiliense, 1985.

——. "O que a Cinderela negra tem a dizer sobre a 'política racial" no Brasil.' *Revista USP* 28 (December–February 1995–1996): 122–35.

Fry, Peter, and Sérgio Carrara. "As vicissitudes do liberalismo no direito penal brasileiro." *Revista brasileira de ciências sociais* 2, 1 (1986): 48–54.

Fundação Casa de Rui Barbosa. *Rui Barbosa: Cronologia da vida e obra.* Rio de Janeiro: FCRB, 1995.

Gabaglia, Laurita Pessoa Raja. *O Cardeal Leme.* Rio de Janeiro: José Olímpio, 1962.

——. *Epitácio Pessoa, 1865–1942.* São Paulo: José Olímpio, 1941.

Gameiro, Mário. "O crime de sedução na exegese de quatro juizes modernos." *Revista criminal* 8, 3 (December 1934): 689–90.

Garcia, Basileu. *Instituições de direito penal.* São Paulo: Grijalbo, 1967.

Garcia, N. Jahr. *Estado Novo: Ideologia e propaganda política.* São Paulo: Edições Loyola, 1982.

García Fuentes, José María. *Inquisición en Granada en el siglo XVI: Fuentes para su estudio.* Granada: Departamento de Historia de la Universidad de Granada, 1981.

Gardel, Luis D. *Escolas de samba.* Rio de Janeiro: Kosmos, 1967.

Goldschmidt, Eliana Maria Rea. "A motivação matrimonial nos casamentos mistos de escravos." *Revista da Sociedade Brasileira de Pesquisa Histórica* 3 (1987): 1–16.

——. "Virtude e pecado: Sexualidade em São Paulo colonial." In *Entre a virtude e o pecado,* ed. Albertina de Oliveira Costa and Cristina Bruschini, 15–36. São Paulo: Rosa dos Tempos and Fundação Carlos Chagas, 1992.

Gomes, Angela de Castro. "Os anos 20: Competição e debate no movimento sindical carioca." Paper presented at the tenth annual meeeting of the Associação Nacional de Pós-graduação e Pesquisa em Ciencias Sociais, Campos do Jordão, October 1987.

——. *A invenção do trabalhismo.* 2d ed. Rio de Janeiro: Relume-Dumará, 1994.

——. "A praxis corporativa de Oliveira Viana." In *O pensamento de Oliveira Viana,* ed. Elide Rugai Bastos and João Quartim de Moraes, 43–62. Campinas: Editora da UNICAMP, 1993.

Gomes, Hélio. *Medicina legal.* Rio de Janeiro: Forense, 1945.

——. "O problema da prostituição sob o ponto de vista sanitário e jurídico." In *Anais da Primeira Conferência Nacional de Defesa Contra a Sífilis,* 423–35. Rio de Janeiro: Imprensa Nacional, 1941.

Gomes, Olívia. "1933: Um ano em que fizemos contatos." *Revista USP/Dossiê Povo Negro—300 Anos* (December–February 1995–1996): 142–63.

Graham, Richard. *Patronage and Politics in Nineteenth-Century Brazil.* Stanford: Stanford University Press, 1990.

Graham, Sandra Lauderdale. *House and Street: The Domestic World of Servants and Masters in Nineteenth-Century Rio de Janeiro.* New York: Cambridge University Press, 1989.

———. "Slavery's Impasse: Slave Prostitutes, Small-Time Mistresses, and the Brazilian Law of 1871." *Comparative Studies in Society and History* 33, 4 (October 1991): 669–94.

———. "The Vintem Riot and Political Culture: Rio de Janeiro, 1880." *Hispanic American Historical Review* 62, 3 (1980): 431–49.

Grazia, Victoria de. *How Fascism Ruled Italy: Italy 1922–1945.* Berkeley: University of California Press, 1992.

Green, James. "Beyond Carnival: Homosexuality in Twentieth-Century Brazil," Ph.D. diss., University of California, Los Angeles, 1996.

Green, Thomas A. "Freedom and Criminal Responsibility in the Age of Pound: An Essay on Criminal Justice." *Michigan Law Review* 93, 7 (June 1995): 1915–2053.

Greene, Margaret Eleanor. "The Importance of Being Married: Marriage Choice and Its Consequences in Brazil." Ph.D. diss., University of Pennsylvania, 1991.

Grimmer, Claude. *La femme et le bâtard: Amours illégitimes et sécrets dans l'ancienne France.* Paris: Renaissance, 1983.

Grinberg, Keila. *Liberata: A lei da ambigüidade—As ações de liberdade da Corte de Apelação do Rio de Janeiro no século XIX.* Rio de Janeiro: Relume-Dumará, 1994.

———. "Slavery, Liberalism, and Civil Law: The Definition of Status and Citizenship in Memorials Regarding the Elaboration of the Brazilian Civil Code, 1855–1916." Paper presented at the "Status, Honor, and Law in Modern Latin America" conference, University of Michigan, December 5, 1998.

Gusmão, Antônio Cardoso de. *Os crimes sexuais.* Rio de Janeiro: F. Briguiet, 1921.

———. "Delitos sexuais." *Arquivos do Departamento Federal de Segurança Pública* 4 (1948): 43.

Gusmão, Crisólito de. *Dos crimes sexuais: Estupro, atentado ao pudor, defloramento e corrupção de menores.* Rio de Janeiro: F. Briguiet, 1921.

Gutiérrez, Ramón. *When Jesus Came, the Corn Mothers Went Away: Marriage, Sexuality, and Power in New Mexico, 1500–1846.* Stanford: Stanford University Press, 1991.

Guy, Donna. *Sex and Danger in Buenos Aires: Prostitution, Family and Nation in Argentina.* Lincoln: University of Nebraska Press, 1991.

Hahner, June. *Emancipating the Female Sex: The Struggle for Women's Rights in Brazil, 1850–1940.* Durham: Duke University Press, 1990.

286

Harris, Marvin. *Town and Country in Brazil.* New York: Columbia University Press, 1956.

Harris, Ruth. *Murders and Madness: Medicine, Law, and Society in the* Fin de Siècle. New York: Oxford University Press, 1989.

Hasenbalg, Carlos A. "Race and Socioeconomic Inequalities in Brazil." In *Race, Class and Power in Brazil,* ed. Pierre-Michel Fontaine. Los Angeles: Center for Afro-American Studies, University of California at Los Angeles, 1985.

Hasenbalg, Carlos A. and Nelson do Valle Silva. "Raça e oportunidades educacionais no Brasil." In *Desigualdade racial no Brasil contemporâneo,* ed. Peggy Lovell, 241–279. Belo Horizonte: CEDEPLAR-FACE/Universidade Federal de Minas Gerais, 1991.

———. *Relações raciais no Brasil contemporâneo.* Rio de Janeiro: Rio Fundo Ed., 1992.

Hellwig, David J. *African-American Reflections on Brazil's Racial Paradise.* Philadelphia: Temple University Press, 1992.

Herzfeld, Michael. "Semantic Slippage and Moral Fall: The Rhetoric of Chastity in Rural Greece." *Journal of Modern Greek Studies* 1 (1983): 161–72.

Holanda, Sérgio Buarque de. *História geral da civilização brasileira.* Vol. 2, pt. 3. São Paulo: Difusão Européia do Livro, 1967.

Holcombe, Lee. *Wives and Property: Reform of the Married Women's Property Laws in Nineteenth-Century England.* Toronto: University of Toronto Press, 1983.

Holloway, Thomas. *Policing Rio de Janeiro: Repression and Resistance in a Nineteenth-Century City.* Stanford: Stanford University Press, 1993.

Hoornaert, Eduardo. "A cristianidade durante a primeira época colonial." In *História da Igreja no Brasil,* ed. Eduardo Hoornaert et al., 2: 248–49. Petrópolis: Vozes, 1979.

Hungria, Nelson. "Crimes sexuais." Part 1. *Revista forense* 70 (April 1937): 8–18.

———. "Crimes sexuais." Part 2. *Revista forense* 70 (May 1937): 216–27.

———. "Do lenocínio e do tráfico de mulheres." *Arquivos do Departamento Federal de Segurança Pública* 3, 7 (1946): 27–32.

———. "Em torno de um parecer." *Revista de crítica judiciária* 21, 2–3 (1935): 81–84.

Hungria, Nelson, and Romão Côrtes de Lacerda. *Comentários ao código penal.* Vols. 1–8. Rio de Janeiro: Revista Forense, 1947.

Ianni, Octávio. *Raças e classes sociais no Brasil.* Rio de Janeiro: Civilização Brasileira, 1966.

Iglesias, Francisco. *História política de Brasil, 1500–1964.* Madrid: Mapfre, 1992.

Irajá, Hernani de. *Adeus! Lapa.* Rio de Janeiro: Gráfica Record, 1967.

———. *Sexo e virgindade: Reconstituição da virgindade física.* Rio de Janeiro: Pongetti, 1969.

Jardim, Germano Gonçalves. "Os recenseamentos e a estatística do estado conjugal." *Revista brasileira de estatística* 15, 57 (January–March, 1954): 165–69.

Johnson, Lyman, and Sonia Lipsett-Rivera. *The Faces of Honor: Sex, Shame, and Violence in Colonial Latin America.* Albuquerque: University of New Mexico Press, 1998.

Juenger, F. K. "The Legal Heritage of the Americas." In *Law and Legal Systems of the Commonwealth Caribbean States*, 57, 63. Washington, D.C.: OAS, 1986. Cited in Thomas H. Reynolds and Arturo A. Flores, *Foreign Law: Current Sources of Codes and Basic Legislation in Jurisdictions of the World* (Littleton: Fred B. Rothman, 1989) 1: 3.

Kamen, Henry. *The Phoenix and the Flame: Catalonia and the Counter Reformation.* New Haven: Yale University Press, 1993.

Kehl, Renato. *Aparas eugênicas: Sexo e civilização.* Rio de Janeiro: Francisco Alves, 1933.

——. *Porque eu sou eugenista: Vinte anos de campanha eugênica, 1917–1937.* Rio de Janeiro: Francisco Alves, n.d.

——. *Lições de eugenia.* 2d ed. Rio de Janeiro, F. Alves, 1935.

Kushnir, Beatriz. *Baile de máscaras: Mulheres judias e prostituição.* Rio de Janeiro: Imago, 1996.

Kuznesof, Elizabeth Anne. *Household Economy and Urban Development: São Paulo, 1765–1836.* Denver: Westview Press, 1986.

——. "Sexuality, Gender and the Family in Colonial Brazil." *Luso-Brazilian Review* 30, 1 (summer 1993): 119–132.

——. "Sexual Politics, Race and Bastard-Bearing in Nineteenth-Century Brazil: A Question of Culture or Power?" *Journal of Family History* 16, 3 (1991): 241–260.

Lacombe, Américo Jacobina. "A cultura jurídica." In *História geral da civilização brasileira*, ed. Sérgio Buarque de Holanda, vol. 2, pt. 3, 356–368. São Paulo: Difusão Européia do Livro, 1967.

Lagenest, H. D. Barruel de. *Lenocínio e prostituição no Brasil.* Rio de Janeiro: Agir, 1960.

Lahdo, Bernardo Elias. *O defloramento da mulher, ignorado pelo marido, é causa de anulação de casamento?* Rio de Janeiro: n.p., 1981.

Largman, Esther. *Jovens polacas.* Rio de Janeiro: Rosa dos Tempos, 1993.

Lavrin, Asunción, ed. *Sexuality and Marriage in Colonial Latin America.* Lincoln: University of Nebraska Press, 1989.

Lavrin, Asunción, and Edith Couturier. "Dowries and Wills: A View of Women's Socioeconomic Role in Colonial Guadalajara and Puebla, 1640–1790." *Hispanic American Historical Review* 59, 2 (1979): 280–304.

Leal, Aurelino de Araújo, ed. *Anais da conferência judiciária-policial.* Rio de Janeiro: Imprensa Nacional, 1918.

——. *Germens do crime.* Salvador: Magalhães, 1896.

Leite, Míriam Lifchitz Moreira. *Outra face do feminismo: Maria Lacerda de Moura.* São Paulo: Ática, 1984.

Lenharo, Alcir. *Sacralização da política.* Campinas: Papirus, 1986.

Lessa, Pedro. *Estudos de filosofia de direito.* 2d ed. Rio de Janeiro: Francisco Alves, 1916.

Lesser, Jeffrey. "Pawns of the Powerful: Jewish Immigration to Brazil." Ph.D. diss., New York University, 1989.

288

——. *Welcoming the Undesirables: Brazil and the Jewish Question.* Berkeley and Los Angeles: University of California Press, 1995.

Lewin, Linda. "Natural and Spurious Children in Brazilian Inheritance Law from Colony to Empire: A Methodological Essay." *Americas* 48, 3 (January 1992): 351–96.

——. *Politics and Parentela e Paraíba: A Case Study of Family-Based Oligarchy in Brazil.* Princeton: Princeton University Press, 1987.

Lewis, Beth Irwin. "*Lustmord:* Inside the Windows of the Metropolis." In *Berlin: Culture and Metropolis,* ed. Charles W. Haxthausen and Heidrun Suhr. Minneapolis: University of Minnesota Press, 1990.

Lima, Agostinho J. de Souza. "Figura do aborto." *Revista da jurisprudência* (July 1898): 251.

——. *Tratado de medicina legal.* 5th ed., 131–37. Rio de Janeiro: Freitas Bastos, 1933.

Lima, Carlos de Araújo. *O júri: Sua atualização e crescente democratização.* Rio de Janeiro, n.p., 1966.

Lima e Silva, Ruy Maurício de. "Iluminação e gás." In *Rio de Janeiro em seus quatrocentos anos,* ed. F. N. Silva, 357–64. Rio de Janeiro: Distribuidora Record, 1965.

Lira, Roberto. *O júri sob todos os aspetos.* Rio de Janeiro: Saraiva, 1950.

——. *O Ministério Público e o júri.* Rio de Janeiro: Jacinto, 1933.

Lira, Roberto. *O amor e a responsabilidade criminal.* São Paulo: Saraiva, 1932.

——. *Direito penal científico (criminologia).* Rio de Janeiro: José Konfino, 1974.

——. *Frutos verdes.* Rio de Janeiro: Brasileira Lux, 1925.

——. *Novíssimas escolas penais.* Rio de Janeiro: Borsoi, 1956.

——. *Novo direito penal.* Rio de Janeiro: Borsoi, 1972.

——. *Polícia e justiça para o amor!* Rio de Janeiro: S. A. A. Noite, 1939.

——. "Psicanálise do sensacionalismo." In *Sensacionalismo,* ed. Cláudio Sussekind de Mendonça, 7–41. Rio de Janeiro: Casa do Estudante do Brasil, 1933.

Lobo, Eulália Maria Lahmeyer. *História do Rio de Janeiro (do capital comercial ao capital industrial e financeiro).* 2 vols. Rio de Janeiro: Instituto Brasileiro de Mercado de Capitais, 1978.

Lombroso, Cesare, and William Ferrero. *The Female Offender.* London: T. F. Unwin, 1895.

Loureiro, Célio. "Conferência na Rádio Sociedade." In *Sensacionalismo,* ed. Cláudio Sussekind de Mendonça, 131–137. Rio de Janeiro: Casa do Estudante do Brasil, 1933.

Lovell, Peggy. "Race, Gender, and Development in Brazil." *Latin American Research Review* 29, 3 (1994): 7–35.

Lovell, Peggy, ed. *Desigualdade racial no Brasil contemporâneo.* Belo Horizonte: CEDEPLAR-FACE/Universidade Federal de Minas Gerais, 1991.

Luizetto, Flávio Venâncio. "Os constituintes em face da imigração." Master's thesis, Universidade de São Paulo, 1975.

Machado Filho, Pinheiro. "Tratamento da blenorragia na fundação Gaffrée-Guinle." Arquivos da Fundação Gaffrée-Guinle 4 (1932–1933): 33–41.

Machado, Roberto, et al. Danação da norma: Medicina social e constituição da psiquiatria no Brasil. Rio de Janeiro: Graal, 1978.

Magalhães Junior, R. Rui, o homem e o mito. Rio de Janeiro: Civilização Brasileira, 1965.

Marcílio, Maria Luíza. Caiçara: Terra e população. São Paulo: Edições Paulinas, 1986.

——. Família, mulher, sexualidade e igreja na história do Brasil. São Paulo: Edições Loyola, 1993.

Martínez-Alier, Verena. Marriage, Class and Colour in Nineteenth-Century Cuba. Ann Arbor: University of Michigan Press, 1989.

Martins, Luís. Noturno da Lapa. Rio de Janeiro: Civilização Brasileira, 1964.

Matta, Roberto da. Carnivals, Rogues, and Heroes: An Interpretation of the Brazilian Dilemma. Trans. John Drury. Notre Dame: University of Notre Dame Press, 1991.

——. A casa e a rua: Espaço, cidadania, mulher e morte no Brasil. São Paulo: Brasiliense, 1985.

Matoso, E. Coisas do meu tempo. Bordeaux: Gounouilhou, 1916.

Mattoso, Kátia de Queirós. "Os baianos no governo central: Origem social e formação." In Bahia, século XIX: Uma província no Império. Rio de Janeiro: Nova Fronteira, 1985.

——. Família e sociedade na Bahia do século XIX. São Paulo: Corrupio, 1988.

Meade, Teresa. " 'Civilizing Rio de Janeiro': The Public Health Campaign and the Riot of 1904." Journal of Social History 20, 2 (winter 1986): 301–22.

——. "Civilizing" Rio: Reform and Resistance in a Brazilian City, 1889–1930. University Park: Pennsylvania State University Press, 1997.

——. "Community Protest in Rio de Janeiro, Brazil, during the First Republic, 1890–1917." Ph.D. diss., Rutgers University, 1984.

Medeiros, Darcy Campos de, and Aroldo Moreira. Do crime de sedução. Rio de Janeiro: Freitas Bastos, 1967.

Médici Filho, Atugasmin. "Doutrina: O crime de sedução no novo código penal." Revista dos tribunais 134 (1941): 399–416.

Meira, Sílvio. O código civil de 1917: O projeto Bevilaqua. Special ed. of Studi in onore di Cesare Sanfilippo. Milan: Giuffré, 1982.

Mello e Souza, Laura de. O diabo e a terra de Santa Cruz. São Paulo: Companhia das Letras, 1987.

Mendes Júnior, Cândido. As mulheres criminosas no centro mais populoso do Brasil. Rio de Janeiro: Imprensa Nacional, 1928.

Mendonça, Cláudio Sussekind de. "Os crimes passionais: A sua repetição, entre nós—algumas das suas causas." Revista criminal 5, 9 (November 1927):

Menezes, Lená Medeiros de. Os estrangeiros e o comércio do prazer nas ruas do Rio, 1890–1930. Rio de Janeiro: Arquivo Nacional, 1992.

Mercadante, Paulo. *A consciência conservadora no Brasil.* Rio de Janeiro: Nova Fronteira, 1985.

Merryman, John Henry. *The Civil Law Tradition: An Introduction to the Legal Systems of Western Europe and Latin America.* Stanford: Stanford University Press, 1969.

Morais, Evaristo de. *A criminalidade das multidões—ensaio de psicologia coletiva.* Rio de Janeiro: Typografia de A Verdade, 1898.

——. *Criminalidade passional: O homicídio e o homicídio-suicídio por amor em face da psicologia criminal e da penalística.* São Paulo: Saraiva, 1933.

——. *Ensaios de patologia social.* Rio de Janeiro: Leite Ribeiro e Maurillo, 1926.

——. *Reminiscências de um rábula criminalista.* Belo Horizonte: Briguiet, 1989.

Morais, Fernando. *Olga.* São Paulo: Companhia das Letras, 1984.

Morais, Manoel Odorico de. "Estado atual da prostituição no Rio de Janeiro." *A folha médica* 23, 3 (July 1942): 148–52.

Moreira, Sônia Virgínia. *O rádio no Brasil.* Rio de Janeiro: Rio Fundo, 1991.

Mortara, Giorgio. "As mães solteiras no Brasil." *Revista brasileira de estatística* 85 (January–June 1961): 1–32.

Mott, Luiz de Barros. *Os pecados da família na Bahia de Todos os Santos.* Salvador: Universidade da Bahia, 1982.

Nachman, Robert G. "Positivism and Revolution in Brazil's First Republic: The 1904 Revolt." *Americas* 34, 1 (1977): 3–23.

Nalle, Sara T. *God in La Mancha: Religious Reform and the People of Cuenca, 1500–1650.* Baltimore: Johns Hopkins University Press, 1992.

Nascimento, Abdias do. *Brazil: Mixture or Massacre? Essays in the Genocide of a Black People.* 2d ed. Dover, Mass.: Majority Press, 1989.

Nazzari, Muriel. "Concubinage in Colonial Brazil: The Inequalities of Race, Class, and Gender." *Journal of Family History* 21, 2 (1996): 107–24.

——. *Disappearance of the Dowry: Women, Families, and Social Change in São Paulo, Brazil, 1600–1900.* Stanford: Stanford University Press, 1991.

——. "An Urgent Need to Conceal." In *The Faces of Honor: Sex, Shame, and Violence in Colonial Latin America,* ed. Lyman Johnson and Sonia Lipsett-Rivera, 103–126. Albuquerque: University of New Mexico Press, 1998.

——. "Widows as Obstacles to Business: British Objections to Brazilian Marriage and Inheritance Laws." *Comparative Studies in Society and History* 37, 4 (October 1995): 781–802.

Needell, Jeffrey D. "History, Race, and the State in the Thought of Oliveira Viana." *Hispanic American Historical Review* 75, 1 (1995): 1–30.

——. "Identity, Race, Gender, and Modernity in the Origins of Gilberto Freyre's Oeuvre." *American Historical Review* 100, 1 (February 1995): 51–75.

——. "Making the Carioca Belle Époque Concrete: The Urban Reforms of Rio de Janeiro under Pereira Passos." *Journal of Urban History* 10, 4 (August 1984): 383–422.

——. "The *Revolta contra vacina* of 1904: The Revolt against 'Modernization' in

Belle Époque Rio de Janeiro." *Hispanic American Historical Review* 67, 2 (1989): 233–69.

———. *A Tropical Belle Époque: The Elite Culture of Turn-of-the-Century Rio de Janeiro.* New York: Cambridge University Press, 1987.

Nogueira, Anderson Perdigão. "Jurisprudência—defloramento." *Revista de direito penal* 16 (1937): 206–25.

Nogueira, Oracy. *Tanto preto quanto branco.* São Paulo: T. A. Queiroz, 1985.

Nogueira, Sérgio Ribeiro. *Crimes passionais e outros temas.* Rio de Janeiro: Itambé, 1975.

Nolan, Mary. *Visions of Modernity: American Business and the Modernization of Germany.* Oxford: Oxford University Press, 1994.

Nye, Robert A. *Crime, Madness, and Politics in Modern France: The Medical Concept of National Decline.* Princeton: Princeton University Press, 1984.

———. "Heredity or Milieu: The Foundations of Modern European Criminological Theory." *Isis* 67 (1976): 335–55.

Oliveira, Lúcia Lippi. *A questão nacional na Primeira República.* São Paulo: CNPq and Brasiliense, 1990.

Oliveira, Lúcia Lippi, Mônica Pimenta Velloso, and Angela Maria Castro Gomes. *Estado novo: Ideologia e poder.* Rio de Janeiro: Zahar, 1982.

Ortega, Sérgio, ed. *De la santidad a la perversión o de por qué no se cumplía la ley de Dios en la sociedad novohispana.* Mexico City: Grijalbo, 1985.

Pang, Eul-Soo. *In Pursuit of Honor and Power: Noblemen of the Southern Cross in Nineteenth-Century Brazil.* Tuscaloosa: University of Alabama Press, 1988.

Peiss, Kathy. *Cheap Amusements: Working Women and Leisure in Turn-of-the-Century New York.* Philadelphia: Temple University Press, 1986.

Peixoto, Afrânio. "Himenolatria." *Arquivos de medicina legal e identificação* 4, 9 (July 1934): 105–17.

———. *Medicina legal.* 5th ed. Rio de Janeiro: Francisco Alves, 1927.

———. *Sexologia forense.* Rio de Janeiro: Guanabara, 1934.

Pena, Eduardo Spiller. "Um romanista entre a escravidão e a liberdade," *Afro-Ásia* 18 (1996): 33–75.

Pena, Maria Valéria Junho. *Mulheres e trabalhadoras: Presença feminina na constituição do sistema fabril.* Rio de Janeiro: Paz e Terra, 1981.

———. "A revolução de 30, a família e o trabalho feminino." *Cadernos de pesquisa da Fundação Carlos Chagas* 37 (May 1981): 78–83.

Pereira, Cristiana Schettini. *Nas barbas de momo: Os sentidos da presença feminina no carnaval das "grandes sociedades" nos últimos anos do século XIX.* Campinas: Instituto de Filosofia e Ciências Humanas, Universidade Estadual de Campinas, 1995.

Pereira, Leonardo Affonso de Miranda. *O carnaval das letras.* Rio de Janeiro: Secretaria Municipal de Cultura, 1994.

Pereira, Virgílio de Sá, Evaristo de Morais, and Mário Bulhões Pedreira. *Projeto do código criminal.* Rio de Janeiro: Imprensa Nacional, 1933.

Peristiany, J. G., ed. *Honor and Shame: The Values of Mediterranean Society.* Chicago: University of Chicago Press, 1966.

Pierson, Donald. *Negroes in Brazil.* Chicago: University of Chicago Press, 1942.

Pinheiro, Paulo Sérgio de M. S. *Estratégias da ilusão: A revolução mundial e o Brasil, 1922–1935.* São Paulo: Companhia das Letras, 1991.

——. *Política e trabalho no Brasil.* 2d ed. Rio de Janeiro: Paz e Terra, 1977.

Pinto, Luís Costa. *O negro no Rio de Janeiro: Relações de raça numa sociedade em mudança.* São Paulo: Editora Nacional, 1953.

Pinto, Ricardo. *Tráfico das brancas: Observações em torno dos caftens franceses que vivem no Rio de Janeiro.* N.p., 1930.

Piragibe, Vicente. *Dicionário de jurisprudência penal do Brasil.* Rio de Janeiro: Freitas Bastos, 1938.

Pitt-Rivers, Julian. *The Fate of Shechem, or the Politics of Sex: Essays in the Anthropology of the Mediterranean.* Cambridge: Cambridge University Press, 1977.

——. "Honor." In *International Encyclopedia of Social Sciences,* 6: 503–11. New York: Macmillan, 1968.

Pontes, Tiago Ribeiro. *Código penal brasileiro comentado.* Rio de Janeiro: Freitas Bastos, 1977.

Portela, Joaquim. "Tese inaugural." Dr. Med. thesis, Faculdade de Medicina do Rio de Janeiro, 1895.

Prandi, José Reginaldo. "Catolicismo e família: Transformação de uma ideologia." *Cadernos Cebrap* 21 (1975): 29–35.

Porto-Carrero, J. P. Preface to *Tratado de medicina legal* by Agostinho J. de Souza Lima. 5th ed. Rio de Janeiro: Freitas Bastos, 1933.

——. "Sexo e cultura." *Arquivos brasileiros de higiene mental* 3, 5 (May 1930): 157–66.

Prestes, Anita Leocádia. *Os militares e a reação republicana.* Petrópolis: Vozes, 1993.

Priore, Mary del. *Ao sul do corpo: Condição feminina, maternidades e mentalidades no Brasil colônia.* Rio de Janeiro: José Olympio, 1993.

Prunes, Lourenço Mário. *Anulação do casamento—erro essencial.* 2d ed. São Paulo: Sugestões Literárias, 1968.

Queiroz, Maria Isaura Pereira de. *Carnaval brasileiro: O vivido e o mito.* São Paulo: Brasiliense, 1992.

Rago, Margareth. *Do cabaré ao lar: A utopia da cidade disciplinar, Brasil, 1890–1930.* Rio de Janeiro: Paz e Terra, 1985.

——. *Os prazeres da noite: Prostituição e códigos da sexualidade feminina em São Paulo, 1890–1930.* Rio de Janeiro: Paz e Terra, 1991.

Ramos, Artur, ed. *Novos estudos afro-brasileiros.* Recife: Fundação Joaquim Nabuco, 1934 (facsimile, 1988).

Ramos, Artur. *The Negro in Brazil.* Philadelphia: Porcupine Press, 1983.

Ramos, Donald. "Marriage and Family in Colonial Vila Rica." *Hispanic American Historical Review* 55, 2 (1975): 200–25.

Ramos, Guerreiro. *Introdução crítica à sociologia brasileira.* Rio de Janeiro: Editorial Andes, 1957.

Raphael, Alison. "Samba and Social Control: Popular Culture and Racial Democracy in Rio de Janeiro." Ph.D. diss., Columbia University, 1981.

Rapp, Rayna, and Ellen Ross. "The Twenties: Feminism, Consumerism and Political Backlash in the United States." In *Women in Culture and Politics: A Century of Change,* ed. Judith Friedlander, 93–107. Bloomington: Indiana University Press, 1986.

Reale, Miguel. "Pedro Lessa e a filosofia positiva em São Paulo." In *Juristas brasileiros,* ed. Instituto Histórico e Geográfico de São Paulo, 55–90. São Paulo: IHGSP, 1960.

Rebelo, Fernando Castro. "Conferência." In *Sensacionalismo,* ed. Cláudio Sussekind de Mendonça, 171–75. Rio de Janeiro: Casa do Estudante do Brasil, 1933.

Reis, João José. *Slave Rebellion in Brazil: The Muslim Uprising of 1835 in Bahia.* Baltimore: Johns Hopkins University Press, 1993.

Reis, José de Oliveira. *O Rio de Janeiro e seus prefeitos: Evolução urbanística da cidade.* Rio de Janeiro: Prefeitura da cidade do Rio de Janeiro, 1977.

Rezende, Astolfo. "As mães solteiras: Sua proteção e dignidade. Pesquisa da paternidade. Penalidade pecuniária na fecundação extra-legal." *Revista de jurisprudência brasileira* 4 (June 1929): 207–18.

Ribeiro, Carlos Antônio Costa. "Clássicos e positivistas no moderno direito penal brasileiro: Uma interpretação sociológica." In *Invenção do Brasil moderno: Medicina, educação e engenharia nos anos 20–30,* ed. Michael Herschman and Carlos Alberto Messeder Pereira, 130–46. Rio de Janeiro: Rocco, 1994.

Ribeiro, C. J. de Assis. *Contribuição ao conhecimento do código criminal brasileiro de 1830: A revolução francesa e suas consequências jurídico-penais.* Rio de Janeiro: Fundação Getúlio Vargas, 1946.

Ribeiro, Leonídio. *Brazilian Medical Contributions.* Rio de Janeiro: José Olympio, 1939.

Roberts, Mary Louise. *Civilization without Sexes: Reconstructing Gender in Postwar France, 1917–1927.* Chicago: University of Chicago Press, 1994.

Rocha, Oswaldo Porto. *A era das demolições: Cidade do Rio de Janeiro, 1870–1920.* 2d ed., Rio de Janeiro: Secretaria Municipal de Cultura, 1995.

Rodd, Laurel Rasplica. "Yosano Akiko and the Taisho Debate over the 'New Woman.' " In *Recreating Japanese Women, 1600–1945,* ed. Gail Lee Bernstein, 175–98. Berkeley and Los Angeles: University of California Press, 1991.

Rodrigues, Ana Maria. *Samba negro, espoliação branca.* São Paulo: Hucitec, 1984.

Rodrigues, José Honório. *Conciliação e reforma no Brasil.* Rio de Janeiro: Civilização Brasileira, 1965.

Rodrigues, Nina. *As coletividades anormais.* Rio de Janeiro: Imprensa Nacional, 1940.

———. "Des formes de l'hymen et de leur rôle dans la rupture de cette membrane." *Annales d'hygiene publique et de médécine légale* (June 1900).

294

——. *As raças humanas e a responsabilidade penal no Brasil.* 3d ed. São Paulo: Editora Nacional, 1938.

Romero, Sílvio. *A América Latina: Análise do livro de igual título do Dr. Manoel Bonfim.* Porto: Chardron, 1906.

Sales, Manuel Ferraz Campos. *Da propaganda à presidência.* São Paulo, 1908.

Sales, Miguel. *Hímens complacentes.* Rio de Janeiro: Imprensa Nacional, 1912.

——. "A perícia médico-legal nos crimes sexuais." *Revista de criminologia e medicina legal* 2, 3–4 (September–October 1928): 59–62.

Samara, Eni de Mesquita. "Casamento e papéis familiares em São Paulo no século XIX." *Revista de estudos e pesquisas em educação* 37 (May 1981): 17–25.

——. *As mulheres, o poder e a família: São Paulo, século XIX.* São Paulo: Ed. Marco Zero, 1989.

Scalon, Maria Celi Ramos da Cruz. "Cor e seletividade conjugal no Brasil." *Estudos afro-asiáticos* 23 (December 1992): 17–36.

Schneider, Jane. "Of Vigilance and Virgins: Honor, Shame and Access to Resources in Mediterranean Societies." *Ethnology* 10, 1 (January 1971): 1–24.

Schwartz, Lilia Moritz. *Retrato em branco e negro.* São Paulo: Companhia das Letras, 1987.

Schwartz, Roberto. "As idéias fora do lugar," *Estudos Cebrap* 3 (1973): 151–61.

Schwartz, Stuart B. "Pecar en colonias: Mentalidades populares, inquisición y actitudes hacia la fornicación simple en España, Portugal, y las colonias americanas." *Cuadernos de historia moderna* 18 (1997): 51–68.

——. "Recent Trends in the Study of Brazilian Slavery." In *Slaves, Peasants, and Rebels: Reconsidering Brazilian Slavery,* 1–38. Urbana: University of Illinois Press, 1992.

Schwartzman, Simon. "A Igreja e o Estado Novo: O estatuto da família." *Cadernos de pesquisa da Fundação Carlos Chagas* 37 (May 1981): 71–77.

Scott, Joan. *Gender and the Politics of History.* New York: Columbia University Press, 1988.

Seed, Patricia. *To Love, Honor, and Obey in Colonial Mexico: Conflicts over Marriage Choice, 1574–1821.* Stanford: Stanford University Press, 1988.

Segurado, Milton Duarte. *Sedução.* Curitiba: Juruá, 1977.

Serrano, Jonathas. *Cinema e educação.* São Paulo: Companhia Melhoramentos de São Paulo, 1931.

Sevcenko, Nicolau. "A capital irradiante: Técnica, ritmos e ritos do Rio." In *História da vida privada no Brasil,* ed. Fernando A. Novais, 513–620. São Paulo: Companhia das Letras, 1998.

——. *Literatura como missão: Tensões sociais e criação cultural na Primeira República.* São Paulo: Brasiliense, 1983.

——. *Orfeu extático na metrópole: São Paulo, sociedade e cultura nos frementes anos 20.* São Paulo: Companhia das Letras, 1992.

——. *A revolta da vacina: Mentes insanas em corpos rebeldes.* São Paulo: Brasiliense, 1984.

Severiano, Jorge. *Código penal da República dos Estados Unidos do Brasil.* Rio de Janeiro: Jacinto Ribeiro dos Santos, 1923.

Sheriff, Robin E. "Negro é um apelido que os brancos deram aos pretos: Discursos sobre cor, raça e racismo num morro carioca." IFSS/UFRJ, 1995. Mimeo.

Silva, Eduardo. *As queixas do povo.* Rio de Janeiro: Paz e Terra, 1988.

Silva, José Luiz Werneck da, Gizlete Neder, and Nancy Naro. *A polícia na corte no Distrito Federal, 1831–1930.* Rio de Janeiro: Pontifícia Universidade Católica, 1981.

Silva, Maria Beatriz Nizza da. "O divórcio na Capitania de São Paulo." In *Vivência: História, sexualidade e imagens femininas,* 151–95. São Paulo: Brasiliense and Fundação Carlos Chagas, 1980.

———. *História da família no Brasil colonial.* Rio de Janeiro: Nova Fronteira, 1998.

———. "A imagem da concubina no Brasil colonial: Ilegitimidade e herança." In *Rebeldia e submissão: Estudos sobre condição feminina,* ed. Albertina de Oliveira Costa and Cristina Bruschini, 17–60. São Paulo: Vértice and Fundação Carlos Chagas, 1989.

———. *Sistema de casamento no Brasil colonial.* São Paulo: T. A. Queiroz, 1984.

Silva, Nascimento. "Defloramento." *Revista siniátrica* 6, 6 (June 1923).

Silva, Nelson do Valle. "Estabilidade temporal e diferenças regionais no casamento inter-racial." *Estudos afro-asiáticos* 21 (December 1991): 49–60.

———. "O preço da cor: Diferenciais raciais na distribuição de renda no Brasil." *Pesquisa e Planejamento Econômico* 10, 1 (1980): 21–44.

———. "Updating the Cost of Not Being White in Brazil." In *Race, Class, and Power in Brazil,* ed. Pierre-Michel Fontaine, 42–55. Los Angeles: Center for Afro-American Studies, University of California at Los Angeles, 1985.

Silverberg, Miriam. "The Modern Girl as Militant." In *Recreating Japanese Women, 1600–1945,* ed. Gail Lee Bernstein, 239–266. Berkeley and Los Angeles: University of California Press, 1991.

Siqueira, Galdino. *Código penal.* Rio de Janeiro: Livraria Jacinto, 1941.

———. *Direito penal brasileiro.* Rio de Janeiro: Jacinto Ribeiro dos Santos, 1924.

Skidmore, Thomas. *Black into White: Race and Nationality in Brazilian Thought.* New York: Oxford University Press, 1974.

Slenes, Robert. *Na senzala uma flor: As esperanças e as recordações na formação da família escrava.* Rio de Janeiro: Nova Fronteira, 1999.

Smith, Bonnie. *Changing Lives: Women in European History since 1700.* Lexington, Mass.: D. C. Heath, 1989.

Soares, Eugênio. *A negregada instituição: Os capoeiras no Rio de Janeiro.* Rio de Janeiro: Secretaria Municipal de Cultura, Departamento Geral de Documentação e Informação Cultural, 1994.

Soares, Luís Carlos. *Rameiras, ilhoas, polacas . . . prostituição no Rio de Janeiro do século XIX.* São Paulo: Ática, 1992.

Soares, Oscar de Macedo. *Código penal da República dos Estados Unidos do Brasil.* 5th ed. Rio de Janeiro: H. Garnier, 1910.

Socolow, Susan M. "Acceptable Partners: Marriage Choice in Colonial Argentina, 1778–1810." In *Sexuality and Marriage in Colonial Latin America*, ed. Asunción Lavrin, 209–46. Lincoln: University of Nebraska Press, 1989.

Sodré, Nelson Werneck. *Do tenentismo ao Estado Novo: Memórias de um soldado*. Petrópolis: Vozes, 1986.

———. *A história da imprensa no Brasil*. Rio de Janeiro: Civilização Brasileira, 1966.

Soihet, Rachel. *Condição feminina e formas de violência: Mulheres pobres e ordem urbana, 1890–1920*. Rio de Janeiro: Forense, 1989.

Sommer, Doris. *Foundational Fictions*. Berkeley and Los Angeles: University of California Press, 1991.

Souza Neto, Paulino José Soares de. "Repressão à fraude nas anulações de casamento." In *Anais do Primeiro Congresso Nacional do Ministério Público*, 9: 123–32. Rio de Janeiro: Imprensa Nacional, 1942.

Spring, Eileen. *Law, Land, and Family: Aristocratic Inheritance in England, 1300–1800*. Chapel Hill: University of North Carolina Press, 1993.

Stepan, Nancy. *Beginnings of Brazilian Science: Oswaldo Cruz, Medical Research and Policy, 1890–1920*. New York: Science History Publications, 1976.

———. *"The Hour of Eugenics": Race, Gender and Nation in Latin America*. Ithaca: Cornell University Press, 1991.

Stern, Steve. *The Secret History of Gender: Women, Men, and Power in Late Colonial Mexico*. Chapel Hill: University of North Carolina Press, 1995.

Sussekind, Flora, and Roberto Ventura, "Uma teoria biológica da mais-valia? Análise da obra de Manoel Bonfim." In *História e dependência: Cultura e sociedade em Manoel Bonfim*, ed. Flora Sussekind and Roberto Ventura, 1–35. São Paulo: Moderna, 1984.

Tannenbaum, Frank. *Slave and Citizen: The Negro in the Americas*. New York: Knopf, 1946.

Telles, J. M. Correa. "Comentário crítico à Lei da Boa Razão." In *Auxiliar jurídico servindo de apêndice à décima quarta edição do código filipino*, ed. Cândido Mendes de Almeida. Rio de Janeiro: Tipografia do Instituto Filomático, 1869.

Thoinot, L. *Medicolegal Aspects of Moral Offenses*. Trans. Arthur W. Weysse. Philadelphia: F. A. Davis, 1919.

Thompson, E. P. "Folklore, Anthropology and Social History." *Indian Historical Review* 3, 2 (January 1977): 247–66.

———. "The Moral Economy of the English Crowd in the Eighteenth Century." *Past and Present* 50 (February 1971): 76–136.

———. "Time, Work-Discipline and Industrial Capitalism." *Past and Present* 38 (December 1967): 56–97.

Tinhorão, José Ramos. *Pequena história da música popular: Da modinha à lambada*. 6th ed. São Paulo: Art Editora, 1991.

Toledo, Francisco Eugênio de. *Atentados ao pudor*. São Paulo: Imprensa Editora Brasileira, 1921.

Torres, Alberto. *O problema nacional brasileiro*. Rio de Janeiro: Editora Nacional, 1914.

Torres, Antônio Eugênio Magarinos. *Processo penal do júri no Brasil.* Rio de Janeiro: Jacinto, 1939.

——. *Diálogos sobre o júri.* Rio de Janeiro: Jacinto, 1933.

——. *A mulher e o júri.* Rio de Janeiro: Jacinto, 1934.

Torres, Londoño Fernando. "El concubinato y la iglesia en el Brasil colonial." *Estudos CEDHAL* (Centro de Estudos de Demografia Histórica da América Latina, Universidade de São Paulo), 1988.

Tupi, Dulce. *Carnavais de guerra: O nacionalismo no samba.* Rio de Janeiro: ASB Arte Gráfica e Editora, 1985.

Vainfas, Ronaldo. "A teia da intriga." In *História e sexualidade no Brasil,* ed. Ronaldo Vainfas, 41–66. Rio de Janeiro: Graal, 1986.

——. *Trópico dos pecados: Moral, sexualidade e inquisição no Brasil.* Rio de Janeiro: Campus, 1989.

Vaz, Lilian Fessler. "Contribuição ao estudo da produção e transformação do espaço da habitação popular: As habitações coletivas no Rio antigo." Master's thesis, Universidade Federal do Rio de Janeiro, 1985.

——. "Notas sobre o 'Cabeça de Porco.' " *Revista do Rio de Janeiro* 1, 2 (1986): 29–35.

Velasques, Muza Clara Chaves. "A Lapa boêmia: Um estudo da identidade carioca." Master's thesis, Universidade Federal Fluminense, 1994.

Veloso, Flora Ferraz. *Sobre a instituição do júri.* Rio de Janeiro: n.p., 1959.

Venâncio Filho, Alberto. *Das arcadas ao bacharelismo.* 2d ed. São Paulo: Perspectiva, 1982.

Venâncio, Renato Pinto. "Nos limites da sagrada família: Ilegitimidade e casamento no Brasil colonial." In *História e sexualidade no Brasil,* ed. Ronaldo Vainfas, 107–24. Rio de Janeiro: Graal, 1986.

Ventura, Roberto. *Estilo tropical: História cultural e polêmicas literárias no Brasil.* São Paulo: Companhia das Letras, 1991.

Viana, Larissa Moreira. "As dimensões da cor—olhares norte-americanos sobre a inserção social dos homens livres de cor (Sudeste—século XIX)." Bachelor's thesis, Universidade Federal Fluminense, 1995.

Viana, Francisco de Oliveira. *Evolução do povo brasileiro.* 3d ed. São Paulo: Editora Nacional, 1938.

——. *O ocaso do Império.* 2d ed. São Paulo: Melhoramentos, 1933.

——. *Populações Meridionais: Pequenos estudos de psicologia social.* São Paulo: Monteiro Lobato, 1921.

——. *Problemas de política objetiva.* São Paulo: Editora Nacional, 1930.

——. *Raça e assimilação.* São Paulo: Editora Nacional, 1932.

——. "Raça e cultura (fragmentos de um ensaio)." In *Ensaios inéditos,* 65–68. Campinas: Editora da UNICAMP, 1991.

Vianna, Hermano. *O mistério do samba.* 2d ed. Rio de Janeiro: Jorge Zahar, 1995.

Viana Filho, L. *A vida de Rui Barbosa.* São Paulo: Editora Nacional, 1943.

Vieira, João. *Código penal comentado.* Rio de Janeiro, 1896.

Vilhena, Cynthia Pereira de Souza. *Família, mulher, prole: A doutrina social da igreja e a política social do Estado Novo.* Ph.D. diss., Universidade de São Paulo, 1988.

Wagley, Charles, ed. *Race and Class in Rural Brazil.* New York: Russel and Russel, 1952.

Walkowitz, Judith R. *City of Dreadful Delight: Narratives of Sexual Danger in Late-Victorian London.* Chicago: University of Chicago Press, 1992.

Weinstein, Barbara. *For Social Peace in Brazil: Industrialists and the Remaking of the Working Class in São Paulo, 1920–1964.* Chapel Hill: University of North Carolina Press, 1996.

Wetzell, Richard Friedrich. "Criminal Law Reform in Imperial Germany." Ph.D. diss., Stanford University, 1991.

Wikan, Unni. "Shame and Honour: A Contestable Pair." *Man,* n.s., 19 (1984): 635–652.

Wood, Charles H. "Categorias censitárias e classificações subjetivas de raça no Brasil." In *Desigualdade racial no Brasil contemporâneo,* ed. Peggy A. Lovell, 93–111. Belo Horizonte: CEDEPLAR-/FACE, Universidade Federal de Minas Gerais, 1991.

Wright, Gordon. *Between the Guillotine and Liberty: Two Centuries of the Crime Problem in France.* New York: Oxford University Press, 1983.

Ypersele, Laurence Van. *Le Roi Albert: Histoire d'un mythe.* Ottignies: Editions Quorum, 1995.

——. "As práticas da justiça no cotidiano da pobreza." Master's thesis, Universidade Federal Fluminense, 1984.

Index

308

Police (cont.)
and venereal diseases, 241 n.23; and
"Vida Policial," 73
Popular masses: in conception of urban
professionals, 52, 54, 61, 63, 66, 77, 91
Popular music, 74
Portela, 67
Porto-Carrero, J. P., 17, 103
Portuguese immigrants, 2, 57, 126
Positivism: and criminology, 32, 192;
influence on Brazilian jurists, 31, 221
n.77; and legal medicine; legal theory
of, 30–34; and opposition to classical
legal doctrine, 31–32, 192; philosophy and August Comte, 31; and the
"positive school" in Europe, 31–33,
222 nn. 78, 79; and positivist church,
31; and republican politics, 31, 61
Private and public criminal law, 44–45
Procedural Code of 1832, 214 n.22
Prostitutes, 5, 36, 57–59, 64, 69–71,
114, 122, 165, 169, 219 n.63; and civil
rights, 40; francesas, 58, 69, 233 n.42;
as French coquettes, 58; mulatas, 58;
national identities of, 58; polacas,
58, 69, 241 n.25; pretas, 69; public
versus "clandestine," 36, 39, 57, 70;
and rape, 24, 40, 41
Prostitution, 12, 38–40, 57–59, 64,
66, 71, 85–88, 118, 141, 142, 168,
242 n.28; and antipimping legislation, 39, 226 nn. 116, 117; and bordellos, 39, 58, 70, 143; in Buenos
Aires, 86; control of, 39, 56, 58, 70,
88, 208 n.26, 225 n.115, 231 n.30;
debates over state regulation, 40, 58–
59, 86, 87; and houses of tolerance,
40; Jewish campaigns against, 86; in
nineteenth-century Rio de Janeiro,
57–59; and pimping, 39, 66, 86, 242
n.28; and police discretionary
powers, 88; regulation of, 40; in
twentieth-century Rio de Janeiro, 12,
69–71, 85–88; and the "white slave

trade," 39, 58, 86, 233 n.43, 241 n.23;
and zoning policies, 58–59, 64, 86, 87
Providência, Morro da, 65. See also
Favelas
Public education, 149
Public health specialists, 39, 149
Public law. See Private and public
criminal law
Pudor, 37, 45, 46, 56

Quality (social status), 7, 23
Queiroz, Narcélio, 80, 271 n.22
Quinta da Boa Vista, 1, 65, 75

Race: relationship to class, 106–107,
166, 167, 169; and absence of racism
in law, 230 n.28; and color classification in criminal records, 154–173;
and ideology of racial "improvement" ("whitening"), 8, 32–33, 146–
151, 162, 179, 181, 260–261 n.17,
262 n.26; and intellectual con-
structions of the "Brazilian race,"
148–154, 188, 260 n.16, 261 n.21;
and mestiçagem (racial mixture), 45,
52, 59, 76, 145, 146, 148, 149, 151,
152, 156, 162, 164, 176, 179, 181,
188, 259 n.10, 261 nn. 19, 23; and the
mulato/mulata, 154–155, 164, 168,
224 n.92; and the myth of racial democracy, 77, 145–153, 173, 181–182,
188, 262 n.26, 263 n.34; and prostitution, 58, 69–70, 169; and racial discrimination in adjudication of sexual
crimes, 173–181; and racial discrimination in employment and education, 158–159, 265 n.55; and racial
ideologies and stereotypes in court
testimony, 145–151; and racism in
turn-of-the-century urban reform,
55–59, 61; and scientific racism, 145,
149; significance in courtship and
marriage choices, 161–173, 176–178,
181–182, 266 nn. 60, 62

Sueann Caulfield is Associate Professor of History at the
University of Michigan.

Library of Congress Cataloging-in-Publication Data
Caulfield, Sueann.
In defense of honor : sexual morality, modernity, and nation
in early-twentieth-century Brazil / by Sueann Caulfield.
Includes bibliographical references and index.
ISBN 0-8223-2377-X (cloth : alk. paper).
ISBN 0-8223-2398-2 (pbk. : alk. paper)
    1. Sex customs—Brazil—History—20th century.   2. Sexual
ethics—Brazil—History—20th century.   3. Virginity—
Brazil—History—20th century.   I. Title.
HQ18.B7C38   1999   306.7'0981'0904—dc21   99-28323 CIP

In this book Sueann Caulfield explores the chan[...] [...]
in early-twentieth-century Brazil, a period that s[...]
liferation of public debates that linked morality [...]
national progress. With a close examination o[...]
offenses and case law in Rio de Janeiro from the [...]
early years of the Estado Novo dictatorship, Caulfield reveals how everyday interpretations of honor influenced official attitudes and even the
law itself as Brazil attempted to modernize.

While some Brazilian elites used the issue of sexual purity to boast
of their country's moral superiority, others claimed that the veneration
of such concepts as virginity actually frustrated efforts at modernization.
Moreover, although individuals of all social classes invoked values they
considered "traditional," such as the confinement of [...]
within marriage, these values were at odds with so[...]
as premarital sex, cohabitation, divorce, and female-headed households—
that had been common throughout Brazil's history. The persistence of
these practices, together with post-World War I changes in both official
and popular moral ideals, presented formidable obstacles to the Estado
Novo's renewed drive to define and enforce public morality and private
family values in the late 1930s.

●

"This is an outstanding work both in terms of its highly original research
and its very sophisticated interpretation."—BARBARA WEINSTEIN, author of *For Social Peace in Brazil: Industrialists and the Remaking of the
Working Class in São Paulo, 1920–1964*

●

"The author is to be applauded for asking hard questions about the ways
in which sexual activity, or the lack thereof, are used to make statements about race and class."—JEFFREY LESSER, author of *Negotiating
National Identity: Immigrants, Minorities, and the Struggle for Ethnicity
in Brazil*

●

SUEANN CAULFIELD is Associate Professor of History at the University
of Michigan.

DUKE UNIVERSITY PRESS Box 90660
Durham, North Carolina 27708-0660

ISBN 0-8223-2398-2